PROTECTION OF HUMAN RIGHTS AND NATIONAL HUMAN RIGHTS COMMISSION REFLECTIONS

PROTECTION OF HUMAN RIGHTS AND NATIONAL HUMAN RIGHTS COMMISSION REFLECTIONS

N.K. PADHI

GYAN

Published by

GYAN

Gyan Publishing House
5, Ansari Road
Daryaganj, New Delhi-110002
Phone: 011-47034999, 9811692060
E-mail: books@gyanbooks.com

Distribution Network
gyanbooks.com
India, USA, Canada, UK, Australia, France

ISBN: 978-93-6280-414-3 (PB)

First Published, 2024

Printed at: Gyan Press, Delhi.

Protection of Human Rights and
National Human Rights Commission Reflections
Author: N.K. Padhi

Dedicated

To

All Those Who are deprived of their inherent rights

Contents

PART - II

Foreword

The framers of the constitution of India who laid emphasis on the protection of human rights and included 27 Articles of Universal Declaration of 1948. After about four decades of the commencement of the constitution it was realised that some more steps need to be taken to reconcile our avowed intentions, with actual practices. Especially in the field of human rights India's deteriorating image owing to the terrorist activities, inter caste and community rivalries, atrocities committed by the police, atrocities on women and children, displacement and many other human rights violation issues needed to be improved. It was at this stage that the National Human Rights Commission came into the existence in 1993 to fulfil the objectives of United Nations Charter as well as those of the Constitution of India.

N.K. Padhi's book Protection of Human Rights and National Human Rights Commission, Reflections is a pioneering work on the subject. Fact -finding is the core of human rights activity. The NHRC as a statutory organisation has to do, this in the pluralistic society of India. Padhi, with his sincere endeavour, presents a comprehensive account of the composition and style of functioning of NHRC. This is likely to promote general awareness on Human Rights in the society and thus facilitate creation of a society free from exploitation and cruelty.

His analysis is spread over six chapters and six appendices. The introductory chapter gives general ideas on the concept of human rights and their violations scenario at the national and international levels. His second chapter discusses the meaning and dimensions of human rights and highlights the original text of some important international documents like UDHR, ICCPR and ICSECR along with a brief overview of each. Padhi has given a holistic view of Indian Culture and its human rights bases. Apart from this the various provisions of human rights contained in the Indian Constitution are analysed in the third chapter. His Chapter IV deals with the structural and functional framework of the National Human Rights Commission. He has made a survey of the activity of the NHRC ever since its creation in 1993 in his Chapter -V. He has cited the many important cases which have been already disposed of or are likely to be decided in the near future by NHRC.

The Chapter VI contains suggestions for making NHRC more and more effective as a statutory body. One of his main suggestions is that the decision of NHRC should not be confined to the recommendations only. It should be executed whole-heartedly by agencies concerned. He has recommended that human rights should be taught at all levels of education to inculcate the culture of human rights in the country. This, I hope, will be an effective remedy to treat the society affected by human rights violation. I hope, this volume will be well - received not only by students and teachers but also by the readers who have a deep concern for Human Rights.

Date- 15-05-2007
(Sukadev Nanda)

Preface

The idea of human rights pre-dates the United Nations. Yet it was only with the setting up this body that it finally achieved formal, universal recognition. The Universal Declaration of Human rights, which was adopted by the UN General Assembly on 10th December 1948, sets a new international standard. It is the greatest effort made by mankind to give society new legal and moral foundations. The two principal international human rights instruments, namely, the International Covenant on Civil and Political Rights, 1966 and the International Covenant on Economic, Social and Cultural Rights, 1966 have given very wide connotation to the concept of human rights and fundamental freedoms. These three universally accepted International documents are often referred to as the **"*Magna carta of Humanity*".**

Respect for human rights makes freedom meaningful. Human rights are meaningless in an environment of poverty and deprivation. These rights are above politics and are part and parcel of life in society concerning humanity. They necessarily signify human values in an absolute sense: but they have greater relevance to the real well-being of the individual if they are applied in the context of society. The whole fabric of society depends upon human rights. Without these society cannot run smoothly, and there could be many chances of crimes and disturbances in society. The protection of human rights is a constant struggle which cannot be won unless every man and woman participates in it.

The National Human Rights Commission was established for the protection of human rights in India in the year 1993 as per the protection of Human Rights Act. It is a statutory body which has touched upon many practical issues relating to application of human rights in various fields. Since the formation, the NHRC has mainly taken initiative to prevent the violation of human rights when the violation is made by the state agency like Armed forces, Security forces and Police forces etc. In this book effort has been made to discuss the composition and functions of NHRC to make the people aware about this effective organisation which can protect their rights and ventilate their grievances as regards the violation of their inherent rights.

The author feels greatly indebted to the works of eminent writers and scholars, particularly those of Darren J. O'Byrne, Geoffrey Robertson, Bryan S. Turner, Dr. Arun Ray, Chiranjivi J. Nirmal, A. K. Pathak, and Dr. U. Chandra, T.S.N. Sastrty and others that have been a source of information and guidance in the compilation of this book.

I must express my heartfelt gratitude to my D. Litt. Supervisor Professor (Dr.) Sukadev Nanda, Vice-Chancellor of F.M. University, Orissa who wrote a foreword to this edition who went through the manuscript and made valuable suggestions. I am also grateful to Prof Anjan Kumar Das of Fakir Mohan College who has made some amendments after going through this volume.

I express my thanks to Mr.Amit Garg, the publisher Gyan Publishing House for co-operating with me and printing this book in an elegant manner. Thanks are also due to Madhu for typing the manuscript neatly within the shortest possible time. Above all, this venture would not have been possible but for the love, patience and moral encouragement of my life partner Jyotsna and my beloved son Samay. Suggestions for the improvement of this book are always welcome.

15-August-2007 **Dr. Nagendra Kumar Padhi**

Abbreviations

AIR	:	All India Reports.
APCL	:	Andhra Pradesh Civil Liberty.
ART	:	Article
ASI	:	Assistant Sub-Inspector.
BSF	:	Boarder Security Force.
CIA	:	Criminal Investigation Agency.
CrPC	:	Criminal Procedure Code.
CRPF	:	Central Reserve Police Force.
CS	:	Charge Sheet.
DG	:	Director General Of Police.
DPSP	:	Directive Principles Of State Policy.
FIR	:	First Information Report.
FR	:	Fundamental Rights.
GA	:	General Assembly.
HC	:	High Court.
HRA	:	Human Rights Association.
HRC	:	Human Rights Cell / Human Rights Court.
HRCPC	:	Human Rights And Civil Protection Committee.
HRO	:	Human Rights Organization.
HROG	:	Human Rights Observer Group.
HRS	:	Human Rights Society.
HRT	:	Human Rights Trust.
HRWPF	:	Human Rights World Peace Foundation.
ICCPR	:	International Covenant On Civil And Political Rights.
ICESCR	:	International Covenant On Economic, Social And Cultural Rights.
IG	:	Inspector General.

IO	:	Investigating Officer.
IPC	:	Indian Penal Code.
IPO	:	International Police Organization.
IPS	:	Indian Police Service.
J & K	:	Jammu And Kashmir.
MAS	:	Manabic Adhikar Sangathan.
NDA	:	National Democratic Alliance.
NGO	:	Non Government Organization.
NHRC	:	National Human Rights Commission.
NSA	:	National Security Act.
OCDR	:	Organization of Civil And Democratic Rights.
OIC	:	Officers – In – Charge.
PHR	:	Protection Of Human Rights Act.
POTA	:	Prevention Of Terrorism Act.
PUCL	:	Peoples Union Of Civil Liberty.
SC	:	Scheduled Caste./Supreme Court.
SCC	:	Supreme Court Cases.
SCR	:	Supreme Court Reports.
SG	:	Secretary General.
SHRC	:	State Human Rights Commission.
SI	:	Sub-inspector Police.
SP	:	Superintendent Of Police.
SSP	:	Senior Superintendent of Police.
ST	:	Scheduled Tribe.
TADA	:	Terrorist And Disruptive Activities. (Protection Act)
UDHR	:	Universal Declaration Of Human Rights.
ULFC	:	United Liberation Front Of Assam.
UN	:	United Nation.
US	:	Under Section / United States.
VHR	:	Violation Of Human Rights.

PART - I

1

Introduction

"It is the obligation of the state to ensure every one the right to adequate food, education and enjoyment of highest attainable standards of physical and mental health. These rights have to be respected and made available to the citizens by the state."

Dr. Justice A. S. Anand Chairperson NHRC.

Man is a social as well as rational animal .The rationality reflects upon him to realise his rights and duties in the society. The concept of human rights is as old as origin of human race and as broad as 'social life'. Human beings are entitled to certain basic and 'natural' rights that define a meaningful existence.[1] Equal dignity of all persons is the central tenet of human rights. These rights have been designated to be universal in application, inalienable in exercise and inherent.

When the United Nations introduced the Universal Declaration of Human rights in 1948, it was seen by many as a sign of optimism, of the possibilities of a better world. Yet, over 58 years later, observers recognise that we live in an age when human rights abuses are as prevalent as they ever have been and in some instances, more prevalent. The world is littered with examples of violations of basic rights: censorship, discrimination, political imprisonment, torture, slavery, the death penalty, disappearances, genocide, poverty, and refugees. The rights of women, children, and other groups in society continue to be ignored in atrocious ways. The environmental crisis takes the discourse on rights to a different level.[2]

The problem of human rights has been receiving the attention and concern of all the wise men and nations since long but society is still deprived of concrete and lasting solutions. In an age of apathy and indifference, the call by Upendra Baxi to 'take suffering seriously' goes beyond the classroom.[3] In remembering and sharing experiences of human suffering, it is difficult to go on as if nothing has happened, as if it is just an academic question and not relevant to our life today. The question remains how much of this experience can stimulate intervention and action. A beginning is made in identifying ourselves as human beings, a consensus that has been renewed and asserted more than ever in this century, making human rights worth defending.

To do what Moses and Jesus Christ did, and in our tradition what Krishna and Mahatma Gandhi did, is to rediscover the meaning of life. In the processes, states can become more democratic. No progress will ever make human rights superfluous or out of date, so long as humans face poverty and cruelty. [4] We live in a Strange World. Strange are the times and Stranger its ways. More than one thousand million people in the World suffer from acute hunger today. Every year more than fifteen million people die of hunger. Twenty-four people die of starvation and hunger every minute; every twenty-four hours 35,000 people die of hunger. Out of twenty-four people who die of hunger in every minute, 18 are children below the age of five years. More people die of starvation every two days than those who died in the bombing of Hiroshima. In 1976 a terrible earthquake in China took a toll of two lakh lives. More people die of starvation in the world every seven days. These startling facts have been reported by Hunger Project, an International Institution set up in 1977. Its object is to spread awareness about the grave situation of starvation and hunger on a global scale, particularly in the context of mankind having developed enough productive power to produce ample food to feed the entire population of the world, if only a proper system of distribution could be worked out.

Apart from millions who die as a result of permanent starvation, many more millions are condemned to life long disabilities. For instance, owing to inadequate intake of certain vitamins children become blind, deaf and dumb. In by the government's own admission, 3000 children become blind in India due to Vitamin –A deficiency every year. We also know how hospital records are inadequate and carelessly complied. According to studies conducted by the National Institute of Nutrition in Hydrabad, 63 percent of children below three years of age and 45 percent in the 3-5 years age group suffer from severe anaemic conditions due to iron deficiency. No matter how startling the facts, they are mere numbers. And numbers in themselves are lifeless. The poverty and hunger of people, as also the animal existence of millions, have become so common that we have inured ourselves to human misfortune and think nothing of the violation of the rights of the poor and the deprived.

The problem of human rights is intrinsically bound up with socio-economic, political environment and the relationship that grow at a given time between a person and the institutions on which his or her existence depends. Indeed, the problems emanating from denial of human rights in various forms are so massive and complex that no single group can adequately provide vigilance and launch movements to redress the grievances concerning human rights. Again, while denial of civil and political rights, arbitrary arrests and extra-judicial executions have attracted worldwide attention of the media and inter-governmental organizations; hunger, poverty, destitution, illiteracy and diseasess, prevalent widely in developing countries, have not succeeded in attracting the attention they deserve. Nor have adequate steps, at national and much less international level, been taken for removal of these social and economic threats all of which amount to negation of basic human rights. Of late, we are witnessing yet another serious threat to human rights. It is not only governments which violate human rights but also non-governmental groups- who detain, terrorise, torture, and kill innocent people including women and children. In fact, the organised violence of such groups is rampant in society.

If we look at the contemporary world from a wide perspective, we find that the most challenging problem of our time is how to utilise the vast knowledge and resources available today for the welfare and development of all mankind. The resolution of other issues- as for instance, international peace and security, arms control and disarmament and equitable management of world resources is not an end itself but a means to achieve the basic objective. It is gratifying to note that there is growing recognition of this basic objective. The international community, as organised and represented at the United Nations has not only taken the initial steps in its long journey towards the goal but also set the meaning and direction of that journey. It has spelt out that the welfare and development of mankind includes universal respect for and observance of human rights and fundamental freedom for all without distinction as to race, colour, sex, language, religion, political and other beliefs, descent, birth or other status.

What is analysed above covers only a part of the grim human rights situation prevalent today. It does not present the whole picture. Indeed, given the complex dimensions of the existing state of human rights, the whole scenario cannot be encapsulated into a single study, whatever its size. One aspect of the situation however is very clear that the promises and aspirations set out in the Universal Declaration of Human Rights and elaborated in several international instruments, remains largely unfulfilled. The rights to life (to an adequate standard of living, to freedom of expression, to protection from torture, inhuman treatment or arbitrary arrest) and many of the "common standards of achievement for all peoples and nations" are as far from realisation now as ever. If this is a depressing evaluation, it is nonetheless a reality for the majority for humankind, particularly those living in poor countries. Among the people of the affluent Western nations also, there is either indifference, or a deeply felt sense of dissatisfaction and frustration about the lack of progress towards universal respect for and observance of human rights. Do we not possess the ability to achieve peace, prosperity and human rights for all'? Have we set standards we can never hope to attend? What is preventing humankind from reaching these standards? And how can the international community contribute to the realization of these fundamental objectives.

Though, the answers to the aforesaid questions are very difficult to find they are certainly not beyond our reach. As regards child marriage, for instance, gradually there is a realisation that child marriage is against the law and it is considered as a gross case of human rights violation. Efforts have been made to protect the rights of the child by making stringent laws and sensitising the people against this evil practice. India has partially achieved this, but we know that even now, in many areas among some communities, child marriage is still quite common because of the lack of education and religious bias. We have not succeeded in providing elementary education to all the children between the age of 6 to 14, as provided in our constitution, and possibly as a consequence we pay a heavy price in terms of population growth, infant mortality, child labour, child marriage and other social evils. There cannot be any two opinions in this regard that we are now giving top priority to this in recent years.

Over a period of time, we have to have a caring society, a sensitive society and a society which does not pay lip service only to human rights but sees to it that they are available to all classes /castes and sections of our society. About 59 years have gone by, after independence.

Democracy in India has struck roots and is accepted and recognised; when a government loses power, and the transfer of power has not posed any problem in this country. Our political parties accept the verdict of the people without question and this is a very big achievement. Agriculture, industry, science and technology, have made progress. In spite of our achievements we are sometimes criticised for human rights violation due to poverty, malnourishment, illiteracy and environmental degradation. Now there are some areas which are of special concern to human rights activists. Custodial death and rape are two of them. The Supreme Court had to intervene and there has been some progress in this respect. The SC has issued several directions from time to time, to prevent human rights violation. Apart from this many public-spirited individuals and Non Government Organisations have done excellent work in this area and PIL has opened a significant avenue too.

India, being a founder member of the United Nations and a signatory to the Universal Declaration of Human Rights, is fully committed to protect the human rights and prevent its violation. Hence, India has made several humanitarian Laws, besides the provisions of constitution .The most significant achievement is the creation of National Human Rights Commission to fulfil the aspirations of the people of India as regards to the protection of human rights. It is seen that within its short span of existence, it has become very popular for its spectacular achievement in the protection and in the promotion of human rights.

This book has been designed to acquent people with the functioning of NHRC and achievements in the past years. The first chapter of the book gives the introduction of human rights and it makes a conceptual treatment of it. The second chapter provides the meaning and kinds of human rights. Besides it also highlights original text of UDHR, ICCPR, ICSECR and the brief analysis of these declarations and covenants. Chapter three deals with Indian culture and human rights and the chronological progress of NHRC. Provision of human rights in the constitution of India has also been reflected in this chapter. Chapter four is devoted to constitution, powers and procedures of function of NHRC and State Human Rights Commissions. Chapter fifth provides the knowledge about the achievements of NHRC since it inception, hence some cases of different nature have been presented to make the reader aware about the style of functioning. The last chapter is the summary. It concludes that NHRC is the most effective body at present in the protection of human rights and through this powerful statutory body the disease India suffers from can be properly treated.

Footnotes

1. South Asia Human Rights Documentation Centre, " Introducing Human Rights" Oxford University Press, New Delhi, 2006.
2. Darren J O' Byrne "Human Rights: An Introduction"Pearson Education Limited, Delhi, 2004.
3. Upendra Baxi " The Future of Human Rights"Oxford University Press, New Delhi, 2002.
4. Chiranjivi J Nirmal (ed) " Human Rights in India" Oxford University Press, New Delhi, 2000.

References

Abraham Henry J., ***"Freedom and The Court: Civil Rights and Liberties in the United States",*** 3rd edn. Oxford University Press, 1977.

Agarwal R.S,, "*Human Rights in the Modern World*", New Delhi, Chetana Publications, New Delhi, 1974.

Aggarwal H.O, *"Implementation of Human Rights Covenants with Special Reference to India*", 1st edn. , Kitab Mahal, Allahabad, 1983.

Gupta V. K, (ed.), *"Perspectives on Human Rights",* Vikas Publishing House Pvt. Ltd., New Delhi, 1996.

Davis Hariss, (ed.), *"International Human Rights Reports",* Vol. 2, no. 1, January 1995, University of Nottingham, Nottingham, U.K.

Ian Brownlie and Guys. Goodwin-Gill (ed.) "Basic documents on Human Rights" Oxford University Press, New Delhi 2007.

Jaswal S.P, and Nishtha Jaswal. "Human Rights and the Law." , APH Publishing Corporation, New Delhi, 1996.

Johari J.C, "*Human Rights and New World Order: Towards Perfection of the Democratic Way of Life",* Anmol Publication, New Delhi, 1996.

2

Human Rights

Human rights are today's buzz phrase. Nevertheless, this concept is as old as the origin of civilized existence of man. Historically the term became very popular after the Second World War. Today the world has become a global society and no man is an island and each should live for the other in order to regard the principle of "Live and Let live". Human rights are indispensable item both in the national and international agenda. The concept has been interpreted in various forms to convey that human rights are essential for human development, without which entire society would suffer.

The concept of Human Rights is not entirely western in origin. It is also not so modern. It is a crystallization of values that are the common heritage of mankind.[1] As ideals, human rights define the community within which people want to live, but have their roots in the community in which they in fact live. Based on our common humanity, human rights differ from rights grounded in domestic law, but in other respects they operate much like rights grounded in domestic law: violation of one of the enumerated human rights would serve as a predicate or justification within the legal system for exercises of the state's coercive power. Human rights might be better viewed more as social ideals than as legal claims.

Meaning

The expression "human rights" denotes all those rights, which are inherent in our nature and without which we cannot live as human beings. In other words, human rights being eternal part of the nature of human beings are essential for individuals to develop their personality, their human qualities, their intelligence, talent and conscience and to enable them to satisfy their spiritual and other higher needs. Further it is described that the rights, which are natural and inherent for the life and happiness of every individual, are called human rights. These rights are indispensable for the maintenance of human dignity and the individual enjoys these rights from birth to death. In fact human rights are the very essence of a meaningful life, and human dignity is the ultimate purpose of Government.

The purpose of securing human rights as such is to provide protection to these rights against the abuse of power committed by the organs of State; to establish institutions for the promotion of living condition of human beings and for the development of their personality; and at the same time, to provide effective remedial measures for obtaining redress when these rights are violated. Karel Vasak has aptly remarked that the human rights are essentially individual in character. They are meant to be enjoyed by individuals and they constitute a social phenomenon by virtue of those for whom they are intended.

Kinds of Human Rights

According to the evolution of the contemporary concept, human rights have been divided into three categories by Louis B Sohn.[2] These are otherwise known as the three generations of human rights. Some western scholars have tried to analyse the 'three generations' of human rights.[3]

The **First generation rights** are those that were concerned mainly with the civil and political rights of the individual or the 'liberty-oriented' rights. These were meant to impose negative obligations on governments to desist from interfering with exercise of individual liberties'. These rights were among the major concerns of all liberal and democratic movements since the nineteenth century.

This generation was led by the classical as well as contemporary Western liberal scholars from John Stuart Mill to John Rawls who conceived civil and political rights as some kind of protection or safeguard against the state power. This generation was greatly influenced by the Magna Carta or the Great Charter of English Liberties granted by King John in 1215 under the threat of civil war, and the English Bill of Rights of 1689, which laid the foundation of parliamentary supremacy over the English Monarchy after the Glorious Revolution of 1688. The generation was rejuvenated and reinforced in the late

18th and the early 19th century with the American Declaration of Independence and French Declaration of the Rights of Man and the Citizen.

Civil and political rights included such rights as the right to freedom of speech and expression, right to freedom of movement and right against arbitrary arrests which are even today considered as the essential safeguards for the citizens against arbitrary government or state power.

The **Second-generation rights** are those, which can be said to be 'security-oriented' and provide for social, economic and cultural security. These rights – social, economic and cultural – are more positive in nature in that they make it the duty of the State to ensure that these rights are realized. The Universal Declaration of Human Rights reflects the consensus on the principles which form the basis of the first and second generation rights.

The post-colonial era witnessed the emergence of the second generation of human rights. The political leaders and thinkers of developing nations, who propagated the ideas that economic, social and cultural rights, were prerequisite for the enjoyment of civil and political rights led to this era. This second category of rights *inter alia* include right against exploitation, right to work, shelter, food, social security, health care and education, the right to freedom of culture and religion.

The concept of human rights in its conprehension has now travelled to encompass what are called **Third generation rights.** They have evolved in response to various new concerns over which international consensus has emerged in recent years. The third generation of human rights was led by the scholars and thinkers of the Socialist and the Third World countries, which conceived human rights as the collective rights of a nation such as the rights to development, the right to peace, the right to one's own natural resources and the right to one's own cultural heritage. In the contemporary context of globalisation and economic liberalization, the collective right of a nation, especially the rights to protect environment and natural resources appear to be most significant for the survival of the developing nations against the economic imperialism of the multinational corporations having their origins in the developed nations.

The third generation of human rights also emphasized on the 'group rights', i.e. rights of the weaker and vulnerable groups such as women, children, aged, minorities, refugees, prisoners, sex workers, etc. The Declaration on the Rights to Development adopted by the UN General Assembly in 1986 is the most important example of these rights.

The term 'generation' in somewhat misleading as it usually implies a succession of phenomena, whereby a new generation takes the place of the previous one. This is not so as far as the three 'generations' of the human rights are concerned. On the contrary, as Baehr has rightly pointed out, 'the idea is rather that the three "generations" exist and should be respected simultaneously'.[4] In other words, this implies that the problem of generation gap does not arise in the case of human rights, as it often happens in the case of human beings.

International Bill of Human Rights

History has witnessed a revolution in the modern moral imagination over the last few decades. The important features of this revolution include the emergence of human rights as the prominent language of the good in international politics and the growth of non-governmental human rights organisations around the world. Until 1945, international protection of individual human rights was confined to the treaties abolishing the slave trade, the laws of war, and the minority rights treaties conclude after Versailles. It is only since 1945,in effect, that the rights of all human beings as individuals have come under the protection of International law.[5]

The Universal Declaration of Human Rights was a great achievement of civilization. It sets out a list of basic rights—a "common standard of achievement" in the words of the Declaration itself – for every one in the world, whatever their race, colour, sex, language, religion, political or other opinion, national or social origin, property, birth or other status. After extensive discussion and debate, two more international instruments were included, i.e. providing legal obligation to States parties through the International Covenant on Civil and Political Rights and the International Covenant on Economic, Social and Cultural Rights. These were both adopted in 1966 and they came into force ten years later. An Optional Protocol to the former Covenant also provided machinery for the handling of complaints from individuals under specified circumstances. These three documents together constitute the International Bill of Human Rights. For details the following original text of UDHR may be referred

UNIVERSAL DECLARATION OF HUMAN RIGHTS 1948

The general Assembly proclaims: -

This Universal Declaration of Human Right as a common standard of achievement for all peoples and all nations, to the end that every individual and every organ of society, keeping this Declaration constantly in mind, shall strive by teaching and education to promote respect for these rights and freedoms and by progressive measures, national and international, to secure their universal and effective recognition and observance, both among the peoples of Member states themselves and among the peoples of territories under their jurisdiction.

Article 1

All human beings are born free and equal in dignity and rights. They are endowed with reason and conscience and should act towards one another in a spirit of brotherhood.

Article 2

Everyone is entitled to all the rights and freedoms set forth in this Declaration, without distinction of any kind, such as race, colour, sex, language, religion, political or other opinion, National or social origin, property, birth or other status. Further, no distinction shall be made on the basis of the political, jurisdictional or international status of the country or territory to which a person belongs, whether it is independent, trust, non-self-governing or under any other limitation of sovereignty.

Article 3

Everyone has the right of life, liberty and security of person.

Article 4

No one shall be held in slavery or servitude; slavery and the slave trade shall be prohibited in all their forms.

Article 5

No one shall be subjected to torture or to cruel, inhuman or degrading treatment or punishment.

Article 6

Everyone has the right to recognition everywhere as a person before the law.

Article 7

All are equal before the law and are entitled without any discrimination to equal protection of the law. All are entitled to equal protection against any discrimination in violation of this Declaration and against any incitement to such discrimination.

Article 8

Everyone has the right to an effective remedy by the competent national tribunals for acts violating the fundamental rights granted him by the constitution or by law.

Article 9

No one shall be subjected to arbitrary arrest, detention or exile.

Article 10

Everyone is entitled in full equality to a fair and public hearing by an independent and impartial tribunal, in the determination of his rights and obligations and of any criminal charge against him.

Article 11

1. Everyone charged with a penal offence has the right to be presumed innocent until proved guilty according to law in a public trial at which he has had all the guarantees necessary for this defence.
2. No one shall be held guilty of any penal offence on account of any act or omission, which did not constitute a penal offence, under national or international law, at the time when it was committed. Nor shall a heavier penalty be imposed then the one that was applicable at the time the penal offence was committed

Article 12

No one shall be subjected to arbitrary interference with his privacy, family, home, or correspondence, or to attacks upon his honour and reputation. Everyone has the right to the protection of the law against such interference or attack.

Article 13

1. Everyone has the right to freedom of movement and residence within the borders of each state.
2. Everyone has the right to leave any country, including his own, and to return to his country.

Article 14

1. Everyone has the right to seek and to enjoy in other countries asylum from persecution.
2. This right may not be invoked in the case of prosecutions genuinely arising from non-political crimes or from acts contrary to the purposes and principles of the United Nations.

Article 15

1. Everyone has the right to nationality.
2. No one shall be arbitrarily deprived of his nationality nor denied the right to change his nationality.

Article 16

1. Men and women of full age, without limitation due to race, nationality or religion, have the right to marry and to found a family. They are entitled to equal rights as to marriage, during marriage and at its dissolution.
2. Marriage shall be entered into only with the free and full consent of the intending spouses.
3. The family is the natural and fundamental group unit of society and is entitled to protection by society and the state.

Article 17

1. Everyone has the right to own property alone as well as in association with others.
2. No one shall be arbitrarily deprived of his property.

Article 18

Everyone has the right to freedom of thought, conscience and religion; this rights includes freedom to change his religion or belief, and freedom, either alone or in community with others and in public or private, to manifest his religion or belief in teaching, practice, worship and observance.

Article 19

Everyone has the right to freedom of opinion and expression; this right includes freedom to hold opinions without interference and to seek, receive and impart information and ideas through any media regardless of frontiers.

Article 20

1. Everyone has the right to freedom of peaceful association.
2. No one may be compelled to belong to an association.

Article 21

1. Every one has right to take part in the government of his country, directly or through freely chosen representatives.
2. Everyone has the right of equal access to public service in his country.
3. The will of the people shall be the basis of the authority of government; this will, shall be expressed in periodic and genuine election, which shall be by universal and equal suffrage and shall be held by secret vote or by equivalent free voting procedures.

Article 22

Everyone, as a member of society, has the right to social security and is entitled to realisation through national effort and international co –operation and in accordance with the organisation and resources of each state, of the economic, social and cultural rights indispensable for his dignity and the free development of his personality.

Article 23

1. Everyone has the right to work, to free choice of employment, to just and favourable conditions of work to protection against unemployment.
2. Everyone, without any discrimination, has the right to equal pay for equal work.
3. Everyone who works has the right to just and favourable remuneration ensuring for himself and his family an existence worthy of human dignity, if necessary, by other means of social protection.
4. Everyone has the right to form and to join trade unions for the protection of his interests.

Article 24

Everyone has the right to rest and leisure including reasonable limitation of working hours and periodic holidays with pay.

Article 25

1. Everyone has the right to a standard of living adequate for the health and well-being of himself and his family, including food,

clothing, housing and medical care and necessary social service, and the right to security in the event of unemployment, sickness, disability, widowhood, old age or other lack of livelihood in circumstances beyond his control.

2. Motherhood and childhood are entitled to special care and assistance. All children, whether born in or out of wedlock, shall enjoy the equal social protection.

Article 26

1. Everyone has the right to education. Education shall be free, at least in the elementary and fundamental stages. Elementary education shall be compulsory. Technical and professional education shall be made generally available and higher education shall be equally accessible to all on the basis of merit.
2. Education shall be protected to the full development of the human personality and to the strengthening of respect for human rights and fundamental freedoms. It shall promote understanding, tolerance and friendship among all nations, racial or religious groups, and shall further the activities of the United Nations for the maintenance of peace.
3. Parents have a prior right to choose the kind of education that shall be given to their children.

Article 27

1. Everyone has the right to freely participate in the cultural life of the community, to enjoy the arts and to share in scientific advancement and its benefits.
2. Everyone has the right to protection of the moral and material interests resulting from any scientific, literary or artistic protection of which he is the author.

Article 28

Everyone is entitled to social and international order in which the rights and freedoms set forth in the Declaration can be fully realized.

Article 29

1. Everyone has duties to the community in which alone the free and full development of his personality is possible.

2. In the exercise of his rights and freedoms, every one shall be subject only to such limitations as are determined by law solely for the purpose of securing due to such limitations as are determined by law solely for the purpose of securing due recognition and respect for the rights and freedoms of others and of meeting the just requirements of morality, public order and the general welfare in the democratic society.
3. These rights and freedoms may in no case be exercised contrary to the purposes and principles of the United Nations.

Article 30

Nothing in this Declaration may be interpreted as implying for any state, group of person any right to engage in any activity or to perform any act aimed at the destruction of any of the rights and freedoms set forth herein.

A brief analysis of the Universal Declaration of Human Rights

The outstanding feature of the Universal Declaration of Human Rights is that it is a simple resolution of the General Assembly in the sense that it does't create binding obligation on the part of State to carry out its enforcement, yet it constitutes a "common standard of achievement for all peoples and all nations." As such it has normative value. "The repeated invocation of the Universal Declaration over more than forty-five years by the United Nations and other international organizations, its use in diplomatic exchange between governments, its incorporation into treaties and national constitutions, and its application by international and national tribunals have given at least some of its rights binding characters custom."[6]

The adoption of Declaration without dissent was considered a remarkable achievement since it was supported by overwhelming consensus of international community as represented in the General Assembly. It has defined and provided contents to the term "human rights and fundamental freedoms" as used in the United Nations Charter. The Declaration consists of a preamble and 30 articles incorporating civil, political, economic, social and cultural rights.

The preamble clearly stastes that "recognition of the inherent dignity and of the equal and inalienable rights of all members of the human family is the foundation of freedom, justice and peace in the world." Thus, the question of maintenance of international peace and security is interlinked with the recognition and protection of human rights.

The first two articles are general in nature providing philosophical assumptions upon which the Declaration is founded. They runs as

Article 1: "All human beings are born free and equal in dignity and rights. They are endowed with reason and conscience and should act towards one another in a spirit of brotherhood."

Article 2: "Everyone is entitled to all the rights and freedoms set forth in this declaration, without distinction of any kind."

Article 3to 21 of the Declaration include civil and political rights: the right to life, liberty and security of person; prohibition of slavery, of torture and cruel, inhuman or degrading treatment; the right to recognition every where as a person before the law; the right to effective judicial remedy; freedom from arbitrary arrest, detention; the right to a fair trial and public hearing by an independent and impartial tribunal; the right to be presumed innocent until provide guilty; freedom from arbitrary interference with privacy, family, home or correspondence; freedom of movement; the right of asylum; the right to nationality; freedom of opinion and expression; freedom of peaceful assembly and to form association; freedom of thought, conscience and religion; right to take part in Government of one's own country; and the right of equal access to public service.

The economic, social and cultural rights, described in Article 22 to 27, are right to education, to social security, to work, to rest and leisure, to an adequate standard of living, and to participate in the cultural life of the community.

Above all the Declaration has realized that everyone is entitled to a social and international order in which the rights and freedom set forth in the Declaration can be fully realized.[7] However, the rights recognized in the Declaration are not absolute. Such limitation as determined by law may be imposed for the purpose of securing due recognition and respect for the rights and freedom of others and of meeting the just requirements of morality, public order and general welfare in a democratic society.[8] These rights and freedoms may in no case be exercised by a State, group or individual contrary to the purposes and principles of the United Nations.[9]

Mary Ann Glendon situates the universal Declaration of Human Rights in this context as follows:

In 1948 the framers of the Universal Declaration achieved a distinctive synthesis of previous thinking about rights and duties. After canvassing sources from North and South, East and West, they believed they had found a core principle so basic that no nation would wish openly to disavow them. They wove those principles into a unified document that quickly displaced all antecedents as the Principal model for the rights instruments in force in the world today.[10]

Right to Information as Part of the UDHR

The Jurisprudence of democracy has been elaborately dealt in Articles23 and 25 of the UDHR, 1948 and in Part-III and IV of the Constitution of India, 1950. It states that every one should be able to enjoy freedom of opinion and expression including the right to "seek, receive and impart information and ideas". This guarantee is now widely understood as including openness on the part of governments and right to access to information in possession of Government. Commenting on the significance of Right to Information once Justice Bhagabati said, " No democratic government can survive without accountability and the basic postulate of accountability that the people should have information about the functioning of the Government. It is only when people know how Government is functioning that they can fulfil the role which democracy assigns to them and make democracy a really effective participatory democracy".

Over fifty countries have adopted comprehensive Right to Information laws, and twenty countries are seriously considering having such laws. The countries are not limited to the advanced western democracies only; but include a wide spectrum ranging from the emerging nation states of Africa through the developing countries of Asia, and Latin America to the recent democracies of Eastern Europe. Countries like South Africa, Mexico and Bulgaria are quite advanced in respect of access to information. India is relatively a latecomer in this respect.

Right to information laws reflect the basic premise that Government is meant to serve the people; and are based on the notion that public bodies hold information not for themselves, but as custodian of public good and that this information must be available to the general public. Access to government recodes and information is a necessary pre-requisite for enhancing transparency. Good governance is only possible where there is transparency and accountability. Access facilitates public knowledge and discussion, and thereby enhances responsiveness in public policy-making and service delivery. It provides an important safeguard against abuses, mismanagement and corruption; it enhances openness and responsiveness in the decision-making process and thereby increases credibility and legitimacy of Government actions essential for a civil and democratic society.

Right to Information Act of India, which has become operational since 12th October 2005, is a milestone in the history of our democracy. The detail provisions of the Act have been referred in Appendix-iv.

INTERNATIONAL COVENANT ON CIVIL AND POLITICAL RIGHTS, 1966

Part-I

Article 1

1. All people have the right of self-determination. By virtue of that right they freely determine their political status and freely pursue their economic, social and cultural development.
2. All peoples may, for their own ends, freely dispose of their natural wealth and resources without prejudice to any obligations arising out of international economic co-operation, based upon the principle of mutual benefit, and international law. In no case may a people be deprived of its own means of subsistence.
3. The parties to the present covenant, including those having responsibility for the administration of Non-self-Governing and Trust Territories, shall promote the realisation of the right of self-determination, and shall respect that right, in conformity with the provisions of the charter of the United Nations.

Part-II

Article 2

1. Each state party to the present covenant undertakes to respect and to ensure to all individuals within its territory and subject to its jurisdiction the rights recognised in the present covenant, without distinction of any kind, such as race, colour, sex, language, religion, political or other opinion, national, or social origin, property, birth or other status.
2. Where not already provided for by existing legislative or other measures, each state party to the present covenant undertakes

to take the necessary steps, in accordance with its constitutional processes and with the provisions of the present covenant, to adopt such legislative or other measures as may be necessary to give effect to the rights recognised in the present covenant.

3. Each state party to the present covenant undertakes:
   (a) To ensure that any person whose rights or freedoms as herein recognised are violated shall have an effective remedy, notwithstanding that the violation has been committed by persons acting in an official capacity;
   (b) To ensure that any person claiming such a remedy shall have his right thereto determined by competent judicial, administrative or legislative authorities, or by any other competent authority provided for by the legal system of the state, and to develop the possibilities of judicial remedy;
   (c) To ensure that the competent authorities shall enforce such remedies when granted.

Article 3

The states parties to the present covenant undertake to ensure the equal right of men and women to the enjoyment of all civil and political rights set forth in the present Covenant.

Article 4

1. In time of public emergency which threatens the life of the nation and the existence of which is officially proclaimed, the state parties to the present Covenant many take measures derogating from their obligations under the present Covenant to the extent strictly required by the exigencies of the situation, provide that such measures are not inconsistent with their other obligations under international law and do not involve discrimination solely on the ground of race, colour, sex, language, religion or social origin

Article 5

1. Nothing in the present Covenant may be interpreted as employing for any State, group or person any right to engage in any activity or perform any act aimed at the destruction of any of the rights and freedoms recognised herein or at their limitation to a greater extent than is provided for in the present Covenant.

There shall be on restriction upon or derogation from any of the fundamental human rights recognised or existing in any State Party to the present Covenant pursuant to law, conventions, regulations or custom on the pretext that the present Covenant does not recognise such rights or that it recognises them to a lesser extent.

Part-III

Article 6

1. Every human being has the inherent right to life. This right shall be protected by law. No one shall be arbitrarily deprived of his life.
2. In countries which have not abolished death penalty, sentence of death may be imposed only for the most serious crimes in accordance with the law in force at the time of the commission of the crime and not contrary to the provisions of the present Covenant and to the Convention on the Prevention Punishment of the Crime of Genocide. This penalty can only be carried out pursuant to a final judgement rendered by a competent Court.
3. When deprivation of life constitutes the crime of genocide, it is understood that nothing in this Article shall authorise any State Party to the present Covenant to derogate in any way from any obligation assumed under the provisions of the Convention on the Prevention and Punishment of the Crime of Genocide.
4. Anyone sentenced to death shall have the right to seek pardon or commutation of the sentence. Amnesty, pardon or commutation of the sentence of death may be granted in all cases.
5. Sentence of death shall not be imposed for crimes committed by persons bellow 18 years of age and shall not be carried out on pregnant women.
6. Nothing in this Article shall be invoked to delay or to prevent the abolition of capital punishment by any state Party to the present Covenant.

Article 7

No one shall be subjected to torture or to cruel, inhuman or degrading treatment or punishment. In particular, no one shall be subjected without his free consent to medical or scientific experimentation.

Article 8

1. No one shall be held in slavery; slavery and the slave trade in all their forms shall be prohibited.
2. No one shall be held in servitude.
3. (a) No one shall be required to perform forced or compulsory labour;

   (b) Paragraph 3(a) shall not be held to preclude, in countries where imprisonment with hard labour may be imposed as a punishment for a crime, the performance of hard labour in pursuance of a sentence to such punishment by a competent Court;

   (c) For the purpose of this paragraph the term "forced or compulsory labour" shall not included:

   (i) And work or service, not referred to in sub –paragraph (b), normally required of a person who is under detention in consequence of a lawful order of a Court, or of a person during conditional release from such detention;

   (ii) Any service of a military character and, in countries where conscientious objection is recognised, any national service required by law of conscientious objects:

   (iii) Any service exacted in cases of emergency or calamity threatening the life or well-being of the community;

   (iv) Any work or service which forms part of normal civil obligations.

Article 9

1. Everyone has the right to liberty and security of person. No one shall be subjected to arbitrary arrest or detention. No one shall be deprived of his liberty except on such grounds and in accordance with such procedure as are established by law.
2. Anyone who is arrested shall be informed, at the time of arrest, of the reasons for his arrest and shall be promptly informed of any charges against him.
3. Anyone arrested or detained on a criminal charge shall be brought promptly before a grudge or other officer authorised by law to exercise judicial power and shall be entitled to trial within a responsible time or to realise. It shall not be the general rule that persons awaiting trial shall be determined in custody, but release may be subject to guarantees to appear for trial, at any other

stage of the judicial proceedings, and, should occasion arise, for execution of the judgement.

4. Anyone who is deprived of his liberty by arrest or detention shall be entitled to take proceedings before a Court, in order that Court may decide without delay on the lawfulness of his detention and order his release if the detention is not lawful.
5. Anyone who has been the victim of unlawful arrest or detention shall have an enforceable right to compensation.

Article 10

1. All persons deprived of their liberty shall be treated with humanity and with respect for the inherent dignity of the human person.
2. (a) Accused persons shall, save in exceptional circumstances, be segregated from convicted persons and shall be subject to separate treatment appropriate to their status as unconvicted persons;
   (b) Accused juvenile persons shall be separated from adults and brought as speedily as possible for adjudication.
3. The penitentiary system shall comprise treatment of prisoners the essential aim of which shall be their reformation and social rehabilitation. Juvenile offenders shall be segregated from adults and be accorded treatment appropriate to their age and legal status.

Article 11.

No one shall be imposed merely on the ground of inability to fulfil a contractual obligation.

Article 12.

1. Everyone lawfully within the territory of a state shall, within that territory, have the right to liberty of movement and freedom to choose his residence.
2. Everyone shall be free to leave any country, including his own.
3. The above mentioned rights shall not be subject to any restrictions except those which are provided by law, are necessary to protect national security public order (order public), public health or morals or the rights and freedoms of others, and are consistent with the other rights recognised in the present Covenant.

4. No one shall be arbitrarily deprived of the right to enter his own country.

Article 13

An alien lawfully in the territory of a State Party to the present Covenant may be expelled there from only in pursuance of a decision reached in accordance with law and shall, except where compelling reasons of national security otherwise require, be allowed to submit the reasons against his expulsion and to have his case reviewed by, and be represented for the purpose before, the competent authority or a person or persons especially designated by the competent authority.

Article 14.

1. All persons shall be equal before the Court and tribunals. In the determination of any criminal charge against him, or of this rights and obligations in a suit of law, everyone shall be entitled to a fair and public hearing of a competent, independent and impartial tribunal established by law. The Press and the public may be excluded from all or part of a trial for the reasons of morals, public order (order public) or national security in a democratic society, or where the interest of the private lives of the parties so requires, or the extent strictly necessary in the opinion of the Court in special circumstances where publicity would prejudice the interests of justice; but any judgement rendered in a criminal case or in a suit at law shall be made public except where the interest of juvenile persons otherwise requires or the proceedings concern matrimonial disputes or the guardianship of children.
2. Everyone charged with a criminal offence shall have the right to be presumed innocent until provde guilty according to law.
3. In the determination of any criminal charge against him, everyone shall be entitled to the following minimum guarantees, in full equality:
   (a) To be informed promptly and, in detail, in a language which he understands of the nature and cause of the charge against him;
   (b) To have adequate time and facilities for the preparation of his defence and to communicate with counsel of his own choosing;
   (c) To be tried without undue delay;

(d) To be tried in his presence, and to defend himself in person or through legal assistance of his own choosing; to be informed, if he does not have legal assistance, of this right; and to have legal assistance assigned to him, in any case where the interests of justice so required, and without payment by him in any such case if he does not have sufficient means to pay for it;

(e) To examine, or have examined the witnesses against him and to obtain the attendance and examination of witnesses on the behalf under the same conditions as witnesses against him;

(f) To have the free assistance of an interpreter if he cannot understand or speak the language used in Court;

(g) Not to be compelled to testify against him or to confess guilt.

4. In the case of juvenile persons, the procedure shall be such as will take account of their age and the desirability of promoting their rehabilitation.

5. Everyone convicted of a crime shall have the right to his conviction and sentence being reviewed by a higher tribunal according to law.

6. When a person has by a final decision been convicted of a criminal offence and when subsequently his conviction has been reversed or he has been pardoned on the ground that a new or newly discovered fact shows conclusively that there has been a miscarriage of justice, the person who has suffered punishment as a result of such conviction shall be compensated according to law, unless it is proved that the non-disclosure of the unknown fact in time is wholly or partly attributable to him.

7. No one shall be liable to be tried or punished again for an offence for which he has already been finally convicted or acquitted in accordance with each country.

Article 15

1. No one shall be held guilty of any criminal offence on account of any act or omission, which did not constitute a criminal offence, under national or internal law, at the time when it was committed. Nor shall a heavier penalty be imposed then the one that was applicable at the time when the criminal offence was committed. If, subsequent to the commission of the offence, provision is

made by law for imposition of a lighter penalty, the offender shall benefit thereby.

2. Nothing in this Article shall prejudice the trial and punishment of any person for any act or omission, which, at the time when it was committed, was criminal according to the general principle of law, recognised by the community of nations.

Article 16

Everyone shall have the right to recognition everywhere as a person before the law.

Article 17

1. No one shall be subjected to arbitrary or unlawful interference with his privacy, family, home or correspondence, or to unlawful attacks on his honour and reputation.
2. Every one has the right to the protection of the law against such interference or attacks.

Article 18

1. Everyone shall have the right to freedom of thought, conscience and religion. This right shall include freedom to have or adopt a religion or belief of his choice, and freedom, either individually or in community with others and in public or private, to manifest his religion or belief in worship, observance, practice and teaching.
2. No one shall be subject to coercion which would impair his freedom to have or to adopt a religion or belief of his choice.
3. Freedom to manifest one's religion or beliefs may be subject only to such limitations as are prescribed by law and are necessary to protect public safety, order, health, or morals or the fundamental rights and freedoms of others.
4. The States Parties to the present Covenant undertake to have respect for the liberty of parents and, when applicable, legal guardians to ensure the religious and moral education of their children in conformity with their own convictions.

Article 19

1. Every one shall have the right to hold opinions without interference.

2. Everyone shall have the right to freedom of expression; this right shall include freedom to seek, receive and impart information and idea of all kinds, regardless of frontiers, either orally, in writing or in paint, in the form of art, or through any other media of his choice.
3. The exercise of the rights provided for in paragraph 2 of his Article carries with it special duties and responsibilities. It may therefore be subject to certain restrictions, but these shall only be such as are provided by law and are necessary:
   (a) for respect of the rights or reputation of others;
   (b) for the protection of national security or of public order (order public), or the public health or morals

Article 20

1. Any propaganda for war shall be prohibited by law.
2. Any advocacy of national, racial or religious hated that constitutes incitement to discrimination, hostility or violence shall be prohibited by law.

Article 21

The right of peaceful assembly shall be recognised. No restrictions may be placed on the exercise of this right other than those imposed in conformity with the law and which are necessary in a democratic society in the interest of national security or public safety, public order (order public), the protection of public health or morals or the protection of the rights and freedoms of others.

Article 22

1. Everyone shall have the right to freedom of association with others, including the right to form and join trade unions for the protection of his interests.
2. No restrictions may be placed on the exercise of this right other than those which are prescribed by law and which are in a democratic society in the interests of national security or public safety, public order (order public), the protection of public health or morals or the protection of rights and freedoms of others. This article shall not prevent the imposition of lawful restrictions on members of the armed forces and the police in their exercise of this right.
3. Nothing in this Article shall authorise State Parties to the international Labour Organisation Convention of 1948 concerning Freedom of Association and Protection of the Right to Organize

to take legislative measures which would prejudice, or to apply the law in such a manner as to prejudice, the guarantees provided for in that Covenant.

Article 23

1. The family is the natural and fundamental group unit of society and is entitled to protection by society and state.
2. The right of men and women of marriageable age to marry and to found a family shall be recognised.
3. No marriage shall be entered in to without the free and full consent of the intending spouses.
4. State parties of the present Covenant shall take appropriate staps to ensure equality of rights and responsibilities of spouses as to marriage, during marriage and at its dissolution. In the case of dissolution, provision shall be made for the necessary protection of any children.

Article 24

1. Every child shall have, without any discrimination as to race, colour, sex, language, religion, national or social origin, property or birth, the right to such measures of protection as are required by his status as a minor, on the part of his family, society and the State.
2. Every child shall be registered immediately after birth and shall have a name.
3. Every child has the right to acquire a nationality.

Article 25

Every citizen shall have the right and opportunity, without any of the distinctions mentioned in Article 2 and without unreasonable restriction:

(a) to take part in the conduct of public affairs, directly or through freely chosen representatives;

(b) to vote and to be elected at genuine periodic elections which shall be by universal and equal suffrage and shall be held by secret ballot, guaranteeing the free expression of the will of the electors;

(c) to have access, on general terms of equality, to public service in his country.

Article 26

All persons are equal before the law and are entitled without any discrimination to the equal protection of law. In this respect, the law shall prohibit any discrimination and guarantee to all person equal and effective protection against discrimination on any ground such as race, colour, sex, language, political or other opinion, national or social origin, property or birth or other status.

Article 27

In those States in which ethnic, religious or linguistic minorities exists, persons belonging to such minorities shall not be denied the right, in community with the other members of their group, to enjoy their other group, to enjoy their own culture, to profess and practice their own religion, or to use there own language.

Part-IV

Article 28

1. There shall be established a Human Rights Committee (hereinafter referred to in the present Covenant as the committee). It shall consist of eighteen members and shall carry out the functions hereinafter provided.
2. The committee shall be composed of nationals of the State Parties to the present to the present Covenant who shall be persons of rights moral character and recognized competence in the field of human rights, consideration being given to the usefulness of the participation of some persons having legal experience.
3. The members of the Committee shall be elected and shall serve in their personal capacity.

Article 29

1. The members of the committee shall be elected by secret ballot from a list of persons possessing the qualifications prescribed in Article 28 and nominated for the purpose by the States Parties to the present Covenant.
2. Each State Party to the present Covenant may nominate not more than persons. These persons shall be nationals of the nominating State.

Article 30

1. The initial election shall be held later than six months after the date of the entry into force of the present Covenant.
2. At least four month before the date of each election to the Committee, other than an election to fill a vacancy declared in accordance with Article 34, the Secretary General of the United Nations shall address a written invitation to the State Parties to the present Covenant to submit their nominations for membership of the Committee within three months.
3. The Secretary-General of the United Nations shall separate a list in alphabetical order of all the persons thus nominated, with an indication of the State Parties which have nominated them, and shall submit it to the State Parties to the present Covenant or later than one month before the date of each election.
4. Elections of the members of the Committee shall be held at the meeting of the State Parties to the present Covenant convened by the Secretary-General of the United Nations at the Headquarters of the United Nations. At the meeting, for which two-thirds of the State Parties to the present Covenant shall constitute a quorum, the persons elected to the committee shall be those nominees who obtain the largest number of votes and an absolute majority of the votes of the representatives of State Parties present and voting.

Article 31

1. The Committee may not include more than one national of the same state.
2. In the election of the committee, consideration shall be given to equitable geographical distribution of membership and to the presentation of the deferent forms of civilization and of the principal legal systems.

Article 32

1. The members of the Committee shall be elected for a term of four years. They shall be eligible for re-election if renominated. However the terms of nine of the members elected at the first election shall expire at the end of two years; immediately after the first election, lot by the Chairman of the meeting referred to in Article 30, paragraph 4, shall choose the names of these nine members.

2. Election at the expiry of office shall hold in accordance with the preceding Articles of this part of the present covenant.

Article 33

1. If, in the unanimous opinion of the other members, a member of the Committee has ceased to carry out his functions for any cause other than absence of a temporary character, the Chairman of the committee shall notify the Secretary-General of the United Nations, who shall then declare the seat of that member to be vacant.
2. In the event of the death or the resignation of a member of the Committee, the chairman shall immediately notify the Secretary-General of the United Nations, who shall declare the seat vacant from the date of death or the date on which the resignation takes effect.

Article 34

1. When a vacancy is declared in accordance with Article 33 and if the term of office of the member to be replaced does not expire within six months of the declaration of the vacancy, the Secretary-General of the United Nations shall notify each of the State Parties to the present Covenant, which may, within two months, submit nominations in accordance with Article 29 for the purpose of filling the vacancy.
2. The Secretary-General of the United Nations shall prepare a list in alphabetical order of the persons thus nominated and shall submit it to the States Parties to the present Covenant. The election to fill the vacancy shall than take place in accordance with the relevant provisions of this part of the present Covenant.
3. A member of the Committee elected to fill a vacancy declared in accordance with Article 33 shall hold office for the remainder of the term of the member of the vacated the seat on the Committee under the provisions of that Article.

Article 35

The member of the Committee shall, with the approval of the General Assembly of the United Nations, receive emoluments from United Nations resources on such terms and conditions as the General Assembly may decide, having regard to the importance of the Committee's responsibilities.

Article 36

The Secretary- General of the United Nation shall provide the necessary staff and facilities for the effective performance of the functions of the Committee of the present Covenant.

Article 37

1. The Secretary- General of the United Nation shall convene the initial meeting of the Committee at the Headquarter of the United Nations.
2. After its initial meeting, the Committee shall meet at such times as shall be provided in its rules of producer.
3. The Committee shall normally meet at the Headquarters of the United Nations or at the United Nations Office at Geneva.

Article 38

Every member of the Committee shall, before taking up his duties, make a solemn declaration in open committee that he will perform his functions impartially and conscientiously.

Article 39

1. The Committee shall elect its officers for a tern of two years. They may be re-elected.
2. The Committee shall establish its own rules of producer, but these rules shall provide, inter alia, that
   (a) Twelve members shall constitute a quorum;
   (b) Decisions of the Committee shall be made by majority vote of the members present.

Article 40

1. The State Parties to the present Covenant undertake to submit reports on the measures they have adopted which give effect to the rights recognized herein and on the progress made in the enjoyment of those rights:
   (a) Within one year of the entry into force of the present Covenant for the State Parties concerned;
   (b) Thereafter whenever the committee so requests.
2. All reports shall be submitted to the Secretary-General of the United Nations, who shall transmit then to the Committee for the consideration Reports shall indicate factors and difficulties, if any, affecting the implementation of the present Covenant.

3. The Secretary-General of the United Nations may, after consultation with the Committee, transmit to the specialized agency concerned, copies of such parts of the reports as may fall within their field of competence.
4. The Committee shall study the reports submitted by the State Parties to the present Covenant. It shall transmit its reports, and such general comments, as it may consider appropriate, to the State Parties. The Committee may also transmit to Economic and Social council these comments along with the copies of the reports it has received from State Parties to the present covenant.
5. The State Parties to the present Covenant may submit to the Committee observations on many comments that may be made in accordance with paragraph 4 of this Article.

Article 41

1. A State Party to the present Covenant may at any time declare under this Article that it recognizes the competence of the Committee to receive and consider communications to the effect that a State Party claims that under State Party claims that another State Party is not fulfilling its obligations under the present Covenant. Communications under this Article may be received and considered only if submitted by the State Parties which has made a declaration recognizing in regard to itself the competence of the Committee. No communication shall be received by the Committee if it concerns a State Party which has not made such a declaration. Communications received under this Article shall be dealt with in accordance with the following procedure:
   (a) If a State Party to the present Covenant considers that another State Party is not given effect to the provisions of the present Covenant, it may, by written communication, bring the matter to the attention of that State Party. Within three months after the receipt of the communication, the receiving State shall afford the state which sent the communication an explanation, or any other statement in writing clarifying the matter which should include, to the extent possible and pertinent, reference to domestic procedures and remedies taken, pending or available in the matter;
   (b) If the matter is not adjust to the satisfaction of both State Parties concerned, within six month after the receipt by

the receiving State of the initial communication, either State shall have the right to refer the matter to the Committee, by notice given to the Committee and to the other State;

(c) The Committee shall deal with a matter referred to it only after it has ascertained that all available domestic remedies have been invoked and exhausted in the matter, in conformity with the generally recognized principles of international law. This shall not be the rule where the application of the remedies is unreasonably prolonged.

(d) The committee shall hold closed meetings when examining communication under this Article.

(e) Subject to the provisions of sub-paragraph (c), the Committee shall make available its good office to the State Parties concerned with a view to friendly solution of the matter on the basis of respect for human rights and fundamental freedoms as recognized in the present Covenant;

(f) In any matter referred to it, the Committee call upon the State Parties concerned, referred to in sub-paragraph (b), to supply any relevant information;

(g) The State Parties concerned, referred to in sub-paragraph (b), shall have the right to be represented when the matter is being considered in the Committee and to make submissions orally and/or in writing;

(h) The Committee shall, within twelve months after the date of receipt of notice under sub-paragraph (b), submit a report;

(i) If a solution within the terms of sub-paragraph (e) is received, the Committee shall confine its report to a brief statement of the facts and the solution reached;

(ii) If a solution within the terms of sub-paragraph (e) is not reached, the Committee shall confine its report to brief statement of the facts; the written submission and record of the oral submission made by the State Parties concerned shall be attached to the report.

In every matter, the report shall be communicated to the State Parties concerned.

2. The provisons of this Article shall come into force when ten States parties to the present Covenant have made declarations under paragraph I of this Article. The State Parties with the Secretary-

General of the United Nations, who shall transmit copies thereof to the other States Parties, shall deposit such declarations. A declaration may be withdrawn at any time by notification to the Secretary-General. Such a withdrawal shall not prejudice the consideration of any matter which is the subject of a communication already submitted under this Article; no further communication by any State Party shall be received after the notification of withdrawal of the declaration has been received by the Secretary-General, unless the State Party concerned has made a new declaration.

Article 42

1. (a) If a matter referred to the Committee in accordance with Article 41 is not resolved to the satisfaction of the States Parties concerned, the Committee may, with the prior consent of the States Parties concerned, appoint an adhoc Conciliation Communication (hereinafter referred to as the Commission). The good office of the Commission shall be made available to the States Parties concerned with a view to an amicable solution of the matter on the basis of respect for the present Covenant.
   (b) The Commission shall consist of five persons acceptable to the States Parties concerned. If State Parties concerned fail to reach agreement within three months on all parts of the composition of the Commission, the member of the Commission concerning whom no agreement has been reached shall be elected by secret ballot by a two-thirds majority vote of the committee from among its members.
2. The members of the Commission shall serve in their personal capacity. They shall not be nationals of the States Parties concerned, or of a state not party to the present Covenant, or of a State party which has not made a declaration under Article 41
3. The Commission shall elect its own chairman and adopt its own rulers of procedure.
4. The meetings of the Commission shall normally be held at the Headquarters of the United Nations or at the United Nations Office at Geneva. However, they may be held at such convenient places as the Commission may determine in consultation with the Secretary-General of the United Nations and the States Parties concerned.

5. The Secretariat provided in accordance with Article 36 shall also service the commissions appointed under this Article.
6. The information received and collated by the Committee shall be made available to the Commission and the Commission call upon the States Parties concerned to supply any other relevant information.
7. When the Commission has fully considered the matter, but in any event not later than twelve months after having been seized of the matter, it shall submit to the Chairman of the Committee a report for communication to the States Parties concerned:
   (a) If the Commission is unable to complete its consideration of the matter within twelve months, it shall confine its report to a brief statement of the status of its consideration of the matter.
   (b) If an amicable solution to the matter on the basis of respect for human rights as recognized in the present Covenant is reached, the Commission shall confine its report to a brief statement of the facts and of the solution reached;
   (c) If a solution within the terms of sub-paragraph (b) is not reached, the Commission's report shall embody its findings on all questions of fact relevant to the issues between the States Parties concerned, and its views on the possibilities of an amicable solution of the matter. This report shall also contain the written submissions and a record of the oral submissions made by the States Parties concerned;
   (d) It the Commission's report is submitted under sub-paragraph (c), the States Parties concerned shall, within three months of the receipt of the report, notify the Chairman of the committee whether or not they accept the contents of the report of the Commission.
8. The provisions of this Article are without prejudice to the responsibilities of the committee under Article 41.
9. The States Parties concerned shall share equally all the expenses of the members of the Commission in accordance with estimates to be provided by the Secretary –General of the United Nations.
10. The Secretary-General of the United Nations shall be empowered to pay the expenses of the members of the Commission, if necessary, before reimbursement by the States Parties concerned, in accordance with paragraph 9 of this Article.

Article 43

The members of the Commission, and of the adhoc conciliation commissions which may be appointed under Article 42, shall be entitled to the facilities, privileges and immunities of exports on mission for the United Nations as laid down in the relevant sections of the Convention on the Privileges and immunities of the United Nations.

Article 44

The provisions for the implementation of the present Covenant shall apply without prejudice to the procedures prescribed in the field of human rights by or under the constituent instruments and the conventions of the United Nations and of the specialized agencies and shall not prevent the States Parties to the present Covenant from having recourse to other producers for setting a dispute in accordance with general or special international agreements in force between them.

Article 45

The Committees shall submit to the General Assembly of the United Nations, through the Economic and Social Council, an annual report on its activities.

PART V

Article 46

Nothing in the present Covenant shall be interpreted as impairing the provisions of the Charter of the United Nations and of the constitutions of the specialized agencies which define the respective responsibilities of the various organs of the United Nations and of the specialized agencies in regard to the matters dealt with in the present Covenant.

Article 47

Nothing in the present Covenant shall be interpreted as impairing the inherent right of all peoples to enjoy and utilise fully and freely their natural wealth and resources.

PART VI

Article 48

1. The present Covenant is open for signature by the State Members of the United Nations or members of any of its specialized agencies, by any State party to the Statute of the

International Court of Justice, and by any other State which has been invited by the General Assembly of the United Nations to become a Party to the present Covenant.

2. The present Covenant is subject to ratification. Instruments of ratification shall be deposited with the Secretary-General of the United Nations.
3. The present Covenant shall be open to accession by any state referred to in paragraph 1 of this Article.
4. Accession shall be effected by the deposit of an instrument of accession with the Secretary–General of the United Nations.
5. The Secretary-General of the United Nations shall inform all States which have signed this Covenant or acceded to it of the deposit of each instrument of ratification or accession.

Article 49

1. The present Covenant shall come into force three months after the date of the deposit with the Secretary-General of the United Nations of the thirty-fifth instrument of ratification or instrument of Accession.
2. For each State ratifying the present Covenant or according to it after the deposit of the thirty-fifth instrument of ratification or instrument of accession, the present Covenant shall come into force three months after the date of the deposit of its own instrument of ratification or instrument of accession.

Article 50

The provisions of the present Covenant shall extend to all parts of federal States without any limitations or exceptions.

Article 51

1. Any State party to the present Covenant may propose an amendment and file it with the Secretary-General of the United Nations The Secretary-General of the United Nations shall thereupon communicate favours such a conference, under the auspices of the United Nations. Any amendment adopted by a majority of the State Parties present and voting at the conference shall be submitted to the General Assembly of any proposed amendments to the State Parties to the present Covenant with a request that they notify him whether they favour a conference of state parties for the porpose of considering and voting upon the

proposals. In the event that at least one-third of the State Parties the United Nations for approval.

2. Amendments shall come into force when they have been approved by the General Assembly of the United Nations and accepted by a two-thirds majority of the State Parties to the present Covenant in accordance with their respective constitutional processes.

3. When amendments come into force, they shall be binding on those State Parties which have accepted them, other State Parties still being bound by the provisions of the present Covenant and any earlier amendment which they have accepted.

Article 52

Irrespective of the notification made under Article 48, paragraph 5, the Secretary-General of the United Nations shall inform all States referred to in paragraph 1 of the same article of the following particulars:

(a) Signatures, ratifications made accessions under Article 48;

(b) The date of the entry into force of the present Covenant under Article 49 and the date of the entry into force of any amendment under Article 51.

Article 53

1. The present Covenant, of which the Chinese, English, French, Russain and Spanish texts are equally authentic, shall be deposited in the archives of the United Nations.
2. The Secretary-General of the United Nations shall transmit certified copies of the present Covenant to all States referred to in Article 48.

A Brief analysis the International Covenant on civil and political rights.

The distinctive feature of this Covenant as described under Article 2 and 4 are:

(I) Each State party undertakes to ensure to all individuals within its territory the rights recognized, in this Covenant without distinction of any kind, such as race, colour, sex, language, religion, political or other opinion, national or social origin, property, birth or other status;

(II) Each State party undertakes to ensure that any person whose rights or freedoms are violated shall have an effective remedy;

(III) Each State party undertakes to ensure that such effective remedy shall be determined by competent judicial, administrative legislative or any other competent authority provided for by the legal system of the State; and

(IV) That such remedies when granted should be enforced by the competent authority.

However, the State parties may take measures derogating form this obligation under the Covenant when the public emergency threatening the life of a nation exist and the existence of which is officially proclaimed. Such measures should be exercised to the extent strictly required by the exigencies of the situation provided they are not inconsistent with State's other obligations or other international law and do not involve discrimination solely on the ground of race, colour, sex, language, religion or social origin.

The rights which are included in this category are; the rights of life; prohibition of torture, cruel, inhuman or degrading treatment or punishment; prohibition of slavery, slave trade, servitude and forced labour; the right to liberty and security of person, freedom from arbitrary arrest and detention; prohibition of imprisonment on the ground of inability to fulfil contractual obligation; the right to liberty of movement and freedom to choose residence; right to equality before law and courts and tribunals; freedom from *ex-post facto* laws; the right to recognition as person; prohibition of arbitrary or unlawful interference with a person's privacy, family, home or correspondence; the right to freedom of thought, conscience and religion; right to hold opinion hold opinion without interference; prohibition of propaganda for war; the right to peaceful assembly and freedom of association; the fight to marry and protection of family; the right to the child to acquire nationality; the right to opportunity to take part in the conduct of public affairs, right to vote and right to be elected by the secret-ballot; the right to equality before law and equal protection of law; and the right of minorities to enjoy their culture, to profess their religion and to use their language.[11]

INTERNATIONAL COVENANT ON ECONOMIC, SOCIAL AND CULTURAL RIGHTS, 1966

Part-I

Article 1

1. All peoples have the right of self-determination. By virtue of that right they freely determine their political status and freely pursue their economic, social and cultural development.
2. All peoples may, for their own ends, freely dispose of their natural wealth and resources without prejudice to any obligations arising out of international economic co-operation, based upon the principle of mutual benefit, and international law. In no case may a people be deprived of its own means of subsistence.
3. The State Parties to the present Covenant, including those having responsibility for the administration of Non-Self-Governing and Trust Territories, shall promote the realisation of self-determination, and shall respect that right, in conformity with the provisions of the Charter of the United Nations.

Part-II

Article 2

1. Each State Party to the present Covenant undertakes to take steps, individually and through international assistance and co-operation, especially economic and technical, to the maximum of its available resources, with a view to achieving progressively of full realisation of the rights recognised in the present Covenant by all appropriate means, including particularly the adoption of legislative measures.
2. The State Parties to the Covenant undertake to guarantee that the rights enunciated in the present Covenant will be exercised without discrimination of any kind as to race, colour, sex, language, religion, political or other opinion, national or social origin, property, birth or other status.
3. Developing countries, with due regard to human rights and their national economy may determine to what extent they would guarantee the economic rights recognised in the present Covenant to non-nationals.

Article 3

The State Parties to the present Covenant undertake to ensure the equal right of men and women to the enjoyment of all economic, social and cultural rights set forth in the present Covenant.

Article 4

The State Parties to the present Covenant recognise that, in the enjoyment of those rights provided by the State in conformity with the present Covenant, the State may subject such rights only to such limitations as are determined by law only in so far as this may be compatible with the nature of these rights solely for the purpose of promoting the general welfare in a democratic society

Article 5

1. Nothing in the present Covenant may be interpreted as implying for any State, group or person any right to engage in any activity or to perform any act aimed at the destruction of any of the rights or freedoms recognised herein, or at their limitation to a grater extent than is provided for in the present Covenant.
2. No restriction upon or derogation from any of the fundamental human rights recognised or existing in any country in virtue of law, conventions, regulations or custom shall be admitted on the pretext that the present Covenant does not recognise such rights or existing in any country in virtue of law, conventions regulations or custom shall be admitted on the pretext that the present Covenant does not recognise such rights or that it recognises them to a lesser extent.

Part-III

Article 6

1. The states Parties to the present Covenant recognise the right to work, which includes the rights of everyone to the opportunity to gain his living by work which he freely chooses or accepts, and will take appropriate steps to safeguard this right.
2. The steps to be taken by the State Party to the present Covenant to achieve the full realisation of this right shall include technical and vocational guidance and training programmes, policies and techniques to achieve steady economic, social and cultural

development and full and productive employment under conditions safeguarding fundamental political and economic freedoms to the individual.

Article 7

The State Parties to the present Covenant recognise the right of everyone to the enjoyment of just and favourable conditions of work, which ensure, in particular:

(a) Remuneration which provides all workers, as a minimum, with:
   (i) Fair wages and equal remuneration for work of equal value without distinction of any kind, in particular women being guaranteed conditions of work not inferior to those enjoyed by men, with equal pay for equal work;
   (ii) a decent living for themselves and their families in accordance with the provisions of the present Covenant;

(b) Safe and healthy working conditions;

(c) Equal opportunity for every one to be promoted in his employment to an appropriate higher level, subject to considerations other than those of seniority and competence;

(d) Rest, leisure and reasonable limitation of working hours and periodic holidays with pay, as well as remuneration for public holidays.

Article 8

1. The State Parties to the present Covenant undertake to ensure:
   (a) The right of everyone to form trade unions and join the trade union of his choice, subject only to the rules of the organisation concerned, for the promotion and protection of his economic and social interest. No restrictions may be placed on the exercise of this right other than those prescribed by law and which are necessary in a democratic society in the interest of national security or public order or for the protection of the rights and freedom of others;
   (b) The right of trade unions to establish national federations or confederations and the right of the latter to form or join international trade-union organisations;
   (c) The right of trade unions to function freely subject to no limitations other than those prescribed by law and which are necessary in a democratic society in the interest of

national security or public order or for the protection of the rights and freedom of others;

(d) The right to strike provided that it is exercised in conformity with the law of the particular country.

2. This Article shall not prevent the composition of lawful restrictions on the exercise of these rights by members of the armed forces or of the police or of the administration of the state.
3. Nothing in this Article shall authorise State Parties to the International Labour Organisation Convention of 1948 concerning freedom of association and Protection of the Right to Organise to take legislative measures which without prejudice, to apply the law in such a manner as would prejudice, guarantees provided for in that Covenant.

Article 9

The state parties to the present Covenant recognised the right of everyone to social security, including social insurance.

Article 10

The State Parties to the present Covenant recognise that:

1. The widest possible protection and assistance should be accorded to the family, which is the natural and fundamental group unit of society, particularly for its establishment and while it responsible for the care and education of dependent children. Marriage must be entered in to with the free consent of the intending spouses.
2. Special protection should be accorded to mother during a responsible period before and after childbirth. During such period working mother should be accorded paid leave or leave with adequate social security benefits.
3. Special measures of protection and assistance should be taken on behalf of all children and young persons without any discrimination for reasons of parentage or other conditions. Children and young persons should be protected from economic and social exploitation. Their employment in work harmful to their morals or health or dangerous to life or likely to hamper their normal development should be punishable by law. State should also set as limits below which the paid employment of child labour should be prohibited and punishable by law.

Article 11

1. The States Parties to the present Covenant recognise the right of everyone to an adequate standard of living for himself and his family, including adequate food, clothing and housing, and to the continuous improvement of living conditions. The State Parties will take appropriate staps to ensure the realisation of this right, recognising to this effect the essential importance of international co-operation based on free consent.
2. The State Parties to the present Covenant, recognising the fundamental rights of everyone to be free from hunger, shall take, individually and through international co-operation, the measures, including specific programmes, which are needed:
   (a) to improve method of production, conservation of food by making full use of technical and scientific knowledge by disseminating of the principles of nutrition and by developing or reforming agrarian systems in such a way as to achieve the most efficient development and utilisation of natural resources;
   (b) taking into account the problems of both food-importing and food-exporting countries, to ensure an equitable distribution of world food supplies in relation to need.

Article 12

1. The State Parties to the present Covenant recognise the right of everyone to the enjoyment of the highest attainable stand of physical and mental health.
2. The steps to be taken by the State Parties to the present Covenant to achieve the full realisation of this right shall include those necessary for:
   (a) the provision for the reduction of the stillbirth-rate and of infant mortality and for the healthy development of the child;
   (b) the improvement of all aspects of environmental and industrial hygiene;
   (c) the prevention, treatment and control of epidemic, endemic, occupational and other diseases;
   (d) the creation of conditions which would assure to all medical service and attention in the event of sickness.

Article 13

1. The State Parties of the present Covenant recognise the right of everyone to education. They agree that education shall be directed to the full development of the human personality and the sense of its dignity, and shall strengthen the respect for human rights and fundamental freedoms. They further agree that education shall enable all persons to participate effectively in a free society, promote understanding, tolerance and friendship among all nations and all racial, ethnic or religious groups, and further the activities of the United Nations for the maintenance of peace.
2. The State Parties of the present Covenant recognise that, with a view to achieving the full realisation of this right:
   (a) Primary education shall be compulsory and available free to all;
   (b) Secondary education in its different forms, including technical and vocational secondary education, shall be made generally available and accessible to all by every appropriate means, and in particular by the progressive introduction of free education;
   (c) Higher education shall be made equally accessible to all, on the basis of capacity, by every appropriate means, and in particular by the progressive introduction of free education;
   (d) Fundamental education shall be encouraged or intensified as far as possible for those persons who have not received or completed the whole period of their primary education;
   (e) The development of a system of school at all levels shall be actively pursued, an adequate fellowship system shall be established, and the material conditions of teaching staff shall be continuously improved.
3. The State Party to the present Covenant undertake to have respect for the liberty of parents and, when applicable legal guardians, to choose for their children schools, other than those established by the public authorities, which conform to such minimum educational standards as may be laid down or approved by the State and to ensure the religious and moral education of their children in conformity with their own convictions.
4. No part of this Article shall be constructed so as to interfere with the liberty of individuals and bodies to establish and direct

educational institutions, subject always to the observance of the principles set forth in paragraph 1 of this Article and to the requirement that the education given in such institutions shall conform to such minimum standards as may be laid down by the State.

Article 14

Each State Party to the present Covenant which, at the time of becoming a Party, has not been able to secure in its metropolitan territory or other territories under its jurisdiction compulsory primary education, free of charge, undertakes, within two years, to work out and adopt a detailed plan of action for the progressive implementation, within a reasonable number of years, to be fixed in the plan, of the principle of compulsory education free of charge for all.

Article 15

1. The State Parties of the present Covenant recognise the right of every one
   (a) To take part in cultural life;
   (b) To enjoy the benefits of scientific progress and its applications;
   (c) To benefit from the protection of the moral and material interests resulting from any scientific, literary or artistic production of which he is the author.
2. The steps to be taken by the State Parties to the present Covenant to achieve the full realisation of this right shall include those necessary for the conservation, the development and the diffusion of science and culture.
3. The State Parties to the present Covenant undertake to respect the freedom indispensable for the scientific research and creative activity.
4. The State Party to the present Covenant recognise the benefits to be derived from the encouragement and development of international contacts and co-operation in scientific and cultural fields.

PART IV

Article 16

1. The State Parties of the present Covenant undertake to submit, in conformity with this part of the Covenant, reports on the

measures which they have adopted and the progress made in achieving the observance of the rights recognized herein.

2. (a) All reports shall be submitted to the Secretary-General of the United Nations, who shall transmit copies to the Economic and Social Council for consideration in accordance with the provisions of the present Covenant;

   (b) The Secretary-General of the United Nations shall also transmit to the specialized agencies copies of the reports, or any relevant parts there from, from State Parties to the present Covenant which are also members of these specialized agencies in so far as these reports, or part there form, related to any matter which falls within the responsibilities of the said agencies in accordance with their constitutional instruments.

Article 17

1. The State Parties of the present Covenant shall furnish their reports in stages, in accordance with a programme to be established by the Economic and Social Council within one year of the entry into the force of the present Covenant after consultation with the States Parties and the specialized agencies concerned.
2. Reports may indicate factors and difficulties affecting the degree of fulfilment of obligations under the present Covenant.
3. Where relevant information has previously been furnished to the United Nations or to any specialized agency by any State Party to the present Covenant, it will not be necessary to reproduce that information, but a precise reference to the information so furnished will suffice.

Article 18

Pursuant to its responsibilities under the Charter of the United Nations in the field of human right and fundamental freedoms, the Economic and Social Council may take arrangements with the specialized agencies in respect of their reports to it on the progress made in achieving the observance of the provisions of the present Covenant falling within the scope of their activities. These reports may include particulars of decisions and recommendations on such implementation adopted by their competent organs.

Article 19

The Economic and Social Council may transmit to the Commission on Human Rights for study and general recommendation or, as appropriate, for information the reports concerning human rights submitted by States in accordance with Article 16 and 17, and those concerning human rights submitted by the specialized agencies in accordance with Article 18.

Article 20

The States Parties to the present Covenant and the specialized agencies concerned may submit comments to the Economic and Social Council on any general recommendation under Article 19 or reference to such general recommendation in any report of the Commission on Human Rights or any documentation referred to therein.

Article 21

The Economic and Social Council may submit from time to time to the General Assembly reports with recommendations of a general nature and a summary of the information received from the States Parties to the present Covenant and the specialized agencies on the measures taken and the progress made in achieving general observance of the rights recognized in the present Covenant.

Article 22

The Economic and Social Council may bring to the attention of other organs of the United Nations, their subsidiary organs and specialized agencies concerned with furnishing technical assistance, any matter arising out of the reports referred to in this part of the present Covenant which may assist such bodies in deciding, each within its field of competence, on the advisability of international measures likely to contribute to the effective progressive implementation of the present Covenant.

Article 23

The State Party of the present Covenant agree that international action for the achievement of the rights recognised in the present Covenant includes such methods as the conclusion of conventions, the adoption of recommendations, the furnishing of technical assistance and the holding of regional meetings and technical meetings for the purpose of consultation and study organised in conjunction with the Governments concerned.

Article 24

Nothing in the present Covenant shall be interpreted as impairing the provisions of the Charter of the United Nations and of the constitutions of the specialised agencies which define the respective responsibilities of the various organs of the United Nations and of the specialised agencies in regard to the matters dealt with in the present Covenant.

Article 25

Every citizen shall have the right and the opportunity, without any of the distinctions mentioned in Article 2 and without unreasonable restrictions:

(a) To take part in the conduct of public affairs, directly or through freely chosen representatives;

(b) To vote and to be elected at genuine periodic elections which shall be by universal and equal suffrage and shall be held by secret ballot, guaranteeing the free expression of the will of the electors;

(c) To have access, on general terms of equality, to public service in his country.

PART V

Article 26

1. The present Covenant is open for signature by any State Member of the United Nations or member of any of its specialised agencies, by any State Party to the Statute of the International court of justice, and by any other State which has been invited by the General Assembly of the United Nations to become a party to the present Covenant.

2. The present Covenant is subject to ratification. Instruments of ratification shall be deposited with the Secretary-General of the United Nations.

3. The present Covenant shall be open to accession by any State referred to in paragraph 1 of this article.

4. Accession shall be affected by the deposit of an instrument of accession with the Secretary-General of the United Nations.

5. The Secretary-General of the United Nations shall inform all States, which have signed the present Covenant and acceded to it of the deposit of each instrument of ratification or accession.

Article 27

1. The present Covenant shall enter into force three months after the date of the deposit with the Secretary-General of the United Nations of the thirty-fifth instrument of ratification or instrument of accession.
2. For each State ratifying the present Covenant or accessing to it after the deposit of the thirty-fifth instrument of ratification or instrument of accession, the present Covenant shall enter into force three months after the date of the deposit of its own instrument of accession.

Article 28

The provision of the present Covenant shall extend to all parts of federal States without any limitations or exceptions.

Article 29

1. Any State Party to the present Covenant may propose an amendment and file it with the Secretary-General of the United Nations. The Secretary-General shall thereupon communicate any proposed amendments to the States Parties to the present Covenant with a request that they notify him whether they favour a conference of States Parties for the purpose of considering and voting upon the proposals. In the event that at last one third of the States Parties favours such a conference, the Secretary-General shall convene the conference under the auspices of the United Nations. Any amendment adopted by a majority of the State Parties present and voting at the conference shall be submitted to the General Assembly of the United Nations for approval.
2. Amendments shall come into force when they have been approved by the General Assembly of the United Nations and accepted by a two-third majority of the States Parties to the present covenant in accordance with their respective constitutional processes.
3. When amendments come into force they shall be binding on those States Parties, which have accepted them, other State Parties still being bound by the provisions of the present, Covenant and any earlier amendment which they have accepted.

Article 30

Irrespective of the notifications made under Article 26, paragraph 5, the Secretary-General of the United Nations shall inform all States referred to in paragraph 1 of the some Article of the following particulars:

(a) Signatures, ratifications and accessions under Article 26;

(b) the date of the entry into force of the present Covenant under Article 27 and the date of the entry into force of any amendments under Article 29.

Article 31

1. The present Covenant, of which the Chinese, English, French, Russian and Spanish texts are equally authentic, shall be deposit in the archives of the United Nations.
2. The Secretary-General of the United Nations shall transmit certified copies of present Covenant to all States referred to in article26.

A brief analysis of the International Covenant on Economic, Social and Cultural Rights.

The distinctive features of this covenant as described under Article 2 are (I) that each State party undertake to take step, to the maximum of its available resources, to achieve progressively the full realization of these rights by all appropriate means including the legislation; (II) that State parties undertake to guarantee that these rights will be exercised without discrimination of any kind as to race, colour, sex, language, religion political or other opinion, national or social origin, property, birth or other status; and (III) Developing countries may determine with due regard to human rights and their national economy as to what extent they would guarantee the economic rights to the non-nationals.

Following rights are included in the list of economic, social and cultural rights; the right to work; the right to the enjoyment of just and favourable condition of work; the right to form and joint trade union of one's own choice; the right to social security including social insurance; the right to protection to family, special protection to motherhood and childhood; the right to adequate standard of living and freedom from hunger; the right to the enjoyment of the highest attainable standard of physical and mental health; the right to education; and the right to take part in cultural life and to enjoy the benefits of scientific progress.

The rights contained in the Covenants are not identical to those contained in the Universal Declaration

As compared to the Universal Declaration of Human Rights, the Covenant on Civil and Political Rights incorporates certain rights which do not found mention in the Universal Declaration, such as, prohibition of imprisonment merely on the ground of inability to fulfil a contractual obligation; human treatment detainees and, certain rights of the child not mentioned the Universal Declaration. At the same time the Covenant on Civil and Political rights do not contain the right to own property, the right to seek and enjoy asylum and the right to nationality. The Covenant on Civil and Political Rights contains the provisions under which State parties may suspend many of the rights "in time of public emergency that threatens the life of the nation."

On the other hand Covenant of Economic, Social and Cultural rights are drafted in broader, and detailed manner. The list of the rights is long and more comprehensive.

Instrumentality of Enforcement of two Covenants

The Human Rights Committee has been established to supervise the State compliance with the provision of the covenant on Civil and Political rights by reviewing and commenting on the periodic reports submitted by the State parties. The committee receives and considers communication to the effect that a State party claims that another State parties are not fulfilling its obligations under the present Covenant. It also considers petition submitted by individuals under the First Optional Protocol to the Covenant on Civil and Political Rights. The Protocol enables the Human Rights Committee to receive and consider petitions from individual claiming to be victims of violations of any of the rights set forth in the Covenant.

The enforcement of the rights contained in the Covenant on Economic, Social and Cultural Rights depend upon the economic viability of the State parties and international economic and technical assistance, particularly to the developing and non-development States.

Declaration on the Right to Development

The General Assembly

Bearing in mind the purposes and principles of the charter of the United Nations relating to the achievement of international co-operation in solving international problems of economic, social, cultural or humanitarian nature, and in promoting and encouraging respect for human rights and fundamental freedoms for all without distinction as to race, sex, language or religion,

Recognizing that development is a comprehensive economic, social, cultural and political process, which aims at the constant improvement of the well-being of the entire population and of all individuals on the basis of their active, free and meaningful participation in development and in the fair distribution of benefits resulting there from,

Considering that under the provisions of the Universal Declaration of human rights everyone is entitled to a social and international order in which the right and freedoms set forth in that Declaration can be fully realized,

Recalling the provisions of the International Covenant of Economic. Social and cultural Rights and of the International covenant on Civil and political Rights,

Recalling further the relevant agreements, conventions, resolutions, recommendations and other instruments of the United Nations and its specialized agencies concerning the integral development of the human being, economic and social progress and development of all peoples, including those instruments concerning decolonisation, the prevention of discrimination, respect for and observance of human rights and fundamental freedoms, the maintenance of international peace and security and the further promotion of friendly relations and cooperation among states in accordance with the charter,

Recalling the right of peoples to self- determination, by virtue of which they have the right freely to determine their political status and to pursue their economic, social and cultural development,

Recalling also the right of peoples to exercise, subject to the relevant provisions of both International Covenants on Human Rights, full and complete sovereignty over all their natural wealth and resources,

Mindful of the obligation of states under the charter to promote universal respect for and observance of human rights and fundamental freedoms for all without distinction of any kind such as race, colour, sex language, religion, political or other opinion, national or social origin, property, birth or other status,

Considering that the elimination of the massive and flagrant violations of the human rights of the peoples and individuals affected by situations such as those resulting from colonialism, neo-colonialism, apartheid, all forms of racism and racial discrimination, foreign domination and occupation, aggression and threats against national sovereignty, national unity and territorial integrity and threats of war would contribute to the establishment of circumstances propitious to the development of a great part of mankind,

Concerned at the existence of serious obstacles to development, as well as to the complete fulfilment of human being and of peoples, constituted, inter alias, by the denial of civil, political, economic, social and cultural rights, and considering that all human rights and fundamental freedoms are indivisible and interdependent and that, in order to promote development, equal attention and urgent consideration should be given to the implementation, promotion and protection of civil, political economic, social and cultural rights and that accordingly, the promotion of, respect for and enjoyment of certain human right and fundamental freedoms cannot justify the denial of other human rights and fundamental freedoms,

Considering that international peace and security are essential elements for the realization of the right to development,

Reaffirming that there is a close relationship between disarmament and development and that progress in the field of disarmament would considerably promote progress in the field of development and that resources released through disarmament measures should be devoted to the economic and social development and well-being of all peoples and, in particular, those of the developing countries,

Recognizing that the human person is the central subject of the development process and that development policy should therefore make the human being the main participant and beneficiary of development,

Recognizing that the creation of conditions favourable to the development of peoples and individuals is the primary responsibility of their states,

Aware that efforts at the international level to promote and protect human rights should be accompanied by efforts to establish a new international economic order,

Confirming that the right to development is an inalienable human right and that equality of opportunity for development is a prerogative both of nations and of individuals, who make up nations,

Proclaims the following Declaration on the Right to Development:

Article 1

1. The right to development is an inalienable human right by virtue of which every human person and all peoples are entitled to participate in, contribute to and enjoy economic, social, cultural and political development, in which all human rights and fundamental freedoms can be fully realized.
2. The human right to development also implies the full realization of the right of peoples to self-determination, which includes, subject to the relevant provisions of both International covenants on Human Rights, the exercise of their inalienable right to full sovereignty over all their natural wealth and resources.

Article 2

1. The human person is the central subject of development and should be the active participant and beneficiary of the right to development.
2. All human beings have a responsibility for development, individually and collectively, taking in to account the need for full respect for their human rights and fundamental freedoms as well as their duties to the community, which alone can ensure the free and complete fulfilment of the human being and they should therefore promote and protect an appropriate political, social and economic order for development.
3. States have the right and the duty to formulate appropriate national development policies that aim at constant improvement of the well-being of the entire population and of all individuals, on the basis of their active, free and meaningful participation in development and in the fair distribution of the benefits resulting there from.

Article 3

1. States have the primary responsibility for the creation of national and international conditions favourable to the realization of the rights to development.
2. The realization of the rights to development requires full respect for the principles of international law concerning friendly relations and cooperation among States in accordance with the Charter of the United Nations.
3. States have the duty to cooperate with each other in ensuring development and eliminating obstacles to development. State

should realize their rights and fulfil their duties in such a manner as to promote a new international economic order based on sovereign equality, interdependence, mutual interest and cooperation among all States, as to encourage the observance and realization of human rights.

Article- 4

1. States have the duty to take stapes, individually and collectively, to formulate international development policies with a view to facilitating the full realization of the rights to development.
2. Sustained action is required to promote more rapid development of developing countries. As a complement to the efforts of developing countries, effective international cooperation is essential in providing these countries with appropriate means and facilities to foster their comprehensive development.

Article-5

State shall take resolute steps to eliminate the massive and fragrant violations of the human rights of peoples and human beings affected by situations such as those resulting from apartheid, all forms of racism and racial discrimination, colonialism, foreign domination and occupation, aggression, foreign interference and threats against national sovereignty, national unity and territorial integrity, threats of war and refusal to recognize the fundamental right of peoples to self-determination.

Article-6

1. All States should cooperate with a view to promoting, encouraging and strengthening universal respect for an observance of all human rights and fundamental freedoms for all without any distinction as to race, sex, language or religion.
2. All human rights and fundamental freedoms are indivisible and interdependent; equal attention and urgent condition should be given to the implementation, promotion and protection of civil, political, economic, social and cultural rights.
3. State should take steps to eliminate obstacles to development resulting from failure to observe civil and political rights, as well as economic, social and cultural rights.

Article -7

All State should promote the establishment, maintenance and strengthening of international peace and security and, to that end, should do their utmost to achieve general and complete disarmament under effective international control, as well as to ensure that the resources released by effective disarmament measures are used for comprehensive development, in particular that of the developing countries.

Article-8

1. States should undertake, at the national level, all necessary measures for the realization of the right to development and shall ensure, inter alias, equality of opportunity for all in their access to basic resources, education, health services, food, housing, employment and the fair distribution of income. Effective measure should be undertaken to ensure that women have an active role in the development process. Appropriate economic and social reforms should be carried out with to eradicating all social injustices.
2. States should encourage popular participation in all spheres as an important factor in development and in the full realization of all human rights.

Article-9

1. All the aspects of the right to development set forth in the present Declaration are indivisible and interdependent and each of them should be considered in the context of the whole.
2. Nothing in the present Declaration shall be construed as being contrary to the purposes and principles of the United Nations, or as implying that any State, group or person has a right to engaged in any activity or to perform any act aimed at the violation of the rights set forth in the Universal Declaration of Human Rights and in the International Covenants on Human Rights.

Article-10

Steps should be taken to ensure the full exercise and progressive enhancement of the right to development, including formulation, adoption and implementation of policy, legislative and other measures at the national and international levels.

A Brief Analysis on Declaration on the Right to Development

The right to self Determination: The Right to self-determination is one of the most basic collective rights. By virtue of the right of self-determination people have right not only to freely determine their political status but also to freely pursue their economic, social and cultural development.[12] Thus, right of self –determination includes right to development.

The right to Development: The right to development encompasses within its ambit all human rights and fundamental freedoms including right of self-determination: Article 1 of the Declaration on the right to Development runs as follows:

"The right to development is an inalienable human right by virtue of which every human person and all people are entitled to participate in, contribute to and enjoy economic, social, cultural and political development, in which all human rights and fundamental freedoms can be fully realised." Further, "The human rights to development also implies the full realisation of the right of people to self determination, which includes, subject to the relevant provisions of both international convents on human rights, the exercise of their inalienable right to full sovereignty over all their natural wealth and resources."

Thus, right to development is of multidimensional character incorporating all civil, political, economic, social and cultural rights necessary for the" full development of individual and the protection of his diginity"[13] Louis B. Sohn has said that the right to development "requires careful balancing of the interests of the community and of the individuals. A healty regard for the rights of the individual is indispensable for a state's success in pursuing its right to development."[14]

The general framework of human rights which were affirmed in international declaration and covenants was mainly concerned with rights of individuals. Various new issues and concerns have led to the emergence of new human rights and their international recognition. A landmark development in the formulation and recognition of new human rights is the Declaration on the Rights to Development which was adopted by the General Assembly of the United Nations on 4 December 1986. This Declaration is particularly significant for its importance to the developing countries even though the necessary means for enforcing it are lacking.

Footnotes

1. T S N Sastry (ed.) "India and Human Rights" Concept publishing Company, New Delhi. (2005).
2. Louis B. Sohan "The new International Law: Protection of the Rights of ndividuals Rater than States"32 Am.ul.Rev.1(1982) reprinted in Thomas Buergenthal and Dinesh Shelton, pp. 9-17.
3. Cess Flinterman,'Three Generations of Human Rights'in Jan Berting et al.(eds),Human Rights in a Pluralistic World:Individuals to Collectivities, Westport & London,Meckler, 1990, pp.75-82;Peter R. Baehr, The Role of Human Rights in Foreign Policy, London, Macmillan,1994.
4. Peter R. Baehr, *op cit*, p. 8.
5. U. Chandra" Human Rights"Allahabad Law Agency Publications.
6. Thomas Buergenthal and Dinesh Shelton,"Protecting Human Rights in the Amerecans, Cases and Materials 1995, pp.18-19.
7. The Universal Declaration of Human Rights, Aart.28.
8. *Ibid.* Article 29 (2).
9. *Ibid*, Article 29 (3).
10. Mary Ann Glendon, A world made New : Eleanor Roosevelt and UDHR, New York : Random House, 2001, p. xviii. It was referred in Arvind Sharma's "Hinduism & Human Rights" Oxford University Press, New Delhi, 2003.
11. U. Chandra. "Human Rights" Allahabad Law Agency Publications, (2004), Allahabad.
12. The International Covenant on Economic, Socialand Cultural Rights, Article1 (1).
13. Report of the working Group to the Commission on Human Rights. U.N. Doc. E CN, 4/1489, p. 9.
14. Thomas Buergenthal and Dinah Shelgton, supra n. 52, p.13.

References

Thakur, Lalit, K. (ed.), ***"Promotion and Protection of Human Rights and Prevention of its Violations",*** New Delhi, Indian Institute of Human Rights.

Thomas, Anna (ed.). "Human Rights in Asia: Women's Perspectives: ***"A Report from the Asian Women's Human Rights Constitution."***

Tripathi, S.C., and Arora, V., ***"Law Relating to Women and Children",*** Allahabad, Central Law Publications, 2004.

Tyagi, Yogesh K. ***"Human Rights in India – An Overview."*** Sage Publications, New Delhi, 1992.

Urik, Peter, ***"Human Rights & Development",*** Kumarian Press, UVC, USA, 2005.

Vasak, Karel (ed.). ***"The International Dimensions of Human Rights",*** 2 Vols. English edn revised and edited By Philip Alston. Greenood Press, Conn., 1982.

Whalen, Mollie. ***"Counselling to End Violence Against Women: A Subversive Model."*** Sage, New Delhi, 1996.

Wronka Joseph, ***"Human Rights and Social Polity in the 21st Century: A History of the Idea of Human Rights and Comparison of the U.N. Declaration of Human Rights With United States Federal and State Constitutions",*** America, Lanham, MD: University Press, 1992.

"Tearbook on Human Rights," United Nations, 1946-, irreg.

"Your Book of the European Constitution of Human Rights", M. Nijhoff, Doidrecht, 1980.

3

Indian Culture and Human Rights

Human rights are what make us human. They are the principles by which we create the sacred home for human dignity. The concept of Human Rights is not entirely western in origin. It is a crystallization of values that are the common heritage of mankind. As Mary Ann Glendon points out, the Universal Declaration of Human Rights did not suddenly drop from heaven engraved on tablets but rather was a milestone on a path on which humanity had already been travelling for centuries.[1] In fact, the language of human rights is a product of the European Enlightenment. But the concepts of human rights are as old as the Indian culture as believed by the people of India. The political thinkers and philosophers have expressed concern over securing human rights and fundamental freedoms for all human beings everywhere since the very early times of *Vedic age.*[2] Philosophy of human rights had already occupied a place of prime importance in ancient Brahmanical society.

The Indian thinkers are of the view that it is not justified to limit the origin of the concept of human rights to only western civilization. What the West has discovered today in the field of human rights has been an accepted principle of India's rich legacy of historical tradition and culture since time immemorial which is evidenced by the declarations made in the Vedas.[3] The *Atharvaveda* declares that just as no spoke of a wheel is superior to other, no individual can claim to be, or regarded as, superior to others. Equality of all human beings and the duty of each individual to strive for the happiness of every other individual as also the equal right to food, water and other natural resources are found incorporated in these declarations.[4]

It may not be out of place to mention here that although the term 'Human Rights' is of twentieth century origin, yet people in India believe that it is as old as the history of human civilization and is known to them as 'Natural Rights' or 'Rights of Man'. Conceptually, the moral values of dharma [righteousness], artha [wealth], kama [desire] and moksha [salvation] were designed to create harmonious social order by striking a balance between inner and outer as well as spiritual and material aspects of life had greater jurisprudential value than the positive law. This aspect of moral value and humanitarian traditions was implied in Vedas, puranas, Mahabharata, Bhagwat Gita and other religious scriptures and aimed to free people from traces of conflicts, exploitation and miseries. Even the "Rulers" enacted Laws in subordination to such natural tenets. It was believed that Laws must aim at helping mankind in enjoying liberty and fundamental freedom and of dignified living free from the omnipotent police state or dictators. Vedic India practised the strong tradition that *sarve vabantu sukhinoh: sarve shantu niramayah: serve vadranee pashyantu maa kashchchit dukhah bhag vabet*! [Let everyone be happy; let everyone be free from all evils; let nobody suffer from grief] and the principle of *vasudheva kutumbakam* [all are of one human family]. The modern utopia of a global village is more or less akin to this concept. [5]

A careful examination of the ancient Indian constitutional and legal system would show that it had established a duty-based society; its postulate was not only the duty of individual towards society but also the duty of rulers towards both individuals and society. The concept of absolutist, monarchies had always been rejected. In stead, there was faith in the supremacy of Dharma (law) and spirit. The doctrine that the king can do no wrong was not accepted. However, the king as head of the state was held in high esteem and people were asked to respect him as God so that he might command the respect and obedience of the people. Dharmashastras impressed upon the kings to look upon the people as God (Praja Vishnu) and regard them with love and reverence.[6] The basic philosophy that for the good of the greater number the interests of individuals or smaller groups should be subordinated and sacrificed to the extent necessary was deeply embodied in and formed the foundation of Dharma. This aspect is evident from the verse in Udyogaparva of (Virduraniti Ch. 37-17) which reads:

"Sacrifice the interest of individual for the sake of the family, Sacrifice the interest of the family, for the sake of the village. Sacrifice the interest of the village, for the sake of the country and lastly for the sake of securing Moksha (eternal bliss) of the Atma reject the world". This was the idea kept before the individual in society.[7]

The duties in the modern welfare state are, first to legislate for the purpose of ensuring social, economic and political justice, second, to provide essential services to the society through its departments or instrumentalities, by way of implementing the politics and programs as directed by the constitution and thirdly, law, to regulate and control the activities of individuals on every relevant sphere to sub-serve common good and fourthly, the ensuring of justice as between individual and individual and between individual and the state through the judicial ring of the state.

An analysis of the ancient Indian policy would show all the responsibilities, except the first which stood determined in the form of Dharma. Law (as explained later) evolved and developed by the people meant to secure the happiness of the people as a whole, as also the welfare and full blossoming of the individuals had been conceived at the earliest period known to human history, and the instrumentality of the state was created and the king, as its head, was entrusted with the duty and responsibility of its implementation. In other words, the Dharma (law) constituted the blue print or master plan for the all around development of the individual and different sections of society. It, therefore, favourably compares with modern public law and constitutional law. The duty of the ancient Indian state was not only to enforce obedience to the law against individuals but also to conform to the law in all its action for the purpose of ensuring the welfare and happiness of the people. This can very well be described as seeds of modern public constitutional law. Dharma is mostly misunderstood as religion. There is no prefix to the word Dharma in any of the smritis of Dharmashastra. It is by using a prefix to the word that it gets a restricted meaning as religion. But the fact remains that the Sanskrit word Dharma is a word of the widest import. There is no corresponding word in any other language. The Mahabharata contains a discussion of this topic as Bhishmah Pitamah explains following a question put by Yudhistira about the meaning and scope of dharma. It is most difficult to define Dharma. Dharma has been explained to be that which helps the uplift of man. Therefore, that which ensures welfare (of living being) is surely Dharma.

Webster Dictionary define Dharma as such:"Dharma – Civil and Criminal Law, the body of cosmic principles by which all things exist. Nature: (1) essential function; It is the nature of stone to be hard, of fire to burn and of a tiger to be fierce, just it is the nature of king to punish and to protect, (2) Natural Law (3) Justice."Hence such Dharma can be called "Every type of welfare of the individuals and the society." It can be classified as follows:

(1) Rules purely personal in nature as *Achar.*

(2) Rules which were to be enforced and observed by the state as civil and criminal law.

(3) Vayahar Dharma and Constitutional Law Rajdharma.

The question of discussion of Achar (conduct) is not relevant for this book, but certainly the others two will be described as ordinary law (Vayahar Dharma) and constitutional law (Raj Dharma). How, when and who propounded Dharma is not known. But certainly it is not the work of individuals. The fact remains Dharma embodies duties and obligations rights, duties, and liabilities of individuals and state. It can be regarded as a product of collective wisdom of the ancient Indian society meant for welfare of the people and accepted as such as by the people. As observed by Fuller, the strength of law in the ultimate analysis lies in the public acceptance. Five fundamental rules of Dharma for observance by individuals were made on the basis for the Indian philosophy and the Indian policy, which was based on the principles of (1) Dharma (2) Artha (Material, wealth required for enjoying life) and finally (3) Karma desired to enjoy life call together as Trivargh. The first controls the second and third. The five rules stated by *Manu* are as follows:"Ahinsa (non-violence), Satya (truethfulness), Asteya (not coveting the property of the others), Shoucham (purity of minds and body) and Indriyanigraha (control of sense) are, for the number, the common dharma. The goal of policy (Rajniti) is the fulfilment of Dharma, Artha and elaborate discussion of the function of the state.[8]

Under the ancient Indian system we find that the importance of doctrine of separation of power had been accepted and involved. As far as law was concerned the fundamental principles of law were to be found in the vedas and corporate provision and division of law was incorporated in the smritis. Sometimes custom was treated as law even if it was not consistent with the fundamental principles of Dharma. The ancient Dharmashastra declared that Dharma, which includes the law, was vested on the king. According to Rajdharma, the king had the power only to ensure the law. Dharmashastra did not confer or recognize any legislative power in the law. This is the most important and distinguishing aspect of the concept of kingship in India.

"The, Hindu conception of kingship was, it would be seen as the arm of Dharma, the unchanging law, the upholder of social order and a limb of the social organism. The king had not the right of changing the laws."

Katyayana recognized the power to issue a Rajshasan and declare any usage to country to Shruti or Smriti, invalid. It reads:"The king could declare a usage invalid if it contravened the superior source of law and on such declaration usage stood overruled by royal command."

The king had the power to issue royal edict (Rajshasan). This was similar to makeing rules for enforcement of law, power that, the king could use for supplementing the law without violating the superior sources of law. Analysing this situation Robert Lingat observes: "Because all the larger sphere was reserved for Dharma and legislative activity of the king was limited very seriously but, there did remain a vast field in which it might operate. The majority of the topics, which come within what we would call administrative law fall under royal authority."

Sukraniti gives several illustrations as to the type of royal edicts which a king was competent to issue. Publicity as a necessary condition to bringing Rajashasan into forces was also laid down by Sukraniti 625.628:

"Rajshasan should be proclaimed to the subject by the beating of drums. It should be written down and displayed wherever four roads meet. It should contain a declaration that branches of the order Rajshasan would entail punishment by leveying of heavy fines.

The Shruti, the Smritis the puranas and customs or usages were the principal sources of law, but there can be a specific situation in respect of which there was no provision in any of these four sources of law and therefore, the creation of new provisions of law was inevitable. To deal with such cases, the procedure for the declaration of new laws was prescribed.

Fundamentals of social justice and various provisions of welfare state had been recognized in the ancient Indian legal system. There was, right to freedom, liberty, equality and fraternity. Freedom and liberty were laid down, as part of law governing association and it was the duty of the king to enforce contracts.

"The king should ensure the observance of contracts settled among associations of heretics believers in the Vedas (Naigamas) guilds of merchant corporations, (pugas) troops of soldiers, assemblages of Kinsmen and other such association".

The restriction, which could be imposed on the right to form association was to be such as was necessary in public interest and in particular in the interest of the state.

(i) The king was to prevent them (association), from undertaking acts, which were injurious to the interest of the king (state).

(ii) He shall also prevent them from bearing arms unlawfully and also from making mutual attacks.

(iii) He shall also take appropriate action against association opposed to the dictates of morality.

The charter of equality has been incorporated in the Vedas, the first and the highest authority among the sources of law. The Vedas define, equality of all in the following words:

No one is superior or inferior. All should strive for the interest of all and should progress collectively.

Again in Atharvaveda, Samjaanaskuta, the right of each individual in respect of natural resources, was declared thus: all have equal rights to articles of food and water. The yoke of the chariot of life is placed equally on the shoulders of all. All live together with harmony supporting one another like the spokes of the chariot connecting its rim and hub.

"The king should protect and support all his subjects without any discrimination in the same manner as the earth supports all living beings."

Kautilya beautifully sums up the entire concept of welfare state: " The happiness of the king lies in the happiness of his subjects; in their welfare, his welfare whatever pleases himself the king shall not consider as good; whatever pleases his subject the king shall consider as good."He disapproved the theory of absolutisim of king and subordinated him to the law and duties. Arthashastra not only affirmed and elaborated the civil and legal rights first formulated by Manu but also added a number of economic rights. He categorically ordained that "the king shall provide the orphan, the aged, the infirm, the afflicted and helpless with maintenance; he shall also provide subsistenence to the helpless expectant mothers and also to the children they give birth to". It is revealed that society in Vedic period was well structured, highly organised and committed to human rights.

Buddism froms an important part of non-Brahmin or non-Sanskritic traditions that stood up for the down trodden in society. Buddha himself debunked the Brahmanical claims to any spiritual superiority on the basis of birth. During the Buddhist period, interest in man, in his image, and man's affairs on this earth, unlike interest in gods and goddesses and good life in heaven after death, his earth being a vale of tears become the primary concern of throughtful men and women. Buddha rejected the caste system for it was based upon inequality and treated some individuals as morally superior purely on grounds of birth.[10]

Buddha's story is known to everybody. Human sufferings made Prince Gautam Siddhartha restless and he left all luxuries and comforts of the King's palace in search of remedies for all human miseries and sufferings on this earth. The basic tenets of Buddhism are non-violence, non-hatred, and friendliness to all. Emperor Ashoka who became a devoted follower of Buddha took to the non-violent and humanist philosophy of Buddhism. Also, he became a great champion of freedom and tolerance. He pleaded for universal tolerance. One of the most significant contributions of Buddhism was the introduction and spread of secular education – education for all. Organised universities came to be established under the direct influence of Buddhism.

Buddha (567 BC-480 BC) rejected the infallibility of the Vedas as well as Brahman, without which no opposition to Brahmin-upanishidic domination was possible. His ***Nirvana*** (liberation from the cycle of life and death) was to be attained in this very world, and it could be attained by anyone, should he or she follow the right conduct. He came out strongly against elaborate Brahmanical rituals and rites involving animal sacrifices on the grounds of non-violence and compassion to all beings. The important philosophical contribution made by Buddhism that should inspire any human right activist for years come.

Along with Buddhism, Jainism constituted another parallel non-Sanskrit tradition that carried forward this all human beings it acknowledged an existence of rights not only of the downtrodden but also plants and animals. Every creature has life and they are all similar in their sensitivity to pain and pleasure. Jainism defined 'sin' as a violence to, and encroachment on, others' right to life. This may have been the first timc in human history that a right to life was laid down as a human right. Likewise, a violation of this right by someone else was considered violence and indeed a sin. What is important is that Jainism extended this right not only to all individuals but also to animals and indeed to all living species.

Another important contribution made by the Jain tradition in the search for truth was evolving a philosophical system known as Syad Ved.[11] The term Syad means perhaps. Syad Vad argued that truth cannot be perceived in totality by anyone and so one should always provide enough space for the possibility of a different understanding and interpretation of truth.

Long before the advent of Buddhism, Indian society had been exposed to another philosophical system called Lokayata, which offered a different and a very radical interpretation of reality. It was a system which persistently rejected the conception of a creator or anything existing prior to matter in one or another form. It however kept company with simple religious beliefs, rites and even cult in daily life.

The Lokayata school of thought was founded by Charvak,[12] who denouneced categorically the karma, Punarjanma, Moksha and Varna System. Some of the Stutras from Lokayat a darshan clearly show their humanist and rationalist nature: "the body, the face and all limbs of all people being similar, how can there be any distinctions of Varna and caste? Such distinctions are unscientific and connot be defended." Lokayata rejected the superiority of ritualistic Brahmanical function over others: "Agriculture, Cattle breeding, trade, state service etc. are occupations of the wise. They should be followed. But those who smear their bodies with ashes and perform Agnihotra and other religious rites are devoid of intelligence and manhood." Lokayata also provided a humanitarian, as against an otherworldly, interpretation of Moksha (liberation from this world): "Real bondage lies in servitude. Real Moksha lies in freedom." The driving impulse of the lokayat was social and not philosophical which is evidenced in various ways. Many of their Sutras were directed against Brahmanical domination embedded in the concept of Chaturvarna.

There were many other non-Vedic-sects – like the *Nath, Yoga, and Siddha* who, too, like the Buddhists, found the key to all religious mysteries in the human body itself. The position of the Nath-panthi siddhas and jogis in Hindu society needs to be understood. Most of the nath-panthi siddhas and jogis belonged to the low castes, opposed caste-based inequalities, denounced the religion espoused by the Brahmins and did not favour image worship. Another important feature of these sects was that Women played a significant part in these sects, particularly in the *Tantra.*

No discussion of human rights and their roots in Indian tradition can be complete without a reference to King Ashoka. His significant contribution lay in translating the philosophy of tolerance into an attitude to be adopted by all. Ashoka is perhaps the first ruler who developed a totally anti-war perspective. Wars have been fought between rulers throughout history, and generally glorified by the victors. Ashoka stands out in history as someone who gave up not only war but also the attitude of war. He equated war not with triumph and glory but with misery and human sufferings. Ashoka looked at war not from the perspective of the vanquished and showed a keen sensitivity towards the all round destruction and suffering brought about by war. His attitude to war has been described in his 13th major rock edict. This rock edict is easily the oldest anti-war statement and should actually be treated as one of the oldest and a very important human rights document.

King Ashoka in Kalinga Edict II inscribes: "All men are my children, and, just I desire for my children that they may enjoy every kind of prosperity and happiness bith in this world and in the next, so also as I desire the same for all men".[13] In fact, after the famous Kalinga war Ashoka worked day and night for the protection of human rights. His chief concern was the happiness of his subjects. It is however,unfortunate that human rights jurisprudence witnessed downfall with the decline of Mauryan Empire.

Gupta period is called as the most glorious epoch in the history of anciant India, which has been compared with the "Elizabethan period of British history" by the hiotorians. It was an age of golry and greatness in every branch of national life. Hieuen Tsang says that administration in Chandragupta period was founded on benign principles. There was no forced labour, crimes were rare, and king personally supervised the whole administration. Harsha Vardhana was the last Emperor of Hindu India. His reign marks the culmination of Hindu culture. He never forgot that the aim of the government was the welfare of the governed. He had made provision to provide free food and drinking water to the poor and stationed physicians with medicines in free of cost for them. He devoted his whole life to promote the welfare of his people. After him the whole India was split up and the society started to degenerate. The philosophy of human rights lost sight.

Human Rights in Medieval Times

The cocept of human rights got lost on its way in the dark and narrow alleys of the middle Ages. In the Medieval period the philosophical and ideal speculaion were replaced by new ideal of chivalry, war and other heroic traditions, which led to confusion and uncertainty. During Muslim era in India, especially in the pre-Mughal period, there were series of cultural, social and political stressed and strain on the style and way of Hindus. The Muslim rulers in India were fundamentalist and despotic who forced upon the Hindus their own laws, customs and religious practices. Hindus were not treated in law on par with the Muslims-the latter being the conquerors and the former being the Kafirs-the non-believers of Islam, special disabilities like jazia, were imposed on Hindus.[14] Both in theory and practice, there was discrimination against Hindus vis-à-vis Muslims. Muslims rule in India was not founded on the basic principles of human dignity, equality and justice, and was essentially autocratic, theocratic and irresponsible, devoid of the idea of rule of law, morality, justice, tolerance and social harmony. So the significance of Muslim rule in India from the point of view of human rights was counter productive to harmony, justice and equality and the concept of human rights got lost on its way in the dark and narrow alleys of the middle ages. It was, however, at later stage that Muslim State in India became considerably modified in its form.

Some of the Moghul rulers, especially Akbar the great brought about a basic change in the style of Moghul administration. He adopted a policy of tolerance and non-discrimination towards Hindus and saw that no injustice is committed in his realm. Hence, it is not wrong to say that, with Akabar a new era begin in Moghul History of India in the field of human rights with his policy of universal reconciliation and tolerance. His policy of tolerance and non-discrimination towards Hindus was followed by his son Jahangir too. There was a popular legend that Jahangir arranged a chain with bells to be hung outside the palace in order to enable petitioners to approach him for the redressal of their grievances. Thus it is clear that it was an easily accessible individual petition system in comparision to our modern lengthy and expensive writ petition system.

The human rights friendly trend initiated by Akbar and Jahangir came to be reversed by Aurangzeb.But during his reign the concept justice was made less intricate and more expeditious than in the former reigns. Corruption in judiciary was made a crime for the first time. If delay in justice resulted in loss to a party, the aggrieved party could be compensated by the judge himself.

The right of an accused to be released on bail did exist during Mughal rule in India.[15] Similarly the right to benefit of doubt was known to Muslim jurisprudence in the administration of criminal justice. The benefit of doubt was known as shuba (doubt), which entitled an accused to be acquitted.

It cannot, however, be denied that the Aurangazeb was the most cruel, fanatic and despotic ruler. He made earnest efforts to convert Kashmiri Pandits to Islam with the use of his governmental machinery. The Ninth Sikh Guru Teg Bahadur had to sacrifice his life, and in 1675 A.D.Guru Gobind Singh (Tenth Sikh Guru) had to sacrifice his four sons in fighting against injustice and repression to save Hindus from conversion. Finally, the Bhakti movement and Sufi movements evolved in later period ultimately revived and regenerated the old Indian values of truth, righteousness, justice and morality.[16] They are remarkable for their simplicity, directness, and for preaching and practising tolerance, love and friendliness.

Bhakti, the path of devotion, implies a belief in the Supreme Person, not a supreme *abstraction*. It is therefore, a very straight forward and unsophisticated belief. It was opposed by the Brahmins for a long time because of its utter disregard for caste divisions, religious rituals and ceremonies. But, later they treated Bhakti with respect. The tradition of Bhakti played an important role among the Tamils as mentioned in the works of the Alvar saints, most of whom came from low castes. In the beginning, the movement was restricted to the lower strata of society who were the chief victims of the Brahmanical tradition. At a later stage, Vaishnavas of even higher castes hailed their literature. One Alvar saint, Andal belonged to a lower caste; she was accepted as a religious leader by the society in general. This is an indication of the popularity of the Bhakti movement. The great scholar, Ramunuja, the best known exponent of this movement, was influenced and inspired by the "works of the Alvars" which were collected by the disciples of Ramanuja at his special, and from which Ramanuja himself drew much inspiration and food for this system of thought.[17]

The devotional Bhakti and the Sufi traditions (the first Sufi teacher, Khwaja Moinuddin Chishti came to India in 1193) had much in common. In medieval north India, mysticism was the product of both the Bhakti movement and the tradition of Sufis. One importantant aspect of this mysticism was its complete independence from orthodox scriptures. These teachers practiced practised and taught tolerance.

The interaction of Bhakti and Islam, specially the Sufi idea, gave rise to a number of progressive movements with the core philosophy of tolerance. Human Rights educationists should give utmost importance to this aspect. It is regrettable at has, with some notable exceptions, been generally studied in isolation. It should, therefore, be emphasised in our text books that relations between Islam and the religions of India were marked by mutual understanding, tolerance and cooperation were, to large extent, promoted by the rise and spread of Sufi and Bhakti ideas.[18]

Namdeva and Tukaram from Maharastra, the former a tailor and the latter a peasant, made the Bhakti movement increasingly acceptable to the people. Namdeva spread the virtues of simplicity and argued forcefully against rituals and superstitions. He said: The stone image speaks not, see the lord within, the Tirthas (holy pilgrimage) cannot wash away sins, clean your hearts instead. Fasting and other observance are futile unless your being is purified. What can ceremonies do if love awake not in your heart?"[19]

In Bengal, the well known Vaishnava Jaidev, Vidyapati and Chandidas, as also Chaitnaya popularised Bhakti movement. It spread to almost all parts if India. Though the movement did not succeed in completely breaking through caste barriers, the very fact that many of its leaders belonged to lower castes, and also that it believed in the equality of men, must be taken note of by human right educationists.[20]

In fourteenth-fifteenth century, Ramananda (1370-1440) challenged caste division, revolted against traditional religious rituals and started preaching in local dialects, and not Sanskrit which was the preserve of the upper castes. His thought is well reflected in his following words: "Wherever I go, I see water and stone, but it is you who had filled them all with your presence. In vain do they seek You in the Vedas..." Ramanada had 12 important disciples. They all belonged to low castes. One of them, Ravidas was a cobbler. "The recitation of the Vedic Mantras, even for many millions of time will not satisfy the longing (to see You)", sang Ravidas.[21]

The most famous disciple of Ramananda was Kabir, who combined in his writings the essence of Sufi and Bhakti traditions. He struck at the roots of ritualism and superstition. "O God, Whether Allah or Rama, I live by the name." sang Kabir. Since Kabir composed song for the common people he chose his own language, which was a combination of many local dialects. He said: Sanskrit is like water in a well, the language of the people is a flowing stream." He practised and preached the gospel of universal tolerance and was one of the exponents of the idea of India with full religious freedom for all. Kabir was utmost importance to human equality and denounced inequality based on caste, religion and wealth.[22]

The founder of the great Sikh religion, Guru Nanak, was greatly influenced by Bhakti and Sufi ideas. Both Kabir and Guru Nanak found a common link between Hinduism and Islam. The Supreme significance of Nanak was that he was the harbinger of Hindu-Muslim unity, for he sought sincerely to reconcile Islam with Hinduism as the following verse will show: Guru Nanak Shah faquir/ Hindu Ka Guru aur/ Musalaman ka pir."(Guru Nanak is a royal pauper. He is a Guru to Hindus and a Pir (saint) to Muslims.)[23]

Apart from the Bhakti and Sufi movement, Baul movement of west Bengal had contributed a lot during the medieval era as regards to the human rights. Bauls are not known outside Bengal.[24] The philosophy of the Baul movement lies in the simple mans's (sahaj) search for the "Man of his heart"- his God. The movement traces its origin to the fall of Buddhism and Vaishnavism. Bauls are like the wind (Baul means wind, vayu)- always free, not tied to any religious traditions. They accepted no caste division, they did not worship any special deity nor did they accept any temple or mosque. Baul devotees belonged to the lowest strata of both Hindus and Muslims. What need have we of other temples, when our body is the temple where the spirit has its abode", they sang. They did not observe asceticism, nor did they believe in celibacy. Earthly love, they argued, helps them to feel divine love, and harmony between material and spiritual needs.

The powerful social movements in medieval India spread the message of secularism by the symbiotic synthesis of core values of different religions to bind the pluralist society. Saints and holy persons propagated the message of the Sufi saints to emphasise that the difference between human beings is manmade, all being born equal. It may be recalled that from time immemorial Indians have called their culture by the name of human culture (Manav Dharam/Manav Samriti). No gain saying the fact that human dignity had universal appeal and Indian culture had tried to be so comprehensive as to suit the needs of every human being, irrespective of age, colour, sex or caste.

Human Rights in Modern India

Broadly speaking the modern period in India started with the advent of the British and the English education in the early nineteenth century. The British came to India as traders, but capitalizing on the disunity and struggle for power among the Indian rulers, they succeeded in securing several parts of the Indian sub-continent under their control. At the initial stage, the Governor Generals ruled the territories. They were the representative of the British East India Company in India and later by the Viceroys, who represented the British crown. The process of the Indian administration and judiciary started with the introduction of Regulating Act of 1773 and continued for 85 long years. This was followed by 89 years of decentralization (1858-1947). This resulted in 174 years of systematic and atrocious suppression of human rights of the Indian subjects, who were actually suffocated under the oppressive burden of these administrative and legislative systems.

The most notable point in the Indian political scenario under the British rule was that the decision making power had been shifted to London, four thousand miles away from Indian soil. As a result, the Indians lost their political decision making rights and were reduced to the status of second-class citizens in their own land. The British never hesitated to project themselves as rulers and discriminated between Britishers and Indians as the ruled. Higher positions in the government, administration and the army were reserved for the English people and the Indians were confined to the low posts like clerks, interpreters and sepoys. At a later stage, this created a severe discontent among the English educated Indian elite. It was quite natural that the Indian boycotted the Simon Commission.

The British never bothered about Indian customs and traditions and denied the native rules their right to adopt a male child, in case they were having no male issues. They adopted the 'doctrine of lapse', through which they tried to annex the territories of those rulers, who died without legal heirs. They never cared for Indian sentiments, while taking decisions like the partition of Bengal (1905), which they tried to justify on the basis of administrative convenience. Moreover, the British involved India in wars which promoted the British to achieve their national interests and imperialistic goals.

The trading company, which was elevated to the status of the rulers of India, conducted its business of administering the country with profit motive and this system of economic exloitation was unashamedly followed by the royal representatives as well. The British believed in the concept of 'eminent domain', which ensures the authority, power and sovereignty of the 'state' over the resources within its boundary and extended it to their Indian colonies thereby pronouncing that all the Indian resource were vested with the British colonial masters. Economic policies, which were beneficial to England, were thrust upon Indians, who supported dearly. 'Colonies for the colonial masters' was the motto and guiding principle for the British colonial policy.

India was involved in the imperialistic wars with the Eastern powers, which were funded by the Indian exchequer. The wealth of India was systematically drained and funnelled out of India to Britain. Indian agriculture and handicraft as well as house hold industries were deliberately suppressed. *Rayatwari* and *Jamindari* systems were introduced which served the interest of local bigwigs and worked against the well-being of both peasants and labourers. Indians were required to grow cash crops like cotton and indigo, which were in demand for the English industries as raw materials. This had seriously affected the native food shortages.

Indians, who were known for their transoceanic commercial contacts with different parts of the world, were reduced to the status of agents and junior partners of the British commercial enterprises in the East. Their once-thriving shipping industry was crippled by putting and imposing several hindrances. Heavy taxes were imposed upon Indian products so that they could not compete with the British manufactured goods. The British monopolized the Indian markets and flooded them with cheap, machine-made goods from home.[25] Every sector of production suffered as a result of British greed.

In the socio-cultural spheres also the rights of the Indians were severely and severally violated. Racialism and the feeling of racial superiority of the colonial masters were manifest in the restrictions they imposed on the native population. Reserved clubs and promenades were rampant in cities like Calcutta and Delhi, into which natives were not allowed. Such was the case of high-class compartments in the Indian Railways. For the same offence, the Whites were punished with leniency while the punishments meted out to the natives were quite severe. Again, for the same nature of work, the Whites were paid more and the locals had to be satisfied with lesser wages. All these go to prove that racial discrimination was rampant under the British colonial rule.

Moreover, the native religion was ridiculed and Indians were denoted as 'copper-coloured pagans'. Their religious practices and rituals were looked down upon. The State encouraged the conversion of Indians carried on by Christian missionaries and patronized their activities by offering favours to the converts in the government services.

The colonial masters ridiculed the culture and literature of the Indians. Lord Macaulay, who introduced the English education in India, is reported to have said that the entire literature in the Sanskrit language could not measure up to a single page of English literature. The natives were regarded as uncivilized barbarians.

Thus, the British colonial masters rode roughshod over the Indian political, economic and socio-cultural rights in all spheres of life. Indians were told that they did not deserve self-rule and that the British rule was a blessing-in-disguise for them. Basic rights such as rights to life and livelihood, right to equality, right to expression and association were denied to them. Their religious freedom their right to belief and their right to practice their own religion were severely restricted and impinged upon by the colonial State.

In such an atmosphere, the leaders and people of India, who were well-aware of the loss of their human rights in the hands of the colonial masters, decided to take on the alien rulers and set to the taste of wresting back their rights. Perhaps the first explicit demand for fundamental rights appeared in the Constitution of India Bill, 1895. The Bill envisaged for India a constitution guaranteeing to every one of her citizen freedom of expression, inviolability of one's house, right to equality before law, right to property, right of personal liberty, and right to free education, etc. A series of Congress resolutions adopted between 1917 and 1919 repeated the demand for civil rights and equality of status with English men. The resolutions called for equal terms of conditions in bearing arms, for a wider application of the system of trial by jury and for the right of Indians 'to claim that no less than one-self jurors should be their own countrymen.

A further resolution to this effect stated the 'emphatic opinion', that parliament should pass a statute guaranteeing 'the civil rights of his Majesty's Indian subjects', which would embody provisions establishing equality before the law, a free press, free speech, etc. The statute should moreover, lay down that political power belonged to the Indian people in the same manner as to any other people or nation in the British empire. By the mid-twenties, Congress and Indian leaders generally had achieved a new forcefulness and consciousness of their Indian ness and of the needs of the people. Some instances like, the experience of the First World War, disappointed provisions of the Montague-Chelmsford Reforms, Woodrow Wilson's support for the rights of self-determination, and above all Gandhi's arrival on the political science of India prompted the Indians to fight for their cause. They no longer aimed at establishing the rights of Indians vis-à-vis Englishmen; the purpose now was to assure liberty among Indians. Another major development in this direction was the drafting of 'Mrs. Besant's Commonwealth of 1925', Art. 4 of this bill contained a list of seven fundamental rights: [26]

(i) Liberty of person;
(ii) Freedom of conscience and the free profession and practice of religion;
(iii) Free expression of opinion and the right of assembly peaceably and without arms and of forming associations or unions;
(iv) Free elementary education;
(v) Use of roads, public places, courts of justice and the like;
(vi) Equality before the law, irrespective of considerations of nationality;
(vii) Equality of the sexes.

The appointment of Simon Commission by British government on November 8, 1927 to undertake a study of the constitutional reforms in India compelled the Indian National Congress to set up a committee to draft a Swaraj Constitution on the basis of a declaration of rights. The resolution was passed in 1927 at the 43rd annual session of the Indian National Congress held in Madras. The committee called for by the Madras Congress resolution came into being in May 1928. Pt. Moti Lal Nehru was its chairman. The Committee's report-known as Nehru Report- contained an explanation of its draft constitution that speaks for itself. The Fundamental Rights, incorporated in the Nehru report, were in several cases taken word for word from the rights listed in the commonwealth of India bill, 1925.The Nehru Report declared that the first concern of Indians was, 'to secure the Fundamental right', that had been denied to them. As regaeds writing of the constitution, the report maintained:

"It is obvious that our first care should be to have our fundamental rights guaranteed in a manner which will not permit their withdrawal under any circumstances..." The Indian Statutory Commission, 1930 did not support the general demand for the enumeration and guaranteeing of Fundamental rights. Sir John in his report observed:

"We are aware that such provisions have been inserted in many constitutions, notably in those of European States formed after the war. Experience, has not shown them to be of any great practical value. Abstract declarations are useless, unless there exist the means to make them effective".

Another landmark in the development of the recognition of fundamental rights was the Karachi Resolution adopted by the Congress Session held in March, 1931. It held that 'in order to end the exploitation of the masses, political freedom must include the real economic freedom of the starving million's. The demand for a declaration of Fundamental Rights in constitutional document was again emphasized by several Indian leaders at the 'Round Table Conference' prior to the making of Government of India Act, 1935. In all the three sessions of this conference, discussions were held on the subject and at the first meeting of the sub-committee held on December 23, 1930. Raja Narendra Nath pointed out the need to make the question of declaration of Rights accessible to the majority. K.T. Paul also emphasised the inclusion of fundamental rights and the need to provide for a machinery to ensure that they were not violated. He asserted that there should be in the statute some declaration of fundamental rights as the case of those constitutions, which have been framed subsequent to the War.

B. Shiva Rao, a representative of the Labour organization of the Round Table Conference placed before the minorities Sub-committee meeting on December 23, 1930, a comprehensive enunciation of a draft declaration of fundamental rights. During the discussion at the sub-committee meeting Dr. B. R. Ambedkar also pointed out the need for the conclusion of selections in the constitution for the enforcement of fundamental rights including the right of redress in case of their violation. The secretary of state for Indiat submitted a report to parliament after the Round Table Conference was over. The report observed that the Government recognized the importance attached by the Indian leaders to the importance attached by the Indian leaders to the idea of making a chapter on fundamental rights, a feature in the new Indian constitution. It also pointed out that some of the propositions discussed at the conference could find their place in the constitution. The joint Select Committee of British Parliament in the "Government of India Bill of 1934", did not view with favour the demand for a constitutional guarantee of fundamental rights to British subjects in India. Expressing its disaggrement with the view of Simon Commission, the committee observed:

"... there are also strong practical arguments against the proposal, which may be put in the form of dilemma; for either the declaration of rights is too abstract in that it has no legal effect of any kind or its legal effect will impose an embarrassing restriction on the power of the legislature and to create a grave risk that a large number of laws may be declared invalid by the court because inconsistent with one or other of the rights so declared".[27]

However, this did not dampen the enthusiasm of Indians to have a list of fundamental rights incorporated in their Constitution. Indians rejected the British view of rights for many reasons. Foremost among them was the belief that independence meant liberty, that rights expressed this liberty and must, both in their positive and negative forms be enshrined in the constitution. During the years when independence had been more of a hope than a reality, the Congress had been loud in demanding written rights. With independence and the Congress's assumption of power near, to reject them would have created a crippling suspicion of the Congress leader's motives. The party leadership, aware of this, was eager to demonstrate its good intentions.

The decade of the 1940's generally was marked by a resurgence of interests in human rights. The denial of liberties under German and Russian totalitarianism and elsewhere resulted in the signing of the Atlantic Charter. It also resulted in the increased activities of the United Human Rights Commission and ultimately to the formation of the U.N. Assembly members were sensitive to these currents, which supported their own faith in the validity of written rights for the Indian people. They belived that if the constitution would contain positive rights as well as negative safeguards, it would nearly be the same as the appearance of the written rights themselves. In fact, the inclusion of negative rights was primarily a product of the national revolution and the minorities situation. So the impetus for the inclusion of the state's positive obligations came, largely from the social revolution and reflected the social consciousness that had increasingly characterized the twentieth century both in India and aboard. The further stage of the development of Fundamental Right in India was the 'Sapru Committee Report', published at the end of 1945. This committee was appointed by and All parties Conference in 1944-45' with Sir Tej Bahadur Sapru as its chairman. The Sapru Report gave a standing suggestion that what constitution demands and expects, is perfect equality between one section of the community and another in the matter of political and civil rights, equality of liberty and security in the enjoyment of the freedom of religion, worship, and the pursuit of the ordinary activities of life.

"Freedom for a nation and a people may be, and is I believe, always good in the long run, but in the final analysis freedom itself is a means to an end, that end being the raising of the people in the question to higher levels and hence the general advancement of humanity" opined Nehru in 1939. It is believed that without freedom no individual can achieve equality or aspire to rise to higher levels of accomplishments and realise his / her full potential. The alien government of India continued to suppress the movement with all powers at its disposal. However, the British Government decided to quit India due to heavy pressure from within and outside. Thus, India became free from British colonial yoke on 15th August 1947, and the centuries-old human rights violations of the Indian people at the hands of the British colonial masters come to an end.

Provision of Human Rights in the Indian Constitution

The struggle for the recognition of human rights and the struggle against political, economic, social and cultural oppression, against injustice and inequalities, have been an integral part of the history of all human societies. The conception of the rights, which every human being is entitled to enjoy by virtue of being a member of the human species, has evolved through history in the course of these struggles.

India has played the most significant role in the promotion of the cause of Human Rights. With the attainment of Independence, a declaration of rights, the most elaborate in the world, was incorporated in the new Constitution. India has made the most sincere efforts for the protection and promotion of human rights the world over and is the greatest champion of Human rights in the Third World. India has not only incorporated an elaborate Bill of Rights in her Constitution but also efforts have been made to translate these into reality. Thus we find that India has incorporated the most elaborate Declaration of Human Rights, 1948 in its Constitution. The spirit of providing for human rights pervaded the minds of the founding fathers of the Indian Constitution as much as it did the minds of the makers of UDHR, 1948.In other words, the framing of the Constitution of India had started about two years before the Universal Declaration of Human Rights was adopted. However, every Article of the Universal Declaration is reflected in the Indian Constitution, which was adopted by India's Constituent Assembly on 26th November 1949, in corporated in the laws of the country.

The Indian Constitution bears the impact of the Universal Declaration of Human Rights and the Supreme Court of India has recognized this. While referring to the Fundamental Rights contained in Part III of the Constitution, Sikri, Chief Justice of the Supreme Court, in Kesavanand Bharati V.State of Kerela (AIR 1973) observed: "I am unable to hold these provisions how that right are not natural or inalienable rights. As a matter of fact, India was a party to the Universal Declaration of Rights.... And that Declaration describes some fundamental rights as inalienable". [28]

The Supreme Court has also recognized the interpretative value of the Universal Declaration of Human Rights in case of Kishore Chand v. State of H.P., 1991 ISCJ 68, 76. The Universal Declaration of Human Rights does not define the term "Human rights," It refers to them as "the equal and inalienable right of all members of the human family."[29] The framers of the Indian constitution were influenced by the concept of human rights and guaranteed most of the human rights contained in the Universal Declaration. The Universal Declaration of Human Rights contained civil and political as well as economic, social and cultural rights. While civil and political rights have been incorporated in part III of Indian constitution, economic, social and cultural rights have been incorporated in part IV of the Constitution.

The following chart is given below to indicate the human rights, which have been incorporated in the Indian Constitution and Law:

However, there are certain rights, which are contained in the Universal Declaration but have not been expressly mentioned in the constitution. These rights are (I) Right to be not subjected to torture, or to cruel, inhuman treatment or punishment (Art.5); (ii) Right to recognition everywhere as a person before the law (Art.6); (iii) Right to full equality to a fair and public hearing by an independent and impartial tribunal (Art. 10); (iv) Right to be presumed innocent until found guilty according to law in a public trial (Art. 11(I); (v) Right to privacy (Art. 12); (vi) Right to leave any country, including one's own, and to return to it (Art. 12); (vi) Right to leave any country, including one's own, and to return to one's own country [Art. 13(2)]; (vii) Right to nationality [Art. 15 (1)]; (viii) Right to marry and found a family [Art.16(1)]; (ix) Right to take part in the government of one's country [Art. 21(1)].

SlNo of Articles	*Declaration of Human Rights*	*Article No.*	*Provisions of the Indian Constitution and Law*
1.	All men are born free and are equal in dignity and in their rights.	14	The State shall not deny to any person equality before the law or the equal protection of the laws within the territory of India.
2.	No Discrimination on the ground of race, colour, sex, language, religion, birth.	15	The State shall not discriminate against any citizen on grounds only of religion, race, caste, sex, place of birth or any of them.
3.	Right to life	21.	No person shall be deprived of his life or personal liberty except according to procedure established by law.
4.	No slavery	23.	Traffic in human beings and beggar and other forms of forced labour are prohibited and any contravention of this provision shall be an offence punishable in accordance with law.
5.	No torture, cruelty, inhuman or Degrading treatment.	21.	State of Maharashtra vs. Ravikant S. Patil. (1991) 2 SCC 373. Handcuffing and parading of under trial prisoner was held violative of rights under Article 21. 3 SCC 161 and (1991) 4 SCC 177. Right to live with human dignity held to be enshrined in Article 21. Maneka Gandhi vs. Union of India (1978) 1 SCC 248.The expression "personal liberty" under Art. 21 is a phrase of wide amplitude and covers a variety of rights which go to constitute personal liberty of man including right to safety of his person.

(Contd. Table)

(Contd. Table)

SlNo of Articles	*Declaration of Human Rights*	*Article No.*	*Provisions of the Indian Constitution and Law*
6.	Right to recognition everywhere as a person before the law.	14&21	
7.	Equality before law	14.	
8.	Right to Effective remedy	32	1.The rights to move the Supreme Court by appropriate proceedings for the enforcement of the rights conferred by part III of the Constitution is guaranteed. 2.Supreme court shall issue directions or orders or writs, including writs in the nature of habeas corpus, mandamus, prohibition, quo warranto and certiorari whichever may be appropriate, for the enforcement of any of the rights conferred by this Part.
		226	Notwithstanding anything in Article 32, every High Court shall have power, throughout the territories in relation to which it exercises jurisdiction, to issue to any person or authority, including in appropriate cases, any Government, within those territories directions, orders or writs, including writs in the nature of habeas corpus, mandamus, prohibition, quowarranto and certiorari, or any of them, for the enforcement of any of the rights conferred by Part III and for any other purpose.

(Contd.)

(Contd. Table)

SlNo of Articles	*Declaration of Human Rights*	*Article No.*	*Provisions of the Indian Constitution and Law*
9.	Arbitrary arrest and detention	22.	1.No person who is arrested shall be detained in custody without being informed, as soon as may be, of the grounds for such arrest nor shall he be denied the right to consult, and to be defended by, a legal practitioner of his choice. 2.Every person who is arrested and detained in custody shall be produced before the nearest magistrate within a period of twenty-four hours of such arrest excluding the time necessary for the journey from the place of arrest to the court of the magistrate and no such person shall be detained in custody beyond the said period without the authority of a magistrate
10.	Public hearing and fair trial	39A	The State Shall secure that the operation of the legal system promotes justice, on a basis of equal opportunity, and shall, in particular, provide free legal aid, by suitable legislation or schemes or any other way, to ensure that opportunities for securing justice are not denied to any citizen by reason of economic or other disabilities.
		304* (CCP)	Where in a trial before the Court, the accused is not represented by a pleader, and where it appears to the Court that the accused has not sufficient means to engage a pleader, the Court shall assign a pleader for his defence at the expense of the State.

(Contd. Table)

(Contd. Table)

SINo of Articles	**Declaration of Human Rights**	**Article No.**	**Provisions of the Indian Constitution and Law**
		303* (CCP)	Any person accused of an offence before a Criminal Court, or against whom proceedings are instituted under this Code, may of right be defended by a pleader of his choice.
		327* (CCP)	The place in which any Criminal Court is held for the purpose of inquiring into or trying any offence shall be deemed to be an open Court, to which the public generally may have access, so far as the same can conveniently contain them.
11.	Presumption of innocence and Criminal Law until prove guilty in public trial .No retrospective declaration of offence nor retrospective objective of higher sentence by retrospective amendements		The principle of common Law, the Doctrine of Rule of Law, Presumption of innocence till guilt is established.
		20	(1) No person shall be convicted of any offence except for violation of the law in force at the time of the commission of the act charged as an offence, nor be subjected to a penalty greater than that which might have been inflicted under the law in force at the time of the commission of the offence.

(Contd.)

(Contd. Table)

SlNo of Articles	*Declaration of Human Rights*	*Article No.*	*Provisions of the Indian Constitution and Law*
12	Privacy, family, home correspondence, reputation, protection of law against interference or of force.		Each one is conversed by the law enacted by Parliament and is protected.
13.	(i) Freedom of Movement and Residence	19.	d. To move freely throughout the territory of India. e. To reside and settle in any part of the territory of India.
	ii) Rights live and return to county.		Provisions of the Passport Act.
14	Rights to Religion	25	All persons are equally entitled to freedom of con-science and free profession, practice and propagation of religion.
15	(i) Right to Nationality (ii) Change of Nationality.	5.	At the commencement of this Constitution, every person who has his domicile in the territory of India and (a) who was born in the territory of India; or (b) either of whose parents was born in the territory of India; or (c) who has been ordinarily resident in the territory of India for not less than five years immediately preceding such commencement, shall be a citizen of India.
		9	No person shall be a citizen of India by virtue of Article 5 or be deemed to be a citizen of India is virtue of Article 6 or Article 8, if he has voluntarily acquired the citizenship of any foreign state.

(Contd.)

(Contd. Table)

SlNo of Articles	*Declaration of Human Rights*	*Article No.*	*Provisions of the Indian Constitution and Law*
		10	Every person who is deemed to be a citizen of India under any of the forgoing provisions of this Part shall, subject to the provisions of any law that may be made by Parliament, continue to be such citizen.
16	Marriage and Family		Covered by suitable legislation applicable to people of different religions.
17	Property	300A	Persons not be deprived of property save by authority of law.
18	Freedom of thought and conscience	25(1)	All persons are equally entitled to freedom of con-science and the right freely to profess, practise and propagate religion.
19	Freedom of information and expression	19(a)	All citizens shall have the right to speech and expression.
20	Peaceful assembly and association	19b)	All citizens shall have the right to assemble peaceably and without arms.
		19c)	To form associations or unions.
21	(i)Democracy	325	There shall be one general electoral role for every territorial constituency for election to either House of Parliament or to the House or either House of the Legislature of a State and no person shall be ineligible for inclusion in any such roll or claim to be included in any electoral roll for any such constituency on grounds only of religion, race, caste, sex or any of them.

(Contd.)

(Contd. Table)

SlNo of Articles	*Declaration of Human Rights*	*Article No.*	*Provisions of the Indian Constitution and Law*
23	(i) Right to work	41	The State shall, within the limits of its economic capacity and development, make effective provision for securing the right to work, to education and to public assistance in case of unemployment, old age, sickness and disablement and in other cases of undeserved want.
	(ii) Right to equal pay	39(a)	The State shall, in particular, direct its policy towards securing-that the citizens men and women equality, have the right to an adequate means of livelihood.
	(iii)Remuneration keeping human dignity	43	The State shall endeavour to secure, by suitable legislation or economic organization or in any other way, to all workers, agriculture, industrial or otherwise, work, a living wage, conditions of work ensuring a decent standard of life and full employment of leisure and social and cultural opportunities and, in particular, the State shall endeavour to promote cottage industries on an individual or cooperative basis in rural areas.
	(iv) Right to form and join unions	19(1)	(c)

(Contd.)

(Contd. Table)

SlNo of Articles	*Declaration of Human Rights*	*Article No.*	*Provisions of the Indian Constitution and Law*
24.	Rights to rest, reasonable working hours	43	
25.	(i) Standard of living adequate for health and well-being.	47	The State shall regarded the raising of the level of nutrition and the standard of living of its people and the improvement of public health as among its primary duties and, in particular, the State shall endeavour to bring about prohibition of the consumption except for medicinal purpose of intoxicating drinks and of drugs which are injurious to health.
(ii)	Motherhood and children	39(f)	The state shall in particular, direct its policy towards securing-that children are given opportunities and facilities to develop in a healthy manner and in conditions of freedom and dignity and that childhood and youth are protected against exploitation and against moral and material abandonment.
		42	The state shall make provision for securing just and humane conditions of work and for maternity relief.
26.	Right to education	45.	The state shall endeavour to provide within a period of ten years from the commencement of this Condition. For free compulsory education for all children until they complete the age of fourteen years.

(Contd.)

(Contd. Table)

SINo of Articles	*Declaration of Human Rights*	*Article No.*	*Provisions of the Indian Constitution and Law*
27.	(i) Free participation in cultural life (ii) Protection of moral material interest	51A(f)	To value and preserve the rich heritage of our composite culture.
28.	Social and international order	38	
		51	That State shall endeavour to (a) promote international peace and security; (b) maintain just and honourable relations between nations; (c) foster respect for international law and treaty obligations in the dealings of organised people with one another; and (d) encourage settlement of international disputes by arbitration.

(Contd.)

(Contd. Table)

SlNo of Articles	*Declaration of Human Rights*	*Article No.*	*Provisions of the Indian Constitution and Law*
29.	Duties	51A	It shall be duty of every citizen of India-(a) to abide by the Constitution and respect its ideals and institutions, the National Flag and the National Anthem: (b) to cherish and follow noble ideas which inspired our national struggle for freedom; (c) to uphold and protect the sovereignty, unity and integrity of India; (d) to defend the country and render national service when called open to do so; (e) to promote harmony and the spirit of common brotherhood amongst all the people of India transcending religious, Linguistic and religional or sectional diversities; to renounce practices derogatory to the dignity of women; (f) to value and preserve the rich heritage of our composite culture: (g) to protect and improve the natural environment including forests, lakes, rivers and wild life, and to have compassion for living creatures; (h) develop the scientific temper, humanism and the sprit of inquiry and reform; (i) to safeguard public property and to adjure violence; and (j) to strive towards excellence in all spheres of individual and collective activity so that the nation constantly rises to higher levels of endeavour and achievement.

* These provisions from the Code of Criminal Procedure ,1973.

Article 32 gave the right to move the Supreme Court by 'appropriate proceedings' for the enforcement of rights guaranteed under the Constitution, which shall not be suspended except as otherwise provided for by the Constitution.

The greatest incidence of human rights violations occurred during the Emergency. Many went unreported, and remedies for enforcement of rights were suspended during the period. The suspension of the Writs of habeas corpus under Article 352 which well legitimised in terms of the greater claim of national security, came up before the Supreme Court in A.D.M. Jabalpur v. Shivakanta Shukla (AIR 1976 SC1207)[30] Chief Justice Ray stated that Liberty is not an abstract or absolute freedom but a regulated freedom, and if extraordinary powers are given to the Government, it is so because the emergency is extraordinary .The court had to give effect to the Presidential Order in force under Article 359. He further claimed that the Emergency provisions were part of the law of the Constitution for such situations.

The 44th Amendment and subsequent judicial interpretations have restored Article 20 and 21 as being capable of enforcement, provided that they cannot be suspended under any situation. The Executive can never deprive a person of his life or liberty without the authority of law. But some habits die hard, and deaths in custody still happen, as do 'disappearances'. Important developments took place in the 1980s and 1990s when the Supreme Court used the power to award monetary compensation where a citizen's constitutional rights had been violated. For wrongful detention after the court acquitted him, Rudal Shah was granted compensation (Rudal Shah v. State of Bihar, 1983-4 SCC 141).[31]

It has consistently been recognised by the Supreme Court that the help of International Covenants on Human Rights, and for that matter all other International Conventions on Human Rights, which have been signed and ratified by India, can be taken into consideration interpreting constitutional provisions relating to human rights. If there is a conflict between the provisions of an international convention and provision of Indian constitution or Indian law obviously the provision of Indian constitution or Indian Law shall prevail. But if there is no conflict between the two and the relevant provision or provisions (relating to Fundamental Rights) are of wide amplitude to encompass the provisions of the International convention thus can be read into the fundamental rights.

No human right is or can be absolute. Human rights like other rights are subject to reasonable restrictions. Liberty is a social contract. If one wants to exercise one's rights in society, one will have to respect similar rights of others. This obviously implies restrictions upon one's rights. This is also clear from the perusal of human rights recognized in the International covenant on Civil and Political Rights. For example, Article 12 (1) of the covenant recognizes everyone's right to liberty of movement and freedom to choose his residence and Article 12(2) incorporates the freedom of everyone to leave any country, including one's own. But Article 12 (3) makes it clear that the above-mentioned shall not be subject to any restrictions except those which are provided by law necessary to protect national interests, security, public order, public health or morals or the rights and freedoms of others, and are consistent with the other rights recognized in the present covenant. Though this provision begins negatively, the purpose in fact is to emphasis the restrictions which can be imposed on the exercise of the freedom. But the restrictions thus imposed cannot be arbitrary and must be reasonable on grounds of restrictions specified in the relevant clause must be satisfied.

To millions of our citizens fundamental rights are teasing illusions. Indeed they are not even aware of them. However, with the development of Public Interest Litigation, fundamental rights have been translated into living realities for some segments of our people. Although the fact of progress in the field of human rights has been slow human rights are no longer in a state of subservience. What we are witnessing today is a gradual emergence of sovereignty of human rights transcending natural frontiers and geographical boundaries.

From the above analysis it is crystal clear that India fully followed International Bill on Human Rights and Indian Constitution protects such rights, according to the philosophy of Universal Declaration. India constitutes the National Human Rights Commissions at the union level and State Human Rights Commissions at the provincial level for the redress of grievances of human rights violations. Besides the Human Rights Courts have been created for the speedy disposal of human rights violation cases. The people of India and other human rights organisations working abroad have appreciated the role of NHRC. It is hoped that the Supreme Court of India and NHRC will help to protect and maintain the dignity of the people of India as enshrined in our

Constitution. The Subsequent Chapter highlights historical background, the compositions and procedure of functioning of National Human Rights Commission.

Footnotes

1. Arvind Sharma "Hundiism and Human Rights, A conceptual Approach" Oxford University Press , New Delhi,2006, p.30.
2. S. C Khare "Human Rights and United Nations" (1978), p. 193.
3. Furquan Ahmad "Human Rights and Developing Nations: Provisions, Problems and Prospective, in Prof Z. A. Nizami and Devika Paul(ed), Human Rights in Third Countries (1994), P. 107
4. Atharvaveda – Sumjuana Sukta, cited in inaugural address of Justice M. Ramajoris, in Judicial Colloquium in Banagalore 24-26 Feb, 1998.
5. Prava Chawala, "Equality and justice in England & West," (1980) P. 85.
6. Study Material "Principles and Theories of Human Rights" Indian Institute of Human Rights, New Delhi.
7. Ibid p. 67.
8. Ibid p. 70-71.
9. Study Material "Human Rights and India" Block –1: Human Rights India's Heritage, IGNOU, New Delhi.
10. *Ibid* p. 5.
11. *Ibid* p. 6.
12. *Ibid* p. 7.
13. *Ibid* p. 7.
14. Sunil Dehta and Lalit Dadwal "Genesis of Human Rights in India" in T. S. N. Sastry, (ed.) "India and Human Rights Reflections", Concept Publishing Company, New Delhi, 2005.
15. Martin Ennals, "The Struggle for Human Rights" in A. R. Desai (ed.), Violation on Democratic Rights in India, (1986), vol. I, p. 37.
16. P. L. Mehta and Neena Verma, Human Rights Under Indian Constitution, (1999), p. 18
17. Study Material "Human Rights and India" Block –1: Human Rights India's Heritage, IGNOU, New Delhi.
18. *Ibid* p. 9.
19. *Ibid* p. 10.
20. *Ibid* p. 10.
21. *Ibid* p. 10.
22. *Ibid* p. 10.
23. *Ibid* p. 11.

24. *Ibid* p. 11.
25. Study Material "Principles and Theories of Human Rights" Indian Institute of Human Rights, New Delhi.
26. *Ibid.*
27. *Ibid.*
28. Keshavananda Bharativ. State of Kerla,AIR 1973 SC 1461.
29. Kishore Chand v.state of Himachal Pradesh,1991 ISCJ,68,76.
30. AIR 1976 SC 1207.
31. AIR 1983 4 SCC 141.

References

Pathak, A. K., "Human Rights" Silver Line Publication, Faridabad, 2005.

Khushyap, S.C., " Human Rights and Parliament, (1978), p. 19.

Altekar, A.S., "State Government in Ancient India" (1985).

Rapson, E. J., "The Cambridge History of India" (1923), Vol.1, p. 436.

Meheta, P. L. & Neena Verma, "Human Rights Under Indian Constitution (1999), p. 18.

Dev, A., I.A. Dev, S. Das (ed) "Human Rights - A Source Book". NCERT, 1996.

Sastry, T.S.N. (ed) "India and Human Rights Reflections" New Delhi, Concept Publishing Company, 2005.

Pal, R.M. and S.Chakraborty (ed) "Human Rights Education in India", New Delhi, Indian Social Institute, 2000.

4

National Human Rights Commission

India is a new State – just 60 years–old- but is admittedly an ancient society.[1] Being the motherland of one of the oldest civilizations of the world and the birthplace of diverse cultures and religions, has a very rich heritage of human rights ideals and values. India is bestowed with all principles and institutions of democratic governance and is also a signatory to the Universal Declaration of Human Rights and international covenants, which fortify India's commitment to and respect for human rights. The Constitution of India, which came into force on 26 January 1950, also has a rich content of human rights in Part III and Part-IV.The historical distinction between fundamental rights and Directive Principles was diluted in a series of constitutional amendments as well as in judicial interpretstions over a period of time.

These developments may be classified into two periods: (1) between 1950 and 1978 and (2) between 1978 and 1993.[2] The year 1978 is important because of the decision given by the Supreme Court in Maneka Gandhi v. Union of India[3]. During the first period, certain basic rights like the right to privacy were held to be part of personal liberty under article 21.[4] The right ot travel abroad was also read into personal liberty in Article 21.[5] The detenu's right to write and be published was held to be part of personal liberty.[6] in the second period, there has been a much faster development in the form of judicial interpretations to protect rights and liberties of individuals against the communications and omissions of the State. In the decision in *Meneka Gandhi v. Union of India*, Justice P.N. Bhagwati observed:

The expression 'personal liberty' in Article 21 is of the widest amplitude and it covers variety of right, which go to constitute the personal liberty of man, and some of them have been rised to the status of distinct fundamental rights and given additional protection under Article 19.

This was turning point for judicial activism in upholding the right and liberties of individuals under the Indian Constitution.

During the period between 1973 and 1993, considerable developments took place in the protection of the rights of individuals. The rights of prisoners and undertrials, which are not mentioned anywhere, were sought to be protected.[7] The rright to livelihood was read into Article 21.[8] Justice Bhagwati observed in *Francis Coralie v. Union Territory of Delhi:*[9]

We think that the right to life includes the right to live with human dignity and all that goes along with it, namely, the bare necessary of life such as adequate nutrition, clothing and shelter over the head and facilities for reading, writing and expressing oneself in adverse forms, freely movion about and mixing and commingling with fellow human beings.

In *Bandhu Mukti Maecha v. Union of India*, in addressing the right of release and rehabilitation of bonded labour, Justice Bhagwati observed: '... these are the minimum requirements which must exist in order to enable a person to live with human dignity, and no State ... has the right to take any action which will deprive a person of the enjoyment of these basic essentials.'[10] in an earlier case, Justice V.R. Krishna Iyer observed:

The high value of human dignity and the worth of human person enshrined in Article 21, read with Articles 14 and 19, obligates the State not to incarcerte except under the law which is fair, just and reasonable in its procedural essence.

In *Sodan Singh v. NDMC,*[11] the Superme Court held that in view of the global developments in the sphere of human rights these judicial decisions are a pointer towards the recognition of an affirmative right to the basic necessities of life under Article 21.[12]

The rights of women and childten housed in protective homes to suitable living conditions and to effective safeguard of their interests was upheld by the Supreme Court.[13] Free legal aid to the accused was held to be a right under Article 21.[14] The court went a step further and said that the trial court is under an obligation to tell an accused who cannot afford legal representation that he is entitled to be represented by a lawyer at the cost of the State.[15] The right to speedy trial was held to be part and parcel of individual rights.[16] The right to claim monetary compensation for thr violation of rights, including the unenumerated rights in Article 21, has been recognized by the Supreme Court.[17] The right to education was also read into the right to life under Article 21.[18]

These decisions are mentioned to indicate that the Supreme Court has been doing an excellent job since 1978 in realizing the Human Rights of all individuals, whether mentioned in the Fundamental Rights chapter or not. In 1993, Justice J.S. Verma in Nilabati Behera v. State of Orissa referred to Article 9(5) of the International Covenant on Civil and Political Rights 1966, which provides: 'Anyone who has been the victim of unlawful arrest or detention shall have an enforceable right to compensation,' and held that it is not alien to the concenpt of enforcement of a guaranteed right.[19] In yet another place, Justice Verma observed:

> It followes that a claim in public law for compensation for contravention of human rights and fundamental freedoms, the protection of which is guaranteed in the Constitution, is an acknowledged remedy for enforcement and protection of such rights, and such a claim based on strict liability made by resorting to a constitutional remedy provided for the emforcement of fundamental rights is 'distinct from, and in adition to the remedy in private law for damages for the tort' resulting from the contravention of the fundamental rights.

India has ratified the International Covenant on Civil and Political Rights.

This brief survey of the attempt to protect, through judicial decisions, the basic human rights, the fundamental rights as well as the Directive Principles of state policiples of State Policy (reflecting social, economic and cultural rights) leads us to the fundamental question, should a separate and independent National Human Rights Commission be established or not? If established, would it not undermine the judicial process through which the rights have got fool protection?[20]

Before the establishment of the NHRC, a series of seminars and workshops were held to identify the method and manners and workshops were held to establiched, its powers and functions, and related legal and constitution euestions. At a seminar organized by the Bar Council of India, several views were presented for and against the NHRC. Justice V.R. Krishna Iyer, reacting to the establishment of NHRC because of criticism from other countries, observed:

It is a creation in panic, a shame that we should think in terms of a Commission on Human Rights only because Sweden or the United State Congress or some other country tells [us]... You are not respecting human rights. Therefore, have a Commission if you really want help from us. The mendicancy to which this nation is reduced not merely financially but even in regard to human rights rights ideology is a matter for pity. We may be proud of our judiciary, we may be proud of our Press but I am not proud of international mendicancy which originates from Delihi.

He went on to describe the NHRC as an optical illusion, cosmetic coloration, opium for the people at home and brower sugar for countries abroad, a legislative camouflage, a verbal wonder which conceals more than it reveals. An ineffectual angel which beats its golden wings in the void in vain.

He also opined that we should have the Human Rights Division of the Supreme Court of India. It will be useful. Similarly we may have at the High Court level and then they can operate with infrastructure which is provided.... We really want, therefore, a commission which is vitalized, a commission which has an independent investigating staff not deputed from the police.[21]

In favour of the NHRC, Justice T.K. Thommen Observed

The proposed National Commission on Human Rights is, in many respects, intended to be an ombudsman to oversee the enforcement of laws and effective protection of human rights. It is the primary responsibility of the legislature to address itself to be enactment of effective laws; it is the responsibility of the executive to implement laws promptly and Justly; it is the function of an independent judiciary to administer justice, according to law. The power of the proposed commission are intended to be so wide as to oversee the functioning of the organs of the state, not with a view to interfering with their constitutionally assigned functions, but to highlighting before them the passing problems endangering human rights in oder that the Commission, which the people of this country have given unto themselves to safeguard a true democratic system of administration, becomes a meaningful instrument of justice and equity and an invigorating force of carry the nation forward. The people of this country, rich or poor, literate or illiterate, forward or backward, demand justice being done to them without fear or favour.... The commission is not a court. Its function is to be the watchdog of human rights. Its procedure is not expected to be adversarial or accusatorial. It must not allow itself to be bogged down by procedural formalities.[22]

With a view to strengthen the process of the protection of human rights in India, the Government of India decided to set up at national level an autonomous National Human Rights system. On 14th May 1993 the Protection of Human Rights Bill was introduced. But on 29th September 1993, the President of India, under Article 123 of the Constitution promulgated an ordinance for setting up a National Human Rights Commission to inquire into the complaints of violations of human rights against the public servants in every part of the country. The Union Parliament promptly passed it. This paved the way for the setting of a National Human Rights Commission. It is a fully autonomous body; its autonomy derived out of the method of appointment of the members, their fixity of tenure, and statutory guarantees thereto, the status they have been accorded; the manner in which the staff responsible to the commission would be appointed and would conduct themselves; as also the autonomy it enjoys in terms of its financial powers. Accordingly the NHRC started its functioning with its first Chairperson Justice Ranga Nath Mishra on 12th October in the same year.

Structure of the National Human Rights Commission

As per the protection of the Human Rights Act, 1993 the NHRC has neately arranged its structural framework inorder to execute its functions. The details of the Protection of Human Rights Act mentioned at appendix-III. It has been systematically arranged for the smooth functioning and to fulfil the objectives of the Act for better protection of human rights.

Composition of the commission

Section 3 of PHR Act envisages that the commission shall consist of one Chairperson and four other members.

(a) The Chairperson of NHRC has been a retired Chief Justice of the Supreme Court;

(b) One Member has to be either a sitting or a retired judge of the Supreme Court;

(c) One Member who is, or has been, the Chief Justice of a High Court;

(d) Two Members to be appointed from amongst persons having knowledge of, or practical experience in, matters relating to human right.

Besides them,the Chairperson of the National Commission for Minorities, the National commission for the Scheduled Castes and Scheduled Tribes and the National Commission for Women shall be deemed to be Members of the Commission for the discharge of certain functions.

There shall be a Secretary-General of the rank of the Secretary to the Government of India who shall function as the Chief Executive Officer of the Commission.

The Headquarters of the Commission shall be at Delhi and there is an enabling provision in the Act to establish offices at other places in India with the previous approval of the Central Government.

The method of appointment envisaged in the Act is unique in as much as it is made by the President on the recommendation of a high-powered committee consisting of the following:

(a)	The Prime Minister	- Chairperson
(b)	Speaker of the House of the People	- Member
(c)	Minister in-Charge of the MHA in the Government of India	- Member
(d)	Leader of the opposition in the House of the People	-Member
(e)	Leader of the opposition in the Council of States	-Member
(g)	Deputy Chairman of the Council of States	-Member

However, no sitting judge of the Supreme Court or a sitting Chief Justice of a High Court shall be appointed without consultation with the Chief Justice of India.

The Chairperson or any other Member of the Commission can only be removed from his office by an order of the President on the ground of proved misbehaviour or incapacity after the Supreme Court has, on an inquiry held in this behalf recommended such removal.

The term of office of the Chairperson and Members will be five years from the date of assumption of office or until the age of 70 years, whichever is earlier. On ceasing to hold office, the Chairperson and

Members shall be ineligible for further appointment under the Government of India or under the Government of any State.

Officers and other Staff of the Commission

The Act provides that besides the Secretary-General, the Central Government shall make available to the Commission such police and investigative staff and an officer not below the rank of Director General of police and such other officers and staff as may be necessary for the efficient performance of the functions of the Commission. The Commission may appoint other administrative, technical and scientific staff considered necessary in conformity with the Rules made by the central Government in this behalf.

Definition of Human Rights

In terms of section 2 of the Act, "human rights" means the rights relating to life, liberty, equality and dignity of the individual guaranteed by the constitution or embodied in the International Covenants and enforceable by courts in India. "International Covenants" means the International Covenant on Civil and Political Rights and the International Covenant on Economic, Social and Cultural Rights adopted by the General Assembly of the United Nations on 16 December 1966.

Functions of the commission

Under the section 12 of PHR Act the NHRC performs the wide range of functions which are mentioned below:

(a) to inquire, on its own initiative or on a petition presented to it by a victim or any persons on his behalf, into complaints of -
    (i) violation of human rights or abetment there of; or
    (ii) Negligence in the prevention of such violation, by a public servant.

(b) Intervene in any proceeding involving any allegation of violation of human rights pending before a court with the approval of such court;

(c) Visit, under intimation to the state Government, any jail or any other institution under the control of the state Government, where persons are detained or lodged for purposes of treatment, reformation or protection to study the living conditions of the inmates and make recommendations thereon;

(d) Review the safeguards provided by or under the constitution or any law for the time being in force for the protection of human rights and recommend measures for their effective implementation;

(e) Review the factors, including acts of terrorism that inhibit the enjoyment of human rights and recommend appropriate remedial measures;

(f) Study treaties and other international instruments on human rights and make recommendations for their effective implementation;

(g) Undertake and promote research in the field human rights;

(h) Spread human rights literacy among various sections of society and promote awareness of the safeguards available for the protection of these rights through publications, the media, seminars and other available means;

(i) Encourage the efforts of non-governmental organisations and institutions working in the field of human rights; and Such other functions as it may consider necessary for the promotion of human rights.

Powers relating to inquiries

(1) The commission shall, while inquiring into complaints under this Act, have all the powers of a civil court trying a suit under the code of civil procedure, 1908 (5 of 1908), and in particular in respect of the following matters, namely:-

(a) Summoning and enforcing the attendance of witnesses and examining them on oath;

(b) Discovery and production of any document;

(c) Receiving evidence on affidavits;

(d) Requisitioning any public record or copy thereof from any court or office;

(e) Issuing commission for the examination of witnesses or documents;

(f) Any other matter which may be prescribed.

(2) The Commission shall have power to require any person, subject to any privilege which may be claimed by that person under any law for the time being in force, to furnish information on such points or matters as, in the opinion of the commission, may be useful for, or relevant to, the subject matter of the inquiry and any person so required shall be deemed to be legally bound to furnish such information within the meaning of section 176 and section 177 of the Indian Penal Code (45 of 1860)

(3) The commission or any other office, not below the rank of a Gazetted Officer, specially authorised in this behalf by the commission has reason to believe that any document relating to the subject matter of the inquiry may be found, and may seize any such document of take extracts or copies there from subject to the provisions of section 100 of the Code of Criminal Procedure, 1973(2 of 1974), in so far as it may be applicable.

(4) The Commission shall be deemed to be a civil court and when any offence as is described in sec. 175, section 178, section 179, section 180 or section 228 of the Indian Penal Code (45 of 1860) is committed in the view or presence of the Commission, the Commission may, after recording the facts constituting the offence and the statement of the accused as provided for in the Code of Criminal Procedure, 1973(2 of 1974), forward the case to a Magistrate having jurisdiction to try the same and the Magistrate to whom any such case is forwarded shall proceed to hear the complaint against the accused as if the case has been forwarded to him under section 346 of the Code of Criminal Procedure, 1973.

(5) Every proceeding before the Commission shall be deemed to be judicial proceeding within the meaning of sections 193 and 228 and for the purpose of section 196, of the Indian Penal Code (45 of 1860), and the Commission shall be deemed to be a civil court for all the purposes of section 195 and Chapter XXVI of the Code of Criminal Procedure,1973(2 of 1974).

Investigation

(1) The Commission may, for the purpose of conducting any investigation pertaining to the inquiry, utilise the services of any officer or investigation agency of the Central Government or any State Government with the concurrence of the Central Government or the State Government as the case may be.

(2) For the purpose of investigating into any matter pertaining to the inquiry, any officer urgency whose services are utilised under sub section (1) may, subject to the direction and control of the Commission:

(a) Summon and enforce the attendance of any person and examine him;

(b) require the discovery and production of any document; and

(c) requisition any public record or copy thereof from any office

(3) The provisions of section 15 shall apply in relation to any statement made by a person before any officer or agency whose services are utilised under sub-section (1) as they apply in relation to any statement made by a person in the course of giving evidence before the commission.

(4) The officer or agency whose services are utilised under sub-section (1) shall investigate into any matter pertaining to the inquiry and submit a report thereon to the Commission within such period as may be specified by the Commission in this behalf

(5) The commission shall satisfy itself about the correctness of the facts stated and the conclusion, if any, arrived at in the report submitted to it under sub section (4) and for this purpose the commission may make such inquiry (including the examination of the person or persons who conducted or assisted in the investigation) as it thinks fit

Statement made persons to the Commission

No. Statement made by a person in the course of giving evidence before the commission shall subject him to or be used against him in, any civil or criminal proceeding except a prosecution for giving false evidence by such statement:

Provided that the statement:

(a) is made in reply to the question which he is required by the commission to answer; or

(b) is relevant to the subject matter of the inquiry.

Persons likely to be prejudicially affected to be heard.

If, at any stage of the inquiry, the Commission:

(a) considers, it necessary to inquire into the conduct of any person: or

(b) is of the opinion that the reputation of any person is likely to be prejudicially affected by the inquiry;

It shall give to that person a reasonable opportunity of being heard in the inquiry and to produce evidence in his defence:

Provided that nothing in this section shall apply where the credit of a witness is being impeached.

Inquiry into Complaints

The commission while inquiring in to complaints of violations of human rights may-

(i) Call for information or report from the central government or any state Government or any other authority or organisation subordinate thereto within such time as may be specified by it;

Provided that-

(a) If the information or report is not received within the time stipulated by the commission, it may proceed to inquire into the complaint on its own;

(b) If, on receipt of information or report, the commission is satisfied either that no further inquiry is required or that the required action has been initiated or taken by the concerned Government or authority, it may not proceed with the complaint and inform the complainant accordingly;

(ii) Without prejudice to anything contained in clause (I), if it considers necessary, having regard to the nature of the complaint, initiate an inquiry.

Steps after inquiry

The commission may take any of the following steps upon the completion of an inquiry held under this Act, namely:

(1) Where the inquiry discloses, the commission of violation of human rights or negligence in the prevention of violation of human rights by a public servant, it may recommend to the concerned Government or authority the initiation of proceedings for prosecution or such other action as the commission may deem fit against the concerned person or persons;

(2) approach the Supreme court or the High court concerned for such directions, orders or writs as that Court may deem necessary;

(3) recommend to the concerned Government or authority for the grant of such immediate interim relief to the victim or the members of his family, as the Commission may consider necessary;

(4) subject to the provisions of clause (5), provide a copy of the inquiry report to the petitioner or his representative;

(5) the Commission shall send a copy of its inquiry report together with its recommendations to the concerned Government or authority and the concerned Government or authority shall, within a period of one month, or such further time as the Commission may allow, forward its comments on the report, including the action taken or proposed to be taken thereon, to the Commission;

(6) The Commission shall publish its inquiry report together with the comments on the concerned Government or authority, if any, and the action taken or proposed to be taken by the concerned Government or authority on the recommendations of the Commission.

Procedure with respect to armed forces

(1) Notwithstanding any thing contained in this Act, while Dealing with complains of violation of human rights by members of the armed forces, the Commission shall adopt the following procedure, namely;

  (a) it may, either on its own motion or on receipt of a petition, seek a report from the Central Government;

  (b) after the receipt of the report, it may, either not proceed with thecomplaint or, as the case may be, make its recommendations to the Government.

(2) The central Government Shall inform the Commission of the action taken on the recommendations within three months or such further time as the Commission may allow.

(3) The Commission shall publish its report together with its recommendations made to the Central Government and the action taken by that Government on Such recommendations.

(1) The Commission shall provide a copy of the report of the report published under sub-section (3) to the petitioner or his representative.

Annual and Special Reports of the Commission

(1) The Commission shall submit an annual report to the Central Government and to the State Government concerned and may at any time submit special reports on any matter which, in its opinion, is of such urgency or importance that it should not be deferred till submission of the annual report.

(2) The Central Government and the State Government, as the case may be, shall cause the annual and special reports of the Commission to be laid before each House of Parliament or the State Legislature respectively, as the case may be, along with a memorandum of action taken or propose to be taken on the recommendations of the Commission and the reasons for non-acceptance of the recommendations, if any.

Basic Standards Recommended by Amnesty International Relating to NHRC

The creation of a national human rights commission can be an important mechanism to strengthen human right protection but can never replace, nor should it in any way diminish, the safeguards inherent in comprehensive and effective legal structures enforced by an independent, impartial, adequately resourced and accessible judiciary. In India, the creation of such a human rights commission should go hand in hand with a through review of existing institutions and mechanisms-including legal aid programs-in order to make these more effective instruments of human rights protection. These initiatives should be accompanied by determined government policy aimed at holding the perpetrators of human rights violations fully accountable, thus ending the impunity now effectively granted to virtually all those who violate human rights.

The commission on Human Rights adopted by consensus Resolution 1992/54 concerning the Principles relating to the status of national institutions and has transmitted these through the Economic and Social Council to the 47th regular session of the General Assembly for adoption. These internationally recognized. Principles should serve as the basic minimum guidelines for the establishment of a national institution for the protection and protection of human rights. In addition, Amnesty International would like to put forward in this discussion document the following key recommendations relating to the establishment and functioning of a national human rights commission.

Mandate and Composition

The basic standards recommended by Amnesty Internatinal and the provisions of the Protection of Human Rights Ordinance as well as the Act(1993) are the same, with a few exceptions.

The Commission should be independent from government and its charter should reflect this. The Commission should be established by law or, preferable, by constitutional amendment. But in India, the NHRC was established by the Ptotection of Hman Rights Act, 1993 and by constitutional amendment.

The Commission should consist of men and women known for their integrity and impartiality of judgement who shall decide matters before them on the basis of facts and in accordance with the law, without any restrictions, improper influences, inducements, pressures, or threats or interferences from any quarter or for any reason. Its members should be independent of government, have a proven expertise and competence in the field of protecting and promoting human rights and should be drawn from a variety of different backgrounds, including relevant professional groups and the non-governmental sector. The method of section of its members should be fair and transparent and should afford all necessary guarantees of independence and broad representation. Commission members should serve in their individual capacity and should be able to serve in their individual capacity and should be able to serve the Commission effectively. The terms of their appointment, tenure and removal should be clearly specified, laid down in the Charter and should afford the strongest possible guarantees of competence, impartiality and independence.

The Commission should be mandated to monitor and report on compliance with and implementation of relevant international human rights standards, including the Universal Declaration of Human Rights, the International Covenant on Civil Political Rights, the UN. Declaration and Convention against Torture, as well as the UN Code of Conduct for Law Enforcement Officials, the UN Body of Principles for the Protection of All Persons under Any Form of Declaration or Imprisonment and the UN Principles in the Effective Prevention and Investigation of Extra-Legal, Arbitrary or Summary Executions.

The commission should be mandated to review the effectiveness of existing legislation and/or administrative provisions in protecting human rights and should be able to make recommendations for the amendment of such legislation or the introduction of new legislation as necessary. The Commission should also examine bills and proposals for new legislation put forward by the government or parliament to verify its conformity with international human rights standards and to ensure the State's compliance with the above international human rights instruments.

Following from the recommendation that the scope of the Commission's concerns be defined in terms of State obligations under international human rights law, Amnesty International believes that the Commission should exclude from its mandate criminal organisations, by political groups which have resorted to arms as a means to achieve their goal criminal actions occurring in the context of domestic violence, to which separate mechanisms can devote special attention.

The Commission should have precisely defined powers to investigate on its own initiative situations and cases of reported human rights violations and set clear priorities for its work in accordance with the seriousness of the violations alleged. Priority should be given to alleged violations of the right to life and security of the person and the right not to be tortured (rights from which no derogation can to be made by any government under any circumstances) as well as the right not to be arbitrarily arrested or detained.

The Commission should be directed to establish effective cooperation with non-governmental organizations with first-hand information about reports of human rights violations.

The Commission should also have the power to conduct wide-ranging national inquiries on human rights concerns of fundamental importance to the nation. One critical analysis which Amnesty International recommends be made is an in-depth study of the factors which have contributed to the persistence of human rights violence in India, including the failure of existing institutions and legal mechanisms adequately to protect human rights. Such a study, which could draw upon authoritative investigations already carried out, such as by the National Police Commission, could recommend institutional and other changes necessary to bring about effective reform to halt these violations.

The Commission should be empowered to investigate the conduct of the police as well as the army and paramilitary security forces in all Indian states. In order to do this effectively, the Commission should have adequate facilities to conduct through investigations independent of the police and other security forces, whose conduct it will be called upon to assess.

Facilities and Methodology

The Commission should have all necessary human and material resources to examine, thoroughly, effectively, speedily and throughout the country, the evidence and other case material concerning specific allegations of violations put before it. The Commission should have its own investigative machinery and should have access to expert assistance whenever required to verify alleged violations. It should have adequate facilities to carry out on-the-spot investigations. The Commission should have immediate and unhindered access to all places where detained persons are held or are suspected to be held. Officials should be obliged to cooperate with the Commission's investigations.

The Commission should have powers to initiate investigations on its own motion. It should be able it receive communications not only from the complainants themselves but also, if they themselves are unable or prevented from doing so, from lawyers, relatives or others acting on their behalf and non-governmental groups. Investigations initiated by the Commission should be adequately published, especially in the state concerned to enable and encourage witnesses to come forward to testify.

The Commission should have full and effective powers to compel the attendance of witnesses and the production of documents.

The Commission should have full and effective powers to protect witnesses, complainants or others providing evidence to the Commission, including bringing about the suspension or transfer of officials allegedly involved to other duties where they would have no power over witnesses or complaints-without prejudice pending completion of investigations. Victims or relatives should have access to all relevant information and documents relating to the investigation and be granted all necessary facilities to present evidence. The Commission should be able to provide financial assistance to witnesses enabling them to travel and be accommodated in order to present their evidence before the Commission.

The Commission should work in an open way with its hearings generally open to the public. Private hearings should be an exceptional measure and be resorted to only in specific pre-established circumstances. The Commission's methodology and the results of its investigations, together with official reports, including post mortem and other expert reports as well as police and court records, should in each case be published in full, in an easily accessible and comprehensible from. The Commission should also prepare regular reports documenting all the complaints it has received, together with the action taken in each case, as well as an account of the its other activities for and protection of human rights. The Commission's reports should be presented periodically to representative bodies such as the National and State Assemblies.

The result of the Commission's investigations should be referred to appropriate judicial bodies without delay. Anyone the Commission alleges to have been responsible for committing human rights violations or for ordering, encouraging or permitting them, should automatically be brought to justice. The government should ensure that any prosecutions for human rights related offences are brought by authorities which are distinctly independent from the police or security force or other bodies allegedly implicated in the human rights violations.

The Commission should have power to ensure that superior officers are held accountable for acts committed under their authority and should be mandated to closely follow subsequent legal proceeding in the case, for example by serving as a 'watchdog' at trials, if necessary appearing before the court to make legal submissions to press for appropriate legal action to be taken within a reasonable time.

The Commission should have power to ensure effectively remedies including interim measures to protect the life and safety of an individual and free medical treatment where necessary; it should ensure that and prompt compensation in paid and other measures of redress and rehabilitation are taken in all cases it has taken up in which the police or the security force are found to have perpetrated human rights violations.

The government should undertake an obligation to respond, within a reasonable time, to the case specific as well as the more general findings, conclusions and recommendation made by the Commission. The government's response should be made public.

From the above analysis, it is clear that NHRC is a fully independent body and based on two important pillars namely automony and transparency. It has been vasted with the powers of quasi- judicial in nature. Fact-finding is the core of human rights activity which has been effectively used by this investigatory body. The status of the Commission is not confined with its status only, rather it has its Constitutional validity under the Commission of Inquiry Act 1952. The status of the commission is also defined in International Law particularly in Paris Principle of 1991 and many international workshops on National Institutions for the Promotion and Protection of Human Rights.[23]

There was wide spread feeling among the general public and the intelligentsia in particular, that with a democratic constitution guranting Fundamental Rights enforceable by the courts and provision for periodical elections on universal adult franchise, there was no need for an institutional mechanism for monitoring and safeguarding human rights. By setting up the Commission like NHRC India has fulfilled not only the objectives as enumerated in the Preamble of the Constitution of India but also the provisions of Article 51 as mentioned in the Part-IV of the Constutititution. Being seen the activities of NHRC of the past years, it will not be any worng if its scope is widened and more power is given to this important mechanism of human rights protection in the era of globalisation.

Footnotes

1. S R Maheshwari, *Public Administration in India*,Macmillan India Ltd. New Delhi,2000.
2. C.J. Nirmal, (ed) *Human Rights in India, Historical,Social and Political Perspectives*, Oxford University Press, New Delhi,2000.
3. Kharak Singh v. State of Uttar Pradesh AIR 1963 SC 1295;
4. Govind v. State of Madhya Pradesh AIR 1975 SC 1378.
5. Satwant Singh Swahney v. Asst Passport Officer, New Delhi AIR 1967 SC 1836.
6. State of Maharastra v. Prabhakar Pandurang AIR 1966 SC 424.
7. Sunil Batra v. Delhi Administration (1978) 4 SCC 494.
8. Olga Tillis v. Bombay Municipal Corporation AIR 1986 SC 280.
9. AIR 1981 SC 746 at 753.
10. AIR 1984 SC 802.
11. Jolly George Varghese v. Bank of Cochin AIR 1980 SC 470.
12. (1989) 4 SCC 155
13. Upendra Baxi v. State of Uttar Pradesh (1983) 2 SCC 308; Sheela Barse v. Secretary, Children Aid Society AIR 1987 SC 656.
14. M.H. Hoskot v. State of Maharastra AIR 1978 SC 1548;Hussainara Khatoon v. State of Bihar AIR 1979 SC 1369
15. Khatri v. State of Bihar AIR 1981 SC 928.
16. Hussainara Khatoon v. Home Secretary, Bihar AIR 1979 SC 1360.
17. Rudalsah v. State of Bihar (1983) 4 SCC 141; Bhim Singh v. State of J &K (1985) 4 SCC 677; M.C. Mehta v. Union of India (1987) 1 SCC 395.
18. Unnikrishnan v. State of Andhra Pradesh (1993) 1 SCC 645.
19. AIR 1993 SC 1960.
20. V. Vijayakumar (Article) "The Working of NHRC-A Perspective" appeared in C.J. Nimal (ed) "Human Rights in India" Oxford University Press. 2000.
21. Indian Bar Review, XX(1), 1993, pp. 23-4.
22. T.K. Thommen, '*Human Rights Commission*', Cochin University Law Review, vol. XVII, nos. 1 and 2 March- June 1993, p. 4., in C.J. Nirmal's (ed) "Human Rights in India "Oxford University Press, 2000.
23. A. Ray," National Human Rights Commission of India, Formation Functioning & Future Prospects" Khama Publishers, Delhi,2005.

References

1. Nirmal, Chiranjivi J.(ed) "Human Rights in India, Historical, Social and Political Perspectives" New Delhi, Oxford University Press,, 2000.
2. Ray, Arun "National Human Rights Commission of India, Formation, Functioning and Future Prospectives" New Delhi, Khama Publishers, 2005.
3. Evas, Tony "Politics of Human Rights : a Global Perspective, London : Photo Press, 2001.
4. Protection of Human Rights Act, 1993. Government of India.
5. Amnesty International "Teaching and Learning about Human Rights", London.
6. Biswal, T "Human Rights Gender and Environment" New Delhi, Viva Books Private Limited, 2006.

5

Achievements of NHRC: An Overview

The creation of National Human Rights Commission under the Protection of Human Rights Act, 1993 marked the beginning of a new era of human governance in India. It is true that the PHR Act did not fulfil the long- cherished desires of human rights activists or other social activists in our country primarily for the reason that it made the NHRC a recommendary or advisory body [1] Even the Commission itself is aware of this fact is evident from the following observation of the Commission it its 1997-98 Report: " It recalls only too well that at the time of its establishment... many were only sceptical as to whether it (Statute of the Commission) provided a sound enough basis on which an effective national institution could be built. The Commission was not however deterred by this, even as it readily shared the view that weakness and ambiguities in its Statute would need to be reminded at the earliest, in the light of Experience gained".[2]

The basic approach of the Commission, namely its determination to come to grips as early as possible, with gravest areas of human rights violation has encouraged people to protect their human rights through the Commission.[3] "Immediately after the Commission was set up, it issued directives to all State governments to ensure that incidents of custodial deaths or rape must reported to the Commission within 24 hours by the district Magistrate /Supertendent of Police , failing which the Commission would presume that threr was an attempt to suppress the incidents. Following these instructions a number of reports have been received from different States in respect of deaths which have occered in police or judicial custody. These reports are studies by the Commission and action recommended against officers found, *prima facie*, guilty. One very siginificant development in this connection has been a higher level of awareness among officials alomg with reports of the commission on incidents of custodial deaths.[4]

Nevertheless, thirteen years after it was established, the NHRC has received popular recognition as indispensable institution of governance due to its sincere and spontaneous efforts to maintain the standards of integrity, efficiency and probity and to ensure accountability and transparency in its functioning. Consequently, it now enjoys great moral authority and the responses to its recommendations by the concerned agencies of central and state governments are overwhelming. By and large, the commission's recommendations for the grant of immediate interim relief to the victims or the members of their families have been adhered to by the concerned governments or authorities, although this is not always so in case of its recommendations for departmental or criminal actions.

The National Human Rights Commission prepares and submits annual report to the Central Government about the position of human rights in the country. From the past years reports it is clear that it has been successfully working from the date of its inception. The NHRC has already received more than four lakhs complaints from various parts of the country. These complaints covered almost all the aspects of the violations of human rights including excesses by armed forces and police, custodial deaths and rape, torture child labour and bonded labour disappearances, dowry deaths and indignity to women, the rights of the disadvantaged sections of society especially of SCs and STs, conditions relating to jails, violence in areas of insurgency and Terrorism spherical problems of minority communities and environmental issue affecting the right to life and dignity and reasonable health. The commission either dismissed or disposed of complaints according the provisions as prescribed by the law and the Protection of Human Rights Act. During the years 1993-2006 (Thirteen years), the NHRC has made great progress in effectively enforcing human rights. It has made many accomplishments and made many sighinificant recommendations for changes in the laws as well as the Protection of Human Rights Act, 1993. Here some cases are mentioned as examples to know how NHRC has been handling the cases since its inception.

Case Study

IMPORTANT CASES (Year 1993-1994)

Atrocity in Police custody

Alleged amputation of male organ of Shri Jugtaram in police custody in Barmer, Rajasthan

On the basis of a press report that appeared in a newspaper dated 10 February 1994 and captioned "cops cut off man's penis", the Commission took cognisance of the incident suo motu and called for a report from the Government of Rajasthan. The State Government sent a preliminary report stating that one A.S.I. and one constable had been arrested in connection with the incident. Simultaneously, they along with one sub-Inspector and two other constables had been placed under suspension. It was further indicated that investigation of the matter had been taken over by CBI on 19 February 1994 and that, for better medical care, the victim had been sent to SMS Hospital, Jaipur where he was undergoing medical treatment in a plastic surgery ward.

On perusing the report, the Commission on 15 March 1994 directed CBI to complete the investigation within 3 months and submit its report to the Commission soon thereafter. The Commission also directed CBI to keep it informed of the progress of the matter from time to time.

The investigation has since been completed and a charge sheet has been submitted.

Beating of Shri Luies, Advocate by Sub Inspector of Police-Complaint by Shri M. Udaya Bhanu, Advocate, Madras

Shri M. Udaya Bhanu, Advocate, Madras had represented to the Commission that on 20 January 1994, an advocate, Shri Luies was mercilessly beaten by Sub-Inspector of Police, Shri Devanesan. According to Shri Udaya Bhanu, Shri Luies had intervened when the Sub-Inspector was physically assaulting some beggars. The Sub-Inspector got violent and started beating Shri Luies. Shri Luies was admitted to hospital. Next morning, Inspector Shri Ranganathan forcibly took away Shri Luies to an unknown place.

On 21 January 1994, members of the Bar passed a resolution condemning the act of the Sub-Inspector and filed a petition before the Court for search of Shri Luies and his production before the Court.

The Commission has called for a report from the Chief Secretary, Government of Tamil Nadu. The Chief Secretary has informed the Commission that a Magisterial Inquiry into the incident has been ordered and that the Sub Inspector, Shri Devanesan has been placed under suspension. The matter remains under the consideration of the Commission.

Year 1997-98

Police torture and death: Rajasthan

The Commission took cognisance of a news item, which reported the death of one Hussain Teli, who was brought to the police station at Bonli in Rajasthan for interrogation in connection with the case of the murder of one Prahlad Yadav. It was alleged that Hussain Teli was tortured to death.

The Commission directed its Investigation Division to investigate the matter. Accordingly, an investigation was undertaken and a report was submitted indicating that this was, indeed, a case of death by torture as a result of police interrogation and that the body of Hussain Teli was buried in unusual circumstances by the police with a view to covering-up their misdeeds.

On an examination of the information before it, the Commission noted that Hussain Teli was called to the police station for interrogation and detained illegally. As Hussain Teli died the very next morning after he was released from police custody and as it was found that blood was oozing from his mouth and nose, there was a nexus between the death and conduct of the police during investigation. Even though no external injuries had been noticed in the inquest and the post-mortem report, the circumstances indicated that Hussain was illegally detained and tortured during the police investigation.

The Commission observed that while steps were being taken to prosecute the concerned officials, a case having already been registered against them, this was a fit case for award of compensation to the dependents. Having regard to the circumstances, the Commission directed payment of interim compensation of Rs.50,000/- to the dependents of the deceased Hussain Teli. The State Government has since complied with the recommendations of the Commission.

Compliance with the Commission's recommendations in the case of torture of Shri A. Ram Singh, a member of the Cuddalore Bar Association: Tamil Nadu

A detailed account of this case was given in the annual report of the Commission for the year 1996-97. It was mentioned that the

Commission had approached the High Court of Madras for appropriate directions to the State Government, as the State had failed to comply with the recommendation of the Commission for the payment of compensation to the torture victim. It was further indicated that the case was pending before the High Court.

By a decision of 19 February 1998, the High Court ordered the State Government to pay Shri Ram Singh the amount of compensation recommended by the Commission, with 18% interest per annum from the date of the Commission's recommendation till the date of payment. Condemning the attitude of the State Government in this case, the Court further ordered payment of an exemplary cost to the Commission as well, with the direction that the State Government was entitled to recover the amounts "from all the officials responsible for the episode".

There has been wide media coverage of the orders of the Court. For its part, Commission also brought the orders of the High Court to the notice of the other State Governments as an indication of the options available to it for enforcing its recommendations.

Year 1998-99

A College Lecturer becomes a Victim of Police Brutality: Kerala (Case 166/11/98-99)

The Commission took suo-motu cognisance of an instance of police brutality, published in the Hindustan Times on 3 September 1998, under the heading "Police brutality again in Kerala". The report stated that a college lecturer was beaten mercilessly by the police as he had dared to question the fare demanded by the driver of an auto rickshaw he had taken while visiting Kozhikode. When the lecturer became unconscious, his legs and hands were tied and he was shifted to a mental hospital, and a case was made out that he was a violent mental patient. The mental hospital did not admit him because of his serious condition and he was taken to the Medical College. The police also assaulted the reporters and photographers, who tried to obtain a first hand account of the torture inflicted upon the victim.

The Commission issued notices to the Chief Secretary and DGP, Government of Kerala. According to the report submitted by the Commissioner of Police, the deeds of the concerned police officials were confirmed. On the basis of this factual confirmation, the Government had suspended the culprits (2 sub-inspectors, 1 ASI, 1 Head Constable, 3 Police Constables) and an enquiry was ordered against them.

Convinced that appropriate steps were being taken against the culprits, the case was closed by the Commission. The Govt. was directed to report the result of the disciplinary action taken against the delinquent officials with utmost expedition.

Year 1999-2000

Torture by Kerala Police which led to Death of Hussain Case No.64/11/1999-2000

A.J. Antony, a resident of Wynad District, Kerala made a complaint to the Commission alleging that one Hussain, a labourer, was brutally beaten by the police on 19 February 1999 during a raid on a gambling place. According to the complaint, Hussain had explained to the police that he had gone there to collect money from one Khalid Mohammad and not to gamble. However, the police ignored his pleas and had beaten him so brutally that his spinal cord broke and he was paralysed from below the neck. Since his family was not wealthy, he was brought home after the initial treatment. The complainant requested the Commission to recommend action against the guilty police officials and to award a compensation of Rs.6 lakhs to the victim.

The Commission immediately called for a report from the DGP Kerala. The report from the DGP stated that during a raid on a gambling den, one of the gamblers, Hussain, was beaten as a result of which he fell down. Shri Hussain made a statement that the police had beaten him and then gone away without providing him any medical treatment. On this basis, a case was registered at the Meppady Police Station. The report added that the victim had since been discharged from hospital and was undergoing treatment at his residence. A police constable had been placed under suspension and an oral inquiry had been ordered against him, as also the concerned Sub-Inspector.

Subsequently, the Confederation of Human Rights Organisations informed the Commission that Hussain had died on 26 November 1999 as a result of the brutal torture inflicted on him by the police. The Confederation also sought action against the policemen for murder and for compensation of at least Rs.3 lakhs to the family of the deceased.

The Commission took note of the report of the DGP Kerala and of the subsequent report of the Confederation of Human Right Organisations. It observed that the Office of the DGP did not dispute the fact that the victim was beaten by the police. The Commission, accordingly, directed the State Government to institute criminal action against the concerned police officials for the murder of Hussain and also to expedite the departmental proceedings against them. The Commission also recommended that a sum of Rs.2 lakhs be paid by the Government to the next of kin of Hussain as immediate interim compensation. The Commission stated that the Government was at liberty to deduct this amount from the salary of the guilty police officials. The Government of Kerala has sanctioned the payment of a sum of Rs. 2 lakhs to the next of kin of Hussain as compensation. The Government has also ordered the Director General of Police to institute criminal action against the guilty officials for murder.

Torture by Tiruchi Police resulting in Death of Shri Mohan, Case No. 4444/95-96/NHRC

The Commission received a telegraphic complaint from Smt. Ayeeponnu stating that her husband was picked up by the police from their home on 3 September 1995, tortured at the police station and was thereafter remanded to judicial custody. While in remand, he was hospitalised in a serious condition and died. The Commission called for a report from DGP Tamil Nadu, Chennai. The DGP stated that Mohan was arrested for selling arrack and had been produced before the Judicial Magistrate the same day and remanded to judicial custody. En-route to jail, he fell down following an epileptic fit and sustained a head injury. He was subsequently hospitalised and died. He also stated that the widow denied having sent a complaint to the Commission.

The matter was further investigated by the Commission through the State Legal Aid and Advice Board, Chennai and an opinion was also sought from the doctor who had performed the autopsy. While the doctor stated that the deceased appeared to have died of shock and haemorrhage due to a head injury, the Legal Aid and Advice Board also reported that the widow denied having sent a complaint. The Commission examined the facts and circumstances and concluded that the telegram itself was a very telling one and it was obvious that the widow, being an illiterate person, wished to avoid a confrontation with the police and therefore, denied having sent the telegram. The post-mortem report also indicated that the injuries could not have been caused by a mere fall to the ground due to an epileptic fit. The deceased also did not have a history of epilepsy.

Based on the facts and clinical evidence available, the Commission came to the conclusion that the death was, indeed, due to head injuries inflicted by the police. The Commission accordingly recommended that in order to compensate for the loss of the precious life of the young man, the Government of Tamil Nadu should pay immediate interim relief in the amount of Rs.2 lakhs to his wife Smt. Ayepponnu within two months of the order. The District Collector was also directed to arrange a house for the widow with Rs.50,000/- and give her a sum of Rs.10,000/- for furniture, and arrange to deposit of the balance amount in her name in a nationalised bank. The State Government was also directed to entrust the matter to the CBI for further investigation, to charge sheet the persons responsible for the death and to take the case to its logical conclusion. The State Government was further asked to submit compliance reports periodically. The State Government has since sanctioned the amount of compensation recommended by the Commission.

Custodial torture of Rakesh Kumar Vij : Uttar Pradesh Case No. 12982/ 96-97

The Commission had received a complaint from one Raj Kumar Vij of Varanasi alleging that his son, Rakesh Kumar Vij had been subjected to severe physical torture by the Uttar Pradesh (UP) Police. This had necessitated the hospitalisation of Rakesh in order to save his life. The complainant alleged that the police had illegally detained his son in connection with a murder investigation. It was mentioned in the petition that the victim was ill-treated and tortured and that electric shocks had been administered to him by making him urinate on a live electric coil – in order to elicit information about the murder. He was also not allowed to meet any family member. The torture had totally incapacitated the victim.

The Commission subsequently received a number of petitions from various non-governmental organisations and social activists regarding this case. Taking Cognisance of the matter, the Commission issued notice to the Director General of Police, UP. The report received from the Senior Superintendent of Police, Varanasi stated that the victim had sustained injuries as a result of a fall while trying to run away from police custody. It also mentioned that Shri Rakesh Vij had a criminal record. The petitioner, when asked to respond, refuted the police version. The Commission then directed its own Investigation Division to inquire into the incident. The report of the Investigation Team affirmed illegal detention and severe torture of the victim. The inquiry by the State CBCID, initiated by the UP Government, substantiated the Investigation Team's report.

The Commission also asked the UP Government to constitute a Medical Board to assess the extent of physical disability suffered by the victim. The Medical Board, gave a report to the Commission, stating that the victim did not suffer from any gross structural damage, and that most of his complaints were subjective. The report also stated that the patient had made a good recovery and that all his medical test results were within normal limits. The complainant, however, in a communication to the Commission, expressed his doubts about the impartiality and trustworthiness of the medical report. He requested the Commission to assess the authenticity of the medical report.

In view of grave apprehensions of miscarriage of justice, the Commission got the victim examined by the Delhi Trauma and Rehabilitation Centre, which gave an entirely different assessment. Due to the discrepancies between the two medical reports, the Commission then directed that Shri Rakesh Vij be referred to the All India Institute of Medical Sciences (AIIMS) for reassessment of his health status. The Commission also directed the State Government to bear all the medical and travelling expenses of the victim.

According to the report from AIIMS, the victim's spinal cord was compressed leading to deterioration of power in his lower limbs and in his neurological functioning in lower limbs, sensory loss of bladder and bowel movement.

There were 60 to 80 per cent chances for improvement, but only if the victim undertook high-risk surgery. He was suffering from hearing loss and some of his teeth were missing. He was suffering from severe Post-Traumatic Stress Disorder with no proven treatment.

The Commission was thus convinced that police officials had perpetrated custodial violence, brutal or savage in nature, on Shri Rakesh Vij. The Commission was also of the opinion that because of this torture, the victim had suffered trauma and stress and had been rendered incapable of living normally for the rest of his life. This was a case of a gross violation of human rights of a citizen resulting from barbaric acts of torture perpetrated on him. The State was, therefore, liable to compensate Shri Rakesh Vij for the damages suffered by him.

The Commission thus directed the UP Government to pay Shri Rakesh Vij Rs.10 lakhs by way of immediate interim relief. It was also directed to arrange for the complete medical treatment of Shri Vij at AIIMS, New Delhi or PGI, Lucknow, as Shri Vij preferred. The expenses of the treatment as well as the travelling expenses of Shri Vij, along with one attendant, from his native place to the place of medical treatment, would also be borne by the State Government.

The Commission also directed the prosecution of the police officers found responsible for perpetrating various acts of torture on Shri Vij. As recommended by the State CBCID, disciplinary action is to be taken against five police personnel, including the Senior Superintendent of Police and a Superintendent of Police, Varanasi. The against them for giving an incorrect report/findings about the status of health and extent of physical disability and incapability suffered by Shri Rakesh Vij.

The Government of Uttar Pradesh reported to the Commission its acceptance of the Commission's recommendations with regard to the prosecution of errant police officials as also in respect of payment of compensation to the victim.

Comment

Under Section 13(1) of the Protection of Human Rights Act, 1993, the Commission shall, while inquiring into complaints under this Act, have all the powers of a Civil Court trying a suit under the Code of Civil Procedure, 1908. Section 13(2) further provides that the Commission shall have power to require any person, subject to any privilege which may be claimed by that person under any law for the time being in force, to furnish information on such points or matters as, in the opinion of the Commission, may be useful for, or relevant to, the subject matter of the inquiry and any person so required shall be deemed to be legally bound to furnish such information within the meaning of Section 176 and Section 177 of the Indian Penal Code.

Section 15 of the Protection of Human Rights Act, 1993 protects those who give evidence before the Commission. It also provides for prosecution of those who give false evidence. Medical personnel have a crucial role in unearthing vital evidence in cases of allegations of torture and custodial violence. They have a duty to ensure that an accurate description of the victim's injuries is provided to the Commission. In this case, the Medical Board constituted by the Government of Uttar Pradesh gave a misleading report to the Commission on the extent of injuries suffered by Shri Rakesh Kumar Vij. The Commission, however, got a further assessment made by the Delhi Trauma and Rehabilitation Centre and then by the All India Institute of Medical Sciences (AIIMS). The Commission, using the powers conferred on it by its Statute, recommended the initiation of appropriate action against those who tried to mislead the Commission.

Article 10(1) the Convention against Torture and Other Cruel, Inhuman or Degrading Treatment or Punishment stipulates that each State Party shall ensure that education and information regarding the Prohibition against Torture are fully included in the training of law enforcement personnel, civil or military, medical personnel, public officials and other persons who may be involved in the custody, interrogation or treatment of any individual subjected to any form of arrest, detention or imprisonment. Article 10(2) further requires each State Party to include this prohibition in the rules or instructions issued in regard to the duties and functions of any such persons. In other words, medical personnel not only have a role in the prevention of Torture but are duty bound to do so.

Death of an Injured Person owing to negligence by the Police: Bihar Case No. 2054/4/1999-2000

The Commission received a complaint from Smt. Phoolwanta Kuwar, a resident of Kamur, Bihar stating that on 16 September 1999, her husband Late Shri Bindeshwar Chaudhary had been brutally beaten by Brij Bihari and others in a false case relating to the theft of a buffalo. In that connection, a case had been registered in the PS Mohania but the police allegedly did not take any action against the accused persons and her injured husband had been kept in the custody of a Medical Officer, Vinay Bahadur Sinha, after being handcuffed. He had allegedly not been provided proper treatment until he contracted tetanus, at which point, he was referred to a hospital in Varanasi. The complainant stated that her husband died there owing to negligence of the doctor and the police. It was further stated that she became a widow at the age of twenty and that her husband had left behind a six-month-old child. The complainant sought a high level inquiry into the matter and justice for herself and her innocent child.

Upon perusal of the complaint, the Commission issued notice to the Chief Secretary and the DGP Government of Bihar to conduct an enquiry and send a report in the matter. The report obtained from the Chief Secretary and the DGP Bihar revealed that an investigation was conducted by Dy. SP Mohania in this case and it was found that on 16 September 1999 at 9.30 PM Sonu Chaudhary brought Bindeshwar Chaudhary in an injured condition to the police station and filed a complaint alleging that the injured Bindeshwar Chaudhary and a few others had been caught red-handed by the locals while stealing a buffalo. The public who gathered on the occasion beat Bindeshwar brutally, thereby injuring him. Following the complaint, a case was registered under Section 379/411 IPC and the injured person was referred to Mohania Hospital for treatment. Owing to excessive injuries on the person of Bindeshwar Chaudhary, he was not produced before a court. On 23 September 1999, his condition had deteriorated and, as a result, he was referred to the hospital in Varanasi, where he succumbed to his injuries. On 27 September 1999, the relatives of the victim had taken away the dead body and filed a complaint which was registered as Case No.263/99 under Section 304(A) IPC against five accused persons. It was also reported that the name of the deceased was in the crime diary Part II in PS Mohania and he was also a suspect in Case No.179/96 under Section 379 IPC. The post-mortem report attributed the cause of death to respiratory failure and to the injuries caused on the body of the deceased.

Upon perusal of the report, the Commission noted serious short-comings in it. No information was forwarded to the Chief Judicial Magistrate in Case No.263/99 for not producing the accused (deceased) within 24 hours of his arrest; when the accused (deceased) was brought to the police station in an injured condition, the police failed to register a complaint against those who had caused injuries; the death of the victim was caused while in police custody and, therefore, a video-graphy of the post-mortem report should have been conducted. An inquest report should also have been prepared by the Judicial Magistrate. While the SHO of PS Mohania was arrested with immediate effect and departmental proceedings were initiated against him, the Commission observed that the police had failed in the performance of their legitimate duties by not registering a case against the wrong doers who had caused serious injuries to the husband of the complainant. The police was also negligent in not referring the seriously injured husband of the petitioner in time to the hospital and in providing proper treatment; this had resulted in his death. The Commission further noted that the report was silent about the allegation of handcuffing of the injured husband. It was also admitted that no information was forwarded to the Chief Judicial Magistrate for not producing the injured husband of the complainant before the said court, which confirmed that there had been deliberate inaction on the part of the police. The Commission observed that the evidence on record proved the allegation of the complainant of ill treatment of her husband by the police.

Having regard to the facts and circumstances of the case and keeping in view that the complainant was widowed at the age of 20 years and left alone with the responsibility of raising a 6 month-old child, the Commission recommended the payment of interim compensation in the amount of Rs. 3,00,000/- to the wife of the deceased. The Commission further directed that a sum of Rs.20,000/ - may be paid by a demand draft to the complainant and the balance deposited in a Nationalised Bank and interest be paid to her every month. The Commission also asked the Government of Bihar to expedite disciplinary action against the errant police officer. The Commission was informed that necessary sanction was issued for payment of compensation.

Year 2000-2001

Fracture Sustained by Sheshrao Rayasing Rathod Following Police Mistreatment: Maharashtra (Case No: 1299/13/98-99)

The Commission received a petition from Shri Shesharao Rayasing Rathod, a resident of Mahuli, Maharashtra, stating that during the course of the Zila Parishad election campaign on 12 December 1998, the petitioner and his friends, Harishchandra and Umesh Sawant, were stopped by a police Sub Inspector and five constables when they were returning from Sawali village. Though they were not within the jurisdiction of these police officials, they were allegedly beaten by them. As a result, the left leg of the petitioner was fractured. It was further alleged that it was done at the instance of one Madharao Nimbalkar of Village Sawali, whose wife was a contestant in the Panchayat Samiti election. In addition, it was alleged that the Sub Inspector had registered a false complaint against the petitioner.

Upon taking cognisance of the complaint, the Commission issued a notice to the Director General of Police, Maharashtra. The report received from his office confirmed the fact that the Sub Inspector of Police Station, Digras had misused his official position and that the incident had occurred outside his area of jurisdiction. An enquiry into the matter indicated that the Sub Inspector had acted at the behest of Madarao Nimbalkar of Sawali Village and that, as a result of merciless beating inflicted on the petitioner, his left leg was indeed fractured. The report also confirmed that a false case had been registered against the petitioner. The report concluded by stating that departmental action was being taken against the Sub Inspector and that it had been recommended that his increments be withheld for two years.

The Commission expressed deep regret over the fact that the police, whose duty it was to protect human rights, was itself involved in the violation of such rights. Having regard to the grievous injuries suffered by the petitioner at the hands of the Sub Inspector, the Commission recommended the payment of immediate interim compensation of Rs. 30,000 to him; it also recommended that this amount may be recovered from the concerned police official if the Government so wished. Further, the Commission asked to be informed of the payment of compensation, as well as the status of the case registered against the Sub Inspector.

The Commission, by its order dated 22 August 2000 had recommended the payment of immediate ognisa compensation of Rs.30,000 to the petitioner, it also recommended that this amount be recovered from the concerned police official if the Government so wished and a criminal case registered against the guilty Sub-Inspector.

Purusant to the Commission's directions the State Government of Maharashtra has indicated that the payment of Rs.30,000/- was made to the petitioner on 19th April 2001. As regards the registeration of a criminal case u/s 325 IPC against the police sub-inspector, Shri B.S.Mahajan, the investigation had been completed and the matter was under consideration of the Director General of Police, Mahrashtra for further necessary action.

Year 2001-2002

Torture of Dayashankar by police: Uttar Pradesh (Case No. 791/ 24/2000-2001)

One Dayashankar Vidyalankar, a resident of Haridwar, Uttranchal submitted a complaint alleging that while he was propagating the teachings of Swami Dayanand at Haridwar Railway Station on 29 February 2001, he was beaten and manhandled by a Constable and, as a result, his left ear was badly injured and a bone behind his right ear was broken. The reports received from the Superintendent of Police Railways, Moradabad and the Director General, Railway Protection Force, Railway Board, in response to a notice issued by the Commission, indicated that the allegations of the complainantagainst the Constable were found to be correct. The Constable was punished by a reduction in his present pay-scale by 3 stages for 3 years, and a case u/s 323/326 IPC and section 145 of Railways Act, 1989 was also registered against him. The Commission, after considering the aforesaid reports and giving a personal hearing to the complainant, as well as after obtaining an opinion from a Medical Board of the All India Institute of Medical Sciences, New Delhi regarding the nature of the injuries suffered by the complainant, recommended a payment of Rs.10,000 to the petitioner by the Ministry of Railways. This has been paid.

In view of the compliance report received from the Ministry of Railways, Govt. of India, the Commission closed the case on 1 April 2002.

Illegal Detention
Year 1995-96

Commission investigates complaints of police high-handedness against the villagers of Mannikere, Karnataka

Investigations into allegations of police excesses against villagers of Mannikere, near Belgaum, Karnataka, by a team from the Commission, have resulted in restoring a sense of confidence among the affected villagers.

The Commission's attention was drawn to this matter by a letter from Shri H.K. Patil, leader of the Opposition, Karnataka Legislative Council. In that letter it was stated that, because of police action on 31 October 1995 and later on 1 November 1995, the villagers of Mannikere had fled their homes. The primary school in the village was closed and milk vendors had not been allowed to enter the village. There was an atmosphere offear and panic all over thearea, the letter added.

Following this complaint, the Commission instructed its Director General (Investigation) and Superintendent of Police to visit the affected area to investigate the matter. They visited Mannikere and the adjoining villages and listened to the grievances of the villagers. They also scrutinized all connected papers.

The investigation team noted evidence of over-reaction by the police. A large number of villagers, including women, had been detained in police custody for more than 48 hours. Because of police high-handedness, many of the villagers had left their hearths and homes in fear and panic. The team found that a land dispute, which was compounded by political rivalry, was at the core of the problem. This coupled with police high-handedness led to a siege of Mannikere village. No immediate and tangible efforts were made by the administration to restore normalcy, the team noted.

The Director General (Investigation) later met the Chief Minister and the Home Minister of the State and conveyed to them the views of the Commission. He also met the Director General of Police, Karnataka and other senior police officers and urged them to take immediate steps to restore normalcy in the affected area and instil confidence in the minds of the villagers.

The State administration has assured the Commission that the cases started against the villagers will be reviewed, and thatmesures will be taken to create a sense of confidence. The Commission has expressed its appreciation of this and is keeping a close watch over developments.

Year 1997-98

Illegal detention/torture by the police – complaint from Shri Baba Khan: Rajasthan

The police received a complaint from Shri Baba Khan of Kota alleging illegal detention and torture. It was alleged that he and his two brothers-in-law were forcibly taken away by the police, illegally detained and tortured. The Commission took ognisance of the complaint, directed the Chief Secretary and Director General of Police, Rajasthan to submit a report. The report submitted by the State police said that the allegations made by Baba Khan were false and baseless. On not being satisfied, the Commission directed its Investigation Division to investigate the matter. The findings of the Investigation Division indicated that the allegations of illegal detention and torture were, prima facie, established. The Commission, accordingly, recommended payment of compensation to the victims: Rs.15, 000/- to Shri Baba Khan, Rs.20, 000/- to Shri Mirza Khan and Rs. 5,000/- to Shri Yousuf Irani. The Commission further recommended that the State Government might consider the report of the investigation team of the Commission with a view to taking action against the errant police officials. The Government of Rajasthan has since complied with the recommendations of the Commission and has intimated that payment of compensation has been made to the victims. It has also reported that a criminal case has been registered against the concerned SHO and disciplinary action initiated against him and two other officers.

Compensation for illegal detention – complaint from Shri Ranbir Yadav: Uttar Pradesh

The Commission took ognisance of a telegraphic complaint received from Shri Inderjit Yadav alleging that his brother Shri Rambir Yadav was forcibly taken away by the police on 23 April 1996 from their milk dairy located at Lal Kuan, District Ghaziabad and illegally detained until 27 April 1996, purportedly for questioning him in regard to the murder of a certain Rajpal.

In pursuance of the Commission's directions, the Investigation Division called for a report from SSP Ghaziabad. The report stated that Rambir Yadav was called to the Police Station on 27 April 1996, in connection with a case and allowed to go the same day. When the police version was communicated to the complainant, he contradicted it and reiterated the allegation, saying that his brother was picked upon 23 April and released on 27 April 1996 after obtaining his signature on a blank paper. Under these circumstances, the Commission directed its Investigation Division to undertake a spot inquiry. On the basis of the report of its Investigation Division the Commission was convinced that this was a case of illegal detention and was a compensatable case. As such, the Commission recommended payment of compensation of Rs.10,000/- to the victim and also directed Inspector General of Police, Meerut to inquire into the matter for fixing the responsibility of officers for the illegal detention. IGP, Meerut inquired into the matter and departmental action has been taken against the two guilty police officials; liberty was sought from the Commission to recover the amount of the compensation from the guilty police officials

Year 1999-2000

Illegal detention/abduction of Rama Rao by Andhra Police Case No.5828/95-96/NHRC

Smt. T. Nagarathnam filed a complaint with the Commission alleging that the police abducted her husband T. Rama Rao from his house on the night of 12/13 November 1995 and that his whereabouts were not known. The Commission immediately called for a report from the State Police. The report received was however not found to be satisfactory and therefore, the Commission directed its own Investigation Team to look into the matter and submit a report.

The NHRC Team upon investigation found that Shri Rama Rao was picked up in the presence of his wife on the night of 12/13 November due to his suspected involvement in an attempt to murder one Tejeshwar Rao, a local CPI leader, on 4 October 1995. He was initially taken to the town police station Srikakulam, from where he was moved to Luvaru Police Station and was tortured to extract a confession. However, when nothing could be established against him, he was produced before an Executive Magistrate on 14 November 1995 and released after he executed a personal bond of Rs.5,000/- Due to the torture that he underwent, Rama Rao's first desire was to be free and he did not, therefore, lodge any complaint immediately. On 13 November, however, the Andhra Pradesh Civil Liberties Committee (APCLC) had submitted a memorandum to the Commission alleging that Rama Rao had been abducted and that his rights had been violated. The police records, on the other hand, stated that he was arrested on 14 November and released on the same day after execution of a personal bond. From the investigation by the NHRC Team, it became clear that the police had manipulated the documents and records to cover their misdeeds. Since the police arrest of Rama Rao was both illegal and malafide, the Commission expressed deep distress at the manner in which the police violated the constitutional rights of Rama Rao, an innocent law abiding person, who was illegally confined and tortured. The Commission recommended that the Government of Andhra Pradesh pay Rs.25,000/- as immediate interim compensation to Rama Rao, that they initiate departmental proceedings against the police officials and take such other appropriate action against them as may be necessary. The Commission has received a compliance report from the Government of Andhra Pradesh with regard to the payment of compensation.

Comment

Article 9 of the Universal Declaration of Human Rights as well as Article 9 of the International Covenant on Civil and Political Rights emphasise that no one shall be subject to arbitrary arrest, detention or exile. In the above case, there is a violation of the fundamental right guaranteed in Article 21 of the Constitution which stipulates that no one shall be deprived of his life or personal liberty except according to procedure established by law.

Arrest involves restriction of liberty of a person arrested and therefore, infringes the basic human rights of liberty. Nevertheless the Constitution of India as well as International human rights law recognize the power of the State to arrest any person as a part of its primary role of maintaining law and order. The Constitution requires a just, fair and reasonable procedure established by law under which alone such deprivation of liberty is permissible.

Although Article 22(1) of the Constitution provides that every person placed under arrest shall be informed as soon as may be the ground of arrest and shall not be denied the right to consult and be defended by a lawyer of his choice and S.50 of the Code of Criminal Procedure, 1973 (Cr. PC) requires a police officer arresting any person to "forthwith communicate to him full particulars of the offence for which he is arrested or other grounds for such arrest". In actual practice these requirements are observed more in the breach.

Likewise, the requirement of production of the arrested person before the court promptly which is mandated both under the Constitution [Article 22(2)] and the Cr. PC (Section 57) is also not adhered to strictly.

A large number of complaints pertaining to Human Rights violations are in the area of abuse of police powers, particularly those of arrest and detention. The Commission has, therefore, found it necessary, with a view to narrowing the gap between law and practice, to prescribe guidelines regarding arrest even while at the same time not unduly curtailing the power of the police to effectively maintain and enforce law and order and proper investigation. The Commission's Guidelines regarding Arrest were sent to Chief Secretaries of all States/ Union Territories on 22 November, 1999 with a request to translate these Guidelines into their respective regional languages and make them available to all police officers and in all police stations for compliance.

Year 2001-02

Illegal detention and torture of Anil Kumar: Maharashtra (Case No.517/13/98-99)

The complainant, Prabhuraj S. Kappikeri, alleged that his brother Anil Kumar, resident of Latur, Maharastra, had come to Udaigiri on 12 January 1997 to meet him and other relatives. He was picked up by the police, beaten and illegally detained. A complaint was made to the Superintendent of Police, but no action was taken.

The Commission issued notice to the Government of Maharashtra and received a report. On consideration of the report, the Commission held that there was truth in the contention of the complainant. The governmental enquiry had also held the public servants to be guilty of misconduct. As the human rights of the victim had been violated, the Commission issued notice to the Chief Secretary,

Government of Maharashtra, to show-cause as to why a sum of Rs.10,000 be not paid as immediate interim relief to Anil Kumar for causing him physical injury and confining him to unlawful custody.

In reply, the Maharashtra Government contended that the erring police officials had been punished and that a fine of Rs.500 had been imposed on each of them. It was therefore urged that the Commission should not grant Rs.10,000 as interim compensation to Shri Anil Kumar. The Commission considered the reply on 28 December 2001 and held that the immediate interim relief u/s 18(3) of the Act was in the nature of compensation to the victim for the violation of his human rights, while the fines imposed as punishment in a disciplinary proceeding on the delinquent public servant served a different purpose. There was therefore no ground to deny the immediate interim relief to the victim. Accordingly, the Commission confirmed that payment be made of immediate relief in the amount of Rs.10,000 to the victim, Anil Kumar. The compensation has since been paid by the State Government.

Illegal detention and torture of D.M. Rege: Maharashtra (Case No.1427/13/98-99)

D.M. Rege, an officer of Shamrao Vithal Co-operative Bank Limited, Versova Branch, Mumbai complained to the Commission that he was illegally detained and tortured by the police in connection with an incident involving the misplacement of cash in the Bank and requested for an inquiry into the matter.

Upon directions of the Commission, a report was received from the DCP, Zone- VII, Mumbai. It indicated that the complainant was indeed innocent, and that his detention and torture were unjustified. The report also mentioned that the guilty Constable had been awarded a minor punishment by way of forfeiture of his increment for one year, while the delinquent Sub-Inspector had been transferred out. After consideration of the report, the Commission directed the Police Commissioner, Mumbai to have the matter re-examined in order to ensure that the erring police personnel were suitably punished in a manner that would be commensurate with the wrong that had been done. The Commission also issued a show-cause notice as to why Rs.30,000 be not awarded as immediate interim relief to the victim.

The State Government, through its letter of 4 January 2001, requested the Commission to reconsider the issue of payment of compensation on the ground that two of the policemen had been immediately transferred, and that the Constable had been awarded punishment of stoppage of his increment for one year for his misconduct. The Commission, in its order dated 10 April 2001, rejected the plea of the State Government, and held that, since the guilt of the public servants had been established, there were no grounds to justify a re-consideration of this matter and directed that compensation of Rs.30,000 be paid by the State Government to the complainant for violation of his human rights.

The State Government has complied with the Commission's directions, the case has been closed.

Illegal detention by Police: Uttar Pradesh (Case No.13161/24/98-99)

Acting on a complaint from one Mohammed Azad, resident of Ghaziabad, Uttar Pradesh, the Commission observed in its Proceedings of 1 November 1999 that the son of the complainant had been illegally detained by the police from 16 – 27 November 1998 and directed the payment of Rs.25,000 immediate interim relief to the complainant; it also recommended that this amount be recovered from the salary of the Sub-Inspector of Police Brij Pal and three other police personnel responsible for the illegal detention. The SSP Ghaziabad sought reconsideration of this decision on the grounds —

(i) that both the petitioner and his son had filed an affidavit denying that the son of the petitioner had been illegally detained; and

(ii) that the petitioner had also denied that any complaint had been submitted to the Commission at any time.

The Commission, while rejecting the stand taken by the police authorities, observed in an order dated 10 December 2001 that a denial made by the petitioner or his son at this stage could not have any weight because the police report had itselfearlier admitted that the son of the petitioner had been illegally detained and kept in lawful custody. Moreover, this crime was committed against society, and not merely against an individual. The Commission observed that the stand taken by the petitioner and his son was an after-thought and could not be accepted.

The Commission therefore directed that compliance be made of its earlier recommendations and also issued notice to the petitioner and his son to show-cause asking as to why action be not taken against them for resiling from their earlier statement by the later filing of an affidavit.

A compliance report was received from Sr. Supdt. Of Police, Ghaziabad stating that the compensation of Rs.25,000/- had been paid to the victim. The case was accordingly closed on 21 June 2002.

False Implication
Year 1999-2000
False implication and torture of Shri Rajiv Rattan by the Police
Case No. 9302/95-96

Shri Rajiv Rattan, a clerk-cum-cashier at the Sahauran Branch of Shivalik Kshetriya Gramin Bank, Hoshiarpur, Punjab made a complaint to the Commission that he was falsely implicated, illegally detained for 13 days and was tortured by the police in a theft case that had taken place in the Bank. The Commission, being unsatisfied with the report of the State Government that the police had neither illegally detained him for 13 days nor had tortured him, directed its Director General (Investigation) to take up a field investigation and submit a report. The NHRC Investigation Team, after considering the statements of independent witnesses, bank correspondence, medical papers and opinion given by the doctors at PGI Chandigarh concluded that the police had tortured the complainant on account of which he sustained the fracture of the neck of the femur bone of his leg.

The Commission expressed its distress at the brutality perpetrated at the police station and the lawless behaviour of those who are duty-bound to maintain law and order and uphold the rule of law, and also took a serious view of the attempt of the Punjab police to cover up its wrongful actions. The Commission held that the police perpetrated brutalities on the complainant causing a fracture of the neck of the femur bone for which he will have to undergo periodic operations after every eight to ten years. While holding that the police of the Ropar Police Station has disabled Shri Rajiv Rattan permanently by its brutal action, the Commission awarded him an immediate interim compensation of Rs.2.5 lakhs and also ordered an in-depth inquiry and initiation of criminal proceedings against the delinquent police officials for falsely implicating and illegally detaining him for 13 days causing him grave physical injuries. The Commission has received a compliance report with regard to the payment of compensation.

Year 2000-01
False Implication of the Complainant and Others and Torture by police: Delhi. (Case No. 3069/30/1999-2000)

The Commission received a petition from one Dara Singh alleging that during the night of 26 March 2000 he, alongwith Manmohan

Singh, Bhim Singh, Anil Sharma and others, was detained in the Anand Parbat Police Station, Delhi at the instance of one Smt. Veero Devi. All of them were brutally beaten by Inspector A.S. Tyagi, Station House Officer. They were later implicated in a false case under section 506, 354 of the Indian Penal Code.

Upon considering the petition, the Commission asked its Director General (Investigation) to enquire into the matter and submit a report. An enquiry was accordingly conducted by an Investigation Team of the Commission, which examined the complainant and his associates, Smt. Veero Devi, Sub Inspector Hari Prasad, Inspector A.S. Tyagi, Constable Sardar Singh and Shri Mohammed Ali, Assistant Commissioner of Police. Documentary evidence perused by the Investigation Team included the medico legal report (MLR) of the injured and the Daily Diary Report etc., maintained at the police station.

Upon considering the detailed report submitted by the Investigation Team, the Commission reached the conclusion that Inspector Tyagi had manipulated the DDR to show his absence from the police station at the time of the illegal detention and torture. Further, it appeared that Inspector Tyagi had taken offence at the conduct of Constable Sansar Singh who had appeared before the Investigation Team of the Commission and disclosed the truth of what had occurred at the police station. The Commission held that Dara Singh and others were illegally detained in the police station during the night of 26 March 2000 and that the Inspector was wholly responsible for this and the torture inflicted on them.

The Commission, therefore, recommended:

- The payment of compensation of Rs. 10,000 each to Dara Singh, Manmohan Singh, Bhim Singh, Anil Sharma and R.K. Mishra for the torture inflicted on them in custody;
- Departmental enquiry be initiated against Inspector A.S. Tyagi to ascertain his liability and that action be taken based on the findings in that enquiry; and
- Constable Sansar Singh may be transferred from the Anand Parbat Police Station to any other police station in view of the apprehension expressed by him, which appeared to be reasonable.

Before the close of the reporting period, the Commission had been informed that compensation had been paid to the victims; that the departmental enquiry was in progress and that Constable Sansar Singh had been transferred from the police station.

In this case, the Commission by its order of 17 August 2000 recommended: (i) the payment of compensation of Rs.10,000/- each to Dara Singh, Manmohan Singh, Bhim Singh, Anil Sharma and R.K.Mishra for the torture inflicted on them while in custody;(ii) initiation of departmental enquiry against Inspector A.S.Tyagi; and (iii) transfer of constable Sansar Singh from Anand Parbat Police station, Delhi to another police station.

Purusant to the Commission's direction, the Commissioner of Police, Delhi, by a letter dated 15 March 2002 informed the Commission that payment of compensation of Rs.10,000/- each had been made to Dara Singh, Manmohan Singh, Bhim Singh, Anil Sharma and R.K.Sharma on 31 March 2000. A departmental enquiry against Inspector A.S.Tyagi, the then SHO Anand Parbat and SI Har Prasad, the IO of the case, had been initiated. The departmental enquiry was in progress. Constable Sansar Singh had been transferred from PS Anand Parbat by an order dated 4 January 2001.

Year 2001-02

False implication of Madhukar Jetley: Uttar Pradesh (Case No.2385/24/2000-2001)

One Madhukar Jetley, an advocate resident in Lucknow, Uttar Pradesh submitted a complaint dated 27 April 2000 alleging false implication and illegal detention in case No.514/1999 u/s 387 IPC. In response to a notice from the Commission, the Government of Uttar Pradesh submitted a copy of the Crime BranchCriminal Investigation Department (CB-CID) inquiry report, which confirmed that the complainant had been falsely implicated and that a report had been filed against the complainant, Smt. Rohini Chandra, u/s 182/211 IPC for filing a false case. Both the Investigating Officers, Shri Narsingh Narain Sharma and the Sub-Inspector Police Station Hazratganj, had been found guilty of falsely implicating the victim and of extorting Rs.1,000 from him. Adverse remarks had, therefore, been made in the confidential reports of the erring police personnel. The Commission, in its proceedings dated 3 November 2000, accordingly awarded compensation in the amount of Rs.50,000 to the victim in respect of his illegal detention and false implication by the police. The DGP, Uttar Pradesh was also directed to inform the Commission of the action taken against the erring police personnel and for the recovery of the compensation amount from them.

Smt. Rohini Chandra, in the meantime, submitted a counter petition alleging that the CB CID had undertaken a wrongful investigation in order to protect the complainant, Shri Madhukar Jetley. The Commission, therefore, directed its Director General (Investigation) to have this matter investigated further by a team of the Commission. The report of that team, as well as further investigations by the Government of Uttar Pradesh came to the conclusion that the allegations made by Smt. Rohini Chandra were false. The Commission therefore reiterated its earlier order of 3 November 2000 directing the Government of Uttar Pradesh to pay Rs.30,000 to Shri Madhukar Jetley. The compliance report was awaited by the Commission.

The Government of Uttar Pradesh had indicated that it has paid the compensation to the victim as directed by the Commission. A report on action taken against the errant police personnel is awaited.

False implication of Rajinder Singh: Haryana (Case No.810/7/98-99)

One Saubhagyawati of Ballabhgarh, Faridabad alleged inaction by the police in regard to her complaint regarding harassment of her daughter, Savita, by her husband and in-laws. She also alleged false implication by the police of Rajinder Singh, husband of Saubhagyawati's second daughter, at the instance of Savita's in-laws. She said that Rajinder had tried to intervene and get the matter settled, upon which Savita's in-laws had lodged a false complaint against him. The report received from the SP, Faridabad admitted that the Police Station House Officer (SHO), Puran Chand, did not investigate the case lodged by the petitioner properly. The case filed against Rajinder Singh was also found to be false and departmental action had been taken against the SHO. The Commission, after considering the report, held that a false case had been registered against Rajinder Singh, and the petitioner and her family had to undergo mental torture. It therefore issued a show cause notice to the SP, Faridabad as to why an amount of Rs.10,000 be not paid to the petitioner and Rajinder Singh. In reply, the Senior Superintendent of Police (SSP) pleaded that the case against Rajinder Singh was cancelled after it was found to be false and that no grounds therefore remained for the award of compensation. Meeting on 18 September 2001, the Commission however held that the very fact that the erring officials had committed lapses and had been dealt with departmentally, was sufficient, prima facie, to establish that there were valid reasons for the grant of immediate interim relief. The

Commission accordingly directed payment of compensation in the amount of Rs.10,000 to the petitioners. The amount was paid soon thereafter.

False implication of Manoj Kumar Tak and Narender Tak: Madhya Pradesh (Case No.667/12/98-99-FC)

The NHRC received a complaint from one Anuradha Tak and her husband Manoj Kumar Tak, both residents of Ramnagar, Sodala, Jaipur, Rajasthan alleging that Manoj Kumar Tak and his brother, Narender Tak, were falsely implicated by SI, C.B.S. Raghuvanshi in case No.70/1998 u/s 392 IPC at the behest of one Sushil Sharma (Advocate), father of Anuradha, who did not approve the marriage of his daughter with Manoj Kumar Tak. The Commission, in its proceedings of 9 May 2001, prima facie found that a gross violation had occurred of the human rights of Manoj Kumar Tak and his brother, Narendera Kumar Tak, as was evident from the findings of the CID inquiry which were not disputed by the State Government. The State Government had further indicated that it had registered a criminal case against the then police station Incharge, SI, C.B.S. Raghuvanshi, Sushil Kumar Sharma, Advocate and some others, and that SI Raghuvanshi had since been removed from service. Based on these findings, the Commission issued a notice to the State of Madhya Pradesh to show-cause as to why immediate interim relief u/s 18(3) of the Act be not awarded to the victims. In response to the show-cause notice, the State Government raised two objections, namely, (i) that only SI C.B.S. Raghuvanshi, the then police station Incharge and Sushil Kumar Sharma, Advocate were held responsible in the CID enquiry for the violation of human rights. Hence only they should be made responsible for paymet of the amount and not the State Government; (ii) that C.B.S. Shri Raghuvanshi had challenged the action of the State Government before the High Court and, therefore, during the pendency of the matter before the High Court, the State Government should not be required to make any payment. The Commission, in its proceedings dated 9 May 2001, while referring to its earlier decisions in Case Nos.91/10/98-99 and 181/95-96/NHRC, reiterated the underlying principle and the object of enacting Section 18(3) in the Protection of Human Rights Act 1993. The Commission observed '(i) the object of Section 18(3) of the Act is to provide immediate interim relief in a case where a strong prima facie case of violation of human rights has been made out, so that the complainant is provided immediate relief which need not await determination in another proceeding of the full compensation awardable or identification of the particular public servant guilty of the violation and determination of his liability in another proceeding. The effect of award of "immediate interim relief" under Section 18(3) of the Act is that the amount so awarded is to be adjusted in the total compensation determined as payable in a proceeding like a Civil Suit so that the same amount is not paid over twice, and no more; (ii) the idea of "immediate interim relief" does not, therefore, presuppose the establishment of criminal liability of the offender in a court of law as a precondition for the administration of the "reliefs" nor does it depend on whether any civil litigation is either pending or prospective. A welfare state recognising its obligation to afford "relief" to its citizens in distress, particularly those who are victims of violations of their human rights by public servants, has made this law under which the Governments seek advice from the National Human Rights Commission as to what in this view, is reasonable "immediate interim relief" in a given case so that the State can act on the recommendation. The recommendations of the Commission are not, no doubt, binding judicial orders; but they cannot be undone and turned to naught by a perverse palpably untenable legal view of the matter. The limiting of such statutory relief only to cases in which criminal liability of the offending public servant is established in a Court of law beyond reasonable doubt by standards of criminal evidence, is to thwart an otherwise civilised piece of legislation by importing totally irrelevant limitations.The Commission desires to point out that the ground urged by the Government in this case is wholly irrelevant; (iii) the meaning to be given to Section 18(3) by any State professing to be welfare state should ensure a liberal construction to promote the philosophy of the statute and to advance its beneficent and benevolent purposes. The view that implies that administration of such "immediate interim relief" could only be at the end of the day, after the guilt of the offending public servant is established in a criminal trial on the standards of criminal evidence would nullify the great humanism the statute seeks to enshrine...' In view of above, the Commission held that the liability of the State of Madhya Pradesh for payment of the amount to be ordered as 'immediate interim relief' u/s 18(3) of the Act cannot, therefore, be doubted and this liability of State does not depend upon and need not be deferred till, fixation of liability of any individual public servant. Accordingly, the Commission awarded a sum of Rs.3 lakhs as immediate interim relief to the two victims. Compliance has since been made, following an intervention with the Chief Minister of the State.

Year 1998-99

Police Harassment of Shri Shakuni Choudhary, MLA, Bihar (Case No.641/95-96/NHRC)

The Commission received a complaint from Shri Shakuni Choudhary and Shri George Fernandes of the Samata Party alleging harassment by police of Shri Shakuni Choudhary and members of his family. The Commission called for reports from the DGP Bihar as well as from its own investigation team.

On considering the investigation reports, the Commission recommended that immediate departmental action be taken against the erring police officers, including a Dy. S.P. and SHO, for harassing Shri Shakuni Choudhary, and attaching his property without justification. The Commission directed the DGP Bihar to report within four months on the results of the departmental inquiry. The Commission, convinced that Shri Shakuni Choudhary and members of his family had been tortured and their dignity lowered, recommended a consolidated sum of Rs.25,000/- by way of compensation and directed the Government of Bihar to make the payment to the complainant. The Government complied with the direction, upon further interventions by the Commission, and paid the sum of Rs.25,000/- to Shri Choudhary. Departmental proceedings against the erring police officers were also initiated.

Policemen turn robbers and kill innocent citizens (Case No. 144/93-94/NHRC)

The Commission received a complaint from one Rita Dhawan that the Maruti van of her husband, while returning from Varanasi, was surrounded by six policemen, near the Police Station Civil Lines, Ranchi, who demanded Rs. One lakh and, on being refused, shot at the petitioner's husband and others in the van from point blank range and killed him. They also removed the gold chain, rings and wrist watch from the body of the deceased. On notice from the Commission, the Under Secretary, Govt. of Bihar submitted a report stating that the SHO of the police station on 5 December 1993, on receiving information that some criminals were absconding in the said van, followed the van along with other police staff and as the persons in the van were firing recklessly, police returned the fire and as a result three of those in the van were killed. A report was lodged about the incident, the police officers were suspended and a case under Section 302/379/201/31 IPC was registered against the SHO and others. The accused persons were arrested and the case was under trial in the Court of the Session Judge, Gaya. The trial ended in a conviction and several persons were sentenced to the extreme penalty of law. But the Commission decided not to close the case and issued notice to the Chief Secretary, Govt. of Bihar, as to why, in the circumstances of the case, Smt. Rita Dhawan should not be awarded an "immediate interim relief of Rs. 10 lakhs without prejudice to her private law rights for damages. The State Government responded contending that as the accused persons had already been convicted and sentenced to death, the Government found no justification for paying a sum of Rs.10 Lakhs as compensation and that it would cause unnecessary financial burden on the State.

In the Commission's analysis, the stand taken by the State Government seemed to have proceeded on the assumption that the establishment of culpability of public servants at a criminal trial and their conviction and sentence puts at rest even the claim for compensation or immediate interim relief' to the dependents of the victim envisaged in Section 18 (3) of the Protection of Human Rights Act, 1993. In the Commission's view the assumption was not only wrong but the position was diametrically opposite. The case for award of interim-relief really became a fortiori. The 'immediate interim relief' envisaged under Section 18 (3) of the Act has to be granted for the injury/loss which the victims or the members of the family have suffered owing to the violation of human rights by public servants and the establishment of culpability of the involved public servants cannot absolve the State of its liability for compensation. The Commission noticed that a welfare State, recognising its obligation to relieve its citizens in distress, particularly those who are victims of violations of their rights by public servants, had enacted the Protection of Human Rights Act, 1993 under which the State sought advice from the Commission as to what, in the Commission's view, was the right thing to do and what immediate interim relief be given in a particular case so that the State could act on that recommendation. Thus, according to the Commission, any State professing to be a welfare State is expected to give a meaning to Section 18(3) of the Act, ensuring liberal construction to promote the philosophy of the Statute and advance its beneficent and benevolent purposes.

Seen in this context, the Commission felt that the stand of the Government of Bihar would only expose it to avoidable legal hassles and investigations. The Commission, accordingly, considered the stand of the State Government wholly untenable and recommended that the State Government pay immediate interim relief of Rs. 10 Lakhs to Smt. Dhawan without prejudice to her private law rights damages. The State Government complied with the recommendations by making payment to Smt. Dhawan

Year 1999-2000

High-Handed acts of Police: Uttar Pradesh (Case No.1970/94-95/ NHRC)

Shri Brijendra Singh in a complaint to the Commission alleged that on 9 April 1994, certain police officials came to his house, destroyed his household articles as well as those of his family members and caused a loss of Rs.2,00,000/- under the directions of the SHO. Despite protest by the local population, the doors and windows of his house were extensively damaged. The police allegedly also took away Rs.18,400/- in cash and 500 gms. Of gold. The complainant supported his allegations by photographs showing the extent of damage done to his properties.

In response to the notice issued by the Commission, the Government of Uttar Pradesh submitted a report stating that in a pending case against the complainant, the police had gone to his home or a number of occasions to apprehend him. Unable to succeed in their effort, a coercive process in the form of an attachment proceeding was obtained from the court. During the course of attachment, the State Government admitted that some police officials had committed irregularities for which censure had been recorded in their personal files and disciplinary action had also been taken against the Inspectors and subordinate police officers.

Upon consideration of the report, the Commission noted that though irregularities were admitted in the report, the State Government did not mention clearly whether the guilty police officials were being prosecuted. The report was also silent regarding the allegation of destruction of property worth Rs.2,00,000/- by the police and the taking away of Rs.18,400/- in cash and 500 gms. Of gold. The Commission found the report very sketchy as it did not respond to all the allegations. The Commission, therefore, rejected the report and called for a fresh report from the Chief Secretary, Government of Uttar Pradesh, requesting him to respond to all the allegations in the complaint and the observations made by it.

In a subsequent report, the State Government of Uttar Pradesh stated that a Circle Officer and three Sub-Inspectors had been found guilty of committing irregularities during the attachment proceeding. A censure entry had been made in the confidential report of the Circle Officer and departmental proceedings had been initiated against three Sub-Inspectors involved in this case. The report denied the taking away of cash and ornaments and also causing damage to the properties of the complainant and his family members. It was reported that during the inquiry, no evidence was found to support the involvement of the policemen in criminal activities and they, therefore, had not been prosecuted.

The Commission noted that the State Government in its report had admitted that during the course of executing the process of attachment, some "irregularities" committed by the police had come to light. The word "irregularities", the Commission observed, was an apologetic euphemism for wanton destruction. The Commission noted that in the successive reports of the State Government, the allegations made by the complainant about the ransacking of his house and the destruction of property have not been traversed and have been admitted without, however, mentioning the extent of the damage so caused. The Commission further noted that the photographs filed along with the complaint corroborate the allegation of damage to the property.

Having regard to the facts and circumstances of the case, the Commission made the following observations and recommendations:

The penalty imposed by giving a "censure" in the service book of the Circle Officer was disproportionate to the gravity of the offences on his part. The DGP, Uttar Pradesh was, therefore, requested to review the departmental proceedings and to initiate proceedings to enhance the punishment in a manner that was commensurate with the misconduct, taking into account the gravity of misconduct.

As there was prima facie evidence to hold that the petitioner had suffered humiliation, harassment and mental torture at the hands of the Circle Officer and three Sub-Inspectors; sustained losses owing to irregularities, admittedly committed by the police officials in the presence of a Gazetted police officer while executing the process of attachment; and keeping in view the ransacking of articles, destruction of property as admitted by the State Government in its report, an interim relief of Rs.1,00,000/- be paid to the complainant Shri Bijendra Singh.

The Commission further observed that the State Government was at liberty to initiate proceedings for the recovery of this sum from the errant officials as their highhandedness had exposed the Government to this liability. The Commission was informed by the State Government that interim relief of Rs. 1,00,000 was sanctioned by it.

Year 2000-01

Harassment by Police Leads to Suicide of Surinder Singh: Uttar Pradesh.(Case No.1929/96-97)

The Commission received a complaint from one Mukesh in May, 1996 stating that a dispute existed between his brother, Surinder Singh, and a certain Chhatar Singh, in regard to a tubewell. He added that the Sub Inspector of Police, R.K.Sharma, in connivance with the latter, had implicated his brother in a false case of theft. He also alleged that though a sum of Rs. 2000 had been paid to the Police upon their demand, but that the Sub Inspector had continued to torture Surinder Singh. As a result of this humiliation, he stated that Surinder Singh had committed suicide on 5 May, 1996, leaving behind a written note blaming Sub Inspector R.K. Sharma for his death.

The Commission directed the Senior Superintendent of Police, Bijnore, Uttar Pradesh to investigate the matter and submit a report. According to the report received, the Sub Inspector had indeed implicated Surinder Singh in a case under Sec. 379/411 IPC. He had then demanded Rs.5000, but only Rs.2000 was paid by him. The Sub Inspector had thereafter threatened the complainant and his family members and, as a result of this harassment and mental torture, Surinder Singh committed suicide. In the course of the investigation, it was learnt that a case had been registered against the Sub Inspector under various sections of the Indian Penal Code. It was also learnt that a Head Constable, Assistant Sub-Inspector and a Station House Officer were also involved in this incident and that disciplinary action had been recommended against them. The Sub Inspector had been suspended and the Head Constable and other police officials had been charge-sheeted under the Police Rules.

After considering the report, the Commission considered it appropriate to award interim relief in the amount of Rs.1 lakh to the legal heirs of the deceased who, by admission of the police itself, were tortured while in custody and forced to commit suicide. The Commission further directed the Senior Superintendent of Police, Bijnore to inform the Commission of the progress in the various proceedings against the police officials.

The Commission by its order dated 11 May 2000, recommended an award of interim relief in an amount of Rs.1 lakh to the legal heir of the deceased who, by admission of the police itself, was tortured while in custody and committed suicide. The Commission has directed the Sr. Supdt. Of Police, Bijnore, to inform the Commission of the progress in the various proceedings against the delinquent police officials.

The State Government reported that the interim relief of Rs.1 lakh has been sanctioned to the next of kin of the deceased on 30 January 2002. As regards action against errant policemen, it was reported that the erring SI had been placed under suspension and departmental proceedings instituted against the other erring policemen by issuing charge sheets against them.

Police High-Handedness Against Agitating Farmers in Ten Villages of C.R. Pattna Taluk,Hassan District: Karnataka (Case No. 91/10/1998-99)

The Commission initiated proceedings in this case on the basis of a petition dated 27 July 1998 from Shri G. Puttaswamy Gowda, former Minister, Karnataka alleging atrocities against farmers of ten villages of C.R. Pattna Taluk, Hassan District, Karnataka who engaged in an agitation on 20-21 July 1998. Similar complaints were also received from Shri D.M. Chandrashekhar, retired Chief Justice of Karnataka High Court; H.K. Patel, former leader of the Opposition; M. Gopal, Secretary, All India Kisan Sabha (Karnataka State Committee); P. Kodanada Ramaiah, ex-MP; M. Veerappa Moily, former Chief Minister, Karnataka and four others.

Upon considering these petitions, the Commission deputed its Special Rapporteur, Shri Chaman Lal, to make an on-the-spot investigation of the situation and submit a report. He met the complainants, the victims, the concerned government officials and various public figures in Hassan and Bangalore and presented his report to the Commission on 2 June 1999. The Commission also received a detailed report from the Government of Karnataka.

Having examined both the reports, the Commission recommended that an assessment be made of the quantum of property loss and the nature of injury suffered by individual victims as a result of the police action. The Commission further proposed that this be done by inviting public claims and that these claims should be examined by a suitably constituted Committee, headed by an officer of the rank of Secretary to the Government. Based on the recommendations of that Committee, the Commission suggested that compensation be paid to the victims. The State Government was asked to report to the Commission on the action taken.

In compliance, the Government of Karnataka informed the Commission that a High-Powered Committee had been constituted by the State Government under the leadership of the Home & Transport Department and had started functioning as of 17 February 2000. The Committee had received as many as 1,343 claims from victims, had visited the concerned villages and inspected the properties in order to verify the authenticity of the claims that had been filed. The Government of Karnataka subsequently reported again, saying that work was well underway and that it was awaiting the final report of the Committee, which was expected shortly.

Acting upon the recommendations of the Commission the State Govt. of Karnataka has submitted the final report of High Powered Committee constituted on 14 January 2000 to consider the amount of compensation for property loss and injury to farmers during the police atrocities at Bagur Naville.

In accordance with the recommendations of the said committee, the Govt. of Karnataka has accorded sanction for the payment of compensation to the victims. Taking into consideration the aforesaid compliance report, the Commission close the case 13 February 2002.

Acts of Police High-Handedness Against Dalits in Ogalure Village : Tamil Nadu (Case No: 772/22/98-99)

A non-governmental organization, Peoples Watch – Tamil Nadu, filed a complaint on 22 December 1998 asserting that serious acts of police high-handedness had occurred against dalits inconsidered it essential to conduct a series of hearings at its Headquarters.

At the conclusion of these hearings, the Commission pronounced its views. The Commission noted that the police had received information that activists of the Dalit Panthers India were planning to destroy public properties in Cuddalore and Perambalur areas. Upon hearing that militants belonging to this organization were hiding in Ogalure village, the police had gone to that village to make preventive arrests. The Commission further noted that the police had initially sent a small party into the village during the night of 30 November 1998. However, as this was repulsed, the police had sent in a large party in the early hours of 1 December 1998, armed at least with lathis. This party appeared to have assaulted the villagers with lathis, injuring some of them and breaking their utensils.

From the evidence available, the Commission observed that the injuries did not appear to be very serious, except in respect of two women. The evidence available clearly indicated that Loganayaki was assaulted by the police and, as a result, suffered injuries on her back and stomach, which required her to take medical treatment. There was no explanation forthcoming from the respondents for the assault on Loganayaki, who was a physically disabled person and inside her hut. Though the respondents had challenged the date on which Loganayaki's affidavit had been recorded by the complainants, the basic fact of Loganayaki having been assaulted and injured by the policemen on the morning of 1 December 1998 could not be doubted. The injuries had resulted in internal bleeding, though the scant medical evidence before the Commission did not satisfactorily establish whether she had suffered an abortion or not. The second injured lady was Muthamil Selvi, who fractured her hand as a result of the police assault on 1 December 1998.

The Commission further noted that the police had rounded up and arrested 69 persons on December 1998. Of these, 34 were women, 3 of them with infants, and there were 4 elderly persons. The rest were men. After considering the reasons and circumstances mentioned by the police in respect of these arrests, the Commission concluded that the guidelines laid down by the Supreme Court in D.K. Basu v. State of West Bengal (1997) 1 SCC 416 in regard to the steps to be taken at the time of making an arrest had not followed by the police. No arrest memos were prepared. While the arrested persons were produced before the Judicial Magistrate at 5 PM on the same day, they were remanded to police custody upto 15 December 1998. Their bail applications were also rejected. However, on 17 December 1998, the High Court granted bail to all the persons arrested, on furnishing a bond of Rs. 5,000 each and they were redressed on 18 December 1998. Charge sheets against these persons were, however, filed only on 29 November 1999, almost a year after the incident and long after the present complaint had been filed before the Commission and notices had been issued to the respondents.

From the explanation given by the police to the Commission for arresting 34 women, infants and elderly persons, the Commission noted that these persons were deprived of their liberty for trying to prevent the arrest of 32 men from the village. There was no allegation that these women, children or elderly persons were armed with any weapon or that they had, in fact, attacked the police party although stones were thrown at the police party by some of the villagers and at least one policeman was injured in stone throwing. The Commission observed that the guidelines issued by the Supreme Court were intended to check the abuse of police power, to ensure transparency and accountability and at the same time efficiency and effectiveness in the police. The Supreme Court had observed that the police force needed to develop a proper work culture, training and orientation consistent with basic human values. Though the guidelines were required to be circulated to every police station, they appeared to have been ignored.

In these circumstances, the Commission took the view that there was need to pay interim compensation to the 34 women, some of them with infants, and the elderly persons who were detained from 1 to 18 December 1998, for no reason, at the insistence of the police.

The Commission also commented on a separate incident, which had a bearing on the present case. On 17 December 1998, one Chandra, daughter of Rasu, who was a dalit, was raped by Ramaraj, a Vanniyar. Chandra was a widow at the time. On the complaint of Chandra, a Crime No. 766/98 was registered by Mangalamedu Police Station under Sections 341, 324 and 376 read with Section 511 of the Indian Penal Code. Ramaraj was arrested. He was, however, released on bail. No complaint under the Scheduled Caste/Scheduled Tribe (Prevention of Atrocities) Act, 1989 was registered. It was only after a year, when a Member of the Commission for Scheduled Castes and Scheduled Tribes visited Ogalure village on 24 December 1999, that an offence under the SC/ST (Prevention of Atrocities) Act was registered against Ramaraj. The respondents were unable to explain why a crime under the SC/ST (Prevention of Atrocities) Act was not initially registered on the complaint of Chandra. Had this been done in good time, she could have received compensation under the Act amounting to Rs. 25,000, which could have helped her in her medical treatment. By the time the compensation was awarded on 6 January 2000, Chandra had died and the compensation could be paid only to her father.

The Commission accordingly condemned the gross negligence of the police in handling such crimes, particularly when the victim was entitled to the benefit of compensation under the SC/ST (Prevention of Atrocities) Act and timely receipt of such compensation could have been of great help to her possibly saving her life. The Commission observed that police officers were expected to know the provisions of this Act and added that they should register complaints under this Act when the complaint clearly relates to the violation of provisions of this Act. The Commission stated that the non-recording of an offence under this Act in the case of Chandra had, therefore, to be condemned. It also asked the State of Tamil Nadu to inquire further into the matter in order to take appropriate action against the errant police personnel.

The Commission concluded that the case represented an instance of lawlessness on the part of the police which had resulted in serious injuries to two women and the arrest and detention of 34 women with children and 4 elderly persons from 1 December 1998 to 18 December 1998, when there was no justification for depriving them of their liberty for such a length of time. It was essential for the preservation of the Rule of Law that legitimate duties assigned to the law enforcement agencies were lawfully discharged and that people who were poor not maltreated or their ognis belongings mindlessly destroyed or damaged by persons who were entrusted by law with the duty of maintaining law and order.

The Commission, therefore, recommended that the State of Tamil Nadu pay to Loganayaki a sum of Rs. 1 lakh, to Muthamil Selvi a sum of Rs. 50,000 and to each of the 34 women and elderly persons arrested a sum of Rs. 10,000 each, and an additional compensation of Rs. 5,000 per child to the women with children, as immediate interim compensation. The State was also directed to take appropriate departmental action to identify the errant police officials, to punish them for not following the D.K. Basu guidelines and to further ensure that the guidelines were circulated to all police stations be followed rigidly. The Commission made the above recommendations without prejudice to the pending criminal prosecutions.

The Commission had recommended in its order dated 26 September 2000 that the State of Tamil Nadu pay the victim, Loganyaki, a sum of Rs.1 lakh, the victim Muthamil Selvi a sum of Rs.50,000/- and a sum of Rs.10,000/- to each of the 34 women and elderly persons arrested, together with an additional compensation of Rs.5000/- per child to the children who were involved. It also called for appropriate departmental action to identify the errant police officials, to punish them for not following the D.K.Basu guidelines and to further ensure that the guidelines were circulated to all police stations rigidly.

The Government of Tamil Nadu has informed the Commission through its letter dated 29 November 2000, that its recommendations regarding award of compensation had been complied with, and that disciplinary proceedings have also been initiated against the guilty officials.

Fake Encounter
Year 1999-2000
Killing of four persons in a fake encounter by police, U.P. (CASE NO:12235/24/98-99)

Shri Panna Lal Yadav, a resident of Village Daulatiya, District Varanasi, Uttar Pradesh, first by means of a telegram dated 19 October 1998 then through a longer complaint, alleged that his son Om Prakash and three others had been killed by the police in a fake encounter on 17 October 1998.

The SP, Sant Ravi Das Nagar, through a communication dated 18 October 1998 also informed the Commission that four criminals had been killed in an encounter with the police in the area of Police Station, Bhadoi on 17 October 1998. It was reported that secret information had been received by the Police that, on 17 October 1998, one Dhanjay Singh, a dreaded criminal carrying a reward of Rs. 50,000/- on his head, would commit a dacoity at the petrol pump of one Satyanarayan Harsh on the Mirzapur-Bhadoi Road. Accordingly, Shri Akhilanand Misra, Circle Officer, Bhadoi constituted three teams to track down the criminals and proceeded to the spot. At about 11.30 am, the police found four persons coming towards the petrol pump who, on seeing the police party, ran away and took shelter in the nearby bushes. They indiscriminately started firing at the police party who returned fire. After 15 minutes of firing, the police party at the site found four dead bodies, including one of the dreaded criminal, Dhanjay Singh, the son of the complainant.

The Commission found the police version unconvincing and therefore, ordered its own Investigation Wing to look into the matter. Accordingly, a team headed by a Deputy Superintendent of Police conducted an inquiry. That report indicated that the alleged encounter was a fake one. The SP, Sant Ravidas Nagar also stated that a magisterial enquiry had been ordered into the matter by the District

Magistrate and the State Government had ordered the Crime Branch Central Investigation Department (CBCID) to conduct an inquiry.

On the basis of the enquiry of the CBCID, a case was subsequently registered against 36 persons including 34 police officials. The CBCID inquiry, on the basis of evidence, opined that the encounter on 17 October 1998 was a fake one and that, in fact, four innocent persons had been taken out by the police from a nearby hotel and later brutally killed.

The Commission ordered, by way of immediate interim relief, the payment of compensation of Rs. 4,00,000 each to the next of kin/ families of each of the victims, namely, Shri Om Prakash alias Munna Yadav, Ajay Kumar Singh, Krisan Harijan and Shamim Natte. The Commission ordered that, in each instance, Rs. 50,000/- should be paid in cash and the remaining amount of Rs. 3,50,000/- should be put in a fixed deposit for five years in the name of next of kin of the victim in a Nationalised Bank, the interest on which should be paid at quarterly intervals to the next of kin. The Commission also recommended to the Government of UP that the CBCID enquiry should be completed expeditiously and a charge sheet filed in the competent court of law for the prosecution of the accused persons. The Commission has received a report from the Government of Uttar Pradesh stating that of Rs. 4,00,000/- recommended by the Commission, Rs. 2,00,000/- has been paid to each of the families of four victims.

The Commission has since been informed by the Government of Uttar Pradesh that the State CID has finalised its enquiry and has sought the State Government's approval for the prosecution of 34 police officials involved in the case. In addition, departmental action is also being taken against 42 police personnel found guilty of various acts of commission and omission in the matter.

Comment

The law in India recognizes the right of a citizen to private defence and in the course of such private defence even the causing of death can be justifiable in some circumstances. The same right of self-defence is available to a policeman. In addition, the use of force if it results in causing of death in the course of an attempt to arrest a person accused of an offence punishable with death or imprisonment for life, can also be justifiable under law. However, if a death is caused in an ecounter that cannot be justified on the ground of a legitimate exercise of the right to private defence, or in proper exercise of the power of arrest under Section 46 of Criminal Procedure Code, the police officer causing the death would be guilty of the offence of culpable homicide. Whether the causing of death in the encounter in a particular case is justified will therefore depend upon the facts established after a proper investigation.

Deeply concerned by complaints of fake encounters, the Commission laid down the procedure to be followed in all cases of encounters in its directions on complaint No.234 (1 to 6)/93-94 brought before the Commission by the Andhra Pradesh Civil Liberties Committee. That procedure, which was spelt out in a letter dated 29 March 1997 from the then Chairperson of the Commission to the Chief Ministers of all the States and Union Territories commended the following steps:

"A. When the police officer in-charge of a police station receives information about the deaths in an encounter between the police party and others, he shall enter that information in the appropriate register.

B. The information as received shall be regarded as sufficient to suspect the commission of a ognisance offence and immediate steps should be taken to investigate the facts and circumstances leading to death to ascertain what, if any, offence was committed and by whom.

C. As the police officers belonging to the same police station are the members of the encounter party, it is appropriate that the cases are made over for investigation to some other independent investigation agency, such as the State CID.

D. Question of granting of compensation to the dependents of the deceased may be considered in cases ending in conviction, if police officers are prosecuted on the basis of the results of the investigation." Information being published on NET

Year 1993-94

Interventions in Court proceedings under Section 12 (b) of the Protection of Human Rights Act, 1993: Cruel, inhuman and degrading punishment of women.

The Commission took ognisance of a press report dated 12 January 1994 concerning the alleged tattooing of the words "Jeb Katri" on the forehead of four women by Amritsar Police personnel. The victims had also filed a Writ Petition before the Punjab and Haryana High Court, Chandigarh, praying for directions to the respondents, viz. Government of Punjab, Superintendent of Police, Amritsar and others to arrange for plastic surgery for removal of the objectionable tattoo, giving adequate compensation for inhuman torture and humiliation and for punishing the guilty police officials. On 17 January 1994, the Commission addressed a letter to the Chief Secretary, Government of Punjab calling for a report in the matter.

As the matter was pending before the High Court, the Commission decided to intervene under Section 12 (b) of the Protection of Human Rights act and, upon intervention being allowed, filed an Affidavit through a Counsel asking forinvestigation to be handed over the CBI as the accused belonged to the State police and investigation by a sister wing may not inspire confidence.

(ii) allow the victims to have their foreheads operated by competent plastic surgeons of their choice at State cost, andallow interim compensation.

The High Court, after hearing Counsel for the parties including Shri Mohinderjit Singh Sethi, Senior Advocate, for the Commission, made a direction accepting all the suggestions of the Commission.

Year 1994-95

Alleged rape in custody by an Assistant Sub-Inspector of Delhi Police

In July 1994, pursuant to its circular of 14 December 1993, the Commission received a report from the Dy. Commissioner of Police, South District. New Delhi, in regard to a custodial rape by an ASI of the Delhi Police force. The victim had been brought to the police station by another ASI, as she had got lost on her way to her parent's home. No report was made in the daily diary of the police station of the victim having been taken to the police station, nor was due care taken to ensure the return of the victim to their family. The ASI who took her to the police station was accordingly placed under suspension. The victim was raped by another ASI who took her to his house in the residential quarters of Paharganj police station. The ASI who committed the rape was arrested and the case was sent to Court for trial. The Commission also received a complaint and a report on this incident from the Peoples Union for Democratic Rights (PUDR), Delhi.

The Commission, on perusal of the report from the Government of NCTD, and also the report of the PUDR, directed the Government of NCTD to explain as to why the woman was detained at the police station for the night, how it was that there was no supporting entry for her detention at the police station, and what steps had been taken or were proposed to be taken to ensure that women were not called to and detained at the police station for investigation, particularly at night. The Commission took serious objection to the persistence of such practices, notwithstanding the decision of the Supreme Court given some 15 years ago in the case of "Nandini Satpathi Vs. State of Orissa".

The Government of NCTD subsequently reported that there had been a lapse on the part of duty officers both at P.S. Hauz Khaz and at P.S. Okhla for not recording the victim's presence in the police station and also for not informing her family members of her whereabouts. Departmental enquiry into the lapses has also been ordered against the concerned police officials. Instructions not to call women for interrogation in the night, and to detail women police officers if a woman is called for interrogation to police station at an odd hour, have reiterated by the Government of NCTD for strict compliance by all concerned officers.

Year 1995-96

Rape in police custody of T. Uma in Tamil Nadu

On receipt of a report from the Collector, Kamarajar District, Tamil Nadu about the custodial rape of T. Uma by the Head Constable of Alangulam police station, the Commission called for a report. The Government of Tamil Nadu, through their letter dated 2 May 1995 stated that the accused was placed under suspension and that acase under section 354 and 376 IPC was registered against him on 30 September 1994. It was also stated that the enquiry report on the alleged rape was under examination and that action would be taken against the delinquents, if necessary, and that a report would be sent in due course.

The Commission considered this report in May 1995 and commented adversely on the long delay; it also called upon the State Government to complete its scrutiny of the report expeditiously and indicate its final view quickly.

Subsequently, the State Government reported to the Commission that it had accepted the findings of the enquiry officer and had come to the conclusion that Uma was indeed raped by the Head Constable and that there was reasonable ground for launching criminal prosecution and simultaneous departmental action against him and other policemen who were involved in this incident. Further, considering the indigent circumstances of the family of Uma, the State Government also sanctioned Rs. 100,000 as compensation to Uma.

While accepting the State Government's report, the Commission recommended that the prosecution should be launched without further delay and that the investigation be entrusted to a senior police officer.

Alleged rape of Jain Sadhvis: Madhya Pradesh Police asked to follow the spirit of law

The Commission has asked the Madhya Pradesh Government to take ognisance of and to start investigating allegations relating to the rape of two Jain Sadhvis, a matter which was the subject of widespread media coverage. Interpreting the relevant provisions of the Indian Penal Code (IPC), the Commission held that it was not necessary for the State Government to wait for a formal report from the victims or anyone on their behalf.

Sakshi, a Delhi-based non-governmental organization, had earlier drawn the attention of the Commission to this incident and requested it to conduct an enquiry into it.

In an initial examination of the complaint on 26 July 1995, the Commission had felt that the act in question did not come within its purview, as it was committed by a private person. The Commission, however, decided to enquire from the Director General of Police, Madhya Pradesh where prosecution had been launched in this case or not.

The Director General of Police, Madhya Pradesh reported to the Commission concerning the efforts made by his Department to enquire into the matter. He indicated that a criminal case had not been registered, as the Sadhvis in question were not willing to report the matter to the police. He added in clarification that neither the Sadhvis nor anyone else on their behalf had ever lodged any complaint at the Police Station, Morena or with the Superintendent of Police, Morena.

As the offence of rape punishable under Section 376 of the Indian Penal Code is a ognisance one, the Commission took the view that "the police would be free under their own information to take ognisance and to start investigation."

Accordingly, theCommission addressed a letter to the Chief Secretary, Madhya Pradesh to look into the matter from this point of view and to advise the police to put the law into motion. The Commission further held that even though the victims of rape had not left the order to which they belonged and were not prepared to come to court, it was the duty of the police to follow the spirit of the law and to take effective steps to ensure that crimes, particularly ognisance ones, did not go unpunished.

Upon the intervention of Commission, a case has now been registered by the Madhya Pradesh Police in this matter. Investigation is in progress.

Torture and sexual assault of a minor tribal girl from Bihar in Maharashtra

The People's Union for Civil Liberties, Singhbhum unit (East and West), Bihar brought to the attention of the Commission six cases of serious violations of human rights which included, among others, an incident of torture and sexual abuse of a minor tribal giril "Baby" by the relatives of an influential officier of the Bihar Police. The girl was working as domestic help in Bombay at the house of the siter and brother-in-law of the police officer, where shewas allegedly tortured by the couple and was also sexually assaulted. There were reports in the press on the hushing up of this matter by the Adityapar police (Bihar) in connivance with the said police officer.

The Commission initially issued notice to the Bihar Government calling for a report. Subsequently, it also sent a Superintendent of Police from its Investigation Division to look into the case.

Upon perusing his enquiry report, the Commission termed the whole episode "shocking"and resulting from "depraved human conduct". As a result of steps taken by the Commission, a case of torture and rape was registered in Raigarh, Maharashtra that was the place of the incident.

The Commission noted down that Baby, an orphan, who is now living with her grandmother in Jamshedpur, would not be in a position to go to Raigad, the place of trial. It further noted that Jamshedpur would also be inappropriate to serve as the venue for a trial as the brother-in-law of the accused was a senior police officer in Bihar. Under these circumstances, the Commission felt that the trial should be transferred to a venue such as Delhi and it moved the Supreme Court in this respect. The Supreme Court has entertained the petition and stayed further proceedings of the trial pending disposal of the transfer petition. Having regard to the trauma of the minor Adivasi girl, the Commission has also provided some interim financial assistance through an NGO, in Ranchi that has agreed to look after her interests

Stripping of Teenagers in Police Lock-up in Kerala

Upon the recommendation of the Commission, the Kerala Government has sanctioned payment of compensation of Rs 10,000 to each of seven boys who were stripped and forced to spend two nights in the police lock-up at Tirunelli in WayanadDistrict. Necessary action has also been initiated by the State Government for recovering, through departmental proceedings, the total compensation amount of Rs. 70,000 from the delinquent police officers, who have been placed under suspension.

The Commission took suo motu ognisance of press reports which stated that some tribal youths, mostly students, were picked up by the police when they were agitating against the opening of liquor shops in Appappara andwho were treated in a very harsh manner. The Commission also subsequently received complaints in this regard from the Kerala Harijan Samajam, Centre for Human Rights, Legal Aid and I, Keralal and Madhya Pradesh Youth Organization, all of them being non-governmental organizations.

In response to the Commission's notice calling for the report, the Karalla Government accepted that certain boys and girls, peacefully demonstrating in front of an arrack shop, were unnecessarily arrested and the police constables behaved indecently with them.

As the allegations were prima-facie found to be true, the State Government suspended four police personnel responsible for this incident and ordered a detailed enquiry.

The Commission, after considering the State Government's report, termed the whole episode "reprehensible" and as yet another case of the violation of human rights of the less fortunate in society. The Commission recommended that Rs 10,000/- be paid as compensation to each of the victims and that the money be recovered from the errant personnel. In its reply, the Government of Kerala has stated that necessary compensation has been sanctioned and that efforts are on to recover it from the delinquent officers through Departmental or other appropriate proceedings

Year 1998-99

Torture of a child labourer: Uttar Pradesh (Case No. 5897/24/98-99)

The Commission took suo-motu ognisance of a report appearing in Nav Bharat Times of 3 July 1998 in which it was stated that two drunken police constables allegedly tortured a young boy, working in a roadside Dhaba. The news item further alleged that the two constables ordered him to fetch his mother to entertain them and when the boy refused, they stripped him and branded him with a hot iron rod used for making "tandoori roti".

On instructions of the Commission, the case was investigated by the Commission's own investigating team and it was found that the boy was beaten with footwear and, later, with a walking stick, by the police constables.

The two constables involved in the incident had been placed under suspension and a criminal case started against them.

In view of the sufferings of the boy, the Commission recommended to the Chief Secretary, Government of Uttar Pradesh, the payment of a sum of Rs.5,000/- to the parents by way of immediate interim relief to be spent on the welfare and education of the boy. At the instance of the Commission, the District Magistrate has initiated action against the Dhaba owner under the Child Labour (Prevention) Act for employing a child in his Dhaba.

Comment

The Convention on the Rights of the Child' (CRC) sets the standards that should prevail for the protection of children. It emphasises in particular, the rights to life, survival and development of the child. Art. 6(2) of the CRC makes it obligatory for the State to ensure the survival and development of the child to the maximum possible extent. This spirit prevails in the Directive Principles of the Indian Constitution, e.g., Art. 39 (e) & (f), which require that the State should direct its policy towards securing for children the opportunities and facilities to develop in a healthy manner, in conditions of freedom and dignity, that childhood is protected against exploitation and the tender age of children is not abused.

The efforts of the Commission seek to give expression to the spirit of Art. 32 of the CRC, the provisions of Constitution of India and judicial pronouncements of the Supreme Court. These provisions recognise that the child has a right against economic exploitation and the performing of any work which is likely to be hazardous or interfere with the child's education or be harmful to the child's health or development.

The Indian Constitution, in its Art. 24, prohibits employment of children in factories and other hazardous enterprises and Art. 45 mandates that the State shall endeavour to provide free and compulsory education for children up to the age of 14 years of age.

Sexual exploitation of woman: Rajasthan (Case No.685/20/97-98)

The Commission received an anonymous complaint alleging that a 24 year old woman had been forcibly detained and was being sexually abused by certain persons at Jaipur for the last 2-3 years. According to the complaint, the woman had a young child and was in a pitiable condition and the culprits were planning to force her into prostitution. The Commission took ognisance of the anonymous complaint. A report submitted by S.P. (Rural) Jaipur on notice from the Commission stated that both the suspected persons had been contacted and that, as they belonged to a respected family, their involvement was ruled out. The report also stated that no such woman as mentioned in the complaint could be located. Not satisfied with the report, the Commission deputed its investigation team for an on-the-spot inquiry. The Commission's team, along with local police, rescued the woman on 13 April 1998.According to the report of the investigation team, she was recovered from the house of one Manoharlal Sharma, a criminal, and was found to be undernourished, in ill health and in traumatized condition. She was sent for medical examination and was found to be pregnant. According to the report, a case under relevant provisions of the IPC was registered and 6 persons, including a police constable, were identified as being responsible for her desperate condition; two of them had already been arrested. The Commission considered the report of its investigation team and noted that the law had been set in motion. Further, taking note of the travails of the victimized woman as well as the trauma that she had undergone, the Commission recommended that the Government of Rajasthan accord her appropriate assistance, inter alia by providing her suitable employment.

Girl Rescued from Captivity: Rajasthan (Case No. 496/20/97-98)

The Commission received an anonymous petition stating that a young girl had been kept in captivity in a house in Dholpur, Rajasthan for about 5 years and, as a result of that, she had become mentally ill and her condition was serious. The Commission, taking ognisance of the matter, directed its investigation team to submit a report after making an on-the-spot inquiry. It also directed the investigation team to take up the matter with the members of the family in case the facts alleged were found to be true. The investigation team, on finding that allegations made in the petition were true, undertook a rescue operation. The team reported to the Commission that, after the Commission's intervention, the victim had been given appropriate care and had been receiving proper medical attention. Noting the report of the investigating team, the Commission further directed the Rajasthan Police to vigorously pursue their efforts to apprehend the culprit, the brother of the victim, and to monitor the progress of treatment of the victim. The Commission also directed the SMS hospital to continue to provide medical assistance to the victim and report to the Commission.

Disparities in Maternity Leave to the Employees of Private Schools: West Bengal (Case No.16295/96-97)

A complaint was received by the Commission alleging that management of certain private schools in West Bengal had not been providing maternity leave benefits to the teaching and non-teaching women employees. The Secretary, Department of Education, Govt. of West Bengal on notice from the Commission submitted a report based on inquires made by the Department with regard to the three specific categories of private schools, where the provisions of maternity leave allegedly were not enforced. The report said that different provisions were made for different categories of schools and that the schools were strictly following the rules which were applicable to each of these categories. On consideration of the report from the Secretary, Department of Education and examining the report of the Ministry of Labour on the subject of maternity leave, the Commission observed that there was no uniformity in the rules/ code framed by different boards like the ICSE and the West Bengal Board of Secondary Education with regard to maternity leave and that they were at variance with the maternity leave rules framed by the Government. It was noted that, in some cases, the existing rules/codes had not been followed. The Commission directed the Government of West Bengal to undertake a review of the existing rules / codes and to bring about uniformity and also to incorporate the provision of grant of 120 days maternity leave to the teaching and non-teaching women employees of various educational institutions. The Commission further stated that it was up to the authorities of the State Government to restrict the facility of maternity leave to two child births, if it thought necessary and appropriate.

Comment

Though women constitute half the world's population, there is still no society in which they enjoy full equality with men. Patriarchal attitudes and consequent power imbalances have adversely affected women culturally, socially, politically and economically. The Universal Declaration of Human Rights, reaffirming faith in the dignity and worth of the human person and in the equal rights of men and women, envisaged the enjoyment of such rights without any distinction of any kind, including discrimination on the basis of sex (Preamble, Article 2). However, gender discrimination constitutes one of the most pervasive forms of violation of human rights. In the light of this fact, the Vienna Declaration of 1993, explicitly asserted that the human rights of women are an inalienable, integral and indivisible part of universal human rights and eradication of all discrimination on grounds of sex are priority objectives of the international community. State Parties have thus undertaken to eradicate this evil under various articles of the Convention on the Elimination of All Forms of Discrimination Against Women, (CEDAW). The Indian Constitution propagates the spirit of equality before law through Art. 14 and mandates the State, through Art. 15, not to discriminate between citizens on certain grounds, including the sex of the person. Art. 15(3) is an ameliorative provision which authorises the State to make special provision for women and children. The Commission thus strives to fulfil the obligation of the State under various human rights instruments and the Indian Constitution to protect and promote the rights of women.

Among these instruments is the UN Declaration on the Elimination of Violence Against Women 1993, which defines 'violence against women' as any act of gender based violence that results in or is likely to result in, physical, sexual or psychological harm or suffering to women, including threats of such acts, coercion or arbitrary deprivation of liberty, whether occurring in public or private life. As regards the latter, further violence against women includes the physical, sexual and psychological violence occurring in the family, including battering, other traditional practices harmful to women, non-spousal violence and violence related to exploitation. For long, due to public and private dichotomy in human rights jurisprudence, violence perpetrated against woman within the four walls of her home remained ignored and could not be brought under the purview of UN instruments and local legislations. However, the international human rights discourse has identified and recognised the 'private sphere' violations of the human rights of women. The Commission's intervention in one of the cases mentioned above is a reflection of this recognition.

The Platform for Action and Beijing Declaration (1995) defines health as a state of complete physical, mental and social well being and not merely the absence of disease or infirmity. The health of women involves their emotional, social, and physical well being and is determined by the social, political and economic context of their lives, as well as by biology. Expecting mothers are therefore entitled to special care and protection and their motherhood should not become a hindrance to their right to favourable conditions of work. Art. 10 of the International Covenant on Economic, Social and Cultural Rights 1966, recognises that special protection should be accorded to mothers during a reasonable period before and after child birth. During such period, working mothers should be accorded paid leave or leave with adequate social security benefits. It is pertinent to note that by virtue of its being a signatory to CEDAW, India is under an obligation, under Art. 11, to protect the right of health and safeguard the function of reproduction in case of working women. Further, the State is under a duty to prevent discrimination on grounds of maternity and to ensure that effective right of women to work is protected by introducing maternity leave with pay, or with comparable social benefits, without loss of employment, seniority or social benefits. The Commission, in fulfilment of Article 11 of CEDAW, directed the State of West Bengal, in one of the above-mentioned cases, to undertake a review of the existing rules/codes and to bring about uniformity by ensuring appropriate provision for the grant of 120 days maternity leave to teaching and non-teaching employees in the schools of that State

Escape of inmates from Juvenile Homes, etc. (Case No.497/13/97-98 & other 86 cases)

In this groups of 87 cases, the attention of the Commission was drawn to the escape of several inmates from the Beggars' Homes/ Juvenile Homes/ Remand Homes situated in different parts of Maharashtra. The Commission pointed out that it was the State Government's duty to take appropriate measures for the safe custody of the inmates. The escape of such a large number of inmates was indicative of the fact that there were either serious infrastructure deficiencies or that security arrangements were faulty.

The Commission directed that the Chief Secretary, Government of Maharashtra should review the functioning of the Beggars' Home/ Juvenile Homes/Remand Homes with a view to ensuring better care in these institutions and avoiding the recurrence of circumstances leading to such instance.

Comment

Progressive criminology propagates the use of non-institutional treatment of offenders. The loss of liberty, separation from the family and the social environment in institutions often results in unwanted consequences. Considering this, Rule 19 of the UN Standard Minimum Rules for the administration of Juvenile Justice (1980) aims at restricting institutionalisation in quantity and in time. Rule 19 lays down that the placement of juveniles in an institution shall always be a disposition of last resort and for the minimum necessary period. Art. 3 of the Convention on the Rights of the Child (CRC) mandates the State to ensure that the institutions responsible for care or protection of children shall conform with the standards established by competent authorities. Art. 19 of that Convention further mandates that the State shall take all appropriate legislative, administrative, social and educational measures to protect the child in all respects, while in the care of parents etc. or any other person. Art 40 of that Convention recognises the state's duty to treat the child offender in a manner consistent with the child's sense of dignity and worth, which reinforces the child's respect for the human rights and fundamental freedoms of others. Rule 26 of the Beijing Declaration says that the juveniles shall receive care, protection and all necessary assistance, e.g. social, educational, vocational, psychological, medical and physical, which they require due to their age, sex, personality and in the interest of their wholesome development.

The order of the Commission sought to review of conditions in the institutions for children, in order to bring them into conformity with acceptable standards.

Sexual Exploitation of Woman: Rajasthan (Case No. 685/20/97-98)

The Commission received an anonymous complaint alleging that a 24-year-old woman had been forcibly detained and was being sexually abused by certain persons at Jaipur for the last 2-3 years. According to the complaint, the woman had a young child and was in a pitiable condition and the culprits were planning to force her into prostitution. The Commission took cognisance of the anonymous complaint. A report submitted by S.P. (Rural) Jaipur on notice from the Commission stated that both the suspected persons had been contacted and that, as they belonged to a respected family, their involvement was ruled out. The report also stated that no such woman as mentioned in the complaint could be located. Not satisfied with the report, the Commission deputed its investigation team for an on-the-spot inquiry. The Commission's team, along with local police, rescued the woman on 13 April 1998.According to the report of the investigation team, she was recovered from the house of one Manoharlal Sharma, a criminal, and was found to be undernourished, in ill health and in traumatized condition. She was sent for medical examination and was found to be pregnant. According to the report, a case under relevant provisions of the IPC was registered and 6 persons, including a police constable, were identified as being responsible for her desperate condition; two of them had already been arrested. The Commission considered the report of its investigation team and noted that the law had been set in motion. Further, taking note of the travails of the victimized woman as well as the trauma that she had undergone, the Commission recommended that the Government of Rajasthan accord her appropriate assistance, inter alia by providing her suitable employment

Year 1999-2000

Rape of a Minor Dalit Girl by Protectors of Law – Uttar Pradsh Case No. 9133/24/98-99

Shri Chandradhas Maurya, a member of Samta Sainik Dal and a resident of District Bulandshar, Uttar Pradesh, in a complaint to the Commission alleged the kidnapping, rape and suicide of a 15 year old dalit girl ABC (name withheld to protect identity). He stated that two firemen, along with a police constable, enticed ABC away on 14 August 1998 and took her to their rented premises in front of the police station where they raped her repeatedly. She was allowed to go away next morning with the threat that she would be killed if she reported the incident to anyone. The girl disclosed the incident to her family members and she along with her family members went to the Police Station, Dibai and met the Sub-Inspector and later the Fire Station Officer both of whom, instead of taking ognisance of the case, abused the girl, passed derogatory remarks and also threatened them with implication in false cases. Upon returning home, ABC committed suicide by setting herself on fire and later succumbed to her burn injuries at 9 AM on 15 August 1998.

As the complaint related to a grave violation of human rights of a dalit girl, the Commission took cognisance of this matter on a priority basis and issued notice to SSP Bulandshar calling for a report. The report dated 6 October 1998 received from SSP Bulandshar stated that the complainant had denied having sent the complaint in question to the Commission but confirmed the averments and allegations made in the complaint with regard to the suicide by ABC after she was raped by the two firemen. It was also reported that, upon a complaint of the grandfather of the victim, a case FIR No.221/98 under Section 363/366/376/306 IPC and under Section 3(1)/12 of SC/ST Act had been registered and efforts were on to arrest the accused persons.

Upon considering the report, the Commission thought it expedient to get the matter inquired into by its own Investigation Division. Pursuant to this decision, an Inspector from the Investigation Division made an on-the-spot inquiry and submitted a report. According to it, ABC had developed illicit relations with the two firemen. On the night of 14 August 1998, she was taken by them to their rented house where she was sexually exploited. The next day, ABC approached the Fire Station Officer and SHO to complain about the rape but neither took cognisance of the case. Thereafter, the girl committed suicide by burning herself. A case was registered on 17 August 1998 only after a protest and road blockade by the residents of the village. The report of the investigation team also indicated that the station diary for 16 August 1998 was tampered with. It was also observed that while the SHO had visited the scene of the crime, he did not record the dying declaration of ABC, though she was capable of giving one at that time.

Upon perusing the report, the Commission held that SHO Dibai and In-charge, Fire Station, Dibai had not conducted themselves in a manner befitting their office and responsibilities and that they had not only shown a lack of sensitivity in a matter of grave importance, namely the protection of a dalit girl subjected to sexual assault, but had been thoroughly negligent in not taking ognisance of the complaint lodged by ABC. Instead, the Commission noted, they had allegedly made derogatory and uncharitable remarks about the girl. The Commission observed that the attitude of these two officers had driven ABC to take the extreme step of ending her life by setting herself on fire, having been left with the impression that she would not get justice. The Commission further observed that the remarks and inaction on the part of the officials might, perhaps, make them liable for the offence of abetment of suicide by ABC, which was punishable under Section 306 IPC and which aspect needed to be investigated.

On a consideration of all the facts and circumstances of the case, the Commission recommended to the Government of Uttar Pradesh that:

While initiating disciplinary proceedings for major penalty against the concerned SHO and Fire Station Officer, they may be placed under suspension with immediate effect;

(ii) It entrust the investigation of the case to the State CID in order to ascertain further the role of these two officers, as also that of another Constable, who was alleged to have aided and abetted in the kidnapping and rape of ABC;

Pay, by way of immediate interim relief, a sum of Rs.1,00,000/- to Shri Narain Singh, grandfather of ABC within a period of one month. Out of the awarded sum of Rs.1,00,000/- a sum of Rs. 25,000/- be paid by way of cash/demand draft and the balance amount of Rs.75,000/- be put in a fixed deposit in a Nationalised Bank for a period of 5 years, periodic interests accruing thereon being payable to him.

Pursuant to the Commission's recommendations, the State Government started a disciplinary inquiry and an inquiry by the State CID. The compensation was also sanctioned.

Illegal detention of three year old child for ten years due to apathy of the Police and other authorities Case No.78/25/98-99

Syed Shahabuddin, former MP, drew the attention of the Commission to the plight of a young girl who had witnessed a murder and was thereafter detained in police custody for about ten years, as a result of which her childhood was lost. The incident had been reported in "The Times of India" under the caption "Witness spent 10 Years in Custody – Case yet to begin". The Commission immediately took note of the letter and called for a report from DGP West Bengal. The Office of the DGP forwarded the report which stated that although the name of the girl had not been mentioned by the complainant or in the newspaper item, the report was presumably about a girl named Kalpana Mistry. According to the report, on 30 March 1990, the learned SJDM Kalyani Nadia had ordered that Kalpana Mistry, who was an eyewitness in a case in which her father had allegedly murdered her own mother, should be lodged at Liluaha Home and produced in the court, as and when required. She was last produced in the court on 20 September 1996 and she failed to identify the accused. She was taken to Liluaha Home on 29 September 1996. In between, in 1992, she was shifted from the Liluaha Home to a Child Care Home (NGO) on the orders of Shri R.M. Zameer, IAS, SP and Ex-Officio Director of Special Welfare, West Bengal for proper upkeep, schooling, protection, care and further rehabilitation. However, when the said NGO moved the learned court for approval of transfer, the learned Sessions Judge termed the act as highly irregular and asked for an explanation from the Director of Social Welfare for having transferred the child without approval and intimation to the court. Subsequently, she was again sent to the Liluaha Home. Though its Memo dated 1 September 1997, the Social Welfare Department again directed transfer of the child to a Government approved/recognised NGO Child Care Home for her education, care and further rehabilitation. The report stated that the court had not passed any order so far.

The gist of the report from the office of DGP West Bengal was sent to Syed Shahabuddin for his comments. Shahabuddin expressed his anguish both at the callousness of the civil and police authorities who, without a thought regarding the tender age of the child, had kept the girl in isolation, and also the court for not even having cared to pass an order for her future guardianship. He suggested that since the State is a guardian in such cases, the child should be handed over to SOS Children Home and NHRC should give suitable compensation which should be deposited in her name as a trust for her future.

The Commission expressed its shock at the inhuman and apathetic manner in which the case was handled by the police and other authorities. The Commission found the very idea of retaining a girl child, who was only three years old at the time of the incident, and considering her competent to be a witness in a court of law and keeping her waiting for the commencement of the trial for ten long years, as shocking. The appalling lack of interest shown by the authorities in the welfare of the innocent child resulted in depriving her of her normal childhood which could never be regained. No amount of compensation, the Commission felt, would be adequate for the loss she had suffered. However, in order to alleviate her suffering to some extent, the Commission recommended to the Government of West Bengal to ensure that child is suitably rehabilitated and educated in the SOS Children's Home or sent to a reputable institute run by an NGO in or around the city of Calcutta, till she became a major. The Commission also recommended that a sum of Rs. 50,000/- be deposited in her name through a court guardian, the interest of which would be paid to the institute looking after her, and the principal amount to be released to her on her becoming a major to enable her to settle in life. A Compliance report from the West Bengal Government has since been received.

Comment

In the Universal Declaration of Human Rights, 1948, the United Nations has proclaimed that the child is entitled to special care and assistance. Article 3 of the Convention on the Rights of the Child, 1989 stipulates that in all actions concerning children, whether undertaken by public or private social welfare institutions, courts of law, administrative authorities or legislative bodies, the best interests of the child shall be a primary consideration

Education of Children of Sex Workers: Delhi CASE NO.16754/96-97/NHRC

The Joint Women's Programme (JWP) and Mashaal Mahila Sangathan (MMS) sent a petition to the Commission on 17 February 1997 complaining about the reluctance of the Municipal Corporation of Delhi (MCD) to allocate one additional room in the MCD Primary School, GB Road, Delhi for the education of children of sex workers and attempts to vacate them from the existing room which was allotted to them.

In response to the Commission's notice, MCD stated that it was not their responsibility to provide accommodation to JWP to educate the children of the sex workers or to provide other health programmes to the sex workers and their children. The MCD added that the terms of the initial allotment to JWP to organize their part-time programme after school hours in room no.9 had been violated and that the MCD was itself providing education to all children in the school run by Corporation. The MCD also said that it would be open to the children of sex workers to get admitted in that school.

The Commission in its proceedings of 7 July 1999 noted that the increased inflow of students every year compelled the JWP to commit a breach of the conditional order of allotment. The breach of the condition was neither volitional nor for any private profit motive but to serve the public cause. The Commission was of the considered view that the breach was inconsequential. Having regard to the circumstances, the Commission held that MCD, being a local authority and an arm of the State, had a duty to implement the programmes of education and health care of the children of sex workers. In the light of the provisions of the Constitution, relevant Supreme Court judgments and the provisions of international instruments, the Commission recommended the allotment of an additional room to the complainant organization, in addition to it retaining possession of the existing room. After repeated efforts to secure compliance of its directive, the Commission received a report from the MCD indicating that appropriate action had been taken in accordance with the view expressed by the Commission.

Comment

In Gaurav Jain vs. Union of India (AIR 1997 SC 3021) the Supreme Court held that, "it is the duty of the State and all voluntary non-government organizations and public spirited persons" to come to the aid of sex workers and "to retrieve them from prostitution, rehabilitate them with a helping hand to lead a life with dignity of person".

The children of sex workers are entitled to facilities and opportunities for their education and health care. Article 19(2) of the Convention on the Rights of the Child stipulates that,'State authorities shall take all legislative, administrative, social and education measures to protect the child from neglect or negligent treatment, mal-treatment or exploitation including sexual abuse'. Articles 28 and 29 of the Convention on the Rights of the Child set out the obligations of States party to the Convention in respect of the education of children.

Year 2000-01

Death of a Girl in VVIP Movement: Uttar Pradesh. (Case No. 13881/24/97-98)

The Commission received a complaint from one Ram Bahadur Singh alleging that his daughter, Vandana Singh, a student of the ninth standard, was crushed by a vehicle which was deployed for the security of an Ex-Prime Minister on 7 November 1997 while she was returning from her school on her bicycle. Though she was rushed to the hospital by the police, she succumbed to her injuries. The complainant further alleged that though this incident was reported to the Thana Cantt, and Crime No. 2006/97 under section 279/304A IPC had been registered, no serious investigation had been carried out owing to the involvement of a police vehicle. He sought an inquiry by an independent agency to punish the errant policemen.

The Commission took ognisance of the complaint and obtained a report from the concerned Senior Superintendent of Police. It stated that, on that particular day, a large number of police vehicles were on duty and it was not possible to identify the vehicle involved in the incident. The report further added that, on completion of the investigation, a Final Report had been filed in the Court on 30 June 1998.

The Commission noted from the above report that the life of a young girl had been lost owing to the negligence of a driver who was deployed on Government duty. The Commission further noted the hazards caused to the public as a result of VIP movement and also the fact that the local administration was casual and insensitive to the tragedy. The Commission observed that no significance was attached to the fact that it was a Government vehicle driven by a Government employee, which knocked down and killed the girl and which gave rise to the Government's vicarious liability as well. It was the duty of the driver involved in the accident to report the accident and those in the motorcade to take necessary action, which they failed to do. Even if it was not possible to identify the delinquent driver at this stage, the Government's liability to pay compensation remained, the Commission noted.

The Commission, therefore, directed the payment of interim compensation of Rs. 2 lakhs to the next-of-kin of the deceased within four weeks. In response, the State Government through its letter dated 31 March 2001 informed the Commission that Rs. 1 lakh has been sanctioned to the next-of-kin of the victim.

The Commission had directed on 22 March 2000 that payment of interim compensation in the amount of Rs.2 lakhs be made to the next of kin of a young girl who had been crushed by a vehicle that had been deployed for the security of a former Prime Minister of the country.

In response the State Government indicated through letters 31 March 2001 and 28 June 2001 that the Rs. 2 lakhs has been sanctioned to the next of kin of the deceased.

Year 2001-02

Sexual Harassment in the Work Place and Suicide of Sangeeta Sharma, Advocate: Andhra Pradesh (Case No.203/1/2000-2001)

Dr Kalpana Kannabiran, President, Asmita Resource Centre for Women, Secunderabad, Andhra Pradesh submitted a complaint in respect of the suicide of an advocate of Andhra Pradesh High Court, Sangeeta Sharma, allegedly as a result of sexual harassment by a fellow lawyer and some senior advocates. The intervention of the Commission was requested in order to ensure proper investigation of the case and action against the accused.

Having regard to the sensitive nature of the complaint, the Commission issued notices to the Chief Secretary and DGP, Andhra Pradesh asking for an indication of the current status of the criminal investigation. The Government of Andhra Pradesh submitted a report dated 11 July 2000, which indicated that a case had been registered u/s 306 IPC. The report added that during the pendency of investigation, a writ petition had been filed in the High Court which granted a stay on further investigations being undertaken by the police pursuant to the FIR and anticipatory bail was also allowed to one of the accused. Subsequently, the High Court vacated the stay on 11 July 2000 and further investigations in the case were handed over to the CID. After completion of investigation by the CID, a charge-sheet was filed in the trial court.

In a parallel action, the Commission also took up the wider question of the sexual harassment of women in legal profession and called for and considered reports/comments from the Secretary, Andhra Pradesh Bar Association, the Secretary, State Bar Council of Andhra Pradesh, the Chairman, Bar Council of India, New Delhi as well as the President, Bar Association of India.

During a meeting with the members and officers of the Commission on 4 May 2001, which was attended amongst others by Shri Soli J. Sorabjee, Attorney General of India, Shri D.V. Subba Rao, Chairman Bar Council of India and Shri R.K. Jain, Senior Advocate, Supreme Court, a decision was taken to constitute a High Power Committee to examine this matter further.

Accordingly, such a Committee was constituted on 21 December 2001, under the Chairmanship of Shri Soli J. Sorabjee in his ex-officio capacity to consider all aspects of the problem of sexual harassment of women in the legal profession and to make suitable recommendations for the penalisation/punishment for those who may be involved. The Committee would also consider whether amendments were needed to the Advocates Act, 1961 and the Bar Council Rules. The other members of this Committee are Shri Raju Ramachandran, Advocate, Supreme Court of India; Shri A.K. Ganguly, Advocate, Supreme Court of India; Ms. Meenakashi Arora, Advocate, Supreme Court of India; Smt. M. Daruwala, Director, Commonwealth Human Rights Initiative, New Delhi and Ms. Naina Kapoor, Director, SAKSHI, New Delhi.

Rape of a Minor Dalit Girl; Failure to Comply with the Law: Haryana (Case No. 390/7/98-99/NHRC)

The Commission received a complaint from Faridabad, Haryana wherein the complainant stated that her daughter aged 7 years was raped by one Lekhraj, who was subsequently sentenced to 10 years of rigorous imprisonment and a fine of Rs.2,500. The complainant added that the crime committed against her young daughter was heinous in nature and that there was great need to rehabilitate her daughter as she was suffering from a deep sense of humiliation and was mentally and psychologically scarred by this experience.

The Commission called for a report from the Home Secretary, Government of Haryana, which indicated that an amount of Rs.6,250 had been given to the complainant as compensation in accordance with a government circular.

On consideration of the report, the Commission took the view that the quantum of immediate relief had to be in accordance with the scale laid down in the Schedule o the rules made under SC/ST (Prevention of Atrocities) Act 1989, which provided the norms to be followed. Under item 17 of Annexure 1, in respect of offences committed under the Indian Penal Code which were punishable with imprisonment for a term of 10 years or more, a victim or his/her dependents were entitled to a minimum amount of relief of at least Rs.50,000, depending upon the nature and gravity of the offence. Further, under Rule 15, the State was required to prepare a model contingency plan for implementing the provisions of the Act and notify the same in the official gazette of the State Government. This plan, inter alia, had to contain a package of relief measures, including a scheme to provide immediate relief in cash or in kind or both.

The Commission observed that the scheme of the Haryana Government appeared to have been framed under the provisions of the Rules. It added that the plan prepared by the State Government under Rule 15 prescribing a scheme for immediate relief in cash or kind could not be in violation of Rule 12(4) read with Annexure 1. The plan had to be prepared within the parameters of the Rules. The Annexure prescribed the minimum amount of the relief to be granted by the State Government. The State Government therefore could not prescribe an amount which was below this minimum. Since rape of a minor girl below the age of 12 years carried a sentence of not less than 10 years rigorous imprisonment and this had been imposed in the present case, the victim would be entitled at least to the minimum compensation of Rs.50,000 in accordance with the norms laid down in Annexure 1 to the Schedule, item 17.

In an order of 18 March 2002, the Commission therefore held that the minimum compensation to be awarded to the victim had to be Rs. 50,000. It also stated that the circular of the Government of Haryana had to be revised in order to bring it in consonance with the statutory requirement.

The State Government, which had initially paid a sum of Rs.6250/- to the victim, has subsequently paid the balance of Rs. 43,750/-.

Death of 12 year old child worker, Naushad: Bangalore (Case No. 452/10/2000-2001)

An NGO of Bangalore, MAYA (Movement for Alternatives and Youth Awareness), made a complaint to the Commission saying that a 12 year old child worker had died in the Silk Filature Unit premises in Ramanagaram town on 14 November 2000 having suffered 79 per cent burns sustained in the unit. It was alleged that the age of the deceased was changed to 17 years by the police, acting in connivance with the doctor who had conducted the post-mortem, in order to save the employer.

Pursuant to a notice issued by the Commission to the Chief Secretary as well as to DGP Karnataka, the Labour Commissioner Karnataka informed the Commission that appropriate cases under the Workmen Compensation Act, 1923 and Child Labour (Prohibition and Regulation) Act, 1986 had been registered in court against the employer. The Commission was also informed that an inquiry had been instituted against the doctors of Victoria Hospital, Bangalore who were involved in falsely certifying the age of the deceased as 17/18 years in the post-mortem report, even though the deceased was aged only about 12 years.

The Commission has been monitoring the progress in respect of the cases that are in court. In addition, after considering the inquiry report submitted against the doctors, the Commission directed the Government of Karnataka to inform it of the action taken by the disciplinary authority on the report of the Inquiry Officer.

The inquiry report submitted by the State Government in respect of the departmental action had been taken up for close scrutiny and comments of the State Government have been called for on discrepancies. The matter is still under consideration.

Commission of rape by a Minister of State in the Government of Assam (Case No.113/3/2000-2001)

The Commission took cognisance of a complaint from a resident of Kokrajhar, Assam alleging that her 16-year-old daughter had been raped by Rajan Mushahary, a Minister of State in Assam in Shantivan Hotel, Barobisa, and West Bengal on 27 February 2000. The victim was, allegedly, raped again after one month and threatened with dire consequences if she divulged the matter. The mother thereafter lodged a complaint and a case was registered at Gosaingaon Police Station. However, no action was taken against the erring Minister, even though the young daughter had conceived. Upon notice being issued to the Government of Assam, a report dated 29 November 2000 was submitted by the DGP, Assam which pointed to the involvement of the Minister in the commission of the offence amongst others. The police had arrested three persons out of the seven who were named. The Commission thereupon asked what action, if any, the Chief Minister proposed to take concerning the continuation of the accused Minister of State in the Government, adding that his continuance in that capacity would run counter to basic rudiments of the rule of law. A further report submitted by the State Government stated that the State CID had directed the SSP to take steps for DNA profiling, in order to complete investigation in the case. In regard to the reservations expressed by the Commission in respect of the accused continuing as a Minister of State, the report indicated that the continuation of Rajender Mushahary in the Council of Ministers was to be based on the result of the investigation. The Commission, however, firmly repeated its view that the continuation of such a person as Minister in the State Cabinet ran counter to the rudiment of the rule of law and was likely to give the impression of interference in the course of investigation and prosecution for the offences. Press reports thereafter appeared indicating that the Chief Minister had taken strong exception to the proceedings and view of the Commission. On 23 April 2001, therefore, the Commission stated that it was constrained to observe that if the newspaper reports were correct, the Chief Minister had completely missed the point made by the Commission and that he had made observations which depicted a lack of appreciation of the role and functions envisaged for the Commission under its Statute. The Commission added that it was 'constituted under the Protection of Human Rights Act, 1993 for the better protection of the human rights and its functions include inquiring into violation of human rights or negligence in prevention of such violation; review of safeguards provided by the Constitution or any law, etc., and such other functions as it may consider necessary for the promotion of human rights.' The Commission then reiterated yet again its earlier observations that 'the continuance of the principal-accused of such an offence as a Minister in the State Cabinet, in its view, is erosion of the rule of law and, as a consequence, it is a serious violation of human rights.' Further investigation reports submitted by the Government of Assam to the Commission indicated that the DNA test established that Shri Rajender Mushahary was the father of the child that had been conceived and that he had been arrested on 6 August 2001. Four others were arrested on 2 January 2002 and two were absconding. In the light of the developments, the Commission did not find it necessary to pursue this matter any further. Accordingly, it closed its proceedings in respect of this case.

Year 1999-2000

Facilities for Foreign Nationals detained at Lamapur Seva Sadan : Delhi (Case No.693/30/97-98)

While considering the petition concerning the possible deportation of Shri Rongthong Kuenley Dorji, it came to the notice of the Commission that he had been detained at Lampur Seva Sadan, an institution for rehabilitation of beggars, administered by the Social Welfare Department of Government of NCT of Delhi. On 24 May 1999, the Commission directed the Director General (Investigation) [DG(I)] of the Commission to visit Lampur Seva Sadan to make an assessment of the conditions prevailing therein. After his visit to Lampur Seva Sadan, DG(I) submitted his report in which he stated that the foreigners were confined to a few barracks in one segregated corner of the campus, with a compound wall and a gate. Security was being provided by a section of the Rajasthan Armed Constabulary.

After considering the report, the Commission recommended that separate enclosures be created for foreign nationals and that the Government of NCT of Delhi undertake immediate repairs and to take the following steps to improve the arrangements:

i. Replace the asbestos sheets roofing with roofing made up of some other material that would not be harmful to inmates.

(ii) Post adequate number of conservancy staff immediately for the cleanliness of the area and for the maintenance of the toilets/ bathrooms.

(iii) Make separate cooking arrangements for the foreigners instead of supplying them food from the beggars home as that might hurt their sentiments and sense of dignity.

(iv) Consider provision of separate STD/ISD booths for use of the foreign detenues.

(v) Establish MI Room where a doctor and the para-medical staff are available round the clock for medical cover.

(vi) Issue proper instructions to ensure regular visits by senior officers to this detention centre.

The Commission also directed the Principal Home Secretary, Secretary and Director, Social Welfare Department and the FRRO of the Delhi Administration to visit the Lampur Seva Sadan and work out a proper strategy for bringing about ameliorative changes not only for the foreign detenues but also for the institutions for beggars located in the campus. The Commission has received a compliance report.

Harassment of denotified and nomadic tribals belong to Pardhis community in Bighwan village, Pune, Maharashtra Case No.512/13/98-99

Shri G.N. Devy, Secretary, Denotified and Nomadic Tribals Rights Action Group, Baroda, Gujarat submitted a complaint to the Commission alleging atrocities on the Pardhis community, a denotified community of tribals living in the backwaters on the banks of the Ujni Dam, Bigwan village, Taluk Indiapur, Pune, Maharashtra by persons in plain clothes serving in the Railway Police on 12 July 1998. It was further alleged that their houses, fishing nets, boats and other materials were burnt. The police had also beaten up the women of the community, including pregnant women and had attempted rape on two teenaged girls.

On consideration of the reports of the Investigation Team of the Commission and the Superintendent of Police, Railways, Pune the Commission found that the police report, sent by the S.P. Railways, Pune also corroborated the report of the Commission's Investigation Team which conclusively established that the Police Anti-Dacoity Team had tortured four innocent women and molested two young women in their zeal to nab male Pardhis who were alleged to have been involved in committing crimes of theft, dacoity, etc. The evidence also established that several huts belonging to the tribals and their fishing nets were destroyed. The Investigation Team had estimated damage amounting to Rs.10,000/- in respect of each family. In addition, innocent women suffered trauma and torture. The highhandedness and misconduct of the police officials was unbecoming of their profession. Two young women, one of them a teenager, were molested by the police. The evidence on record indicated that, in their zeal to nab certain criminals alleged of belonging to the denotified Pardhi tribe, the police had behaved in a shocking and brutal manner.

In view of the facts and circumstances, the Commission recommended: of the four women victims, namely, Smt. Shalan Pratap Kale, Smt. Manda Latif, Kum. Jyoti and Smt. Alka Chandrasal Kale, the first three be paid Rs.1 lakh each and Smt. Alka Chandrasal Kale, Rs.1,50,000/- as immediate interim relief; a sum of Rs.10,000/- may be paid to each of the families of the Pardhis who were staying on the bank of Ujni Dam, near the backwaters, whose huts, utensils and fishing nets were destroyed, as compensation by way of 'immediate interim relief'; in case a charge-sheet had not yet been filed in the court against the erring police personnel, the case may be entrusted to the State CID and a charge-sheet be filed thereafter against all the culprits in the appropriate court; (d) disciplinary action may be initiated against the erring police personnel. The State Government has sent a compliance report with regard to the payment of compensation

Atrocities inflicted on a family Maharashtra Case No.1361/94-95/ NHRC

Shri A.R. Antulay, Member of Parliament (MP) filed a petition dated 12 September 1994 before the Commission highlighting the case of the Haspatel family of village Walwati, Shrivardhan Taluk, Raigad District, Maharashtra, who were allegedly subjected to serious atrocities by the police during the communal riots that took place in Maharashtra in December 1992 – January 1993. The complainant stated that the act of the police against an innocent family had the distinct tinge of communal bias.

On consideration of the matter, the Commission noted from the report of the State Government that departmental action had been ordered against the police officials involved in the matter. The Commission accordingly recommended that, keeping in view the nature of findings in the departmental proceedings, appropriate prosecution should be launched in respect of all or such of the persons who were found responsible for the conduct which had been indicted in the Government order.

The matter was again considered again by the Commission on 17 January 2000. The Commission observed that from the conclusions reached and the findings recorded by the State CID, it was evident that Shri Iqbal Ismail Haspatel, his wife, three sons and a daughter-in-law, i.e. in all six members of that family, were not only humiliated and harassed but also unlawfully tortured. Some of them were subjected to illegal arrest. All of these persons were subjected to several indignities wholly inconsistent with norms of decency. It was also noted that allegations had been made to the effect that valuable property estimated at Rs.1.87 lakh, owned by the victims of the incident, had also been taken away or destroyed by the police officials; this required further verification. The Commission directed the Government of Maharashtra to pay an amount of Rs.5 lakhs as compensation by way of 'immediate interim relief' to Shri Ismail and his family members. The Government of Maharashtra has complied with the Commission's recommendations on the payment of compensation of Rs. 5 lakhs to the victims.

Death of workers in silicon factories of Madhya Pradesh Case No.7894/96-97/NHRC

A news-item appeared in the "Sunday Observer" in September 1996 captioned "Death in the Air". The Commission took suo motu ognisance of the news item and called for a report from the Government of Madhya Pradesh. The report indicated that there were 134 slate factories which were set up in Mandsaur District of Madhya Pradesh. The health of the majority of the workers employed in these factories was affected due to inhalation of silicon dust. The Government had taken steps to provide medical facilities and ensure that all these workers were covered under the Employees State Insurance (ESI) scheme. There was a mobile van in operation to provide medical facilities to the workers. They were unable to meet the cost of the sophisticated machinery, this resulted in the spread of silicosis dust and affected the workers' health. The Labour Inspectors were visiting the factories and prosecuting those who were not applying the minimum standards laid down for prevention of this pollution.

Having regard to the provisions of the Indian Constitution as well as to the International Human Rights instruments with regard to the right to life. The Commission gave the following directions to the State for compliance in future:-

(i) To ensure the establishing of BHEL machinery in the factories to prevent dust pollution and to ensure that pollution free air is provided to workers.
(ii) Periodic inspection, on a monthly basis, by the Labour Department and reports made to the State Human Rights Commission for monitoring.
(iii) Widows and children of deceased workers to be taken care of by the factory owner by providing assistance.
(iv) To ensure that child labour is prevented by the following methods:
(v) Establishing schools at the cost of factory owners, with assistance from the State for the education of workers' children.
(vi) The provision of periodic payments for their education and insurance coverage at the cost of factory owners.
(vii) IThe position of mid-day meals and clothing to dependent children or children of deceased workers.

Comment

In examining this matter, the Commission observed that the Right to Health and Medical Care is a fundamental right under Article 21, read with Articles 39(e), 41 and 43 of the Constitution. The Right to Life includes protection of the health and strength of workers and is a minimum requirement to enable a person to live with human dignity. The Universal Declaration of Human Rights as well as other International Instruments also speak of this right. Continuous exposure to the corroding effect of silicon dust can result in the silent killing of those who work in such an environment. The duty of the State, under the Directive Principles of the Constitution, is to ensure the protection of the health of workers employed in such Slate factories in Mandsaur and elsewhere in the State.

Rehebilitation of Physically Handicapped : Madhya Pradesh Case No.1528/96-97/NHRC

Shri Bihari Lal Thevait, a resident of District Bilaspur, Madhya Pradesh sent a petition to the Commission wherein he said that he was a 26-year old man whose lower limbs had not been affected by polio. He also suffered from a cardiac problem. He had approached the District Collector for assistance and employment. Although the District Collector arranged for his operation at a private hospital, free of cost, the operation was not successful and even after four to five years he was not cured. He alleged that the operation was suggested instead of providing him with a tricycle. The then District Collector also provided him with assistance at the rate of Rs.2,000/- per month and this continued until such time as that Collector was in office. The Collector also passed an order for his appointment as an Assistant Teacher. However, this did not materialise. He, therefore, sought compensation of Rupees Fifty lakhs for violation of his fundamental rights, treatment of his heart ailment, management of his disability and employment as an Assistant Teacher.

Though the Commission does not normally take action on petitions which relate essential to service matters, the Commission in this case issued a notice to the Collector and called for a report as the petitioner was a disabled person. The Collector responded saying that the complainant was affected by polio when he was one-and-a-half years old and that both his feet were deformed. The opinion of Orthopaedic Doctors was sought, and they had certified that the complainant would have to move on hands and knees, in a crawling position, unless he was operated upon. Accordingly, he was operated upon in 1988 and his limb deformity was corrected to a large extent. In five months time, he was fitted with ognisanc and a walking frame to help him stand erect. The Collector also stated that the complainant was entitled to be considered for a job under the quota for persons with disabilities. According to the Collector, the complainant had tried to obtain a certificate of complete recovery to enable him to get the job of an Assistant Teacher. He was advised to obtain a disability certificate from the competent authority. The petitioner apparently made the complaint as he was aggrieved by this advice. The report of the Collector was sent to the complainant for his comments. However, the petitioner stood by his complaint and stated that the operation, which was performed, was not successful and his defect was not cured even after four years. The complainant claimed Rupees Twenty lakhs as compensation for mental and physical torture he had undergone and Rupees Thirty lakhs for protection of his rights and for his living.

(i) The Commission considered the matter To grant ex-gratia monetary relief to the tune of Rupees One lakh to the petitioner, either from the fund established by the State Government for the welfare of the handicapped persons, or from the Chief Minister's Relief Fund.

(ii) To offer a job to the petitioner commensurate with his academic qualifications and physical ability, in accordance with the provisions of Persons with Disabilities (Equal Opportunities, Protection of Rights and Full Participation) Act, 1995, or on compassionate grounds.

carefully and expressed appreciation of the action taken by the District Collector. The question whether the condition of the petitioner worsened after the operation, as claimed by him, was not probed further. However, the Commission felt that the State Government, in a Welfare State, should help alleviate the suffering of such disabled persons. Accordingly, the following recommendations were made by the Commission to the State of Madhya Pradesh:

The State Government has intimated the Commission that it has paid a sum of Rs. 1 lakh as compensation to the petitioner

Violation of human Rights of Members of Reang Community of Mizoram Case No.40/16/97-98

The President, Akhil Bharatiya Vanwasi Kalyan Samiti and seven other such like-minded persons submitted petitions to the Commission wherein they alleged that since September-October 1997, the Reang community members had been living in an atmosphere of terror created by the Mizos, with the tacit support of the local administration and police. As a result of this, over 30,000 Reangs left Mizoram for Tripura. There were apparently several incidents of killing, rape, abduction and burning of houses by the Mizos. The condition in the refugee camps established by the Government of Tripura was also not satisfactory. The petitioners requested intervention by the Commission.

The Commission called for reports from Governments of Mizoram, Tripura and Assam. The Government of Tripura in their report stated that although the influx of Reangs started with about 10,000 people in October 1997, the number had gone up to 30,000. The Government of Tripura was finding it difficult to bear the burden though they were financially helped by the Government of India. They mentioned that efforts made to persuade the refugees to return to Mizoram had failed.

The Government of Assam in their reply stated that some families had gone into the Karimganj and Balkandi districts of Assam and were living there in forest villages, earning their living by labour on daily wage basis. No refugee camps had been set up. However, medical aid was being provided.

The Government of Mizoram in their reply stated that the administration was making efforts to take action against the local Mizos who had indulged in burning of houses of some Reang families. It was the demand of the Group National Union of the Reangs for an autonomous district council and the murder of a Mizo forest guard by suspected Bru-Reangs militants, which led to violence between the two communities. Some arrests had been made in this regard. The refugees had been requested by the Home Minister of Mizoram to return and they were also given Rs.2,000/- for reconstruction of their houses and a week's ration. However, some of the Reangs received the amount and again went back to the refugee camp in Tripura. The Ministry of Home Affairs also confirmed this position and stated that the matter was being closely monitored.

Shri Sudarshan Agarwal, Member, NHRC and Shri R.C. Jain, Registrar General visited the spot to make an assessment of the situation. The Special Rapporteur Shri Chaman Lal was also deputed to meet the Reang refugees and make a report on their problems. According to his report there were certain inadequacies in the arrangements made at the refugee camps. The Special Rapporteur made certain recommendations to improve the situation. Shri Agarwal, Member, NHRC held a meeting with Chief Secretary, Tripura and other concerned officers who were requested to implement the recommendations of Shri Chaman Lal on a time bound basis. The Member, NHRC also held separate meetings with the petitioners who emphasised the urgency for settlement of the issue since they had serious apprehensions about their security in Mizoram. The Member, NHRC subsequently held meetings with Chief Secretaries of three States and the Additional Secretary of the Ministry of Home Affairs. It was made clear to the Government of Mizoram that there is a specific provision in the Mizoram Accord regarding the protection of rights and privileges of minorities of their economic and social development by the Government of Mizoram. The Ministry of Home Affairs assured Government of Mizoram that para-military forces in adequate strength would be provided to the Government for ensuring safety and security of the repatriated families. The Government of Mizoram was reminded of their constitutional obligations to take back the refugees and ensure their peaceful settlement in the villages.

The Commission, taking into consideration the reports from Member, NHRC and Special Rapporteur made the following recommendations:

(i) The Reangs are lawful inhabitants of Mizoram and the Government of Mizoram should not only take them back in accordance with the agreement made in November 1997, but should also instill in them a sense of confidence and security.

(ii) The Government of India should play an active role to arrange repatriation of the Reangs to Mizoram and should also give special attention to the safety and security of the Reangs on their return to Mizoram.

(iii) The Ministry of Home Affairs and the State Governments of Mizoram and Tripura shall keep the Commission informed of the progress made at regular intervals.

The Commission has received reports from the Governments of Tripura, Mizoram and the Government of India with regard to the action taken on its recommendations.

Year 2000-01

Atrocities on Dalit Women by Forest Officials: Uttar Pradesh (Case No. 2731/96-97/NHRC)

The Commission took suo-motu ognisance of a news item entitled "Girls paraded naked by the Daroga" on the basis of a report in a newspaper on 21 June 1996 and called for a report from the Director General of Police, Uttar Pradesh.

In his report, the Director General of Police, Uttar Pradesh mentioned that a case No.49/96 under the relevant sections of the Indian Penal Code and the Scheduled Castes and Scheduled Tribes (Prevention of Atrocities) Act, 1989 had been registered against the concerned Forest Officer and four Forest Guards. Upon preliminary investigation, the charges had been proved against all the five accused persons and the State Government had been requested to sanction the prosecution of these persons.

Upon considering the above report, the Commission directed the State Government to grant sanction for the prosecution of the errant officials expeditiously.

In response, Shri Bhagwan Shankar, Special Secretary, Government of Uttar Pradesh informed the Commission that a chargesheet dated 16 July 1998 had been filed in court by the Investigation Officer, Naraini, District Banda. The report of the Superintendent of Police, Banda indicated that the concerned Forest Officer had taken two ladies into his custody. He had later apprehended two more women. The four women were disrobed and later beaten by the Forest Sub Inspector. They were released only after they had agreed to pay a sum of Rs.1000 and give honey to the Forest Department officials. The Commission noted that the involvement of the officials had been proved during investigation and that a chargesheet had been filed. In view of the fact that dignity of the four women had been violated by the Forest Sub Inspector and five officials, the Commission held that the State was vicariously liable for the payment of compensation. Accordingly, the Commission recommended the payment of a sum of Rs. 50,000 as interim compensation to each of the four women. The Director General (Investigation) of the Commission was asked to monitor the trial of the case closely.

The Commission has since been informed, however, that the errant officials have filed a case in the High Court of Allahabad, where the matter is now pending.

In this case, the Commission by its order dated 2nd June 2000 had recommended the payment of Rs. 50,000/- as interim compensation to each of 4 women.

The State Government has stated that immediate interim relief of Rs.2 lakhs @ Rs. 50,000/- for each of the 4 women has been sanctioned. However, payment had been made to only two of the women. The other two women were yet to be identified and they had not yet come forward to make a claim. The State Government has assured the Commission that, as and when the remaining two women come forward or are identified, the payment would be made to them on the basis of sanction already issued.

Upon being satisfied with the response of the State Government, the Commission closed the case on 2nd July 2001.

Seven Boys from Balmiki Community Paraded Naked by Police: Haryana (Case No:393/7/1999-2000)

In a complaint to the Commission, one B. Jit Singh stated that on 2 June 1999, an Assistant Sub Inspector and two Constables from the Police Post Khandsa Road, Gurgaon, Haryana had picked up seven boys aged between 7 and 12 years, taken them to the Police Post, stripped them naked and paraded them on the streets. They were also forced to clear garbage from nearby areas. The parents of the children were also insulted. The only fault of boys, it was stated, was that they were playing cricket in their locality and that their ball had landed in the premises of the Assistant Sub Inspector.

Pursuant to the Commission's directions, two reports were received from the Superintendent of Police, Gurgaon. In view of the inherent anomalies and contradictions in these reports, the Commission, however, directed its own Investigation Division to inquire into the matter and submit a report.

After a thorough investigation, the Commission's team reported that seven children belonging to Balmiki Community were humiliated, stripped naked, and paraded in the locality and also beaten up by police personnel. In its proceedings dated 2 May 2000, the Commission accordingly held that the concerned police personnel had abused their power. Apart from exhibiting depraved conduct, the Commission held that the behaviour of the concerned police personnel constituted a gross violation of the rights of the children involved. The Commission therefore directed the Superintendent of Police, Gurgaon to file charge sheets against the three errant police personnel under the appropriate provisions of the Indian Penal Code and the Scheduled Castes and Scheduled Tribes (Prevention of Atrocities) Act, 1989, to pursue the case diligently and also initiate disciplinary action. In addition, the Commission recommended the payment of a sum of Rs. 20,000 as compensation to each of the seven boys. The Commission also observed that the State Government was at liberty to recover this amount from the salaries of the concerned police personnel.

The State Government has subsequently reported to the Commission that it has paid the compensation to the children and was complying with its recommendations.

In this case, the Commission in its proceedings dated 2 May 2000 came to the conclusion that seven children, belonging to the Balmiki community, were humilitated, stripped naked, and paraded in the locality and also beaten up by the police personnel of Gurgaon, Haryana. It held that the concerned police personnel had abused their power and, accordingly directed the Supdt. Of Police, Gurgaon to file charge-sheets against them under the appropriate provisions of the Indian Penal Code and the Scheduled Castes and Scheduled Tribes (Prevention of Atrocities) Act, 1989, to pursue the case diligently and also intitiiate disciplinary action against delinquent police personnel. In addition, the Commission recommended the payment of a sum of Rs. 20,000/- as compensation to each of the seven boys. It also observed that the State Government was at liberty to recover this amount from the salaries of the concerned police personne.

The State Governmennt has, through its letter dated 23 October 2000, reported to the Commission that it has paid the compensation to the children as directed, and that disciplinary proceedings/ prosecution had been initiated against the delinquent public servants.

Attacks on Members of the Christian Community in Several States (Case Nos.289/6/1999-2000; 351/6/1999-2000; 295/6/1999-2000; 481/6/1999-2000; 1873/4/1999-2000;1933/4/1999-2000)

Previous reports of the Commission have indicated in detail the steps taken by the Commission to protect the rights of members of the Christian community in the aftermath of the killing of the Australian priest, Mr. Graham Stewart Staines and his two sons in Orissa, as well as attacks on members of the community in Madhya Pradesh and Gujarat. During the year under review, the Commission continued to pay the closest attention to instances when atrocities were reported to have been committed against Christians. At the time of the writing of this report, the Commission had intervened, often by invoking its suo-motu jurisdiction, in twenty incidents in which persons professing the Christian faith had been mistreated, assaulted or even killed in different parts of the country.

In each instance, the Commission called for reports from the highest echelons of the concerned State Governments and pursued matters thereafter. A number of incidents related to Uttar Pradesh. But the intervention of the Commission was also required in respect of incidents that occurred in Indore, Madhya Pradesh; in various locations of Gujarat; in Rewari, Haryana and in Nashik, Maharashtra. Further, the Commission intervened following the killing of a Christian priest, Ashish Prabhash, in Batala, Punjab and the bomb blasts that rocked Churches in the States of Goa, Andhra Pradesh and Karnataka.

In addition to issuing directives as required in these cases, the Commission also received and considered a number of petitions, both from organizations and individuals complaining that such incidents disclosed a pattern of violence against Christians and their institutions, particularly in some States, which created a reasonable apprehension in the minds of Christians throughout the country of victimization and the violation of their human rights. The Commission took careful note of similar apprehensions that were voiced in editorials, articles and news items in the media and the general feeling that they conveyed that there was need to better protect the human rights of the Christian community and the safety of their institutions, as also to ensure that such acts of violence were prevented from occurring in the future. The Commission observed that such apprehensions were of serious concern, that they were shared by many in the country, and that they must be addressed by all the authorities. For this reason, the Commission considered it essential to make an in-depth scrutiny of the situation, not merely by inquiring into the violation of human rights of the section of people involved in the specific incidents on which suo-motu ognisance had already been taken, but also by exploring the avenues necessary for the prevention of any such violations in future, and ensuring that there was no neglect on the part of the public authorities concerned in the performance of their duties.

The Commission therefore issued notice on 21 June 2000 to the Chief Secretaries of all States and Union Territories as well as to the Ministry of Home Affairs, Government of India, calling for reports on the measures already taken in this behalf and the plans of action drawn up by them to meet the situation. Urging all of them to accord top priority to this matter, the Commission pointed out that it was necessary to preserve "the secular credentials of the nation and to ognis the promise of fraternity and common brotherhood" envisaged in the Constitution. The Commission's decision was based on the need to take a holistic view of the situation as well as to inspire the requisite confidence amongst persons of the Christian community. In response to the notice issued by the Commission, reports were received from all the concerned authorities, who sought to answer in full the concerns raised by the Commission.

On 18 October 2000, the Commission directed the issue of fresh notices to all State Governments inviting their attention specifically to letter No. 9/42/96-CHC dated 22 October 1997 of the then Union Home Minister, Shri Indrajit Gupta, with an annexure thereto addressed to all Chief Ministers of States/Union Territory Administrations and D.O. letters No. 14013/35/98-US (D.V) dated 2 January 1999 and No. 5/98-NIMC dated 28 January 1999 of the then Union Home Secretary, Shri B.P. Singh to the Chief Secretaries/Administrators of all the States/Union Territories. The State Governments were requested to indicate the follow-up action, if any, taken by them to comply with the directions contained in the above-mentioned letters of the Union Home Minister and the Union Home Secretary. The Home Minister had enclosed with his letter the revised "Guidelines To Promote Communal Harmony" with a request to the States to take urgent action in accordance with those Guidelines.

Based on an analysis of all the responses received, the Commission is taking steps to call a meeting of the senior officers of the States principally concerned to discuss and monitor all aspects of this matter. It is important, in this report, to recount illustratively the specific action that the Commission took following the murder of Brother George, during the night of 6-7 June 2000, in St. Francis Public School, Mathura, Uttar Pradesh, in respect of which crime a case was registered under section 396 IPC. On 11 June 2000, the cook of Brother George, Vijay Ekka was picked up by the police for interrogation. He remained in police custody but was found dead on 17 June 2000. On 19 June 2000, in response to a press report entitled "Cleric's cook dies in police custody", the Commission issued notice to the Chief Secretary and Director General of Police, Uttar Pradesh calling for a report within one week. The Commission also directed the Director General of Police, Uttar Pradesh to have a video recording made of the post-mortem examination conducted in this case. Pursuant to the Commission's orders, a team from its Investigation Division also conducted an on-the-spot inquiry into this incident and submitted a report to the Commission.

On 26 September 2000, the Commission asked the Government of Uttar Pradesh, through its Chief Secretary, to show-cause, if any, why an amount of Rs. 2.00 lakhs be not granted as 'immediate interim relief' to the next of kin of Vijay Kumar Ekka. As there was no response from the Government of Uttar Pradesh, the Commission on 20 November 2000 recommended that an amount of Rs. 2 lakhs be granted as immediate interim relief under section 18(3) of the Protection of Human Rights Act, 1993 to the next kin of Vijay Ekka.

The Commission continues to keep a close watch on all incidents and reports expressing an apprehension regarding the violation of rights of members of the Christian community. The situation in this respect is under the constant monitoring of the Commission.

Year 2001-02

Killing of 7 Dalits by Upper Castes: Karnataka (Case No.628/10/99-2000)

The Commission received complaints from a number of organisations concerning the killing of 7 Dalits in Karnataka on 11 March 2000 by persons belonging to the upper castes. They requested a probe by the Commission and called for the granting of compensation to the victims.

The Commission took cognisance of the matter and, in response to a notice, received a report from DGP Karnataka. The report stated that there was a clash between two groups. To escape from the fury of the clash, the members of one group, who were Dalits, entered the house of a relative and bolted the door from inside. The accused persons bolted the door from outside and set the house ablaze. In this criminal act, 6 persons were burnt alive and another person, who was in a neighbouring house, also sustained severe burns and died while being taken to the hospital. A case had been registered against the accused. Inquiry into the incident indicated that a police Sub Inspector (PSI) had failed to take precautionary measures and to arrange appropriate 'bandobust' to avoid untoward incidents. The PSI had exhibited gross negligence and dereliction in the discharge of his duties. He had been placed under suspension and a departmental enquiry had been intitiated against him.

The Commission, in its proceedings dated 19 December 2000 held that the failure of the Government of Karnataka to protect Dalits was, in this instance, beyond doubt. It therefore issued a show cause notice to that Government asking as to why immediate interim relief u/s 18 (3) of the Act be not awarded to the next-of-kin of the deceased.

A further report was then received from the State Government. It stated suitable 'bandobast' had been arranged in the village; that an amount of Rs.1.5 lakh had been paid to the next-of-kin of each of the deceased as compensation, and that disciplinary proceedings had been instituted against the delinquent public servant. The Commission took note of the action taken and closed the case on 30 June 2001.e for any inadvertent error that may have crept in the Information being published on NET.

Year 2000-01

Release of Bonded Labourers and their Rehabilitation: Punjab.(Case No. 663/19/1999-2000)

The Commission took suo-motu ognisance of a press report which appeared in the 'Indian Express' dated 17 December 1999 entitled "84 Bonded Labourers Freed, Narrate Shocking Tales of Torture, Molestation". In the press report, it was stated that 84 bonded labourers, who were freed from a cold storage construction site, stated that they were beaten and were given third degree treatment. The woman workers alleged rape and molestation. None of the workers were paid their wages.

The Commission directed the Director General of Police, Punjab and the Senior Superintendent of Police, Jallandhar to send reports to the Commission on this article. The latter responded saying that one Mohan Singh, who was constructing a cold storage, was providing labourers with clothes, food, free accommodation and Rs. 600 per month. The labourers, however, had stated that they had been working for the last four months and were not given wages because the owner had promised to pay them when they returned to their native places. When the Sub Divisional Magistrate, Shahkot and Station House Officer, Police Station, Shahkot visited the spot, the labourers told them that they did not wish to work with the cold-storage owner as his behaviour was insulting. A woman labourer, named Saloni stated that one Pappu had beaten her husband and locked him in a room. The owner could not, himself, be contacted. However, his employees agreed to pay the wages to the labourers. The report added that the Labour Inspector had been directed to ensure the payment of wages to the labourers so that they might go wherever they wanted. The labourers had been brought to the office of the Sub Divisional Magistrate where food had been arranged for them. The labourers were then set free and they went back to their homes. The report concluded by saying that a case, FIR No. 236 dated 15 December 1999, had been registered under section 16, 17 of the Bonded Labour System (Abolition) Act and under Sections 342/323/354 of the Indian Penal Code.

Upon perusing the report, the Commission noted that it was not clear whether the District Magistrate, Jallandhar had issued release certificates and ensured that the bonded labourers would be rehabilitated. By proceedings dated 23 March 2000, the Commission therefore directed its Director General (Investigation) to contact Senior Superintendent of Police (SSP), Jallandhar and to secure the relevant details. The further report, received from the SSP, indicated that the 65 bonded labourers had been released and that the minimum wages due to them had been collected from Mohan Singh, owner of the cold storage. However, release certificates under the relevant Act and the rehabilitation package envisaged under it had not been provided. The Commission, therefore, directed the District Magistrate, Jallandhar:

To issue release certificates to all the 65 bonded labourers, namely the 42 men and 23 women involved. Further, a sum of Rs. 20,000 was to be paid to each of the 65 released bonded labourers under the relevant legislation, of which a sum of Rs. 5,000 may be paid in cash or by demand draft to each labourer.

Form a cooperative society; have it registered under the State Cooperative Societies Act as a Released Bonded Labourers Cooperative Society; treat the balance amount of Rs. 15,000 per head as share capital of each of the members of the society.

Under the appropriate Rozgar Yojana or any other appropriate scheme available, provide governmental work to the cooperative society.

An Inspector of the Cooperative Societies should monitor the working of the society. The work allotted to it would be jointly done by all the members of the cooperative society and the returns from their labour would be enjoyed by them in equal proportion.

In case any Government land was available in the village, the district administration shall take steps to allot the same to the cooperative society and all the members would collectively cultivate the land and reap the benefit in equal proportion. The District Administration would also, in that event, arrange appropriate loans for reclamation of land, its cultivation, and supply of seeds or saplings for agricultural operations, manure etc., for the successful working of the society. The Agriculture Department should be directed to help them in the farming.

In case all the members of the Society were illiterate, the Inspector belonging to the Cooperative Department should assist them in writing the accounts regularly and ensuring its successful working.

The District Labour Officer should ensure the successful prosecution of the offender for the offences charged against him. The District Labour Officer should act in collaboration with the concerned Public Prosecutor/District Attorney, as the case may be, and take the case to its logical conclusion.

The report received from the Deputy Commissioner, Jalandhar was placed before kthe Commission on 29 April 2002 when the Commission observed that partial compliance had been made, but it appeared that inadequate steps had been taken to comply fully with the directions of the Commission. It was added that the District Magistrate, Jalandhar should not take the directions of the Commission casually but should make strenuous efforts to trace the labourers who had been released, issue them the release certificates that were required under the law and provide them with other benefits directed by the Commission in its proceedings dated 18 September 2000.

NHRC's Initiative Results in the Release of Bonded Labourers: Haryana (Case No. 513/7/98-99)

The Commission received a complaint from Prof. Sheotaj Singh, General Secretary of the Bonded Labour Liberation Front, Delhi alleging that 20 persons including men, women and children were being kept as bonded labourers in a stone quarry in Gurgaon, Haryana. According to the complaint, though the Sub Divisional Magistrate of the area had visited the site and admitted that minimum wages were not being paid to the labourers, he had refused to issue release certificates to them.

On 21 September 1999, the Commission directed the Chief Secretary, Haryana, to look into the matter and submit a report. In response to the Commission's notice, the Labour Commissioner of Haryana stated that this was not a case of bonded labour but a dispute between workers and their employer regarding wages. Both the parties had reached an agreement, after which the labourers had been sent back to their home district, namely, Jaipur in Rajasthan. The report further stated that the complaint of Prof. Sheotaj Singh alleging non-release of the bonded labour was false.

The Special Rapporteur of the Commission, Shri Chaman Lal, was asked to look into the matter. He recommended that the Commission's own investigation team should meet the bonded labourers who were now living in Jaipur district in order to ascertain the facts.

Accordingly, an investigation team of the Commission, along with senior representatives of the Rajasthan University Women's Association and an officer deputed by the District Magistrate of Jaipur, visited Durgapura, 10 kilometers away from Jaipur city where about 29 persons including 10 children were found camping in the open. They had been living there since their return from Haryana in the second half of September 1999. They belonged to the Banjara Nomadic Tribe and had gone to Haryana in 1994 to market their products. While they were there, one Balkar Singh lured them to work in a stone quarry, offering them attractive wages. After a year, they were denied payment of wages and in lieu of wages; arrangements were made with a local general merchant to provide them daily rations on credit. When the labourers objected and demanded full wages, they were forcibly confined in their hutments after working hours and were guarded by armed musclemen. In August 1999, they somehow managed to establish contact with Prof. Sheotaj Singh. When word spread that

Prof. Singh had lodged a complaint, labourers were made to put their thumb impressions on papers of agreement declaring that they had received Rs.5,000 each towards the settlement of their wages. This was done in the presence of the local Sub Divisional Magistrate and police officials. The money was, however, not given to the labourers and, instead, it was adjusted against the items taken by them from the local merchant. In the third week of September 1999, they were transported away from Haryana, escorted by policemen, and later dumped in the outskirts of Jaipur city.

The Sub Divisional Magistrate, when questioned by the team of the Commission, reiterated that the issue related to a wage dispute in which he had worked out a compromise and that, to avoid any further chance of exploitation, he had made arrangements for the transportation of the labourers to Jaipur on their request. He claimed ignorance of the legal interpretation of the Supreme Court verdict wherein the word "bonded labour" had been given a wider interpretation, covering all cases where wages paid to the labourers was less than the minimum fixed by the Government. The Deputy Commissioner, Gurgaon, was also not fully aware of the whole episode. However, after discussions with the officials of the Commission, the district officials dispatched 19 Release Certificates to the Commission to be handed over to the labourers. The District Magistrate, Jaipur assured the Commission that immediate steps would be initiated to render all help to rehabilitate these Banjaras under various welfare schemes of the Government.

The Release Certificates were handed over to the labourers in December 1999 at a small function held in Jaipur. To rehabilitate these labourers, arrangements were made to shift their families temporarily to a Government housing building in Sanganer, near Jaipur city. Thereafter, they would be permanently settled under the Indira Awas Yojna. The Government of Rajasthan informed the Commission that efforts are also being made to allot them cultivable land. Employment is being given to them under the Rural Development Schemes near Sanganer Airport to help them earn their immediate livelihood. A cooperative is being created for them, to which stone mines would be leased in order to generate work in which the tribals had experience. Of the Rs10, 000 given to each of the 19 labourers, along with their Release Certificates, Rs. 2,000 was given in cash and rest of the money was deposited in their respective bank accounts. The District Magistrate had sanctioned Old Age Pensions to two elderly women. A pension was also announced to a person who became disabled following serious leg injuries while working in the Gurgaon mines. Cash relief of Rs. 5,000 from the Chief Minister's Relief Fund was also announced for his treatment.

The Commission expressed its appreciation of the role of the officers who were involved in the release of the bonded labourers and the subsequent effort to rehabilitate them.

Year 1993-94

Firing by Security Forces in Bijbehara, Jammu & Kashmir

On 1 November 1993, the Commission, suo motu, took Cognisance of press reports about the death of about 60 persons in and around Bijbehara in Jammu & Kashmir, as a result of firing by security forces operating in the areas and called for reports from the Ministries of Defence and Home Affairs as also the Government of J&K.

While the Ministry of Defence clarified that the army was not involved, the Ministry of Home Affairs sent a report to the Commission on the basis of the Magisterial Inquiry ordered by the State Government into the incident and the Staff Court of Inquiry ordered by B.S.F. authorities. On examination of the report, the Commission felt that perusal of copies of evidence given by six witnesses was necessary and accordingly called for additional material viz, the evidence given by the witnesses. That evidence having been made available to the Commission and considered by it, together with the report and material provided earlier, the Commission made the following observations/ recommendations:

(a) The Commission noted that disciplinary proceedings had been initiated under the Border Security Force Act against 14 members of the Force, and further that, on the basis of a Magisterial Inquiry, steps may be initiated to launch prosecutions. The Commission expected that the dual proceedings would be pursued their respective logical ends and that it would be kept informed of the action taken against those found guilty.

(b) Payment was recommended of interim compensation on a graded scale.

(c) It was recommended that a thorough review should be undertaken by Government of the circumstances and conditions in which Units of the Border Security Force are deployed and expected to operate in situations involving only civilian population.

These were communicated to the Central Government and the Commission has since been informed that the recommendations made by it have been accepted.

Year 1994-95

Alleged killings of civilians in Ukhrul town, Manipur, in crossfiring between 20 Assam Rifles and NSCN

On a complaint dated 9 June 1994, received from the Committee on Human Rights (COHR), Manipur regarding the death of civilians caught in cross-fire between the 20 Assam Rifles and elements of the NSCN, the Commission called for a report from the Ministry of Defence. The COHR complaint alleged that the firing by the Assam Rifles had been indiscriminate, that civilians had been detained illegally, that there had been acts of physical torture and the looting of cash and valuables and the destruction of properties by the Assam Rifles. It was further alleged that this was in retaliation, consequent to the killing of two Assam Rifles Officers earlier by NSCN ognisance.

In their report of 6 December 1994, Army Headquarters stated that NSCN insurgents had shot two Assam Rifles Officers on duty, in an ambush in Wino Bazar of Ukhrul town, without any provocation. When the wounded officers were being rushed to hospital, the insurgents fired at them again, as a result, the two officers succumbed to their injuries and four others sustained injuries. The Quick Reaction Team of the Assam Rifles cordoned off the area to search for the insurgents. Peace meetings were arranged with prominent church leaders and others of Ukhrul town, along with the District Collector and Superintendent of Police; these gestures were appreciated by all. The Court of Inquiry set up by the General Officer Commanding also expressed the opinion that maximum restraint was exercised by the armed forces and that, contrary to the allegation that 20 mortars were fired, only 2 fired, and that the Assam Rifles unit had not engaged in torture, illegal detentions or looting.

After considering the report of the Ministry of Defence (Army Headquarters) the Commission was satisfied with the response of the armed forces, including the follow-up action taken by them to restore peace. The Commission, however, recommended in its proceedings of 9 February 1995, that compensation of Rs. 50,000/- be paid to the next of kin of each of the 3 civilians killed in the cross firing.

The Ministry of Defence issued instructions on 31 March 1995 for the payment of the compensation, as recommended by the Commission.

Alleged death of Muhammad Akbar Sheikh in armed forces custody, Baramulla district, Jammu & Kashmir

Inhabitants of a cluster of villages in Barwah tehsil of Baramulla district, Jammu & Kashmir, submitted a written complaint to the Commission alleging the death, in the custody of the armed forces, of Muhammad Akbar Sheikh on 27 December 1993. It was asserted that he was seized during an army crackdown in the area on that date and that his dead body was handed over to the police in Baramulla on 29 December 1993.

Proceeding under Section 19 of the Protection of Human Rights Act 1993, the Commission called for reports from the Defence and Home Ministries. The reply of the Defence Ministry, dated 6 September 1994, forwarded a report from Army Headquarters. According to that report, the 15 Punjab Regiment was involved in an operation against militants on 27 December 1993 around the village of Fategarh. Tehsil Barwah, District Baramulla. A cordon was established at 0700 hours and a search started at about 0900 hours.

All male adults were collected at the local government high school. Muhammad Akbar Sheikh agreed to assist one of companies of the unit in the matter of the search. Five hideouts were shown to the search party and weapons and ammunition too were recovered. The search continued till 1800 hours. The period being the last week of December 1993, the weather was harsh and the terrain difficult. The report attributed the death of Muhammad Akbar Sheikh to exhaustion.

After carefully Cognisanc the report, the Commission observed that it was apparent that the deceased had been totally exhausted. The valley was in the grip of severe cold at that time. The record further indicated that Muhammad Akbar Sheikh was not a man in normal health. In such circumstances, it was the obligation of those who wanted to utilize his services for the purpose of the search, to take proper care of him. It was evident that exhaustion in this case was the result of the strain put upon him by the search party. Though the case was not one of custodial death, the situation was more or less akin to it.

After considering all aspects of the case, factual and legal, the Commission was of the opinion that Muhammad Akbar Sheikh's life could have been saved if appropriate care had been taken of him by the armed forces. Holding the latter responsible for negligence in the death of Muhammad Akbar Sheikh, the Commission directed the Ministry of Defence to pay Rs. 50,000/- as compensation to the legal heirs of the deceased.

Accepting the recommendations of the Commission, the Ministry of Defence issued a sanction order on 2 December 1994 for the payment of the compensation. The Commission took note of this on 22 December 1994.

Alleged death of Allen Kuki of Khoijang village, Manipur, in custody of the armed forces

On the basis of a press report appearing in The Statesman of 9 March 1994, alleging that a Kuki rebel had died in the custody of the armed forces, the Commission called for a report from the Ministry of Defence.

The latter replied, providing a report from Army Headquarters. According to that report, during the night of 5-6 March 1994, village Kholjang was cordoned by the 4th Regiment of the Assam Rifles for apprehending certain persons who were reportedly hiding in the village. Around 0330 hours, three persons where seen coming towards a group of the security forces. On being challenged, those persons opened fire and the security forces returned fire. One of those persons, later identified as Allen Kuki, jumped into a nullah full of boulders and bamboo stumps to evade capture. The report mentioned that Allen succumbed to injuries at about 1530 hours on that day.

After a thorough examination of the facts stated in the report, the Commission noted that Allen had been taken into custody at about 0330 hours but that no medical help had been provided to him, nor any attempt seemingly made in this respect, until his death about 12 hours thereafter. The Commission observed that it was the obligation of the security forces, who held Allen n custody, to take steps for his immediate treatment and that the obligation arose the moment Allen came into their custody in an injured condition.

Quoting from the Supreme Court's observations in the case of Pandit Paramanand Katia versus Union of India and others (1989), the Commission's order pointed out "there can be no second opinion that preservation of human life is of paramount importance. That is so on account of the fact that once life is lost, the status quo ante cannot be restored. Whether he be an innocent person or a criminal liable to punishment under the laws of society, it is the obligation of those who are in charge of the patient to preserve life so that the innocent may be protected and the guilty may be punished. Social laws do not contemplate death by negligence to be tantamount to legal punishment".

The Commission was of the view that what the Apex Court held in the aforesaid decision, applied equally to the situation where a public authority had physical custody of an injured person. The Commission observed "There is no material in the report to indicate the nature of injuries he had received by jumping into the nullah. We have, in the circumstances, to assume that if timely treatment had been provided to Allen, his life could have been saved and the captors have failed to conform to their obligation under the law. In such circumstances, compensation is payable to the next of kin of Allen. Ordinarily, for loss of life, compensation of Rs. 50,000/- to Rs. 1,00,000/- is being given depending upon the different situations in which death occurs. From the report, it appears that Allen had voluntarily jumped into the nullah to avoid capture. We are of the view that compensation of the sum of Rs. 50,000/- would meet the ends of justice".

The Army authorities have indicated that the amount of compensation recommended by the Commission has been paid to the mother of the deceased.

Year 1995-96

Death of Kheshiho Sumi in the custody of the armed forces (Assam Rifles) in Nagaland

Upon the intervention of the Commission, the Ministry of Defence has sanctioned a sum of Rs. 100,000/- to the next of kin of Kheshiho Sumi, who died in the custody of the Assam Rifles.

The Commission initiated a proceeding on the basis of a report received by it from the Superintendent of Police, Dimapur, Nagaland indicating the custodial death of Kheshino Sumi. Upon notice, the Ministry of Defence reported to the Commission that Kheshiho Sumi was arrested on 12 November 1994 from Purana Bazar as he was observed to be movingaround in a suspicious manner. Two days later, while he was reportedly being taken by the Assam Rifles on a mission to uncover the hide out of insurgents, it was stated that Kheshiho jumped from a running vehicle with a view to escaping andwas injured in the process. After being found in a ditch, the report added that Kheshiho was taken to the civil hospital, Dimapur but that the doctor on emergency duty declared him dead. According to the defence authorities, the salient fact which emerged from the court of enquiry proceedings was that Kheshiho was actively involved in the activities of the outlawed National Socialist Council of Nagaland (IM) and that he was neither maltreated nor beaten after his apprehension.

Upon perusing the report, the Commission noted that, under the Armed Forces (Special Powers) Act, 1958, admittedly in force in the area,"Any commissioned officer warrant officer, non-commissioned officier or any other person of equivalent rank in the armed forces may, in a disturbed area, arrest without warrant, any person who has committed a ognisance offence or against whom a reasonable suspicion exists that he has committed or is about to commit a ognisance offence and may use such force as may be necessary to effect the arrest". Section 5 however requires that any person arrested and taken into custody under the Act shall be made over to the officer in charge of the nearest police station with the least possible delay, together with a report of the circumstances ognisance the arrest.

The Commission also noted that the Guwahati High Court in a judgement in the case of Purnima Barua vs. Union of India (1991 CRI.L.J 2675) and others interpreted the term "least possible delay" in the following manner:"Whenever the question "least possible delay" arises for decision in computing the period of time, the Court has to have regard to the particular circumstances of the case-physical impossibility or otherwise-to make over the arrested person to the nearest police station, and how, where and in what circumstances the arrest was effected."

The Commission observed that it was the obligation of the Assam Rifles to hand over Kheshiho to the Dimapur police on 12 November itself after he was arrested, and that they were not entitled to keep him in their custody for carrying out any investigation. The Commission held that the act of keeping Kheshiho in their control after arrest was contrary to the provisions of Section 5 of the Armed Forces (Special Powers) Act 1958 (Act 28 of 1959). The Commission noted that the obligation to make over the arrested person to the civil police without delay itself ruled out the legal authority of the investigation by the Assam Rifles. The Commission, therefore, observed that the attempt to engage the deceased in the search of hideouts of insurgents for two days following his arrest was an unauthorized act. It was also felt that, as custodians of Kheshihi, who was injured, the Assam Rifles were under legal obligation to provide prompt and adequate medical care. They were found to benegligent in discharging this obligation.

After a detailed analysis of all the facts stated in the report, the Commission observed that:

(i) the"detention of Mr. Kheshiho from 12 to 14 November 1994 was unauthorized and illegal;

(ii) taking him out for recoverieswas a part of an attempt to investigate into the alleged offences andwas a matter without jurisdicition so far as Assam Rifles are concerned; and

(iii) the explanation about death is not very impressive and at any rate, if due care had been taken, even accepting the fact that he was found unconscious at 5.30 P.M with the injuries said to have been suffered, he might have been saved."

In the absence of positive evidence of assault, theCommission noted that it was not in a position to hold that Kheshiho died on account of physical torture. However, the Commission pointed out that this case involveda violation of law and therefore, recommended compensation of Rs. 100,000/- to the next of kin of Kheshiho Sumi. The Commission has received a report from the Ministry of Defence indicating that its recommendation has been complied with. As indicated in paragraph 4.3 of this report, the Commission has also begun a process of examining the Act and has asked for the comments of the Central Government on it.

Year 1999-2000

Jawan Rapes mentally disturbed girl in public – Assam Case No.27/3/1999-2000

The Commission took suo motu cognisance of a news item published in "The Statesman" dated 20 April 1999 entitled "Jawan rapes mentally disturbed girl in public" and directed that a report be had from the Secretary, Ministry of Defence in the matter.

The report from the Ministry of Defence confirmed the allegation that one Ajit Singh had raped ABC (name withheld to protect identity), a 15 year old mentally deranged girl and that an FIR was lodged by a civilian. The girl was examined medically and the Medical Officer had confirmed the offence. Ajit Singh was arrested and placed in military custody. Summary General Court Martial tried Ajit Singh and awarded him 8 years rigorous imprisonment and dismissal from service.

The Commission while taking note of the action taken by the Military authorities against the accused, expressed the view that the victim, ABC, a mentally disturbed girl also needed to be compensated. It accordingly directed the District Magistrate, Kokrajhar to pay a sum of Rs.25,000/- to the parents of ABC by way of immediate interim relief. The Commission has received a compliance report with regard to the payment of compensation.

Year 2000-01

Complaints Against Security Forces: High-Handed Acts of Army Personnel: Andhra Pradesh.(Case No. 67/1/1999-2000)

In a decision dated 1 November 2000, the Commission made far-reaching recommendations to the Ministry of Defence, Government of India to compensate farmers of Andhra Pradesh who were victims of actions taken against them by personnel of the army.

The Commission had, on 19 May 1999, taken suo-motu ognisance of a report stating that some 300 army personnel had gone on a pre-dawn rampage in Hyderabad and had attacked farmers who had come to sell their produce at Rythu Bazaar in that city on 12 May 1999. They threatened the farmers who were sleeping in the compound and severely beat up four of them who had protested. The losses incurred during the incident were estimated by the district administration to amount to some Rs. 12 lakhs. The farmers had occupied sheds set-up at the Bazaar by the State Government on military land with the permission of the army authorities. The State Government had condemned the action of the army personnel for taking the law into their own hands and had lodged a strong protest with the Defence Minister and Army Headquarters.

In reply to a notice from the Commission, the Ministry of Defence had justified the action of the army men in forcibly evicting the farmers. The reply stated that the State Government had backtracked on its assurance to vacate the area within the specified period for which it had been given on lease by the army. The Ministry denied the violation of any human rights by the army.

On the other hand, the report of the Collector of Ranga Reddy District, who was an eyewitness to the whole incident, said that despite her pleadings, hundreds of military personnel had demolished the property erected at Rythu Bazaar while she and the police personnel who were present at that time could only remain silent spectators. Around 80 farmers who were at the site at the time of the incident were manhandled and four of them were seriously injured. Vegetables worth Rs. 1.7 lakhs were strewn around and the temporary structures erected were irreparably damaged. The total damage worked out to Rs. 11.26 lakhs. Photographs supported the Collector's eyewitness report.

The Commission, on considering both these responses, recorded in its proceedings of 20 September 1999 that the two reports, from two responsible and highly placed functionaries of the Central and

State Governments, were in total variance. It observed that the pertinent question was whether or not the army personnel had committed high-handed acts. Therefore, it requested the Secretary, Ministry of Defence, to get the entire matter examined, including the aspect of the propriety of the Ministry in making such sweeping denials of events in the face of an apparently authentic report of senior officers of the State Government.

The Commission also requested the Chief Secretary, Government of Andhra Pradesh to examine both the responses and give his own report. The report of the Chief Secretary clearly pointed to the high-handedness of the army personnel and made the disturbing observation that the role of the Andhra Pradesh Sub-Area Commander in the incident had been questionable. The Chief Secretary's report was also sent to the Ministry of Defence for its response.

The Ministry of Defence, however, reiterated its earlier version and asked the Commission to call the concerned officers of the Army and State Government and take a view in the matter. However, in the meeting called by the Commission on 6 September 2000, the concerned army officials chose not to come and were represented only by the Civilian Staff Officer of Army Headquarters.

The Commission therefore had to formulate its opinion and consider the allegation of the violation of human rights of the victims based on the facts and circumstances of the case. The Commission had no hesitation in rejecting the version of the army authorities, which was in direct conflict with the version of the State Government. Certain admitted facts and circumstances also supported this conclusion of the Commission.

The Commission also learned that the State Government, keen to ensure the continuance of the Bazaar in the same location, had already moved for this land to be exchanged with some other land of the State Government, which could be given to the army instead. Discussion in this regard was in progress between the State Government and the Army and the Sub-Area Commander had been requested to await the final outcome of this discussion. Thus, there was no occasion for the District Collector to tell the Sub-Area Commander to carry out the eviction, as had been alleged by the Army. Moreover, the unusual time of early morning chosen for carrying out the surprise action, without any prior notice to the occupants or to the District Collector, supported the allegation of high-handedness by the Army men and their intention to take even the State Government by surprise.

Rejecting the clandestine and unlawful action of the army men, the Commission said, “a civilised legal system does not permit even a trespasser with settled possession to be thrown out in this manner without resort to the procedure established by the law”.

The Commission thus directed the Ministry of Defence, Government of India to pay a sum of Rs. 12 lakhs as compensation for loss to property, a sum of Rs.10,000 to each of the four farmers beaten up by the army men and a sum of Rs. 5000 to each of the farmers forcibly evicted. The Government of India was asked to pay the above amounts, granted as ‘immediate interim relief’ under section 18(3) of the Protection of Human Rights Act, 1993, to the Government of Andhra Pradesh. The calculation of the total amount was to be made by the Chief Secretary, Andhra Pradesh and intimated to the Secretary, Ministry of Defence within one month. The Government of India was asked to pay this amount to the Government of Andhra Pradesh within one month thereafter, for disbursement among those entitled, within one month.

The Government of India was also asked to consider initiating proceedings to identify the army personnel responsible for the violation of human rights in the above incident and to take appropriate action against them. The Ministry of Defence was, further, asked to formulate necessary guidelines for the observance of human rights of the civilian population by the Armed Forces while performing their duties in non-combat areas.

In concluding, the Commission emphasised the urgency and need for amending the Protection of Human Rights Act, 1993 to empower the National Human Rights Commission to inquire more effectively into human rights violations by the Armed Forces. Any further delay or inaction, it observed, was likely to erode the credibility of the Government of India in its commitment to respect human rights.

The Commission has since been informed of compliance with its directives in this case.

Year 2001-02

Procedure with respect to complaints against Armed Forces: Disappearance of Mohammed Tayab Ali, who was last seen in the company of para-military forces (Case No. 32/14/1999-2000)

The Commission received a complaint from Smt. Mina Khatoon, resident of District Imphal (East), which was referred to it by the Manipur State Human Rights Commission, alleging the disappearance of her husband Mohammed Tayab Ali on 25 July 1999 after he was taken away to the headquarters of the 17 Assam Rifles Battalion. He had not been seen thereafter.

The Commission considered the report submitted by the Ministry of Defence and, in the light of the evidence on record, including the deposition of witnesses, who stated that they had seen Mohammed Tayab Ali being picked-up by security men, held that the security forces were liable for the disappearance of Mohammed Tayab Ali. The Commission accordingly awarded a sum of Rs.3 lakhs as immediate interim relief, u/s 18(3) of the Act, to the complainant. A compliance report is awaited.

Given the importance of this case, particularly in respect of the procedure to be followed in regard to complaints submitted against the armed forces, relevant extracts of the proceedings of the Commissions in this case are being reproduced verbatim below:

Mohammed Tayab Ali was seen being picked up in the Maruti van and being taken to the battalion headquarters of 17 Assam Rifles. His relatives and friends also made attempts to reach him at 17, Assam Rifles on the same day, but failed. Pursuant to a notice issued by the Manipur State Human Rights Commission to the Inspector General of Police (Law and Order) to ascertain the whereabouts of Mohd. Tayab Ali, the Inspector General of Police (Law and Order), Manipur submitted his inquiry report to the State Commission. It stated that the Director General of Police, Manipur, Imphal had issued crash messages to all concerned police authorities in the State of Manipur for flashing the information regarding whereabouts of Mohd. Tayab Ali. It had also taken up the matter with the Commander, Manipur Range. On 22 August 1999, the Staff Officer of Commander, Manipur Range, Imphal informed the Director General of Police, Manipur that the case of the alleged arrest of Mohd. Tayab Ali of Kairang Muslim village was investigated and inquiries were made from 17 Assam Rifles and all other units in that behalf. It was confirmed by them that no individual by the name of Mohd. Tayab Ali was picked up by 17 Assam Rifles or any other Assam Rifles unit.

After receipt of this report, the State Commission summoned the complainant Smt. Mina Khatoon in order to find out if her husband had been located. She appeared before the Commission and reiterated that her husband was last seen being carried in a Maruti van to 17

Assam Rifles campus at Kangla, Imphal. She also filed some photographs of her husband.

On consideration of the entire matter, the State Commission referred the case to this Commission as it relates to the 'armed forces'. On receipt of the reference from the Manipur State Human Rights Commission this Commission issued notices to the Ministries of Defence and Home Affairs, Government of India and called for a report in accordance with Section 19 of the Protection of Human Rights Act, 1993. The report of the Ministry of Defence received with their letter dated 11 April 2000 stated that on 25 July 1999, at around 9.45 hours, information was received that some valley based insurgents after firing on CRPF personnel at Langjing were fleeing towards Dimapur. A column of 17 Assam Rifles accordingly established a Mobile Check Post. Apparently, one of the vehicles attempted to speed towards Dimapur. The security team stopped the vehicle. There was an exchange of fire and one individual died. The driver of the vehicle managed to escape with the vehicle. This body was later identified as that of Mohd. Tayab Ali. It was handed over to Kangpokpi police station on 25 July 1999. Thus the Defence Ministry's report concluded that Mohd. Tayab Ali had died in retaliatory fire opened by the personnel of the armed forces. Hence no cognisance could be taken of the complaint submitted by Smt. Mina Khatoon. This was a totally different and inconsistent stand taken by the Defence authorities from the earlier report of DGP Manipur which had denied that any person by the name of Mohd. Tayab Ali was picked up by 17 Assam Rifles or any other Assam Rifles unit. As per the report of the Defence authorities, the body of the person killed in the encounter was handed over to Kangpokpi police station. No attempt seems to have been made by Kangpokpi police station to identify the body despite information having been flashed to all the police stations about the disappearance of Mohd. Tayab Ali. The body was disposed of as unidentified. This Commission, therefore, directed by its order dated 13 December 2000, that the photographs of the dead body of the person killed in the encounter on 25 July 1999 should be shown to the complainant to ascertain whether the photographs were of Mohd. Tayab Ali. The Commission received a letter dated 15 January 2001 from the Director General of Police, Manipur, Imphal stating that the Kangpokpi police station had shown the photographs of the unidentified dead body to the close relatives of Mohd. Tayab Ali, i.e. the complainant Mrs. Mina Khatoon, his wife, Mohd. Tahir Ali, the father and Mohd. Vazir Ahmed, the elder brother of Mohd. Tayab Ali. But none of them could identify the deceased in the photograph and they stated that the body was not of Mohd. Tayab Ali. Thus, it is proved that the person who was killed in an encounter on 25 July 1999 was not Mohd. Tayab Ali.

Thus, facts clearly indicate that Mohd. Tayab Ali while he was travelling on a Luna Moped was picked up apparently by some armed forces men in a Maruti van without any registration number and was taken to the Headquarter of 17, Assam Rifles. There is the unrebutted testimony of several witnesses who had seen him being taken in this fashion. Since then Mohd. Tayab Ali is missing. The stand taken by the Defence authorities that Mohd. Tayab Ali was killed in an encounter on 25 July 1999 must be rejected since the dead body of the person killed in that encounter was not that of Mohd. Tayab Ali. It must, therefore, be concluded that 17 Assam Rifles in whose custody Mohd. Tayab Ali was last seen, has failed to account for him, thereafter. In the case of the Union of India vs. Luithukla (Smt.) and Others, (1999) 9 SCC 273, the Supreme Court considered a similar case where the husband of the first respondent had been taken away by the army personnel. His brother had visited the army camp on the next day and inquired about his brother but no information was given to him. Thereafter, a complaint was lodged with the officer in charge of the local police station. Various attempts were made to locate the missing person but to no effect. The Supreme Court upheld the High Court's finding that the missing person was last seen in the custody of security forces and was not seen since then. The security forces were, therefore, held liable for his disappearance, and payment of compensation to the wife of the missing person. In the present case also, the facts are similar. The security forces in the present case are, therefore, liable to pay 'immediate interim relief' to the complainant for the disappearance of her husband Mohd. Tayab Ali while in the custody of 17, Assam Rifles.

Since the violation of human rights is by members of the armed forces, it is appropriate to examine the provisions of sections 17 to 19 of the Protection of Human Rights Act, 1993 Sections 17, 18 and 19 are contained in Chapter IV relating to the procedure to be followed by the Commission for inquiry into the complaints of violation of human rights, which is one of the functions of the Commission specified in sub-section (a) of section 12 of the Act. Section 17 prescribes the general procedure for inquiring into the complaints; section 18 specifies the steps after inquiry that may be taken by the Commission; and section 19 prescribes the special procedure with respect to armed forces while dealing with such complaints. These sections have to be read together for a proper understanding of the scope of section 19 and the limitations in the special procedure. Sections 17 to 19 are as follows:

Section 17. Inquiry into complaints. The commission while inquiring into the complaints of violations of human rights may:

(i) call for information or report from the Central Government or any State Government or any other authority or organisation subordinate thereto within such time as may be specified by it; Provided that:

(ii) if the information or report is not received within the time stipulated by the Commission, it may proceed to inquire into the complaint on its own;

(iii) if, on receipt of information or report, the Commission is satisfied either that no further inquiry is required or that the required action has been initiated or taken by the concerned Government or authority, it may not proceed with the complaint and inform the complainant accordingly;

(2) without prejudice to anything contained in clause

(i) if it considers necessary, having regard to the nature of the complaint, initiate an inquiry. Section 18. Steps after inquiry The Commission may take any of the following steps upon the completion of an inquiry held under this Act namely:

(ii) where the inquiry discloses, the commission of violation of human rights or negligence in the prevention of violation of human rights by a public servant, it may recommend to the concerned Government or authority the initiation of proceedings for prosecution or such other action as the Commission may deem fit against the concerned person or persons;

(2) approach the Supreme Court or the High Court concerned for such directions, orders or writs as that Court may deem necessary;

(3) recommend to the concerned Government or authority for the grant of such immediate interim relief to the victim or the members of his family as the Commission may consider necessary;

(4) subject to the provisions of clause

(5) provide a copy of the inquiry report to the petitioner or his representative;

(6) the Commission shall send a copy of its inquiry report together with its recommendations to the concerned Government or authority and the concerned Government or authority shall, within a period of one month, or such further time as the Commission may allow, forward its comments on the report, including the action taken or proposed to be taken thereon, to the Commission;

(i) the Commission shall publish its inquiry report together with the comments of the concerned Government or authority, if any, and the action taken or proposed to be taken by the concerned Government or authority on the recommendations of the Commission.

Section 19. Procedure with respect to armed forces

(ii) Notwithstanding anything contained in this Act, while dealing with complaints of violation of human rights by members of the armed forces, the Commission shall adopt the following procedure, namely:

(2) (a) it may, either on its own motion or on receipt of a petition, seek a report from the Central Government;

(b) after the receipt of the report, it may, either not proceed with the complaint or, as the case may be, make its recommendations to that Government.

(3) The Central Government shall inform the Commission of the action taken on the recommendations within three months or such further time as the Commission may allow.

(4) (3) The Commission shall publish its report together with its recommendations

made to the Central Government and the action taken by that Government on such recommendations.

(4) The Commission shall provide a copy of the report published under subsection

(3) to the petitioner or his representative.

Section 17 which prescribes the general procedure for inquiry into complaints of violations of human rights says that the Commission may call for information or report from the concerned government or authority etc.; and on receipt of information or report, if the Commission is satisfied that no further inquiry is required or the necessary action has been taken, it may not proceed further with the complaint. It further says that if it considers necessary, then the Commission may initiate an inquiry. Section 18 mentions the steps after completion of the inquiry.

It empowers making of recommendations by the Commission, which include that for initiation of action against the concerned person and also for grant of such immediate interim relief to the victim as may be considered necessary. In the case of armed forces, section 19 prescribes the special procedure, which to the extent indicated therein overrides the general procedure. It is necessary now to examine the restriction made by section 19.

Section 19 begins with the non-obstante clause which indicates that the special procedure prescribed therein overrides the general procedure in its application to complaints of violation of human rights by members of the armed forces. The first step in this procedure prescribed by clause (a) of sub-section (1) is to seek a report from the Central Government as against calling for 'information' or 'report' prescribed in section 17. Clause (b) of sub-section (1) of section 19 then prescribes the next step, that 'after the receipt of the report, it may, either not proceed with the complaint or, as the case may be, make its recommendations to that Government.' Thus, on receipt of the report there are two options: the first is not to proceed with the complaint, and the other is to make 'recommendations' to the Central Government. The first option of not proceeding with the complaint is similar to that in proviso (b) to clause (i) of section 17. Obviously, it refers to the situation where on receipt of the report the Commission is satisfied that there is no need to proceed further with the complaint in order to make its recommendations to the Government. This situation being similar under both provisions, it presents no difficulty. The question is of the scope of Commission's powers when it is not satisfied with the report received from the Central Government and there is need to adopt the second course, which may lead to making its recommendations to the Government. It is this area which needs a closer look. It is clear that the function of the Commission prescribed in clause (a) of section 12 to inquire into any complaint of violation of human rights includes the power to inquire into such complaints made even against members of the armed forces; and section 19 merely prescribes the special procedure for dealing with such complaints overriding the general procedure under section 17. The power to make recommendations, when necessary, in section 19 must be read along with subsections (1) and (3) of section 18 which deal with the nature of recommendations on conclusion of the inquiry, when closure of the complaint is not considered appropriate. There is nothing restrictive in section 19 to curtail this power of the Commission and the express power to make recommendations leads necessarily to this conclusion. In other words, the only limitation in section 19 vis-à-vis section 17, is that under section 19, the Commission cannot proceed to 'initiate an inquiry' itself, as it can under section 17(ii) of the Act. Implicit in section 19 is the responsibility of proper investigation by the Central Government to enable it to make the report required under section 19 after examination of the complaint in a fair and objective manner in the light of all relevant facts. This requires ascertainment of the relevant facts and examination of the material disclosed by the complainant. The conclusions reached in the Report forwarded by the Central Government to the Commission, must be the logical outcome of the materials and duly supported by the reasons given in its support. It is settled, that when there is power to do an act, there is power to do all that is necessary for the performance of that act. This is implicit in the provision conferring the power to act. Thus, all that is necessary to make 'recommendations' for compliance by the Central Government is implicit in the power conferred in section 19(1)(b) to make recommendations, in case the Commission is not satisfied with the report that it is not necessary to proceed with the complaint. To decide whether to accept the report and not proceed with the complaint or to proceed further, itself requires an objective determination which must be based on relevant materials. The 'report' of the Central Government must, therefore, satisfy this requirement and contain all relevant materials to enable performance of the exercise by the Commission. The dictionary meaning of the word 'report' includes: 'to write an account of occurrences; to make a formal report; a statement of facts.' There is nothing in the context to alter the ordinary meaning. The 'report' required to be submitted by the Central Government to the Commission must contain a statement of facts and an account of occurrences and not merely the findings or conclusions reached by the Central Government on facts which are not disclosed to the Commission. This meaning given to the word 'report' in section 19 is in consonance with its purpose of enabling the Commission to perform the task of dealing with such a complaint against members of the armed forces. The object of enacting the Protection of Human Rights Act, 1993 (POHRA) is the better protection of human rights and constitution of National Human Rights Commission (NHRC) is for this purpose. Jurisdiction of the NHRC to deal with the complaints against armed forces is subject only to a restricted procedure. The construction made of section 19 and the meaning given to the word 'report' therein, promotes the object of the enactment. It has to be preferred. This is a settled canon of interpretation of statutes. Another aspect needs mention. A complaint of violation of human rights is based invariably on the allegation of harm to the victim resulting from some act or omission of the alleged violator. Once the harm attributed to the violator is proved or admitted, the burden of proving that the harm resulted from a justified act permitted under the law, is on the person against whom the allegation is made. Unless that burden is discharged by proof of facts or circumstances, which provide justification for the act under the law, the initial presumption of the violators' accountability remains unrebutted. An obvious illustration is the case of unnatural death caused by use of force or disappearance from custody. As soon as it is proved or admitted that the victim was in the custody of someone, the burden is on that person to prove how he dealt with the detainee, and unless it can be satisfactorily shown that the custodian is not responsible for the harm or disappearance from the custody, the initial presumption of accountability remains unrebutted. The present case is of that kind.

Mohd. Tayab Ali, husband of the complainant is proved to have been taken in custody by the 17 Assam Rifles, and the custodian has been unable to prove satisfactorily the lawful termination of custody, when he was alive. These facts alone are sufficient to uphold the liability of 17 Assam Rifles and to hold it accountable for his disappearance.

Section 105 of the Indian Evidence Act, 1872 places the burden of proving the existence of circumstances bringing the case within any of the General Exceptions in the Indian Penal Code or any other justification on the 17 Assam Rifles, which burden it has failed to discharge. Section 106 of Evidence Act places the burden of proving the facts especially within knowledge of any person upon him, irrespective of the general burden of proof being on the other side. This provision also casts the obligation on the custodian to prove how he dealt with the detainee or the victim. Viewed at, in any manner, the 17 Assam Rifles has failed to discharge the burden and the initial presumption of its liability for the disappearance of Mohd. Tayab Ali remains unrebutted. This case falls within the ambit of the second part of section 19(1)(b) since on receipt of the report from the Central Government the Commission is of the considered opinion that it is a fit case for making recommendations in terms of subsection (1) and (3) of section 18 of the Act. The Commission therefore, makes the necessary consequential recommendations. The complainant has lost her husband at a young age. At the time of her husband's disappearance, she had five children and she was pregnant. The loss of the sole breadwinner rendered the family destitute. Since the violation of human rights in the present case is by members of the armed forces, the Commission, in exercise of its powers under section 19 of the Protection of Human Rights Act recommends that it would be just and proper in the circumstances of the case to award immediate interim relief of Rs.3 lakhs to the complainant and her children. We make this recommendation to the Ministry of Defence and the Ministry of Home Affairs, Government of India for compliance. The action taken should be communicated to the Commission within three months.

The Ministry of Defence reported compliance with the Commission's directions and made payment of the amount of compensation by cheque dated 18 February 2002. The case was therefore closed.

Year 1993-94

Appeal for expeditious arrangements for heart surgery of Harihar Behara lodged in Central Jail, Berhampur, Ganjam (Orissa)

The Commission received a representation from Shri D.N. Panda, Advocate, Cuttack, stating that prisoner Harihar Behera in Central Jail, Berhampur, in the State of Orissa needed immediate heart surgery as advised by the Cardiology Department, S.C.B. Medical College Hospital, Cuttack, and asked for the intervention of the Commission.

The Commission called for a report from the inspector General of Prisons, Cuttack and directed him to make provision for medical assistance in the manner asked for, if the matter was urgent.

The Inspector General of Prisons responded to the Commission's directions and stated that the Government of Orissa had been moved to approve the journey of Shri Harihar Behera outside the State and that sanction of funds and orders to that effect were awaited.

On 24 March 1994, the I.G. Prisons further informed the Commission that on the petition of the wife of Shri Harihar Behera for release of her husband on special parole for a period of 90 days for open heart surgery at C.M.C. Vellore or at AIIMS, New Delhi at her own cost, the Government of Orissa had sanctioned 90 days special parole. Accordingly, Shri Harihar Behera had been released on special parole for 90 days with effect from 28 February 1994.

Murder of Dinesh Pathak, editor of a newspaper in Baroda

The Writers in Prison Committee of International P.E.N. had in February 1994 taken up with the Commission, inter alia, the case of Shri Dinesh Pathak who was stabbed to death reportedly by Shiv Sena activists on 22 May 1993. The Commission took ognisance of the case and directed the authorities concerned to submit a report.

The Commission has since been informed that 19 Shiv Sena activists were involved in the crime and they have all been arrested. One of the arrested persons was killed when he tried to escape from police custody. Out of the accused who were arrested, 16 are still in judicial custody. The trial is likely to commence shortly.

Year 1994-95

Illegal chanining of a patient in a hospital in Orissa

The Commission received a complaint from the Kalahandi Consumers Welfare Organization alleging that, in a misuse of poer by public servants, a social worker, Shri Radhanath Pradhan, had been chained to his hospital bed. The complaint was accompanied by photographs of the incident. The Commission accordingly called for a report from the Collector and District Magistrate, Kalahandi.

On perusing that report, the Commission noted that Shri Radhanath Pradhan had been prosecuted for offences committed under Sections 448/294/353 of the IPC in regard to incidents which were mentioned in the complaint. The Chief Judicial Magistrate had found him guilty and had sentenced him to imprisonment of one year and a fine of Rs. 1,000/-. It was also noted that Shri Pradhan had filed an appeal in the Court o the Sessions Judge. Without taking a position on Shri Pradhan's arrest, as that issue was before the Sessions Judge, the Commission expressed grave displeasure over the changing of Shri Pradhan to his hospital bed. The Commission added that, unless there wire special reasons and a judicial order in support of such action, patients under treatment in hospitals must not be chained.

Following these directions, the State Government has issued appropriate instructions to all concerned officials in the State

Conditions of Chakma & Hojong refugees settled in Arunachal Pradesh

The Commission received representations from the Peoples Union for Civil Liberties (PUCL) and Amnesty International regarding the plight of Chakma and Hajong refugees living in Arunachal Pradesh.

It was stated that these groups, comprising respectively Buddhists and Hindus, fed for fear of persecution on grounds of their religion from the Chittagong Hill Tracts, in what was formerly East Pakistan, between the years 1964-1971. Onginally welcomed to India and to parts of NEFA, which today form Arunachal Pradesh, they were now increasingly being harassed and threatened in that State. When some of them tried to flee to Assam, it was alleged that the Government of Assam threatened to shoot them if they did so. Allegations regarding threats to the life and property of Chakmas and Hajongs were also conveyed directly to the Chairperson of the Commission through representatives of their communities who had ognisanc to Delhi from Arunachal Pradesh.

The Commission, in a communication to the State Government on 29 September 1994 stated that it was the obligation of that Government to accord protection to the person and property of the members of the two communities and to ensure that their human rights were not violated. In addition, the Commission called upon the State Government to take prompt action to restore normalcy. It also urged the Ministry of Home Affairs to ensure prompt and necessary action by the State Government.

The "Committee for Citizenship" of the Chakmas in Arunachal Pradesh also sent a representation to the Commission asserting that while the Chakmas and Hajong communities settled in other North-Eastern States of India were enjoying the full-fledged rights of Indian Citizenship, those settled in Arunachal Pradesh were not being granted such citizenship because o the State Government's adamant opposition to the Central Government's policies in this respect in consequence, the Committee stated, human rights abuses were being constantly perpetrated against the Chakmas in Arunachal Pradesh. In respect of this complaint, too, the Commission called for reports from the State Government and the Home Ministry.

The State Government stated that there is no threat to the life and property of members of the two communities in question and that an adequate police force has been deployed to protect them. The Home Ministry reported that the State Government had been advised to ensure normalcy in the law and order situation as also to supply needed essential commodities and medical facilities to the Chakma and Hajong refugees. As regards the granting of citizenship to them, the Home Ministry reported that the matter was under consideration, in consultation with the State Government.

The Chairperson addressed a further letter on 7 December 1994 to the Union Home Minister and also to the Chief Minister, Arunachal Pradesh, stressing the need to provide adequate protection to the members of these two communities with a view not only towards instilling a sense of safety and security in their minds but also in order to ensure that their human rights were fully respected.

Enhanched compensation to persons affected by the activities of extremists in Andhra Pradesh

During the Commission's visit to certain districts in Andhra Pradesh in August 1994, a number of representations were received by the Commission from the victims of Naxalite and extremist activities. A majority of these representations sought adequate compensation to the next of kin of the deceased, or for those permanently disabled or seriously injured at the hands of extremists. A number of other petitioners sought profection for their life and property, consequent upon violence resulting from the actions of extremists.

By an order of the Government of Andhra Pradesh issued on 2 April 1991, compensation to victims of Naxalite violence was paid at the rate of Rs. 25,000/- in case of death, Rs. 10,000/- in case of permanent incapacitation, and Rs. 5,000/- in case of injury. The Commission discussed this issue with the Chief Minister of Andhra Pradesh, stressing the inadequacy of these levels of compensation. The Commission impressed upon him the need to increase the amounts on the lines of a similar scheme existing in Punjab. As a result of this discussion, the State Government issued an Order on 20 August 1994 enhancing the compensation to Rs. 50,000/-, 20,000/- and 10,000/- in respect of the three situations mentioned above, with the order to come into effect from 1 April 1994.

The Commission, however, in its proceedings held in September 1994, insisted that a uniform rate of compensation be adopted in respect of the three situations, namely, death, permanent disablement and serious injury, irrespective of and without reference to the date of occurrence of the event on the ground. It was of the view that a "widow" of a person killed on 31.1.1994 and another killed on 1.4.1994 should stand on no different footing:. The State Government thereafter amended its Order on 21 November 1994 providing for payment of the enhanced compensation of Rs. 50,000/- in all cases of death, effective from 1 January 1991 instead of 1 April 1994.

The Commission them took up 616 petitions which had been received by it during its visit to Andhra Pradesh, and that requested enhanced compensations. It forwarded these complaints to the Collectors of Karimnagar, Nalgonda, Warangal and Medak districts with a direction to pay the compensations, at the enhanced rates, to the affected petitioners of their respective districts, before 31 March 1995. Action-taken reports from the Collectors of these districts are awaited.

Another batch of 140 petitions were forwarded by the Commission to the State Government with the direction that necessary protection be provided to the petitioners against extremist violence. The State Government had sent a report recently, furnishing a statement giving the details of the protection provided to these petitioners.

Complaint of Dr. Subramanian Swamy, President, Janata Party, alleging systematic denial of permission to him and to his party, by the Government of Tamil Nadu, to hold public meetings in the State

On receipt of a complaint from Dr. Subramanian Swamy, President, Janata Party alleging the systematic denial of permission to him and to his party, by the Government of Tamil Nadu and its officers, to hold public meetings in the State, the Commission fixed 17 February 1995 as a date of hearing. Notices were accordingly issued to both the parties, namely, the complainant Dr. Subramanian Swamy and the State of the Tamil Nadu. The complainant appeared in person on the said date, but there was no appearance on behalf of the State of Tamil Nadu. On the basis of the papers available, the matter was disposed of by the Commission by its order of 24 February 1995 with the following recommendations:

(a) application made for permission should ordinarily be disposed of within three days of making;
(b) permission granted could be recalled, if there be sufficient and justifiable cause of be stated;
(c) in such cases, where request for permission is not intended to be accorded, the applicant may be given an opportunity of interacting of with the authority either in person or through writing;
(d) granting of permission should be the rule, subject to the requirement of maintenance of law and order.

The Commission has been informed by the complainant that the recommendations issued by it are now being followed by the State Government.

Year 1995-96

End to discriminatory treatment in the remission of unexpired portion of life sentence in Orissa

Upon the intervention of the Commission, the Orissa Government has remitted the unexpired portion of thesentence passed on a life convict, Gopal Banerjee, and has ordered his release. The wife of Gopal Banerjee complained to be Commission stating that discriminatory treatment was shown by the Orissa Government in regard to her husband's premature release.

In a sessions trial in 1975, four persons, Gopal Banerjee, Ashit Dey, Amulya Rai and one other were convicted and were sentenced to life imprisonment by the Sessions Judge of Cuttack, Gopal Banerjee was lodged in cusody at the Dum Dum Central Jail, Calcutta. Ashit Dey and Amulya Rai were released prematurely in 1989 and 1993 respectively, upon the State Government remitting the unexpired portion of their sentence.

In response to a writ petition filed by the wife of Gopal Banerjee in 1992, the Supreme Court had asked the Orissa Government to take a decision on his release. Thereupon, the StateGovernment, which considered the mercy petition of Smt. Gopal Banerjee praying for premature release of her husband, had rejected the same.

The Commission examined the matter following an application of Smt. Gopal Banerjee and felt that the State Government's stand in the case affected the right to equlity of treatment.

The Chairperson of the Commission, in a letter to the Chief Minsiter of Orissa, drew his attention to the fact that Gopal Banerjee, like the other co-accused, was from West Bengal. As he had spent more than 20 years in a jail situated in another State, there was no occasion for the Orissa police to make any assessment of the possible impact of his release prematurely. While considering the claim of Gopal Banerjeefor premature release, the fact that two other co-accusedhad been so released, had perhaps not been kept in view, the letter noted. The State Government responded in December 1995 saying that the unexpired portion of the sentence passed on Gopal Banerjee has been remitted, and orders passedfor his release.

Compensation to the next of kin of riot victims in Gujarat

Upon the intervention of the Commission, a sum of Rs. 2,00,000/- was sanctioned to the heirs of Gulab Nabi Bandey and Zahir Ahmad Bandey, who died in communal riots in Surat, Gujarat, following the demolition of Babri Masjid.

The Commission received arepresentation from Bashir Ahmed Mir of Jammu & Kashmir stating that thedeceasedwere his relatives and that they were trading in Kashmiri shawls in Surat, Gujarat where they were killed in communal riots which broke out in December 1993.

Giving details of the efforts made by him to find the where abouts of his uncle and cousin, Bashir Ahmed Mir complained of inaction on the part of the concerned government authorities and prolonged delay in the dispensation of justice.

The Commission issued notices to the Jammu & Kashmir Government and to the Gujarat Government. The Home Department of Gujarat reported to the Commission that the matter pertained to the Revenue Department and that it was transmitting the papers to the latter for necessary action.

As no response came from the State Government for about four months, the Commission issued summons to the Chief Secretary and the Revenue Secretary to appear in person before the Commission, which they did. Following that hearing, the Gujarat Government reported to the Commission that ex-gratia payment of Rs, 2,00,000/- had been sanctioned to each of the heirs of the decased.

Year 1997-98

Release of foreign nationals in Indian jails

A complaint was received from Shri Sazwara Khan and four other nationals of Pakistan, alleging that they were confined illegally and unconstitutionally by the Government of Rajasthan under Section 100 Cr.P.C. and were confined in different jails of Rajasthan. The Commission took ognisance of the matter and issued notice to the Government of Rajasthan and the Government of India.

The External Affairs Ministry vide its communication dated 24 December 1997 intimated that the Government had decided to repatriate Shri Sazwara Khan in view of his advanced age.

Right to form Association: State Government's orders prohibiting teachers and other faculty members of Universities from associating with Andhra Pradesh Civil Liberties Committee (APCLC) : Andhra Pradesh

The Commission received a number of complaints from NGOs and academic institutions from India and abroad stating that the Government of Andhra Pradesh issued a circular ordering universities to prevent teachers and other faculty members of Universities from associating themselves with the Andhra Pradesh Civil Liberties Committee (APCLC). It was alleged that such a directive was violative of the Freedom of Association and Political Rights. Five academics of Osmania Krishnadevaraya and Nagarjuna Universities were asked to resign from the membership of APCLC, a non-governmental organisation. The State Government had issued such a direction, apparently based on a rule that bars university employees from participating in political activities. It was stated by the NGOs that membership of a human rights organisation could not be construed as political activity.

The Commission took ognisance of the matter and issued notice to the Chief Secretary, Andhra Pradesh. In response to the notice from the Commission, the Secretary, Department of Higher Education, Government of Andhra Pradesh sent a communication to the Commission informing it that the Government had reviewed the whole matter and decided not to take any further action in pursuance of the letter issued by the Education Department, Government of Andhra Pradesh.

Killing of 29 bus Passengers in Peren Sub-Division: Nagaland

Proceedings in this case were initiated on a communication from the Chairperson of the Assam State Human Rights Commission. This related to an incident in which 29 persons had lost their lives in an attack by certain insurgent elements when the latter intercepted a Dimapur bound passenger-bus and opened indiscriminate fire on the passengers. On notice being issued, the Ministry of Home Affairs, Government of India, submitted a report. The report did not dispute that the deaths occurred as a result of violent activities of insurgents. On examination of the report, the Commission considered it reasonable to infer that the State Government had failed to protect the lives of these innocent citizens. It further observed that the State Government itself had sanctioned ex-gratia relief of Rs.10,000/- to the dependents of the deceased and Rs.5,000/- to those severely injured and Rs.2,500/- to those who had sustained minor injuries.

The Commission felt that ex-gratia payment of Rs.10,000/- sanctioned to each of the families of the deceased was not adequate; and recommended to the State Government that it enhance the quantum of ex-gratia relief from Rs.10,000/- to Rs.50,000/- to the families of the 29 persons killed in the incident and make the payment accordingly.

The State Government of Nagaland intimated that the amounts of ex-gratia payments of Rs.50,000/- each to the next to kin of 28 victims have since been made on 1.4.1998.

Year 1998-99

Protection of right of victims in cases of industrial hazards: Uttar Pradesh (Case No.19900/24/97-98)

The petitioner, Ms. Subhashini Ali, drew the attention of the Commission to the occurrence of a ghastly incident in the factory premises of Jyoti capsules on 4 January 1998 in Kanpur, in which 8 workers had lost their lives. The accident occurred due to an explosion caused by the leakage of an inflammable chemical, hexane. The petitioner alleged that the factory had resumed production without taking due care of safety conditions.

The Special Rapporteur of the Commission investigated the case and stated that the accident was the result of criminal negligence by the factory owner in handling and storing explosive chemicals and that he had failed to maintain safe working conditions in the factory. A major contributory factor was supervisory lapse on the part of the Inspectorate of Factories. The Commission directed the Government of Uttar Pradesh to finalise criminal cases registered against the owner and also ordered that the factory should not be permitted to resume production without complying with all safety requirements. The Labour Department of the Government was directed to investigate the reasons for the supervisory lapse and to penalise the culprits. The District Magistrate, Kanpur was directed to ensure early payment of all financial benefits in case of death and injuries. The intervention of the Commission brought about the award of immediate relief of Rs. 5000/- each to the victims apart from the compensation which was sanctioned to them by the State.

Comment

The Directive Principles contained in Art. 48A of the Constitution direct the State to endeavour to protect and improve the environment.

Principle 13 of the UN Declaration on Environment and Development (Rio Declaration, 1992) proclaims that States shall develop national laws regarding liability and compensation for the victims of pollution and other environmental damage. The Public Liability Insurance Act 1991 is in consonance with the spirit of principle 13 of the Rio Declaration, in as much as it aims at providing for public liability insurance for the purpose of providing immediate relief to persons affected by accident occurring while handling any hazardous substance or matters connected therewith or incidental thereto. Under the Act, any person handling any hazardous substance is required to take out insurance policies so that he is insured against liability to give relief in case of death or injury to a person, or damage to any property, arising from an accident occurring while handling any hazardous substance. This Act has been enacted subsequent to the Bhopal Gas leak disaster where MIC leaked from the plant of Union Carbide India Ltd. And caused the death of over 3000 persons and serious injuries to a large number of others.

It is important to mention here that in the case brought before the Commission by Ms. Subhashini Ali, negligence was involved on the part of the factory owner. In such cases, exemplary compensation and damages are to be awarded to the victims. The Supreme Court of India has modified the English rule of strict liability in M.C. Mehta vs. UOI (AIR 1987 S.C. 1087) and has laid down the concept of 'absolute liability' in the case of industrial hazards, even though there might not have been any negligence on the part of the enterprise owner. By providing additional relief and ordering the expeditious criminal trial of the culprits, the Commission has kept in mind the constitutional obligations of the State and also the UN Declaration on the Environment and Developments.

Year 1999-2000

Negligence of a Medical Officer : Uttar Pradesh Case No.7122/24/98-99

Smt. Ram Kumari in her complaint to the Commission stated that her late husband, Shri Krishan Kumar, died in a road accident when his truck collided with a tree and caught fire thereafter. The police prepared an inquest report and sent the burnt body of her husband for post-mortem to Rai Bareilly. A team of three doctors performed the autopsy of the dead body on 17 May 1998 but were unable to give an opinion on the cause and time of death and, therefore, sought the opinion of the State Medico-Legal Expert. The opinion was delayed by six months, as a result of which the complainant was made to rush from Allahabad to Rai Bareilly to plead with the authorities to hand over the remains of her husband's dead body for performing the last rites. The complainant sought the Commission's assistance in getting the dead body released early.

In response to a notice issued by the Commission, the Special Secretary (Medical), Government of Uttar Pradesh, by his letter dated 28 December 1998 admitted the delay in the submission of papers to the Medico-Legal Expert. The Medico-Legal Expert examined the case and found radio opaque shadows of metallic density and referred the matter for examination to check for presence of gunpowder. However, these papers remained lying in the office for about three months. The report of the Medico-Legal Expert also indicated certain deficiencies in the inquest report, site-plan and photographs of the truck. After the report, the bodily remains of the deceased were re-examined on 13 January 1999 by the Chief Medical Officer, Rae Bareilly who did not find metallic particles as indicated in the report of the Medico-Legal Expert.

A supplementary report was filed by the Special Secretary (Medical), Government of Uttar Pradesh stating that the remains of the deceased were handed over to the complainant on 15 February 1999. By a final report dated 19 April 1999, the Commission was informed that the Chief Medical Officer (CMO) Rae Bareilly was found negligent for not obtaining the Medico Legal Expert Report promptly. An adverse remark had also been noted in his confidential file.

From the reports, the Commission noted that the bodily remains of the deceased were handed over to the complainant nine months after the death; this had resulted in mental agony to her and forced her to rush to Rai Bareilly to contact the authorities. The Commission held that this avoidable delay was directly attributable to the gross negligence of the State authorities at different levels. In the circumstances, the Commission recommended the payment of interim compensation of Rs.10,000/- to the complainant by the Government of Uttar Pradesh within two months. The State Government has since paid the compensation.

Death of an Innocent person owing to Negligence of State Electricity Board : Bihar Case No. 2010/4/98-99

The Commission received a complaint from Smt. Ranjana Singh alias Ranju, a resident of Daltonganj, Palamu, Bihar alleging that on 2 August 1996, her husband Satyabrat Narain Singh came in contact with a live electric wire lying in front of Morehouse, Patna as a result of which he was electrocuted and died. She attributed the death of her husband to the negligence of the Bihar State Electricity Board (BSEB). She also stated that BSEB had failed to award her any compensation though in a similar case the Supreme Court had awarded compensation. The complainant stated that she was facing an acute financial crisis and was on the verge of starvation and was unable to meet the expenditure required for the education of her minor sons. She sought an inquiry into the matter and award of suitable compensation to her.

In response to the notice, the Government of Bihar in its report stated that the late Satyabrat Narain Singh, husband of the complainant, died of electrocution at Rajinder Nagar, Patna for which a case dated 5 August 1996 was registered in Kadam Kuan Police Station, Patna. The report also brought out that the post-mortem on the body of the deceased was conducted at Patna Medical College and Hospital and that the cause of death was stated to be electrocution. The report of the Secretary, BSEB confirmed that the L.T. line and live wire of the Transmission/Distribution line of the Bihar State Electricity Board was broken due to a heavy storm on 2 August 1996 and that Shri Satyabrat Narain Singh touched the live wire and died due to electrocution. The report also stated that no compensation was paid to the wife of the deceased by the BSEB, as her husband died following a natural calamity.

The Commission noted that there was no material on record to show that the storm, which had allegedly led to the breaking of the live wire, was of such intensity or unprecedented severity in nature that the concerned authorities responsible for the installation and maintenance of the transmission/ distribution lines could not have foreseen a storm of the intensity that occurred. On the contrary, all transmission/ distribution lines lying there, by their very hazardous nature, were expected to have been so installed as to withstand the vagaries of nature/ weather like rain, high velocity wind/storm, etc. Even if it were assumed that the storm was in fact of such a high intensity as could have broken the live wire, the Commission observed that an imperative obligation was cast upon the concerned authorities to take immediate measures to switch off the power so as to prevent disastrous consequences. There was also nothing on record to show that adequate safeguards were taken by the BSEB to guard the live wire of the transmission/distribution line falling on the ground, even if it had broken down as a result of the alleged storm. The authorities of the State Electricity Board had a duty to see that the live wire was removed immediately and/or that the power was switched off so as to make a public place safe. The Commission thus noted that there was a clear breach of duty on the part of the State Electricity Board which had resulted in the death of Shri Satyabrat Narain Singh. The Commission was, therefore, of the opinion that the State and Electricity Board Authorities were liable to the victim for damages.

The Commission accordingly recommended a compensation of Rs. 2,00,000 to the wife of the deceased by way of immediate interim relief, without prejudice or detriment to her right to claim damages under the civil law. However, in case such a claim is put forth, the Commission said that the concerned adjudicatory authority might take into account the payment of the above interim relief to the complainant while awarding damages. Further, the Bihar State Electricity Board was directed to constitute an inquiry into the matter and to frame adequate regulations/ guidelines to take appropriate and prompt measures to prevent the recurrence of such incidents involving human life.

The compliance report with regard to the payment of compensation has been received in the Commission.

Comment

In Manohar Lal Sobha Ram Gupta vs. M.P. Electricity Board (1975 ACJ 494), the High Court held that it was negligence to omit to use all reasonable means to keep electricity from harming a person. The standard of care required was held to be high owing to the inherently dangerous nature of electricity, and the burden of proving that there was no negligence was on the authorities. The principle was reiterated in Angoori Devi vs. Municipal Corporation, Delhi (AIR 1998 Delhi 305) and in Padma Behari vs. Orissa State Electricity Board (AIR 1992 Orissa 68).

The main plank of defence of the State Government and BSEB was that it was an Act of God (Vis major). The Commission was, however, of the considered view that the said defence was not available to them for the following reasons:

(i) Act of God (Vis major) is defined to be such a direct, violent, sudden and irresistible act of nature as could not, by any amount of ability, have been foreseen, or if foreseen, could not by any amount of human care and skill have been resisted.

(ii) Vis major, to afford a defence, must be the proximate cause, the causa causans, and not merely a causa quanon of the damage complained of. The mere fact that vis major co-existed with or followed on the negligence is not an adequate defence. Before an Act of God may be admitted as an excuse, the defendant must himself have done all that he was bound to do.

A more stringent rule of strict liability than the rule in Rylands vs. Fletcher was laid down by the Supreme Court recently in the case of M.C. Mehta vs. Union of India. The case related to the harm caused by escape of Oleum gas from one of the units of Shriram Foods and Fertilizer Industries. The Court held that the rule of Rylands vs. Fletcher which was evolved in the 19th century did not fully meet the needs of a modern industrial society with highly developed scientific knowledge and technology where hazardous or inherently dangerous industries were necessary to be carried on as part of the development programme and that it was necessary to lay down a new rule to adequately deal with problems arising in an industrialised economy. The Court laid down the rule as follows: Where an enterprise is engaged in a hazardous or inherently dangerous activity and harm results to anyone on account of an incident in the operation of such hazardous or inherently dangerous activity resulting, for example, in escape of toxic gas, the enterprise is strictly and absolutely liable to compensate all those who are affected by the accident and such liability is not subject to any of the exceptions which operate vis-à-vis the tortuous principle of strict liability under the rule in Rylands vs. Fletcher. The Court earlier pointed out that this duty is 'absolute and non-delegable' and the enterprise cannot escape liability by showing that it had taken all reasonable care and there was no negligence on its part. The bases of the new rule as indicated by the Supreme Court are two: (1) If an enterprise is permitted to carry on an hazardous or inherently dangerous activity for its profit, the law must presume that such permission is conditional on the enterprise absorbing the cost of any incident (including indemnification of all those who suffer harm in the accident) arising on account of such hazardous or inherently dangerous activity as an appropriate item of its over-heads; and (2) the enterprise alone has the resources to discover and guard against hazardous or dangers and to provide warning against potential hazards. (AIR 1987 SC 965).

Year 2000-01

Killing of 35 Members of Sikh Community in Anantnag District of Jammu & Kashmir by Militants. (Case No. 206/9/1999-2000)

The Commission took suo motu ognisance of a newspaper report in 'The Times of India' dated 22 March 2000 in respect of the killing of

35 persons of the Sikh community in Anantnag District, Jammu & Kashmir by militants.

Upon notice being issued to the State Government, a report was received saying that a Commission of Inquiry consisting of Justice Shri S.R. Pandian, a retired Judge of Supreme Court, had been appointed by the Government of Jammu & Kashmir to enquire into causes and circumstances leading to the event of firing on 3 April 2000 which led to the death of 8 persons, justification for use of force and fixation of responsibility for use of excessive force, if any.

On considering this report, the Commission observed that Justice Pandian Commission of Inquiry had not been mandated to enquire into either the incident of 20 March 2000 in respect of the massacre of 35 innocent Sikhs or the incident of 25 March 2000 in which reportedly 5 foreign mercenaries were killed by the Security Forces.

A subsequent report submitted by the Director General of Police, Jammu & Kashmir indicated that a case had been registered in respect of the killing of the 35 Sikhs and that investigation was in progress. The report further indicated that, of the twenty accused persons identified in connection with the killing of 35 Sikhs, 6 were killed in subsequent encounters; 2 were further detained under the Public Safety Act and 12 were absconding. A chargesheet had been filed in the case on 13 November 2000. The report stated that three Pakistan nationals belonging to Lashkar-e-Toiba had confessed their involvement in the killings. The State Government had made adequate security arrangements for the protection of villagers residing in vulnerable areas and provided an ex-gratia payment of Rs. 1 lakh to the next of kin of the deceased and Rs. 75,000 to those permanently disabled.

The Commission had directed the State Government to furnish a report on the action taken on the findings and recommendations of the Justice Shri S.R.Pandian Commission, as well as to furnish a progress in respect of the case before CJM Anantnag in respect of the killings of 5 persons on 5 March 2000, allegedly in a fake encounter.

The State Government in its letter dated 4 July 2001, informed the Commission that it had decided to accept the report of the Justice S.R.Pandian Committee of Inquiry in toto, in terms of the recommendations of the Commission. It further informed the Commission that the concerned personnel of Jammu and Kashmir police personnel had been formally charge sheeted and a full-fledged departmental enquiry was being conducted. The State Government added thazt an FIR had been registered against them and that a special team of investigators had been appointed to complete the investigation. In respect of the police personnel of the Central Security Forces, the Ministry of Home Affairs, Government of India, had been requested to take disciplinary action. Ex-gratia relief at Rs. 1 lakh to the next-of-kin of each of the deceased, and at Rs.5,000/- per head to the injured persons, had been paid by the concerned District Magistrate.

In view of this report, the Commission closed the case before it in its proceedings recorded on 25 July 2002.

Year 2001-02

Death due to Electrocution — Strict Liability of the State: Jharkhand (Case No.1509/4/2000-2001)

The Commission took cognisance of a complaint from Maku Murmur, resident of Dumka, Jharkhand alleging that her husband, Babu Ram, had died on 9 July 2000 as a result of being electrocuted by a live transmission wire. She stated that the death was the result of negligence of the Bihar State Electricity Board.

Upon a notice sent to the Chairman, Bihar State Electricity Board as well as to the District Magistrate, Dumka, it was confirmed that the victim had died after being electrocuted. It was, however, contended that a severe storm had occurred on the date of the incident and that deceased might have come into contact with the electricity wires, which would have fallen to the ground because of the storm and rain. It was stated that the death had not resulted from the fault of any person of the electricity department or any other authority.

The Commission, while over-ruling the contentions of the State, held that the Bihar State Electricity Board could not be absolved of its responsibility of properly maintaining the whole system; that rain and storms were not an unusual phenomenon and care was needed to avoid such situations. Accordingly, the Commission in its proceedings dated 29 August 2001 issued a notice to the State of Bihar to show cause why immediate interim relief u/s 18(3) of the Protection of Human Rights Act, 1993 be not awarded to the petitioner.

The Bihar State Electricity Board sought a review of the matter on two grounds, namely, (i) that the State of Bihar had been bifurcated with the formation of the State of Jharkhand with effect from 15 November 2000 and that this had transferred the liability to the State of Jharkhand; and, (ii) that the death of Babu Ram Tudu was in an accident, resulting from heavy rains and a storm which led to the snapping of a hightension wire and the lowering of its height.

The Commission did not find any justification in these submissions. In a decision of 11 January 2002, it referred to the doctrine of strict liability recognised and applied by the Apex Court in a similar situation in the case of M.P. Electricity Board vs. Shail Kumari and Others. The Commission accordingly recommended the payment of Rs.2 lakhs by the Bihar State Electricity Board as immediate interim relief u/s 18(3) of the Protection of Human Rights Act, 1993 to the next of kin of the deceased.

As regards the bifurcation of the State of Bihar following the creation of the State of Jharkhand, the Commission held that this was now a matter for adjustment between the two States, it did not however exonerate the State of Bihar of its liability to a third party, which had been incurred on a date prior to bifurcation of the State.

In view of the compliance report received from the Bihar State Electricity Board, the case was closed on 29 January 2003.

Cases where decision of the Commission has been upheld by Court — Shri Mohammed Khan: Haryana (Case No.7/21/96-LD)

This case relates to a complaint received from one Sher Mohammed Khan, alleging beating and torture at the hands of police officials in Gurgaon, Haryana. The Commission called for a report from the DGP, Haryana and after considering the report, recommended on 20 February 1998 that a case be registered against the SHO Police Station, Sadar, Gurgaon and compensation in the amount of Rs.25,000 be paid to the complainant. Feeling aggrieved by the recommendation of the Commission, Shri Sheodan Singh, the then SHO PS Sadar, Gurgaon, filed a petition Crl. Misc. No.12078/98 — Sheodan Singh vs. State of Haryana and others before the High Court of Punjab and Haryana. The High Court, by its order dated 30 November 2000, dismissed the petition directing that it would be wholly inappropriate to exercise the extraordinary jurisdiction of the court u/s 482 of the Code of Criminal Procedure in the instant case. Shri Sheodan Singh then moved a special leave petition in the Supreme Court against the order of the High Court of Punjab and Haryana in Crl. Misc. No.12078 – M/ 1998. The Supreme Court took the view that since the police had registered an FIR against Shri Sheodan Singh, and that FIR had been transformed into a final report and the Magistrate had taken action on the said final report, it did not feel inclined to interfere in the matter and disposed of it accordingly. The amount of compensation has since been paid by the State Government.

Shocking cases has issued notices to the IG (prison) and Chief Secretary, Assam asking them to submit reports of five undertrial prisoners presently lodged at the LGB Regional Institute of Mental Health, Tezpur, Assam.

The five cases are that of Machang Lalung who has been a undertrial prisoner for 54 years, Khalilur Rehman who has been lodged in the Mental Hospital for 35 Years, Anil Kumar Burman a undertrial prisoner for 33 years, Sonamani Deb a undertrial prisoner for 32 years and a woman Parbati Mallik who has been a undertrial prisoner for 32years.

Killing of 15 villagers by naxalites in Chhattisgarh

The Commission has asked for comments from the Chief Secretary, Government of Chhattisgarh on a news report which said 15 villagers were killed by naxalites on 29 April 2006 in the State. Taking suo-motu cognisance based on the report, which said out of 52 villagers of Chattisgarh staying in Dornapal relief camp, 15 were killed by the naxalities after being abducted. These villagers had been participating in a peace campaing against the Maoists in Dantewada and Bijapur Districts.

After observing the contents of the news report, the Commission said that if the contents are true, there is a serious issue of violation of human rights.

CGHS case

The Commission has asked for comments from Secretary, Ministry of Health and Family Welfare and Director General, Health Services on a news report, which said that Central Government pensioners at Noida are supplied medicines 8 to 10 days after they have been indented. Taking suo-motu cognisance of a media report the Commission observed that the Contents, if true, raise serious issue of violation of right to health.

The press report had also said the medicines were in short supply. According to the Secretary, Central Government Pensioners' Welfare Association, the CGHS authorities had appointed a chemist based in Ashok Vihar, New Delhi making it difficult for old and sick pensioners to travel far to get the urgent medicines. The report further highlighted that retired MPs were getting medicines on top priority on the same day following arrangements made by the Additional Director.

Police firing on students in Meghalaya

The Meghalaya Government has informed the Commission that an amount of Rs. 5 lakh each had been paid as a special assistance to the family of those killed in police firing in Tura and Williamnagar districts of the State on 30 September 2005. The State Government also said that this was in addition to the ex-gratia payment of Rs.10 lakh.

The Commission was also informed that Rs. 10 lakh had been sanctioned by the State Government for meeting the hospital bills of those injured. The Commission, reacting to a media report, which said 11 students were killed and a number of others injured in police firing in the two districts last year, had asked for comments from the State Chief Secretary. The news story published in the Pioneer had state that the firing was unprovoked.

Taking cognisance of the matter, the Commission shout comments from the Chief Secretary, Meghalaya. Following this, the State Government constituted a Commission of Inquiry. As per the report of the State Government, the rallies were organized by the Garo Students' Union to oppose plans by the State Government to shift the headquaters of the Meghalaya Board of Secondary Education from Tura to Shillong. A day earlier, the District Administration of WestGaro Hills decided not to allow the rally and withdrew the permission granted earlier with prior intimation and announcement on the issue. Williamnagar district administration also promulgated prohibitary orders. However at both the places a large crowd gathered the next day and did not disperse despite the warning of the District Magistrates. Soon the crowd became violent and pelted stones injuring the Magistrates and a number of police personnel. The police used teargas followed by the lathi charge. This however failed to disperse the unlawful assembly and ultimately police resorted to firing. Which resulted in the death of 11 people.

After going through the report of the State Government, the Commission held, that in view of the appropriate action taken by the State Government with respect to the ex-gratia compensation, no further intervention is called for.

The asks Chief Secretary, Delhi Government for Factual report on 55 Child Labours

The Commission has asked for the Chief Secretary, Delhi Government for a factual report on 55 child labours who were rescued from embroidery units in South Delhi. Taking suo-motu ognisance of the news reports, which appeared on 9 January 2006, and said that these children belonging to Bihar, West Bengal and Uttar Pradesh were rescued by the authorities during raids with the assistance of Bonded Labour Liberation Front Activists.

The Commission, after observing the contents of the report, said if found true it raises the issue of bonded Child Labour, which is worst affront to human dignity and constitutes an offence under the Bonded Labour Act. Taking note that the children were lodged at the Ashraya Kendra in the capital, the Commission further said that the matter could not be stopped at mere lodging the rescued children in the Kendra. The Commission said that the news reports should be sent to Chief Secretary, Delhi Government, Commissioner Police, Delhi, Labour Secretary, Delhi Government, for factual report in four weeks. It also asked the Delhi Government to inform the Commission the rescued children.

NHRC orders compensation to the next of kin of 45 more persons in the Punjab Mass Cremation Case

The national Human Rights Commission has directed the Punjab Government to pay Compensation to the next of kin of 45 more persons who died in police custody in its anti-terror drive during 1984-I994. The Counsel for State Government of Punjab appeared before the Commission and informed that on scrutiny of record, 45 more deceased have been identified who fall within the parameters of the order of NHRC dated 11 November 2004. in its first order dated 11 November 2004, the Commission had Granted a compensation of Rs. 2.5 Lakhs each to the next of kin of 109 persons who admittedly died in police custody. The Commission found the state of Punjab accountable and responsible for the infringement of the right to life of the deceased. Again on 8th March 2006 the Commission granted compensation in respect of 38 more persons. In this regard, the counsel for the State of Punjab informed the Commission that the state Government has already deposited Rs.95 Lakhs with the Deputy Commissioner concerned as compensation for disbursal to the next of kin of 38 deceased. Out of this, the next of kin of 20 deceased have been paid the amount while the process for disbursal in respect of 18 was on.

Accordingly the Commission has directed the State of Punjab to pay compensation of Rs. 2.5 Lakhs each to the next of kin of 45 deceased. With this, the Commission was so far provided compensation to 194 people.

Sex determination tests by doctors in Rajasthan

The Commission has taken a serious view of a news report which appeared in the Hindu dated 5 May 2006 and revealed that 21 doctors in Rajasthan have been involved in sex determination tests. A TV news channel under its sting operation recently exposed these doctors. A number of women groups had been demonstrating immediate action against the accused doctors. These groups alleged that the State Government had failed in implementing the Pre-Conception and Pre-Natal Diagnostic Techniques (Regulation of Prevention of Misuse) Act, 1994. The report also said that 19 of these doctors had agreed to abort foetus after sex determination and three of them were posted in Government Hospital, Chittorgarh.

The Commission, after observing the contents of the report, said it raises a serious human rights issue concerning gender discrimination. It has asked for comments from the Chief Secretary, Government of Rajasthan on the report.

NHRC calls for report from UP Government regarding Meerut fire tragedy

Taking suo-Motu cognisance of reports in the print and electronic media of the fair tragedy in Victoria Park in Meerut, Utter Pradesh on 10 April 2006, the National Human Rights Commission (NHRC) has called for a report from the Chief Secretary and DGP, Uttar Pradesh.

One of the newspapers had reported on 12 April 2006 that nearly 50 persons were Killed and 110 injured in the tragedy. However, the administration, it quoted, had put the death toll at 34 and claimed that 27 bodies had been identified. Of the 40 injured sent to various hospitals in Delhi, 2 had died at the Safdarjung hospital. Further the news report mentioned allegations of laxity on the part of the local administration in ensuring that the fair organizers obtained proper fire safety clearance. Relatives of those killed, it stated, had alleged that adequate fair-fighting equivalent was not in place despite the fact that highly combustible material was used as canopy for the pandals and even the floor of the premises was made of wood.

It was further reported that the organizers, Mrinal Events and expositions, had got 24 air-conditioning ducts installed in the three pandals and they kept just a single entry and exit to the fair premises. Besides, there was an eating joint inside the pandals that had LPG cylinders.

The Commission observed that the contents of the news item, if true, raise a serious issue of violation of human rights of the citizens. While calling for a report from the Chief Secretary and DGP, UP, it has asked that information be furnished to the Commission regarding:

- Number of persons who died in the incident and details thereof.
- Whether proper identification of the dead bodies had been made and if so whether the dead bodies had been handed over to the relatives of the deceased.
- Number of persons injured in the incident and details thereof.
- Whether proper medical arrangements had been made for providing medical aid to the injured at the State's cost.
- Whether any amount of relief was disbursed to the next of the kin of the deceased or the injured persons.
- Whether any person had been reported missing and if so, details thereof.
- What efforts had been made by the administration to trace out the missing persons.
- Whether all the requirements and necessary procedures were followed before granting license/permission for organizing the consumer exhibition.
- Whether any case had been registered with the police relating to the incident. If so, the status of investigation.

Commission calls for comments of J&K Government on minors languishing in Jammu Jails

The Commission has taken suo-motu Cognisance based on a distressing news story reported in the Kashmir Times Dated 14 March 2006 of 'Minors languishing in Jammu Jails'. It has directed that a copy of the news item be sent to be Chief Secretary, Jammu and Kashmir and I.G. (Prison), Jammu and Kashmir to look into the allegations contained in it and submit their comments.

The news report indicated that inmates belonging to various age groups are serving sentence in various jails in Jammu and Division. While some of them are above the age of 60 years.

Besides, there are inmates who are minors and languishing in the jails Jammu region. It was reported that the High Court Bar Association after visiting the jails of Jammu Division, had submitted a report in this regard. The report revealed that 275 people are lodged are lodged in court Bhalawal Jail under the Public Safety Act, PSA including Pakistani and Afghan Inmates.

Gowhar Amed Bhat, Wasim Raja Dar and Jaladdin Shah, all aged 16 years, are also lodged in the jails. The report further adds the persons who are serving their detention under PSA have been detained twice and thrice on the same ground which have already been relied upon by the concerned authority or have been quashed by the court. The courts also fixed dates for hearing beyond two months, which is alleged to be contrary to Cr PC. Harassment by the public prosecutors is also alleged, resulting in prolonged trial of the cases. The under trial prisoners are not being produced in various jails of Jammu division due to absence of escorts.

NHRC seeks report from AP Government on Stone Quarrying in Ambedkar Nagar

Acting on a news report which was telecast on E-TV, of the difficulties faced by the residents of Ambedkar Nagar near Warangal, in Andhra Pradesh due to a stone quarry, the National Human Rights Commission has asked the District Magistrate, Warangal, to send a factual report.

The TV channel had quoted the residents as complaining that blasting at the Quarries take place any time of the day and at night as will, due to which they are unable to sleep. Students/children also face problems. The blasting of the residents and the dust emitting from the stone, blasted by the quarry owners, had caused health hazards for the residents.

The Commission stated if the contents of the report are true, it raises serious issue of violation of human rights.

NHRC takes suo-motu cognisance of the marathon run by child Budhia Singh

The NHRC has taken suo-motu cognisance based on media reports that a 4-years old boy Budhia Shingh was made to run a 65 km marathon in Orissa on 2nd May 2006. The commission after considering the contents of various reports appearing in different newspapers observed that if the contents of the reports are true it raises serious issue of violation of human rights of the child.

The newspapers said that the Orissa Government had imposed curbs on Budhia Singh's running, yet the district authorities in Puri allowed the boy to run th 65 kms distance in sweltering heat, as CRPF was associated with the event. Reports also said that the Sports Minister of Orissa Sh. Debashis Nayak, Archana Nayak, MP and and Additional

Director of CRPF Mr. B.S. Gill were present at the stadium in Bhubaneshwar to receive Budhia Singh.

It was also reported that before Budhia could run the full length he was exhausted and had to interrupt the run. Reacting to the incident a number of doctors had also voiced their concern saying, long distance runs could make heart beat faster to meet the extra oxygen need which could lead to heart failure. Further they said that Budhia's cartilages could face serious wear and tear, ultimately affecting his normal growth.

The Commission directed that the news report be sent to the Chief Secretary, Orissa Government and DG, CRPF, New Delhi for comments in two weeks.

Shocking cases of undertrial neglect in Tezpur Mental Hospital Comes to the attention of the NHRC

The Commission has issued notices to the IG (Prisons) and Chief Secretary, Assam asking them to submit reports of five undertrial prisoners presently lodged at the LGB Regional Institute of Mental Health, Tezpur, Assam.

The five cases are that of Machang Lalung who has been a undertrial prisoner for 54 years, Khalilur Rehman who has been lodged in the Mental Hospital for 35 years, Anil Kumar Burman a undertrial prisoner for 33 years, sonamani Deb a undertrial prisoner for 32 years and a women Paebati Mallik who has been a undertrial prisoner for 32 years.

The plight of these undertrial prisoners was reported to the NHRC by its Special Rapporteur Shri Chaman Lal who had visited the LGB Regional Institute of Mental Health on 31 March and 1 April 2005. While the Statw Government is yet to respond, the media has reported that Lalung has now been set free.

Maharastra government asked on follow-up action of rescued Child Labours

The Commission has asked the Chief Secretary, Maharastra as to whether action has been taken against the employers of the nearly 400 child labours of Madanpura in Central Mumbai who were rescued recently. It has directed that if any action has been taken against the employers, then the information on whether the childwelfare committee has made any orders, and if the children were produced before such a committee.

The Commission has taken suo-motu cognisance based on reports that appeared in the media on 2nd June 2005. it has directed that the news story be sent to the Chief Secretary, Maharastra to look into the allegations and submit his comments.

Comments sought from Delhi Government and DJB on sewer deaths

Taking suo-motu cognisance of the recent case of two Delhi Jal Board (DJB) workers dying in a sewer in Giri Nagar area of Delhi reported by the media on 25 May 2005, the Commisstion directed that the copies of the news reports be sent to the Chief Secretary, Delhi and the Chairman of the Delhi Jal Board to look into the allegations and submit their comments

It has also asked the Chief Secretary, Delhi and Chairman, Delhi Jal Board to state clearly whether the guidelines and safety codes for operation and maintenance of the sewage system issued by the Commission have been followed scrupulously or not. These guidelines and safety codes were conveyed to the Government of Delhi through a letter dated 18 October 2002. the Commission stated that it would also like to know what steps have been taken by the State Government of Delhi on the recommendations of the Commission in this regard.

Report on Child Workers in mines; NHRC takes suo-motu cognisance

The Commission has taken suo-motu cognisance of a news item quoting a report stating that lakhs of children are employed State Mines in Karnataka.

The news story appeared in a national daily dated 16th May 2005 wherein it was reported that an NGO named HAQ-Centre for Children Rights published a report alleging that several lakh children starting from the age of five are working in the mines at Hospet, Sandur and Ikal belt of Karnataka in horrible and hazardous conditions and in violation of child and Labour laws.

The Commission has directed that a copy of the news story be sent to the Chief Secretary, Karnataka and Secretary, Department of Women and Child Development, New Delhi to look the allegations and submit their comments.

Police Lathicharge Tribals including children in Orissa; NHRC asks its Special Rapporteur to enquire

Following the direction of the Commission, its Special Rapporteur, Shri A.B. Tripathy has begun enquiring into the allegation of lathicharge on tribals by police of Orissa, ehich was reported in the Asian Age Newspaper of 17 May 2005.

The new story had state that a group of tribals numbering around 5000 from the Kalinganagar area of Orissa had gathered on 9th May 2005 to protest against non-payment of dues for land acquired for the construction of Steel Plants and delay in rehabilitation by the State Government. They were brutally assaulted by the police and the barbarous, uncivilized act of police had left four tribals including two children dead.

UP Govt. asked to comment on Panchayat ordering rapist to web victim

The Commission has asked for the comments of the Chief Secretary , U.P. and District Magistrate, Pratapgarh, U.P. regarding a media report of a Panchayat ordering a rapist to web a victim.

The media had reported on 18 May 2005 that a village panchayat at Takia village in Partapgarh district of Uttar Pradesh had ordered a young man accused of raping a minor to marry her in order to make amends for his crime. The district police officials, it quoted, when contacted feigned complete ignorance about the incident.

AP Government submits report on tribal deaths in Visakhapatnam, says precaution and medical care taken

Deeply concerned by a report carried in a newspaper alleging deaths of hundreds of tribals in Visakhapatnam due to unknown factors and lack of medical facilities, the Commission taking suo-motu cognisance had sought the comments of the Chief Secretary, Andhra Pradesh.

The news report, which appeared in the Telugu daily 'Enadu' on 24 June 2004, had alleged that about 476 people had died over a three month period. These deaths, it stated, had taken place despite the State Government setting up health camps. The news story drew attention to the poor medical facilities in the Agency area.

In response, a report was received from the State Government of Andhra Pradesh from the Department of Home forwarding a report from the Principal Secretary, Health, Medical and Family Welfare Department, Government of Andhra Pradesh. The report refuted the changes that appeared in the newspaper. It outlined the measures the State Government had taken to control malaria especially after the issue was highlighted in the media.

Taking note of the report the Commission expressed hope that Government of Andhra Pradesh continue to take measures for providing medicare and to improve the health status of the tribal. It stated it expects that the state should take all such measures as are available to it, to prevent death of the tribals due to causes mentioned in the news report.

It has also pointed out that continuous monitoring of the facilities available in the sub-centres and PHCs particularly in the tribal areas would be useful.

Maharastra Government gives financial assistance in the case of suicide of farmers after intervention of NHRC

The Commission has requested the State Government of Maharastra that it would be desirable and appropriate to put in place a mechanism to ensure that there is no recurrence in future of farmers' suicides on account of drought or indebtedness. It also directed the State Government to take all appropriate steps to mitigate the hardships faced by farmers due to drought or indebtedness. The State Government had acknowledged that 140 farmers had committed suicide on account of indebtedness, drought ect. And who were found to be eligible for financial assistance of Rs. 1.00 lakh, an amount the Commission had recommended.

These directions were issued following the report by the State Government submitted to the Commission in connection with the death of 2 farmers by suicide. The deaths were reported in a national daily on 18 July 2004 and on the basis of which the NHRC had directed the Chief Secretary, Government of Maharashtra to take appropriate action and submit a report on the action taken.

Participants of 39th Professional Course for Foreign Diplomats organized by Ministry of External Affairs, Government of India Visited the Commission on 24 November 2005.

Schoolboy kept chained; NHRC asks for AP Govt.'s comments

The Commission has called for the comments of the Chief Secretary, Government of Andhra Pradesh regarding the news report of a schoolboy being kept chained.

The news story under the caption "Residential school keeps boy chained" carried in a national daily on 19 December 2005 stated "the management of a Rsidential Bridge School set up under Sarva Siksha Abhiyan, chained a second standard boy, Daniel, at Veldurthy to prevent him from running away from school.

The Commission observed that if the news report is true, it raises a serious issue of violation of rights of child by an NGO with a view to ensure fund to the school run by them under the Sarva Siksha Abhiyan claim.

Visually impaired students to get Braille Textbooks on time;12 States/UTs assure NHRC

The Commission was shocked to learn that blind students routinely receive their Braille textbooks towards the fag end of the academic sessions and what is worse is that a majority does not have access to these books at all. Upon delving deep into the matter, it was found that the non-availability of book is because many State and Union Territories had not established a Braille press, in places where it existed, obsolete technology and an inefficient distribution system together make the service as good as redundant.

The Commission has written to the Chief Ministers of all the state requesting them to ensure availability of Braille book to blind students. The Commission recommended that State Education Broads may take steps to print book in Braille and work on proper distribution system so that books prescribed by the Broads are available to visually impaired children at the brining of each academic session, at the same time as their sighted counter parts.

Responding positively to the suggestions of the Commission around 12 states and UT have assured it of timely availability of the Braille books. The Governments of Haryana, Madhya Pradesh, Uttar Pradesh, Rajastan, Jammu & Kashmir and Manipur have initiated positive steps. West Bengal, Gujarat and Karnataka are also amongst those who have developed the necessary capacity.

On similar lines, the Commission in working towards availability of a child appropriate sign language to be used in the education of children with hearing important in the country.

NHRC take suo-motu cognisance of reports of Mass grave in Gujarat

The Commission has taken suo-motu cognisance of media reports about the unearthing of a mass grave in Lunawada village of Panchmahal District of Gujarat. The Commission has sought reports from the State Government and CBI.

According the news reports eights skulls belived to be those of victims of post-Godhra riots of 2002, have been recovered. The bodies were reportedly discovered by the relatives of riot victims who claim there are at least 21 bodies in the grave. The State Government has confirmed the discovery.

Two kidnapped girls recovered by the NHRC's Investigation Team

Due to swift and timely action of the Commission, two kidnapped minor girls have been recovered from Mumbai and Pratapgarh, Uttar Pradesh.

The Commission took cognisance of a dated 7 October 2005 from a serving Head Constable of Border Security Force alleging that his two minor daughters aged 17 years and 13 years were kidnapped from the market of Kishan Ganj town (Bihar) on 19 September 2005 and the police despite a formal report, was not taking the required action.

The Commission Immediately deputed its Investigation Team, which conducted on-the-spot investigation at Varanasi, Amritsar, kishan Gandhi and Mumbai. During the course of investigation at Mumbai, the team came to know that both the girls have married persons from other communities and were staying at Pratapgarh, UP. As a result of the initiative of the NHRC team the girls were recovered on 14 December and 17 December 2005. The elder of the two was recovered from Mumbai while the younger one surrendered before the police in Pratapgarh. On the advice of the Commission the Bihar Police took possession of both the girls and produced them before the competent Court. The elder girl has been sent by the Court to Patna Remand Home, while her younger sister has been handed to the father for safe custody. The Bihar Police in investigation the matter further.

Non-availability of disabled friendly cars; NHRC seeks comments from the Government

Nothing the concern of disabled persons over the non-availability of disabled friendly care in India, the Commission has sought comments from the Government. The Commission took cognisance of a complaint from a person with physical disability that car manufacturing companies have discontinued manufacturing of the vehicles for physically challenged persons which is causing hindrance to those who want to be independent.

The Commission has forwarded a copy of the complaint to the Secretary, Ministry of heavy Industries for comments.

NHRC recommends post-quake measures to Centre and J&K Government

The NHRC made a series of recommendations to the Home Ministry has made a series of recommendations to the Home Ministry, Government of India and the Jammu and Kashmir government on post-quake measures. The recommendations are based on a report by its three-member team, which had toured the quake-affected areas of the J&K including Tangdhar and Uri. Parts of J&K has been devastated following an earthquake on the morning of October 2005.

Some of the key recommendations made by the NHRC to the Governments at the Centre and the State of J&K are

- Ensure equitable distribution of relief in kind.
- Consider having centralized collection and distribution centers at various place in the affected areas where relief material could be received from NGOs, civil society and other private agencies.
- Take steps to ensure that building material for repairing damaged property or restoring destroyed is available at the affected places.
- Where tents are not available, temporary shelter with all essential amenities be provided to the local population.
- Consider feasibility of construction houses in the affected areas with pre-fabricated building material.
- Prepare computerized list of orphaned children, widows and young girls.
- Prepare computerized list of dead and missing person to enable relief to next of kin.

The NHRC Team consisting Dr. G.S. Rajagopal, DG (I), Shri Ajit Bharihoke, Registrar (Law) and Shri A.K. Parashar, Dy. Registrar (Law) had visited Kashmir valley between 11 and 13 October 2005. It held meeting with the Chief Secretary, the DGP, Additional DGP (HR) and other State official beside the Corps Commander, the officials of the Central Government and some member of the civil society, including a sitting MLA and a former MLC. Apart from meeting officials of the Central agencies, security force and the civil society, the team visited the area of Tangdhar and Uri for on the spot assessment of relief and rehabilitation measures.

The team on its return apprised the Commission of the situation prevalent in the areas of Tangdhar and Uri in the and in the valley in general. The team found that the Central Government and State Government as also the security forces and civil society did rise to the occasion to provide some 'immediate relief' to the affected persons. In its assessment, the task of rehabilitation is a daunting one and more particularly, at this time of the year when the areas of Tangdhar and Uri are likely to be affected by the winter which is already seeting in. thus, immediate attention to the provision of shelter by the authorities is imperative. The team learned from the Civil Society as well as the authorities that some children had been apparently rendered orphans. According to the assessment made by the team the possibility of parents of some such children being still alive could not be ruled out as some injured persons has been shifted for treatment elsewhere.

NHRC takes suo-motu cognisance of students' death in police firing in Meghalaya

The Commission has taken suo-motu cognisance on the basis of a media report of the killing of students in police firing in Meghalaya on 30 September 2005. The news report published in a national daily on 1 October 2005 reported that at least 11 students were killed and nearly 90 wounded when police opened fire to quell thousands of student protestors who had taken to the streets in Tura and William Nagar districts of Meghalaya. The Chief Secretary, Maghalaya has been asked to give his comments.

Boy's torture: Haryana DGP asked to comment

The Commission has taken suo-motu cognisance of the alleged torture of children during enquiry conducted by the CID in Chandigarh, Haryana as reported by a section of the media on 9 October 2005. It was alleged that one of the boys, a 12-year-old called Mukesh, who is a resident of Jhuggi colony situated in the compound of Mansa Devi was beaten and even shown hanging from a tree with both his hands tied. In addition, the media reports stated that earlier the Police also tortured two other children.

The Commission stated that if the contents of the media reports are true it raises issues of violation of human rights of innocent children and brings to fore the need for police reforms. No civilized State can allow such brutalities to go unpunished, it observed.

It directed that the press report and copy of transcript of the TV channel be transmitted to the Director General of Police, Government of Haryana to look into the matter and send his comments.

Rs. 2.5 Lakh relief for Punjab Mass Cremation victim

The Commission, on 4 October 2005, ordered the Punjab Government to pay a compensation of Rs. 2.5 lakh to the next of kin of a man who died in police custody in 1992 during its anti-terror drive, thus rejecting the administration's claim that this was not a case of custodial death. Paramjit Singh was one of the victims of the "secret mass cremations" in Punjab.

However, the Punjab Government had field an affidavit that Paramjit was not in the custody of the police prior to his death. Dismissing affidavit, a Bench comprising the Chairperson Justice A.S. Anand and Members justice Shivaraj V. Patil, Justice Y. Bhaskar Rao and Shri R.S. Kalha said a statement of a senior police officer showed that Paramjit had been arrested in an injured condition and had died in the police custody.

The Punjab Government will have to pay half of the compensation money to the next of kin of Paramjit and the rest would be kept in a fixed deposit for a period of five years. A compliance report would have to be sent to the NHRC, in November last year, had announced compensation of Rs. 2.5 lakh each to be paid to the next of kin of 109 persons who had died while in the custody of police.

Sadashiva Panel Report and copies of responses of Karnataka and Tamil Nadu State Govts. to be sent to the Complainants

The National Human Rights Commission has directed that the report of the justice A.J. Sadashiva Panel constituted to look into the alleged excesses perpetrated by the Joint Special Task Force during the anti-Veerappan operations be sent to the complainants along with the responses received from the Governments of Karnataka and Tamil Nadu. The complainants will have to send their comments, if any, to the responses fron the Government of Karnnataka and Tamil Nadu within 8 weeks.

On the recent representation dated 13 October 2005 submitted by Shri Henri Tiphagne, the Commission has directed that its copies be forwarded to the Chief Secretaries of Karnataka and Tamil Nadu for their comments in 4 weeks.

The Justice Shri A.J. Sadashiva Panel, had been constituted by the Commission vide its proceedings dated 28 June, 1999, and had submitted its report to be Commission on 2 December, 2003

After getting the report examined, the Commission on 23 February, 2004, directed that copy of the report of the Panel be sent to the Chief Secretaries of Government of Karnataka and Government of Tamil Nadu.

Report of interesting Cancer deaths in Punjab draws Commission's attention

The Commission has taken suo-motu cognisance of a story titled "interesting cancer death in Punjab" which was published in a national daily on 1 October 2005.

The report indicted that Malwa region of Punjab was turning into toxic hot spot and villages of Jajjal and Giana in the Talwandi Saboo block of Bhatinda District have reported increased cases of cancer over the last 5 years. People attributed the cases of cancer to the use of pesticides and quality of ground water. The report further indicates that a study carried out by the Community Medicine Department of PGI of Chandigrah has shown that lack of education and awareness, use of tobacco and improper storage of pesticides may have also contributed to the causes. The news report alleged that the Punjab Health Department and Punjab Agriculture University scientists have neglected the study saying that it was not adequate and there was need to have the study corroborated with various labs and agencies to get the truth.

The Commission has directed that the newspaper report be transmitted to the Chief Secretary, Government of Punjab for his comments.

Poor condition Kerala Hospitals

The Commission has taken Suo-motu cognisance of a news story captioned "No life saving equipments; Hospitals are gateways to death" published in the Delhi edition of the Malayala Manarama on 3 October 2005. The news report commented on the lack of infrastructure especially shortage of ventilators and adequate medical staff across a number of hospitals in Kerala.

The hospitals being the Medical College Hospitals, at Alleppy, Calicut, Thiruvananthapuram, Kottayam and the district hospitals at Manathavady in Wayanad, Kanjangad in Kasargode in Kasargode and Kannur. It also stated that to this a number of deaths have taken place.

The Commission has directed a copy of the news item be sent to the Chief Secretary, Kerala and Health Secretary, Kerala for their Comments.

NHRC appreciates action taken by Haryana Government for Gohana victims

The Commission has appreciated the sensitivity and promptness shown by the State Government of Haryana in awarding compensation, repairing/reconstructing of the houses for the victims whose houses were torched by a mob in Balmiki Colony in Gohana, Sonepat during September 2005. The Haryana Government had also initiated a CBI inquiry and departmental proceeding against errant officers in connection with this incident.

The incident was widely reported in the media based on which the Commission had taken suo-motu cognisance. It was reported in the media that a mob belonging to upper caster castes most of them Jats, burnt several houses of the Dalits situated in Balmiki Colony, near Baroda Chowk in a violent backlash to murder of Gharwal villageg youth Baljeet Siwach which had taken place a few days ago.

Following the directions of the Commission, reply was received from the Chief Secretary to the Government of Haryana which while giving details about the incident also mentioned that cash compensation to the tune of Rs. 1.00 lakh has been paid to each of the 54 affected families. Investigation in respect of the cases registered in relation to the unfortunate incident has been handed over to CBI on 11 September 2005. The 54 demaged/burnt houses have been reconstructed by the Government at the cost of Rs. 49 Lakh Affected families have also been given compensation for the damage to their household articles Besides, cash assistance of Rs.5,000/- was also provided to 54 families immediately after the incident and a sum of more than Rs. 2.00 lakh has been spent for providing free food, medicine, text books, TA/DA etc. to the victims. Regarding the status of disciplinary proceedings, it was submitted that the then DSP, Gohana and the then SHO, Police Station Sadar Gohana, have been placed under suspension and departmental action is being taken against them.

The Commission observed that from the above report, it transpires that the affected families have not only been paid monetary compensation but the Government has got their damaged houses repaired/reconstructed. CBI investigation into the cases registered in relation to the incident has also started besides the delinquent police official have been suspended and departmental action against them is being initiated.

With the observation that no action on the part is called for, the NHRC has closed the file. The Commission also stated that it is expected that the State authorities will expeditiously complete the departmental proceedings and take appropriate action against the delinquent officials on the basis of the outcome of department enquiry. It holed that other State Governments also would act promptly and with all sensitivity as regards the violation of human rights wherever required.

AP Government submits report on tribal deaths in Visakhapatanam, says precaution and medical care taken

Deeply concerned by a report carried in a newspaper alleging deaths of hundreds of trials in Visakhapatanam due to unknown factors and lack of medical facilities, the Commission taking suo-motu cognisance had sought the comments of the Chief Secretary, Andhra Predesh.

The news report which appeared in the Telugu daily 'Enadu' on 24 June 2004, had alleged that about 476 people had died over a three-month period. These death, it stated, had taken place despite the State Government setting up health camps. The news story drew attention to the poor medical facilities in the Agency area.

In response, a report was received from the State Government of Andhra Pradesh from the Department of Home forwarding a report from the principal Secretary, Health, Medical and Family Welfare Department, Government of Andhra Pradesh. Refuted the charges that appeared in the newspaper. It outlined the measures the State Government had taken to control malaria especially after the issue was highlighted in the media.

Taking note of the report the Commission expressed hope that Government of Andhra Pradesh continue to take measures for providing medicare and to improve the health status of the tribal. It stated it expects that the state should take all such measures as are available to it to prevent death of the tribals due to causes mentioned in the news report.

It has also pointed out that continuous monitoring of the facilities available in the sub-centre and PHCs particularly in the areas would be useful.

Maharashtra Government gives financial assistance in the case of suicide of framers after intervention of NHRC

The Commission has requested the State Government of Maharashtra that it would be desirable and appropriate to put in place a mechanism to ensure that there is no recurrence in future of farmers' suicides on account of drought or indebtedness. It also directed the State Government to take all appropriate steps to mitigate the hardships faced by farmers due to brought or indebtedness. The State Government had acknowledged that 140 farmers had committed suicide on account of indebtedness, drought etc. and who were found to be eligible for financial assistance of Rs. 1.00 lakh, an amount the Commission had recommended.

These directions were issued following the report by the State Government submitted to the Commission in connection with the death of 2 farmers by suicide. The deaths were reported in a national daily on 18 July 2004 and on the basis of which the NHRC had directed the Chief Secretary, Government of Maharashtra to take appropriate action and submit a report on the action taken.

Killing of 3 boys by Security Forces in J&K, NHRC seeks report

The Commission had taken suo-motu cognisance based on media reports of the recent killing of three boys security forces in Kupwara District of Jammu & Kashmir. It has asked the Secretary, Ministry of Defence, Government of India to send a factual report on the incident to the Commission.

The print and electronic media dated 25 July 2005 carried reports of the killing of three innocent minor boys and of a fourth being seriously injured in a shoot out allegedly by security forces in village Bagargund, district Kupwara in north Kashmir on the night of intervening 23 and 24 July 2005.

Reacting to the media reports of the incident, the Commission taking a serious view of the matter stated that it has always maintained and reiterates that "Right to life" is of crucial significance for every person, every group of people, every class, every nation and as a matter of fact for all humanity. No person who supports human rights can support terrorism, which is a grave violation of human rights. The Commission, however, has always maintained that while terrorism is a clear danger to the world today, it being the most vicious, irrational and senseless kind of violence and, therefore, the war against terrorism has to be fought relentlessly, but that there is no conflict between respect for human and combating terrorism. International Humanitarian Law is a part of human rights law applicable even in armed conflicts. Action of the State must be guided by human rights principles, which strike a balance between the enjoyment of freedom and the legitimate concerns for national security. It is necessary for the State and the Agencies to strike the balance between the liberty of an individual and the requirement of security of state and sovereignty and integrity of the nation. A proper balance between the need and the remedy requires respect for the principles of necessary and proportionality. Since fundamental rationale for anti-terrorism measure has to be to protect human rights and democracy, counter terrorism measures should, therefore, not undermine democratic values, violate human rights and subvert the rule of law or chill civil liberties of the citizens. The battle against terrorism needs to be carried out in keeping with the international human rights obligations and basic tenets of the rule of law.

NHRC recommends independent investigation into assault by Gurgaon police

The Commission has strongly recommended to the Government of Haryana to take effective steps to get an independent investigation preferably by the CBI commenced into the reported brutal assault by the Haryana police on agitating workers of the Honda Motorcycles and Scooters India, which took place at Gurgaon on 25 July 2005. it has asked the Chief Secretary, Haryana to send an action taken report in this regard to the Commission. The NHRC is of the opinion that in order to instill public confidence in the rule of law an impartial investigation into the police assaults and the related incidents by an agency independent of the State is called for.

The disturbing news item about the alleged brutal by the Haryana Police at Gurgaon on the agitating workers of Honda Motorcycle and Scooters India (HMSI) on 25 July 2005 was widely publicized both by the print and electronic media.

The Commission voiced its deep concern at the events, which took place in Gurgaon. The issue before us, it stated is of grave concern as it affect human rights of a large number of persons belonging to vulnerable section of the society-industrial workers. Where or not the police assault on 25 July 2005 at Gurgaon was justified or whether more force than was necessary was used can only be found out by conducting an investigating through an agency independent of the State machinery, it observed.

The Commission has since received reports from the Superintendent of Police and the District Magistrate, Gurgaun which were forwarded by the Chief Secretary, Haryana and are being examined by it.

Inhuman treatment of inmates of a mental asylum in Bihar

The Commission took suo-mptu cognisance of a media report, which showed gory details of inhuman treatment meted out to inmates of an unlicensed mental asylum run by a quack at Saharsa in Bihar. Reacting to the CNN-IBN news report, the Commission said that the treatment methods shown in the report are primitive as the patients are tied to the tree and buckets of cold water poured on them. The video clipping also showed mental patients being kept in chain and brutally beaten up.

The Commission said the contents of the story, if true, were an affront to human dignity and raise an issue of violation of human rights of mental patients.

The Commission directed the Chief Secretary, Bihar to get the matter enquired into and submit a factual report within two weeks. It further directed that if the contents of the story were found to be true, the Chief Secretary would intimate the Commission regarding the steps being taken for the release of the mental patients and the steps taken to ensure that they are provided proper medical and psychiatric treatment.

Over 30 years later 4 undertrial prisoners at the Mental Hospital in Tezpur, Assam freed

A visit by the Commission's Special Repporteur Shri Chaman Lal to the LGB Regional Institute of Mental Health in Tezpur, Assam on 31 March and 1 April 2005 had revealed the plight of 6 mentally ill persons who had been undertrial prisoners for years together. They were Machang who has been lodged in the Mental Hospital for 35 years, Anil Kuman Burman a undertrial prisoner for 33 years, Sonamoni Deb a undertrial prisoner for 32 years, a women Parbati Mallik who has been a undertrial prisoner for 32 years and Hemakanta Changmai. On coming to know about this, the Commission had taken sou-motu cognisance and asked the authorities concernd for a report.

In reply, the IG (Prisons) sent a communication on the status of 4 of the undertrials. The report on Anil Kumar Burman is still awaited.

- Machang Lalung had been released on a personal bound of Re. 1.00 by the Chief Judicial Magistrate, Kamrup on 1 July 2005. He has been handed over to the custody and care of his nephew.

Lalung transferred to the Mental Hospital on 14 April 1951, from the Guwahati Jail, where he was loged as an undertrial prisoner. As per information, prima facie, the accused was never produced in the trial court for trial even though he was fit to stand for trial after 9th Aughtst 1967. While as undertrial prisoner, he had received no visitors for more than 40 years.

- Sonamoni Deb had been certified fit for discharge. He has since been handed over to his brother. Shri Deb was acquitted by Sessions Judge, Lakhmipur on 8 November 1971 in a murser in a case on the ground of insanity and he was ordered to be detained in jail for observation and necessary action. He was transferred to Tezpur mental hospital, now called LGB Religional Institute of Mental Health, on 5 July 1972 from Dibrugarh jail. Deb, a destitute was wrongly treated as a prisoner after 8th Nov. 1971, even after the Sessions Judge, Lakhmipur found him "not guilty" of the offence.
- Khalilur Rehman has been releted. He is new in the care and custody of his sister who took change of him on 24 Jume 2005. Rehman was sentenced to imprisonment for by the Sessions Judge, Cachar on 23 July 1965. he was acquitted of the changes on the ground of insanity by the Guwahati High Court on 30 April 1968. thereafter, he was transferred to Tezpur mental hospital on 1 December 1969 under the orders of the State Governemt.
- Parbati Mallik's brothers have been traced and ther have expressed their willingness to take care of her on her release form jail. Her case was fixed for 4 July 2005 for her protection and order before the Sessions Judge, Cachar. Mallik who was acquitted in a murder case was ternsfered to LGB Regional Institute of Mental Health on 9 May 1977 form silchar jail.

The Directorof the LGB Regional Institute of Mental Health in Tezur in his report on the condition of

- Hemakanta Changmai stated that the undertrial prisoner needs continuous supervised medication and he is not fit for discharge. A progress report has been sent to the Hon'ble Sessions Judge, Dhemaji.

The NHRC noted the report and closed the matter. At the same time, it requested the Director to ensure that full periodical reports as required under the Mental Health Act, 1987 be sent to be Court regularly.

Other measures taken by NHRC to Prevent Human Rights Violation NHRC Chairperson calls on State machinery to be sensitive to human rights issues

Dr. Justice A.S Anand, chairperson, National Human Rights Commission (NHRC) has expressed concern of NHRC to the chief Secretaries and Directors General of Police towards human rights sensitivity. Speaking at the meeting of the Chief Secretaries and Directors General of Police held in New Delhi on 17 March 2006, he stressed that unless they show sensitivity, this sentiment can not be expected to percolate to the lower levels. Pointing out to the diminishing level of sensitivity shown by some of the state machinery and the absence of promptness in addressing human rights Hconcerns, Justice Anand stressed that sensitivity towards human rights issues is important. He stated that the purpose of holding this meeting is not to find faults but to appreciate and understand each other's point of view.

In his address Justice Anand highlighted that the Commission has been receiving complaints of cases of alleged human rights violations. The number of complaints has steadily increased over the years ever since its inception. The Commission is consistently attempting to develop a culture of human rights in the Country, the NHRC strongly advocates that enjoy civil and political rights, economic, social, cultural rights cannot be put on the backburner, he said. He requested the Chief Secretaries and Directors General of police to give proper importance to Economic, Social, Cultural Rights.

On the conditions of jails, Justice Y. Bhaskar Rao, Member, NHRC highlighted the need for State Governments to be factually correct in their reports to he Commission. He also observed that there was a need for filing of charge sheets in time as per the judgement of the Supreme Court in the Sheela Barse case. The case of a ninety-year-old undertrial languishing in a jail in Chhattisgarh, underscored the need for urgent attention to the problems in jails. Shri P.C. Shrma, Member, NHRC mentioned the need for proper planning to ensure that additional facilities, which are provided for the inmates, are not at the cost of increased congestion.

Shri R.S. Kalha, Member, NHRC in his remarks outlined the changes taking place globally and its impact on the domestic situation of a country. He cautioned all administrators on the need to reckon with international safeguards that are available and being increasingly invoked by citizens in their quest for justice.

Earlier Shri Nirmal Shing, Secretary General of the NHRC, in his welcome address outlined the focus areas of the meeting.

The daylong meeting was a follow up of the earlier meeting held on 14 December 2004. The meeting deliberated on Civil a Political rights especially crimes committed by persons in uniform such as non-registration of FIR and violence being used during investigation while in custody. It also took up Economic, Social and Cultural Rights such as eradication of manual scavenging by 2007, spreading of awareness regarding child marriages, policy regarding rehabilitation of internally displaced persons, duties of the state in protecting Economic, Social and Cultural Rights Implementation of the Bonded Labour Act and Child Labour Prevention Act, Right to health especially 100% vaccination for Children, female foeticide, health care of senior citizens, Human rights and HIV/AIDS, rights of the disabled, trafficking in women and children and rights to food.

Chief Secretaries from 7 States, Representatives of Chief Secretaries from 25 States, the Administrator from Lakshadweep, DGPs from 11 States and represent of DGPs from 21 States attended the meeting.

Workshop for Jail Superintendents of Tripura

A one-day sensitisation workshop for the Jail Superintendents of Tripura was conducted by Shri Chaman Lal, Special Rapporteur, NHRC at Agartala on 24 March 2006. The workshop was inaugurated by Shri R.K. Mathur, Chief Secretary, Tripura and was attended by Jail Superintendents or jailors of all the 11 Jails of Tripura. Besides apprising the Jail officials about their human rights objectives towards prisoners, the workshop proved useful in removing some of their doubts and misgivings about the Commission. It also provided them an opportunity to project the difficulties and hardships of their working and living conditions.

NHRC recommends extension of Long Term Action Plan for KBK Area

The NHRC has recommended extension beyond March 2007 of the Revised Long Term Action Plan (RLTAP) for the on-going relief and development programmes in Kalahandi, Bolangir and Koraput (KBK) region of Orissa. The Commission has been dealing with this matter since December 1996, under a mandate from the Supreme

Court by carrying out periodical monitoring of relief and development programmes in these regions though its Special Rapporteur Shri Chaman Lal. In the last hearing in July 2006, the Commission took final assessment/stock of the State Government satisfactory in sectors of Rural Water Supply, Social Security targeted public distribution system, Rural Development and Afforrestation. Deficiencies were however, observed in Public Health Care, execution of Soil Conservation Projects and implementation of Land Reforms The Commission expressed its distress over the failure of the State in dealing effectively with the menace of Malaria and even Diarrhoea in KBK region.

The Commission recommended improvement in Primary Health Care by filling up vacancies of Medical Officers and posting of Specialists, opening of additional Sub-Centres, strengthening of Immunisation Programme and intensification of drive against Malaria. It requested the Government of India to suitable enhance the allocation of BPL rice to the State to enable it to meet its commitment of providing 35 Kg- per month to all the BPL households. Besides the launching of a special campaign to direct the cases of alienation of tribal land, under the amended provisions of Regulation 2/56, the State Government has been asked to bring forth similar amendments in Orissa Land Reforms Act so as to completely ban the transfer of tribal to non-tribals.

It recommended that all the students in the schools run by ST/SC Department should receive the benefit of the scholarship scheme and Government if India should allot BPL rice in sufficient quantity to meet full requirements of rice for hostels run by ST/SC Departments. A through review of the educational infrastructure and position of teachers especially in predominantly tribal pockets of these Districts was another important recommendation made by the Commission.

A special system of monitoring with peoples' involvement was recommended for ensuring efficiency and transparency in the execution of all developmental projects in the region.

Protest on proposed reservation in higher education

The National Human Rights Commission has recommended to the Government that it should get examined the issue of reservation thoroughly. Reacting to the media reports that showed some of the students and doctors on hunger strike being removed for medical care during the agitation, the Commission said that the Government should ensure that fairness and justice is not denied to any section or class of the society. Describing the reservation issue as a complex one, the Commission felt that Government should also ensure a balance and orderly development of all sections and classes of society while implementing its policy.

While expressing concern over the deteriorating health of students and doctors who were on hunger strike in protest against the reservation, the Commission also expressed concern for the denial of health care facilities to the sick and ailing due to strike in Government hospitals. It appealed to the doctors to resume their work in the interest of ailing patients and asked those who were on hunger strike to call off their strike.

Earlier, the Commission called for factual reports from the Commissioners of Police, Delhi and Mumbai in respect of the unprovoked lathi charge on the students in the two place during the agitation. Taking note of newspaper reports and electronic media coverage about the alleged police action on medical and engineering students indulging in peaceful protests, the Commission said, the allegations of police action raise a serious issue of violation of human rights. The commission also said that no civilized State could justify use of brutal force on peaceful demonstrations.

Eradition of Manual Scaverging

The Commission had called a meeting with the Senior Officials of the Ministry of Urban Employment &Poverty Alleviation (MOUE&PA) and Ministry of Social Justice & Empowerment (MOSJ&E) , Government of India in New Delhi recently eradication of the demeaning practice of Manual Scavenging in the country. Smt. Chitra Chopra, Secretary, MOUE&PA and Srhi Narayanamurthy, joint Secretary, MOUSJ&E attended the meeting, which was held on 21 June 2004.

Dr. Justice A.S. Anand, Chairperson, derew attention to the commitment made by the representatives of the State Governemnts at an earlier meeting held on 6 November, 2003 that they would conduct a survey within a year and report to be Commission. A Survey, he said, is vital as in the absence of accurate data, the extent of the problem cannot be judged and the 2007 deadline for the eradication of Manual Scavenging as envisaged in the National Action Plan for total eradication of manual scavenging cannot be met.

He stated that the survey should throw some light on the fact whether the person is the only one engaged in manual scavenging or his dependents or family members are also engaged in it. The Chairperson emphasized the need to involve the NGOs and Safai Karamcharis working in the area and not be restricted itself to the individuals employed as scavengers, but take into account their dependents and the number of household where this practice exists.

The Chairperson said that the feedback received by the Commission from various State is scanty and implementation wanting and there is number mention by the State Government as to whether manual scavenging exists in rural areas, a point which needs to be addressed, considering a large part of India's population lives in the rural area. He also expressed his concern that the responses elicited from the State do not indicate whether training and rehabilitation have been given to the indentified scavengers.

The ongoing case studies reveal the achievement of NHRC since its inception. It has proved that it is a unique statutaty body and has performened its duties according to the norms fixed by the Protection of Human Rights Act. By disposing the different cases of human hights violation of divergent nature, it has conpelled the cynics to think otherwise and change their attitude towards the NHRC which they had developed initially. In some cases the NHRC has taken a bold stand to defend human rights and created havoc among the agencies where human rights violation is rampant. It is seen that within the thirteen of its exestance it has proved its excellence where it has got co-operation. Hence it can be concluded that no organisation like National Human Rights Commission can flourish in the environment of human rights violation if it does not get a congenial atmosphere of co-opration and awareness.

Footnotes

1. Chakrabarty &Mohit Bhatacharys (ed.) "Public Administration, A Reader"Oxford University Press,New Delhi(2003).
2. NHRC, Annual Report 1997-98, paras 17.4 and 17.5,p.79.
3. A. Ray " National Human Rights Commission of India, Formation, Functioing & Future Prospects" Khama Publishers, Delhi, 2005.
4. R.V. Pillai," Protection of Huamn Rights", Presented at UNESCO branch office, in Arun Ray's National Human Rights Commission of India, Formation, Functioing & Future Prospects" Khama Publishers , Delhi,2005.p.129

References

Annual Report of NHRC,1993-94.
Annual Report of NHRC,1994-95.
Annual Report of NHRC,1995-96.
Annual Report of NHRC,1996-97.
Annual Report of NHRC,1997-98.
Annual Report of NHRC,1998-99.
Annual Report of NHRC,1999-2000.
Annual Report of NHRC,2000-2001.
Annual Report of NHRC,2001-2002.
Annual Report of NHRC,2003-2004.
Annual Report of NHRC,2004-2005.
www.nhrc.nic.in
News Letter, Human Rights, Vol. 12 No-07 July. 2005 NHRC.
News Letter, Human Rights, Vol. 12 No-08 August. 2005 NHRC.
News Letter, Human Rights, Vol. 12 No-09 Sept. 2005 NHRC
News Letter, Human Rights, Vol. 12 No-11 Nov. 2005 NHRC.
News Letter, Human Rights, Vol. 12 No-12 Dec. 2005 NHRC.
News Letter, Human Rights, Vol.13 No-2 Feb 2006 NHRC.
News Letter, Human Rights, Vol. 13 No-4 April 2006 NHRC.
News Letter, Human Rights, Vol.14 No-5 May 2006 NHRC.
News Letter, Human Rights, Vol.14 No-6 June 2006 NHRC.
News Letter, Human Rights, Vol. 13 No-7 July 2006 NHRC.
News Letter, Human Rights, Vol. 13 No-9 Sept. 2006 NHRC.
News Letter, Human Rights, Vol. 13 No-11 Nov. 2006 NHRC.
News Letter, Human Rights, Vol. 13 No-12 Dec. 2006 NHRC.
News Letter, Human Rights, Vol. 14 No-1 January 2007 NHRC.
News Letter, Human Rights, Vol. 14 No-2 February 2007NHRC.

6

Summing Up

The world conference on Human Rights in 1993 noted in the Vienna Declaration and protection and Programme of Action, the responsibilities of all States, in conformity with the charter of the UN, to develop and encourage respect for human rights and fundamental freedoms for all, without distinction as to race, sex, language or religion. The Programme of Action stresses the primary responsibility for human rights by stating that their protection and promotion is the first responsibility of government. Although this statement seems self-evident, it was no doubt considered useful to recall states' obligations as the protagonists in guaranteeing respect for human rights and as being accountable in the event of their violation.

It is the responsibility of the institutions set up by the state to guarantee respect for human rights. During the last five and half decades, the Indian government has set up several special institutions under different acts of parliament to give effect to the constitutional provisions of human rights of all persons, including those of the disadvantaged and weaker sections of the society. The National Human Rights Commission is one of such institutions, which was established on 12th October 1993 following constant international criticism of human rights record in the country. Additionally the NHRC fulfils the constitutional obligations. It has more members and broader powers compared to other commissions in the field of human rights.

The National Human Rights Commission of India is a statutory and autonomous body, which works independently. It has the status and power of a civil court and all its actions are sanctified by law. The Commission has the responsibility of bringing to light the violations of human rights by any government agency or official as well as of taking remedial action for punishing the guilty and compensating the victims. It can move the Supreme Court or any High Court for this purpose. It can even become a party to any case involving a violation of human rights. The NHRC of India is even more powerful than its counterparts working in other countries in so far as it has been given the power to investigate the actions of the armed forces of the country if necessary. The NHRC has already completed more than thirteen years of its life and it has been successful in demonstrating its teeth

Further, the establishment of the NHRC has added an entirely new and additional dimension to the efforts of the country for the protection and promotion of human rights. While the courts have, through formal decisions, interpreted the constitution and the law of the land in terms of the Universal Declaration of Human Rights, and various covenants to which India is a party, and have come to the rescue of victims of human rights, it is envisaged that the NHRC would undertake a variety of tasks aimed at promoting a culture of human rights. As a watchdog body the NHRC has so far done a credible job not only in promoting human rights in the country, but also in enhancing the image of the nation in the community of states. The initial scepticism, that sooner or later the NHRC will end up as another government-type institution with its usual quota of lethargy and indifference has withered, as the commission has successfully maintained its image of objectivity, impartiality and integrity and, in fact, assume the role of a model institution that will act as a catalyst in keeping with the executive and legislative wings of the government and to stick in helping to their task. Indeed, the NHRC has become the central focal point for enforcement of the new generation of human rights while protecting the basic social order, and in a given threat perception, the integrity and security of the state. However, it cannot be said that the commission's achievements have been miraculous or extraordinary in promoting and protecting human rights ethos of the country or that human rights violations have ceased to occur. But one can honestly agree on the point that it has brought a fresh hope to those who seek redress for their grievances. Furthermore, there is awareness now, as perhaps never before, of the meaning of human rights in India.

Recently the National Human Rights Commission completed 13 years of its existence on October 12th, 2006. Over these years the commission has endeavoured to give a positive meaning and content to the objectives set out in the protection of Human Rights Act, 1993 for better protection of human rights. During this period the commission has worked vigorously and effectively to create awareness and to sensitise public authorities for promoting and protecting human rights in the country.

Consistent with its mandate, the commission has been taking up issues of human rights violation that are of significance, either suo-motu, or when brought to its notice by the civil society, the media, concerned citizens or expert advisers. The primary focus of the commission has been on strengthening and extension of human rights to all sections of the society. The vulnerable groups and weaker sections of the society, particularly, are guarded by the commission against violation of human rights.

The commission's purview covers the entire range of civil and political, as well as economic, social and cultural rights. The issues emerging from terrorism and insurgency, custodial death, rape and torture, reform of police, prison conditions and other institutions such as juvenile homes, mental hospitals and shelters for women, along with the issues of health care and exploitation of children and their education have assumed special focus and attention. Basic needs such as drinking water, food and nutrition, and equity and justice to the less privileged, namely SCs and STs and prevention of atrocities perpetrated against them also form a part of the Commission's work. Rights of the disabled access to public services by the disabled, displacement of population and especially of tribals by mega projects, food scarcity and allegation of death from starvation, rights of the children, rights of women subjected to violence, sexual harassment and discrimination, and rights of minorities, have been the focus of the Commission's action on numerous occasions.

The Commission has taken up the cause of relief and rehabilitation of Kashmir migrants, provision of relief to the victims of devastating tsunami, cyclone and earthquake in certain parts of the country during recent years. The spectacular achivement of NHRC is its interim relief work. Since inception, the Commission has directed that interim relief to the extent of Rs.10, 47.58,643/- be paid in 707 cases. It has also recommended, in a significant number of cases disciplinary action and prosecution against the public servants *who were prima- facie* found responsible for their acts of omission or commission resulting in violations of human rights of the people.

In spite of its sincere endeavour it has been remarked that the National Human Rights Commission has only been able to touch the tip of the iceberg of the problem of Human Rights Violation. But National Human Rights Commission can't be blamed, when the entire society is culpable in respect of Human Rights violations in one-way or the other. In his presidential address, on 12th October 2006, NHRC Chairperson Dr. justice A.S. Anand said that the commission has maintained that the main obligation to protect human rights is that of the state itself. He said the commission acts as a facilitator and there are numerous challenges, which we have to meet. He pointed out that poverty, neglect of social, economic and cultural rights, corruption are some of the biggest violators of human rights. He said the present day terrorism has cast a pall on efforts to promote human rights. In fact, it is not possible on the part of National Human Rights Commission to keep vigil on every human being in the country.

It is the duty of the State to guarantee what is said in the constitution. But the shocking evidence is that the state is itself the culprit, according to justice J.S. Verma the former Chairman of NHRC. According to a statement made by him on January 15, 2003, "it is often the state which is the violator of human rights in maximum cases in the country. But the maximum responsibility to protect and safeguard the rights of its citizens also lies with the state."

However, the creation of National Human Rights Commission has brought about a qualitative change in the observance of human rights in India. As a result of its consistent efforts, there is now greater awareness to follow human rights principles among the police, army and security forces. Yet there are a number of constraints and constitutional limitations that have made the NHRC look rather like a toothless body. For example, while the NHRC's role in probing the Gujarat riots issue created ripples, yet, precious little has been done to act upon its recommendations. This is basically because the commission's powers have been limited to mere recommendations. It is basically an investigative and reporting body, imbued with powers of a civil court. It lacks judicial power, so far as meeting out punishment to offenders is concerned. Secondly, the commission's investigating powers have been restricted by the fact that if a state government institutes an investigative commission on a case of human rights violation, the commission cannot carry any investigation on its own. Third, the NHRC has no financial independence of its own. It is dependant on central Government grants. The grants are so limited that they often restrict the commission's activities. Fourthly, the Commission cannot interfere in service matters. Consequently, several human rights violation cases are going unheard. Fifthly, the commission functions in a situation of interdependence. It functions along with other statutory bodies like National Minorities commission, National commission for women and SC/ST commission. Sixthly, the commission is unable to take prompt action due to lack of adequate number of staff especially in the field of investigation. Now the commission has a sanctioned strength of 343 officers and staff for more than 102 crore people but the rate of violation of human rights cases are increasing day by day.

Last but not the least, the commission has no power to entertain the complaints about events that have occurred over one year prior to the date of the filing the complaint. But this limitation has been overlooked in mass cremation of more than 2,000 bodies of persons killed by the Punjab police during 1991-93 in fake encounters. When the matter was under investigation by the NHRC, the union government in fact questioned its jurisdiction in view of one-year time limit set by the Protection of Human Rights Act. When the commission rejected the objection, the government had got the inquiry stayed to enable it to appeal to the Supreme Court. The apex court subsequently ruled, “Any compensation awarded by the commission (to the dependants of the victims) shall be binding and payable”.

From the on going discussion it is crystale clear that NHRC has achieved a lot within the short span of its existence in spite of its constraints. The structure and the style of functioning and its point of view is such that every one will agree that it is the most effective statutory body in comparison to other commissions. Within the last 13 years it has proved its excellence by protecting human rights. However, some suggestions may be made here to make the commissions more viable to fulfil its objectives and the aspirations of the people. The suggestions are :

1. The commission is vested with the power of civil court and its decisions are confined to recommendations. It does not have the powerful teeth to prevent the violators from escaping easily. Hence the commission should be provided with some power of punishment to create a phobia among the violators.
2. In several cases, due to inadequate investigating staff of its own it depends upon the state agencies for investigation. Consequently the investigation process is being delayed and sometimes it is not free from doubt. Therefore, the commission should be provided efficient, expert and active manpower to deal with the human rights violation.

3. It is a matter of great concern that till date only 15 states have established State Human Rights Commissions where as the Human Rights Protection Act has been in force since 1993. Now nearly half of the states and all Union Territories have no commissions at all. As a result it is difficult for NHRC to deal with the human rights violation issues in those states and Union Territories. Hence the Union Government should pressurise the States and Territories to establish their own mechanisim to deal with human rights issues as early as possible.
4. The NHRC should organise a workshop every year inviting the eminent human rights activists, public-spirited citizens, human rights advocates, trade union leaders and persons who have done outstanding work in the field of human rights. This will help to collect the opinion from the grassroots level and if necessary they should be provided training to deal with human rights violation cases and promote human rights in their respective areas.
5. It has a research division to promote human rights education which is one of the objectives of the commission. The government should make enough budgetary provision for NHRC as it is being provided to University Grants Commission for research fellowship in order to explore new means to prevent human rights violation and protect human values.
6. During the recruitment of the officers and staff the NHRC should take extra care and provide opportunities to those who have tremendous inclination for human dignity and values. The canididature of those persons having some sort of experience in the field of human rights should be taken into consideration because the wearer knows where the shoe pinches.
7. The Annual Report of the NHRC and SHRC should be placed in the Parliament and State Legislatures respectively not only for the sake of principle but it should also be properly analysed and efforts should be made to stop human rights violation further. In the areas where human rights have been violated brazenly, the laws should be seriously enfored. If necessary, the law has to be amended as per the demands of the situation.
8. As the decision of NHRC is limited to recommendations it is the duty of the Union Government and State Governments to implement the Commission's recommendations whole-heartedly until the power of punishment is not given to the Commission.

9. The Information and Public Relation Division of the Commission should become more and more active as per the need of the hour. Their work should not be confined to the publication of Annual Report and Monthly Newsletter. Time has come to popularise the human rights education through electronics and print media. The achievements of the commission should appear in the headlines of the News Papers and Television News in all vernacular languages so that the Commission's work will be popular and people can retain their confidence in the functioning of the commission. Apart from this efforts should be made by both public and private parties to produce films and serials highlighting the performance of the Commission to make common people vigilant.
10. Above all, in order to protect and promote human rights, efforts should be made to impart human rights education at all levels, starting from the schools to the university level and in all branches of study so that a culture can be created which will be the panacea to prevent human rights violation.

The commission's role, no matter how advisiory in application, has raised a new hope for thousands, who earlier had no hope to get justice. "No Commission or no Police station can police every nook or corner of the country, no NGO, no agency can be present everywhere to protect the Human Rights. It is, we the people, who are the sovereign authority according to our constitution; it is the duty of every citizen to rise to the occasion. This can be brought about only through general awakening and, where necessary, by forming civil society organisations, which make every one understand the eternal values of life and dignity of individual irrespective of cast, creed or sex. Swami Vivekananda's concept that "the self in you is the self everywhere" should be our ideal. We still have promises to keep and miles to go. There is no doubt the NHRC will play a crucial role in future years if every body comes forward forgetting his or her distinctive identity. In a nutshell a co-operative venture is necessary to make the commission break new grounds in the arena of human rights and help it to keep abreast of globalisation.

References

Vienna Declaration and programme of Action, UN, A/CONF. 157/23, preamble (5th Sub Paragraph), and Part 1, para. 1(subpara. 3): also para. (Sub para.!).

Human Rights Newsletter,Vol.13 No.11 November,2006,NHRC.

PART - II

PART-II

Appendix-I

Land Marks of Human Rights Development

26 June 1945

Signing of the Charter of the United Nations and statute of the International Court of Justice, in San Francisco.

21 June 1946

Establishment of the commission on Human Rights under Economic and Social Council resolution 9 (11). At its first session, in 1947, the Commission establishes the Sub commission on prevention of Discrimination and Protection of Minorities on the basis of that resolution.

21 June 1946

Establishment of the Commission on the Status of Women under resolution 11 (II) of the Economic and Social Council.

9 December 1948

Adoption by the General Assembly of the Covenant on the Prevention and Punishment of the Crime of Genocide.

10 December 1948

Adoption by the General Assembly of the Universal Declaration of Human Rights.

2 December 1949

Adoption by the General Assembly of the Convention for the Suppression of the traffic in Persons and of the Exploitation of the Prostitution of Others.

4 November 1950

Adoption by the members of the Council of Europe of the Convention for the Protection of Human Rights and Fundamental Freedoms (European Convention on Human Rights).

1 December 1950

Creation of the Committee on Crime Prevention and Control under General Assembly resolution 415 (v). The Committee is responsible for preparing the United, Nations Congresses on the Prevention of Crime and the Treatment of Offenders. It is institutionalised in the form of the Commission on Crime Prevention and Criminal Justice by the Economic and Social Council on 6 February 1992.

28 July 1951

Adoption by a United Nations Conference of Plenipotentiaries of the Convention relating to the Status of Refugees.

20 December 1952

Adoption by the General Assembly of the Convention on the Political Rights of Women.

23 October 1953

Adoption by the General Assembly of the Protocol amending the Slavery Convention Signed at Geneva on 25 September 1926.

28 September 1954

Adoption by a Conference of Plenipotentiaries; of the Convention relating to the Status of Stateless Persons.

30 August 1955

Adoption by the First United Nations Congress on the Prevention of Crime and the Treatment of Offenders of the Standard Minimum Rules for the Treatment of Prisoners.

7 September 1956

Adoption by a Conference of Plenipotentiaries; of the Supplementary Convention on the Abolition of Slavery, the Slave trade, and Institutions and Practices Similar to Slavery.

29 January 1957

Adoption by the General Assembly of the Convention on the Nationality of Married Women.

25 June 1957

Adoption by the General Conference of the International Organization of the Convention on the Abolition of Forced Labour.

30 July 1959

Adoption by the Economic and Social Council of resolution 728 F (XXVIII), given the Commission on Human Rights certain responsibilities with regard to the treatment of communications dealing with human rights.

20 November 1959

Adoption by the General Assembly of the Declaration of the Rights of the Child.

14 December 1960

Adoption by the General Assembly of the Declaration on the Granting of Independence to Colonial Countries and Peoples.

30 August 1961

Adoption by a Conference of Plenipotentiaries of the Convention on the Reduction of Statelessness.

7 November 1962

Adoption by the General Assembly of the Convention on Consent to Marriage, Minimum Age and Registration of Marriages.

14 December 1962

Adoption by the General Assembly of resolution 1803 (XVII) on permanent sovereignty over natural resources.

20 November 1963

Adoption by the General Assembly of the United-Nations Declaration on the Elimination of All forms of Racial Discrimination.

21 December 1965

Adoption by the General Assembly of the International convention on the Elimination of All forms of Racial Discrimination. This convention provides for the establishment of the committee on the Elimination of Racial Discrimination.

16 December 1966

Adoption by the General Assembly of the International covenant on Economic, social and cultural Rights. Adoption of the International covenant on civil and political Rights and of the corresponding-optional protocol. This covenant provides for the establishment of the Human Rights committee.

6 June 1967

Adoption by the Economic and Social Council of resolution 1235 (XLII), authorizing the Commission on Human Rights and the Sub commission on Prevention of Discrimination and Protection of Minorities to examine information relevant to gross violations of human rights and fundamental freedoms.

7 November 1967

Adoption by the General I Assembly of the Declaration on the Elimination of Discrimination against Women.

13 May 1968

Proclamation by the International Conference on Human Rights of the Protection of Teheran.

26 November 1968

Adoption by the General Assembly of the Convention on the Non-Applicability of Statutory Limitation to War Crimes and Crimes against Humanity-

22 November 1969

Adoption of the American convention on Human Right!

11 December 1969

Adoption by the General Assembly of the Declaration on Social, Progress and Development.

27 May 1970

Adoption by the Economic and Social council of resolution 1503 (XLVIII), establishing procedures allowing the Commission on Human Rights and the Sub commission on Prevention of Discrimination and Protection of Minorities to hold private meetings to consider communications relating to violations of Human rights and fundamental freedoms.

13 August 1971

Adoption by the Sub commission on Prevention of Discrimination and Protection of Minorities of resolution 1 (XXIV), concerning procedures for the implementation of Economic and Social Council resolution 1503(XLVIII).

30 November 1973

Adoption by the General Assembly of the International Convention on the Suppression and Punishment of the Crime of Apartheid. The Convention provides for the establishment of the Group of Three, which is to monitor its implementation.

9 December 1975

Adoption by the General Assembly of the Declaration on the Protection of All Persons from Being Subjected to Torture and Other Cruel, Inhuman or Degrading Treatment or Punishment.

8 June 1977

Adoption by the Diplomatic Conference on the Reaffirmation and Development of International Humanitarian Law applicable in Armed Conflict of the Protocol Additional to the Geneva Conventions of 12 August 1949, and relating to the Protection of Victims of Non-international Armed Conflicts (Protocol 11).

27 November 1978

Adoption by the General Conference of UNESCO of the Declaration on Race and Racial Prejudice.

17 December 1979

Adoption by the General Assembly of the Code of Conduct for Law Enforcement Officials.

18 December 1979

Adoption by the General Assembly of the Convention on the Elimination of All Forms of Discrimination against Women. The Covenant Provides for the establishment of the Committee on the. Elimination of Discrimination against Women.

June 1981

Adoption of the African Charter on Human and Peoples' Rights, by the Eighteenth Conference of Heads of State and Government of the Organization of African Unity.

25 November 1981

Adoption by the General Assembly of the Declaration on the Elimination of All Form of Intolerance and Discrimination Base on Religion-or Belief.

25 May 1984

Approval by the Economic and Social Council of the Safeguards Guaranteeing protection of the rights of those facing the death penalty.

12 November 1984

Adoption by the General Assembly of the Declaration on the Right of Peoples to Peace.

10 December 1984

Adoption by the General Assembly of the Convention against Torture and Other Cruel, Inhuman or Degrading Treatment or Punishment. The Convention provides for the establishment of the Committee against Torture.

28 May 1985

Adoption by the Economic and Social Council of resolution 1985/17 establishing the Committee on Economic, Social and Cultural Rights, responsible for –monitoring the implementation of the International Covenant on Economic, Social and Cultural Rights.

29 November 1985

Adoption by the General Assembly of the United Nations Standard Minimum Rules for the Administration of Juvenile Justice (The Beijing Rules).

29 November 1985

Adoption by the General Assembly of the Declaration of Basic Principles of Justice for Victims of Crime and Abuse of Power.

29 November 1985

Adoption by the Seventh United Nations Congress on the Prevention of Crime and the Treatment of Officers of the Basic Principles on the Independence of the Judiciary.

10 December 1985

Adoption by the General Assembly of the International Convention against Apartheid in Sports. The Convention provides for the establishment of the Commission against Apartheid in Sports.

13 December 1985

Adoption by the General Assembly of a resolution on the implementation of the Nairobi Forward-looking Strategies for the Advancement of Women.

4 December 1986

Adoption by the General Assembly of the Declaration on the Right to Development.

9 December 1988

Adoption by the General Assembly of the Body of Principles for the Protection of All Persons under Any Form of Detention or Imprisonment.

24 May 1989

Adoption by the Economic and Social Council of the Principles on the Effective Prevention and Investigation of Extra-legal, Arbitrary and Summary Executions.

20 November 1989

Adoption by the General Assembly of the Convention on the Rights of the child. The Convention provides for the establishment of the Committee on the Rights of the Child.

15 December 1989

Adoption by the General Assembly of the Second Optional Protocol to the International Covenant on Civil and Political Rights, aiming at the Adoption of the Death Penalty. The Human Rights Committee is the monitoring body for the Protocol.

7 September 1990

Adoption by the Eighth United Nations Congress on the Prevention of Crime and the Treatment of Offenders of the Basic Principles on the Use of Force and Firearms by Law Enforcement Officials.

7 September 1990

Adoption by the English United Nations Congress on the Prevention of crime and the Treatment of Offenders of the Principles on the Role of Lawyers.

7 September 1990

Adoption by the English United Nations Congress on the Prevention of Crime and the Treatment of Offenders of the Guidelines on the Role of Prosecutors.

30 September 1990

Adoption by the World Summit for Children of the World Declaration on the Survival, Protection and Development of Children and of the Plan of Action for Implementing the World Declaration.

14 December 1990

Adoption by the General Assembly of the United Nations Standard Minimum Rules for Non-custodial Measures (The Tokyo Rules); Basic Principles for the treatment of prisoners; the United Nations Guidelines for the Prevention of Juvenile Delinquency (The Riyadh Guidelines) and the United Nations Rules of the Protection of Juveniles Deprived of their Liberty.

18 Docombor 1990

Adoption by the General Assembly of a resolution deciding to convene a World Conference on Human Rights in 1993.

18 December 1990

Adoption is the General Assembly of the International Convention on the Protection of the Rights of All Migrant Workers and Members of Their Families. The Convention provides for the establishment of the Committee on the Protection of the Rights of all Migrant Workers and Members of Their Families.

20 May 1991

Adoption by the Security Council of a Resolution establishing the United Nations Observer Mission in EL Salvador (ONUSAL).

7 April 1992

Adoption by the Security Council of a resolution deciding to deploy the United Nations Protection Force (UNPROFOR) in the former Yugoslavia.

30 May 1992

Adoption by the Security Council of a resolution demanding that the parties to the conflict in Bosnia and Herzegovina allow the unimpeded delivery of humanitarian supplies.

14 September 1992

Adoption by the Security Council of a resolution authorizing the enlargement of the mandate of UNPROFOR.

16 November 1992

Adoption by the Security Council of a resolution condemning "ethnic cleansing" in Bosnia and Herzegovina.

18 December 1992

Adoption by the Security Council of a resolution demanding that the detention camps in-Bosnia and Herzegovina should be closed.

18 December 1992

Adoption by the General Assembly of the Declaration on the Protection of All Persons from Enforced Disappearance.

18 December 1992

Adoption by the General Assembly of the Declaration on the Rights of Persons Belonging to National or Ethnic, Religious and Linguistic Minorities.

22 February 1993

Adoption by the Security Council of a resolution establishing an International Tribunal for the Prosecution of persons responsible for serious violations of international humanitarian law committed in the territory of the former Yugoslavia since 1991.

20 April 1993

Adoption by the General Assembly of a resolution authorizing the participation of the United Nations jointly with the Organization of American States in an International Civilian Mission to Haiti (MICIVIH).

25 May 1993

Adoption by the Security Council of a resolution adopting the statute of the International Tribunal for the Prosecution of Persons Responsible for Serious Violations of International Humanitarian Law Committed in the Territory of the Former Yugoslavia since 1991.

14 June 1993

The Secretary-General, at the opening of the World Conference on Human Rights in Vienna, describes human rights as "the quintessential values through which we affirm together that we are a single human community".

25 June 1993

Adoption of the Vienna Declaration and Programme of Action at the closing of the World Conference on Human Rights.

20 December 1993

Adoption by the General Assembly of resolution 48/91, proclaiming the Third Decade to Combat Racism and Racial Discrimination.

20 December 1993

Adoption by the General Assembly of resolution 48/163, proclaiming the International Decade of the World's Indigenous People.

20 December 1993

Adoption by the General Assembly of resolution 48/141, establishing the post of United Nations High Commissioner for Human Rights.

23 February 1994

Adoption by the Security Council of a resolution establishing the civil police component of the United Nations Operation in Mozambique (ONUMOZ).

1 July 1994

Adoption by the Security Council of a resolution establishing a Commission of Experts to investigate violations of human rights in Rwanda.

19 September 1994

Adoption by the General Assembly of a resolution establishing the United Nations Mission for the Verification of Human Rights and of Compliance with the Commitments of the Comprehensive Agreement on Human Rights in Guatemala (MINUIGUA).

23 September 1994

Adoption by the Security Council of a resolution re-emphasising that "ethnic cleansing" constitutes a clear violation of international humanitarian law.

8 November 1994

Adoption by the Security Council of resolution 955 (1994), establishing an International Tribunal for Rwanda.

23 December 1994

Adoption by the General Assembly of resolution 49/184, Proclaiming the United Nations Decade for Human Rights Education (1995-2004).

3 March 1995

Adoption by the Commission on Human Rights-of a resolution establishing a working group to elaborate a draft declaration on the rights of indigenous people (resolution 1995/32), i.e (1994-2004).

1995

Bejining Declaration & platform for Action, Fourth World Conference on Women: Action for Equality, Development and peace.

1997

Guiding principles on International Diplacement, 1997.

1998

Declaration on the Right & Responsibility of Individuals, Groups and Organs of Society to Promote and Protect Universally Recognized Human Rights and Fundamental Freedom, 1998.

2000

U.N. millennium Declaration, 2000.

2000

Declaration of Articles on Nationality of Natural persons in relation to the succession of states, 2000.

2000

General Assembly Declaration of commitment on HIV/AIDS, 2000.

2003

Norms on the Responsibilities of Trasnational Corporation and other Business Entyerprises with regard Human Rights, 2003.

2005

Basic principles of Guidelines on the Right to a Remedy and Reparation for victims of gross violations of International Human Rights Law and serious violations of International Humantarian Law, 2005.

Human Rights and Human Genome

1. Universal Declaration on the Human Genome and Human Rights 1997.
2. European convention for the protection of Human Rights and Dignity of the Human Being with Regard to the Application of Biology and Medicine (Convention on Human Rights and Biomedicine), 1997.
3. Additional Protocol to the European convention on Human Rights and Biomedicine, on the prohibition of cloning Human Beings, 1998.
4. Additional Protocol to the European Convention on Human Rights and Biomedicine, concerning Transplantation of Organs and Tissues of Human origin, 2002.
5. Additional Protocol to the European convention on Human Right and Biomedicine, concerning Biomedical Research, 2005.

6. UNESCO International Declaration on Human Genetic Data, 2003.
7. United Nations Declaration on Human Clonning 2005.
8. Universal Declaration on Bioethics and Human Rights, 2005.

Appendix-II

Optional Protocol to the International Covenant On Civil and Political Rights

The state parties to the present protocol

Considering that in order further to achieve the purposes of the covenant on civil and political Rights (hereinafter referred to as the covenant) and the implementation of its provisions it would be appropriate to enable the Human Rights committee set up in part IV of the covenant (hereinafter referred to as the committee) to receive and consider, as provided in the present protocol, communications from individuals claiming to be victims of violations of any of the rights set forth in the covenant.

Have agreed as follows:

Article 1

A state party to the covenant that becomes a party to the present protocol recognizes the competence of the committee to receive and consider communications from individuals subject to its jurisdiction who claim to be victims of a violation by that state party of any of the rights set forth in the covenant. No communication shall be received by the committee if it concerns a state party to the covenant, which is not a party to the present protocol.

Article 2

Subject to the provisions of Article 1, individuals who claims that any of their rights enumerated in the covenant have been violated and who have exhausted all available domestic remedies may submit a written communication to the committee for consideration.

Article 3

The committee shall consider inadmissible any communication under the present protocol which is anonymous, or which it considers to be an abuse of the rights of submission of such communications or to be incompatible with the provisions of the covenant.

Article 4

1. Subject to the provisions of Article 3, the committee shall bring any communication submitted to it under the present protocol to the attention of the state party to the present protocol alleged to be violating any provisions of the covenant.
2. Within six months, the receiving state shall submit to the committee written explanations or statements clarifying the matter and the remedy, if any, that may have been taken by that state.

Article 5

1. The committee shall consider communications received under the present protocol in the light of all written information made available to it by the individual and by the state party concerned.
2. The committee shall not consider any communication from an individual unless it has ascertained that:
   (a) The same matter is not being examined under another procedure of international investigation or settlement;
   (b) The individual has exhausted all available domestic remedies. This shall not be the rule where the application of the remedies is unreasonably prolonged.
3. The committee shall hold closed meetings when examining communications under the present protocol.
4. The committee shall forward its views to the state party concerned and to the individual.

Article 6

The committee shall include in its annual report under Article 45 of the covenant a summary of its activities under the present protocol.

Article 7

Pending the achievement of the objectives of Resolution 1514(XV) adopted by the general Assembly of the United Nations on 14 December, 1960 concerning the Declaration on the Granting of Independence to colonial countries and peoples, the provisions of the present protocol shall in no way limit the right of petition granted to these peoples by the Charter of the United Nations and other international conventions and instruments under the United Nations and its specialized agencies.

Article 8

1. The present protocol is open for signature by any state, which has signed the covenant.
2. The present protocol is subject to ratification by any state, which has ratified or acceded to the covenant. Instruments of ratification shall be deposited with the secretary-General of the United Nations.
3. The present protocol shall be open to accession by any state, which has ratified or acceded to the covenant.
4. Accession shall be effected by the deposit of an instrument of accession with the secretary-General of the United Nations.
5. The secretary-General of the United Nations shall inform all states which have signed the present protocol or acceded to it of the deposit of each instrument of ratification or accession.

Article 9

1. Subject to the entry in to force of the covenant, the present protocol shall enter into force three months after the date of the deposit with the Secretary-General of the United Nations of the tenth instrument of ratification or instrument of accession.

2. For each state ratifying the present protocol or acceding to it after the deposit of the tenth instrument of ratification or instrument of accession, the present protocol shall enter in to force three months after the date of the deposit of its own instrument of ratification or instrument of accession.

Article 10

The provisions of the present protocol shall extend to all parts of federal states without any limitations or exceptions.

Article 11

1. Any state party to the present protocol may propose an amendment and file it with the Secretary-General of the United Nations. The Secretary-General shall thereupon communicate any proposed amendments to the state parties to the present protocol with a request that they notify him whether they favour a conference of state parties for the purpose of considering and voting upon the proposal. In the event that at least one-third of the state parties favour such a conference, the Secretary-General shall convene the conference under the auspices of the United Nations. Annual amendment adopted by a majority of the state parties present and voting at the conference shall be submitted to the General Assembly of the United Nations for approval.
2. Amendments shall come in to force when they have been approved by the General Assembly of the United Nations and accepted by a two-thirds majority of the state parties to the present protocol in accordance with their respective constitutional processes.
3. When amendments come in to force, they shall be binding on those state parties, which have accepted them, other state parties still being bound by the provisions of the present protocol and any earlier amendment which they have accepted.

Article 12

1. Any state party may denounce the present protocol at any time by written notification addressed to the Secretary-General of the United Nations. Denunciation shall take effect three months after the date of receipt of the notification by the Secretary-General.
2. Denunciation shall be without prejudice to the continued application of the provisions of the present protocol to any communication submitted under Article 2 before the effective date of denunciation.

Article 13

Irrespective of the notifications made under Article 8, paragraph 5, of the present protocol, the secretary-General of the United Nations shall inform all states referred to an Article 48, paragraph 1, of the covenant of the following particulars:

(a) Signatures, ratifications and accessions under Article 8:

(b) The date of the entry into force of the present protocol under Article 9 and the date of the entry in to force of any amendments under Article 11:

(c) Denunciations under Article 12.

Article 14

1. The present protocol, of which the Chinese, English, French, Russian and Spanish texts are equally authentic, shall be deposit in the archives of the United Nations.

2. The Secretary-General of the United Nations shall transmit certified copies of the present protocol to all states referred to in Article 48 of the covenant.

Declaration by the Government of India

Whereas the international covenant on Economic, social and cultural Rights and the International covenant on civil and political Rights were adopted by the General Assembly of the United Nations in Resolution 2200(XXI) of 16 December 1966, which covenants are reproduced in the Annexure to this Document:

And whereas it is fit and expedient to accede to the aforesaid covenants subject to the following Declarations:

Declarations

1. With reference to Article 1 of the International covenant on Economic, Social and cultural Rights and Article 1 of the International covenant on Civil and political Rights, the Government of the Republic of India declares that the words "the right of self-determination" appearing in those articles apply only to the peoples under foreign dominations and that these words do not apply to sovereign independent states or to a section of a people or nation-which is the essence of national integrity.

2. With reference to Article 9 of the International covenant on Civil and political Rights, the Government of the Republic of India takes the position that the provisions of Article shall be so applied as to be in consonance with the provisions of clauses (3) to (7) of Article 22 of the constitution of India. Further under the Indian Legal System, there is no enforceable right to compensation for persons claiming to be victims of unlawful arrest or detention against the state.

3. With respect to Article 13 of the International covenant on civil and political Rights, the Government of the Republic of India reserves its right to apply its law relating to foreigners.
4. With reference to Article 4 and 8 of the International covenant on Economic, Social and cultural Rights, and Article 12, 19 (3), 21 and 22 of the International covenant on Civil and political Rights, the Government of the Republic of India declares that the provisions of the said Articles shall be so applied to be in conformity with the provisions of Article 19 of the constitution of India.
5. With reference to Article 7 I of the International covenant on Economic, Social and cultural Rights, the Government of the Republic of India declares that the provisions of the said Article shall be so applied as to be in conformity with the provisions of Article 16 (4) of the constitution of India.

Now, there fore, be it known that the Government of the Republic of India, having seen and considered the said covenants, do hereby accede to the same, subject to the a fore-mentioned Declarations.

In testimony where of I, Neelam Sanjiva Reddy, president of India, have signed these presents and affixed here into my seal at New Delhi this the sixth day of chaitra of the same year one thousand nine hundred and one corresponding to the twenty-seventh day of March of the year one thousand nine hundred and seventy-nine A.D. in the Thirtieth year of the Republic of India.

Deposited with the U.N. O

Sd /-
(Neelam Sanjiva Reddy)
President of India.

Appendix- III

The Protection of Human Rights Act, 1993

(10 OF 1994)

(8th January 1994)

An Act to provide for the constitution of a National Human Rights Commission, State Human Rights Commissions in states and Human Rights Courts for better protection of human rights and for matters connected therewith or incidental thereto.

Be it enacted by Parliament in the Forty-forth Year of the Republic of India as follows: -

Chapter 1
Preliminary

1. Short title, Extent and Commencement

(1) This Act may be called the Protection of human rights Act, 1993.

(2) It extends to the whole of India:

Provided that it shall apply to the State of Jammu and Kashmir only in so far as it pertains to the matters relatable to any of the entries enumerated in list I and III in the Seventh Schedule to the Constitution as applicable to that state.

(3) It shall be deemed to have come into force on the 28th day of September 1993.

2. Definition

1. In this Act, **unless** the context otherwise requires.

    (a) "Armed forces" means the naval, military and air force and includes any other armed forces of the Union.

(b) "Chairperson" means the Chairperson of the Commissioner of the State Commission, as the case may be;

(c) "Commission" means the National Human Rights Commission constituted under section 3;

(d) "Human rights" means the rights relating to life, liberty, equality and dignity of the individual guaranteed by the Constitution or embodied in the International Covenants and enforceable by courts in India;

(e) "Human Rights Courts" means the Human Rights Court Specified under section 30;

(f) "International Covenants" means the International Covenant on Economic, Social and Cultural rights adopted by the General Assembly of the United Nations on the 16th December, 1966;

(g) "Member" means a Member of the Commission or of the State Commission, as the case may be, and includes the Chairperson;

(h) "National Commission for Minorities" means the National Commission for Minorities constituted under section 3 of the National Commission for Minorities Act, 1992; 19 OF 1992

(i) " National Commission for the Scheduled Cast and Scheduled Tribes" means the National Commission for the Scheduled Caste and Scheduled Tribes referred to in article 338 of the Constitution;

(j) "National Commission for Women" means the National Commission for Women constituted under section 3 of the National Commission for Women Act, 1990;

(k) "Notification" means a notification published in the official Gazette;

(l) "Prescribed" means Prescribed by rules made under this Act;

(m) "Public Servant" shall have the meaning assigned to it in section 21 of the Indian Penal Code;

(n) "State Commission" means a State Human Rights Commission constituted under section 21.

2. Any reference in this Act to a law, which is not in force in the State of Jammu and Kashmir, shall, in relation to that State, be

constructed as a reference to a corresponding law, if any, in force in that State.

Chapter II

The National Human Rights Commission

3. Constitution of a National Human Rights Commission

1. The Central Government shall constitute a body to be known as the National Human Rights Commission to exercise the powers conferred upon, and to perform the functions assigned to it, under this Act.
2. The Commission shall consist of:
   (a) a Chairperson who has been a Chief Justice of the Supreme Court;
   (b) one member who is or has been, a Judge of the Supreme Court;
   (c) one Member who is, or has been, the Chief Justice of a High Court;
   (d) two Members to be appointed from amongst persons having knowledge of, or practical experience in, matters relating to human rights.
3. The Chairpersons of the National Commission for Minorities, the National Commission for the Scheduled Castes and Scheduled Tribes and the National Commission for Women shall be deemed to be Members of the Commission for the discharge of function specified in clauses (b) to (j) of section 12.
4. There shall be a Secretary-General who shall be the Chief Executive Officer of the Commission and shall exercise such powers and discharge such functions of the commission as it may delegate to him.
5. The headquaters of the Commission shall be at Delhi and the Commission may, with the previous approval of the Central Government, establish officers at others in India.

2. Appointment of Chairperson and other Members

1.The Chairperson and other Members shall be appointed by the President by warrant under his hand and seal.

Provided that every appointment under this sub-section shall be made after obtaining the recommendations of a Committee consisting of :

(a) The Prime Minister - Chairperson
(b) Speaker of the House of the People - Member
c) Minister in-Charge of the MHA in the Government of India - Member
(b) Leader of the opposition in the House of the People -Member
(c) Leader of the opposition in the Council of States -Member
(f) Deputy Chairman of the Council of States -Member

Provided further that on sitting Judge of the Supreme Court or sitting Chief Justice of a High Court shall be appointed except after consultation with the Chief Justice of India.

(2) No appointment of a Chairperson or a Member shall be invalid merely by reason of any vacancy in the Committee.

5. Removal of a Member of the Commission

1. Subject to the provisions of sub-section (2), the Chairperson or any other Member of the Commission shall only be removed from his office by order of the President on the ground of proved misbehavior or incapacity after the Suprme Court, on reference being made to it by the President, has, on inquiry held in accordance with the procedure prescribed in that behalf by the Supreme Court, reported that the Chairperson or such other Member, as the case may be, ought on any such ground to be removed.
2. Not withstanding anything in sub-section (1), the President may be order remove from office the Chairperson or any other Member if the Chairperson or such other Member, as the case may be-
   (a) is adjudged an insolvent; or
   (b) engages during his term of office in any paid employment outside the duties of his office; or
   (c) is until to continue in office by reason of infirmity of mind or body; or
   (d) is of unsound mind and stands so declared by a competent court; or
   (e) is convicted and sentenced to imprisonment for an offence which in the opinion of the President involves moral turpitude.

6. Term of office of Members

(1) A person appointed as chairperson shall hold office for a term of five years from the date on which he enters upon his office or until he attains the age of seventy years, whichever is earlier.

(2) A serson appointed as a Member shall hold office for a term of five years from the date on which he enters upon his office and shall be eligible for re-appointment for another term of five years.

Provided that no Member shall hold office after he has attained the age of seventy years.

(3) On ceasing to hold office, a Chairperson or a Member shall be ineligible for further employment under the Government of India or under the Government of any State.

7. Member to act as Chairperson or to discharge has function in certain circumstances

(1) In the event of the occurrence of any vacancy in office of the Chairperson by reason of his death, resignation or otherwise, the Presicent may, by notification, authorise one of the Members to act as the Chairperson until the appointment of a new Chairperson to fill such vacancy.

(2) When the Chairperson is unable to discharge his functions owing to absence on leave or otherwise, such one of the Members as the President may, by notification, authorise in this behalf, shall discharge the functions of the Chairperson until the date on which the Chairperson resumes his duties.

8. Terms and conditions of service of Members

The asaries and allowances payable to, and other terms and conditions of service of, the Member shall be such as may be prescribed.

Provided that neither the salary and allowances nor the other terms and conditions of service of a Member shall be varied to his disadvantage after has appointment.

9. Vacancis, ect., not to invalidate the proceedings of the Commission

No act or proceedings of the commission shall be questioned or shall be invalidated merely on the ground of existence of any vacancy or defect in the constitution of the Commission.

10. Procedure to be regulated by the Commission

(1) The Commission shall meet at such time and place as the Chairperson may think fit.

(2) The Commission shall regulate its own procedure.

(3) All orders and decisions of the Commission shall be authenticated by the Secretary-General or any other officer of the Commission duly authorised by the Chairperson in this behalf.

11. Officers and other staff of the Commission

(1) The Central Government shall make available to the Commission:-

  (a) an officer of the rank of the Secretary to the Government of India who shall be the Secretary-General of the Commission; and

  (b) Such police and investigative staff under an office not below the rank of a Director General of Police and such other officers and staff as may be necessary for the efficient performance of the functions of the Commission.

(2) Subject to such rules as may be made by the Central Government in this behalf, the Commission may appoint such other administrative, technical and scientific staff as it may consider necessary.

(3) The salaries, allowances and conditions of service of the officers and other staff appointed under sub-section (2) shall be such as may be prescribed.

Chapter III

Functions and Powers of the Commission

12. Functions of the Commission

The Commission shall perform all or any of the following function, namely:-

(a) inquire, Suo Motu or on a petition presented to it by a victin or any person on his behalf, into complaint of

  (i) Violation of human rights or abetment thereof or

  (ii) Negligence in the prevention of such violation, by a public servent.

(b) intervene in any proceeding involving any allegation of violation of human rights pending before a court with the approval of such court' (c) visit, under intimation to the State Governmant, any jail or any other institution under the control of the State Governmant, where persons are detained or lodged for purpose of treatment, reformation or protection to study the living conditions of the inmated and make recommendations thereon;

(d) review the safeguards provided by or under the Constitution or any law for the time being in force for the protection of human rights and recommend measures for their effective implementation;

(e) review the factors, including acts of terrorism that inhibit the enjoyment of human rights and recommend appropriate remedial measures;

(f) study treaties and other international instruments on human rights and make recommendations for their effective implementation;

(g) undertake and promote research in the field of human rights;

(h) spread human rights literacy among various sections of society and promote awareness of the safeguards available for the protection of these rights through publications, the media, seminars and other available means;

(i) encourage the efforts of non- Governmantal organisations and institutions warking in the field of human rights

(j) such other functions as it may consider necessary for the promotion of human rights.

13. Powers relating to inquiries

(1) The Commission shall, while inquiring into complaints under this Act, have all the powers of a civil court trying a suit under the Code of civil Procedure, 1908 (5 of 1908), and in particular in respect of the following matters, namely:-

(a) summoning and enforcing the attendance of witnesses and examining them on oath;

(b) discovery and production of any document;

(c) receiving evidence on affidavits;

(d) requisitioning any public record or copy thereof from any court of office;

(e) issuing commission for the examination of witnesses or documents;

(f) any other matter which may be prescribed.

(2) The Commission shall have power to require any person, subject to any privilege which may be clained by that person under any law for the time being in force, to furnish information on such points or matter as, in the opinion of the Commission, may be useful for, or relevant to, the subject matter of the inquiry and any person so required shall be deemed to be legally bound to furnish such information within the meaning of section 176 and section 177 of the Indian Penal Code (45 of 1860).

(3) The Commission or any other office, not bellow the rank of a Gazatted Offocer, specially authorised in this behalf by the Commission may enter any building or place where the Commission has reason to believe that any document relation to the subject matter of the inquiry may be found, and any seize any such document of take extracts or copies therefrom subject to the provisions of section 100 pf the Code of Criminal Procedure, 1973 (2 of 1974), in so far as it may be applicable.

(4) The Commission shall be deemed to be a civil court and when any offence as is described in section 175, section 178, section 179, section 180 or section 228 of the Indian Penal Code (45 of 1860) is committed in the view or presence of the Commission, the Commission may, after recording the facts Constituting the offence and the statement of the accused as provided for in the Code of Criminal Procedure, 1973 (2 of 1974), forward the case to a Magistrate having jurisdiction to try the same and the Magistrate to whom any such case is forwarded shall proceed to hear the complaint against the accused as if the case has been forwarded to him under section 346 of the Code of Criminal Procedure, 1973.

(5) Every proceeding before the Commission shall be deemed to be a judicial proceeding within the meaning of sections 193 and 228 and for the purpose of section 196, of the Indian Penal Code (45 of 1860), and the Commission shall be deemed to be a civil court for all the purposes of section 195 and Chapter XXVI of the Code of Criminal Procedure, 1973 (2 of 1974).

14. Investigation

(1) The Commission may, for the purpose of conducting any investigation pertaining to the inquiry, utilise the services of any officer or investigation agency of the Central Government or any State Government with the concurrence of the Central Government or the State Government at the case may be.

(2) For the purpose of investigation into any matter pertaining to the inquiry; any officer or agency whose services are utilised under sub-section (1) may, subject to the direction and control of the Commission:

(a) summon and enforce the attendence of any person and examine him;

(b) require the discovery and production of any document; and

(c) requisition any public record or copy thereof from any office

(3) The provisions of section 15 shall apply in relation to any statement made by a person before any officer or agency whose services are utilisd under sut-section (1) as they apply in relation to any statement made by a person in the course of giving evidence before the Commission.

(4) The office or agency whose service are utilised under sub-section (1) shall investigate into any matter pertaining to the inquiry and submit a report thereon to the Commission within such period as may be specified by the Commission in this behelf.

(5) The Commission shall satisfy itself about the correctness of the facts states and the conclusion, if any, arrived at in the report submitted to it under sub-section (4) and for this purpose the Commission may make such inquiry (including the examination of the person or persons who conducted or assisted in the investigation) as it thinks fit.

15. Statement made by persons to the Commission

No statement made by a person in the course of giving evidence before the Commission shall subject him to, or be used against him in, any civil or criminal proceeding except a prosecution for giving evidence by such statement:

Provided that the statement:

(a) is made in reply to the question which he is required by the Commission to answer; or

(b) is relevant to the subject matter of the inquiry

16. Persons likely to be prejudicially affected to be heard

If, at any stage of the inquiry, the Commission:

(a) considers, it necessary to inquier into the conduct of any person; or

(b) is of the opinion that the reputation of any person is likely to be prejudicially affected by the inquiry;

It shall give to that person a reasonable opportunity of being heard in the inquiry and to procedure evidence in his defence:

Provided that nothing in this section shall apply where the credit of a witness is being impeached.

Chapter IV
Procedure
17. Inquiry into Complaints

The Commission while inquiring into complaints of violations of human rights may-

(i) call for information or report from the Central Government or any State Government or any other authority or organisation subordinate thereto within such time as may be specified by it;

Provided that-

(a) if the information or report is not received within the time stipulated by the Commission, it may proceed to inquire into the complaint on its own;

(b) if, on receipt of information or report, the Commission is satisfied either that no further inquiry is required or that the required action has been intitled ro taken by the concerned Government or authority, it may not proceed with the complaint and inform the complainant accordingly;

(ii) without prejudice to anything contained in clause (i), if th consideres necessary, having regard to the nature of the complaint, initiate an inquiry.

18. Steps after inquiry

The Commission may take any of the following steps upon the completion of an inquiry held under this Act, namely:

(1) where the inquiry discloses the commission of violaion of human rights or negligence in the prevention of violation of human rights by a public servent, it may recommend to the concerned Government or authority the initiation of proceeding for prosecution or such other action as the Commission may deem fit against the concerned person or Persons;

(2) approach the Supreme Court or the High Court concerned for such directions, others or writs as that Court may deem necessary;

(3) recommend to the concerned Government or authority for the grant of such immediate interim relief to the victim or the members of his family as the Commission may consider necessary;

(4) subject to the provisions of clause (5), provide a copy of the inquiry report to the petitioner or his representative;

(5) the commission shall send a copy of its inquiry report together with its recommendations to the concerned Governemnt or authority and the concerned Governemnt or authority shall, within a period of one month,or such further time as the Commission may allow, forward its comments on the report, including the action taken or proposed to be taken thereon, to the Commission;

(6) the Commission shall publish its inquiry report together with the comments on the concerned Government or authority, if any, and the action taken or proposed to be taken by the concerned Governemtn or authority on the recommendations of the Commission.

19. Procedure with respect to armed forces

(1) Notwithstanding any thing content in this Act, while dealing with complaints of violation of human rights by members of the armed forces, the Commission shall adopt the following procedure, namely;

- (a) it may, either on its won motion or on receipt of a petition , seek a report from the Central Government;
- (b) after the receipt of the report, it may, either not proceed wuth the complaint or, asd the case may be , make its recommendations to the Governemnt.

(2) The Central Government shall inform the Commission of the action taken on the recommendations within three months or such further time as the Commission may allow.

(3) The Commission shall publish its report together with its recommendations made to the Central Government and the action taken by the Government on such recommendations.

(4) The Commission shall provide a copy of the report published under sub-section (3) to the petitioner or his representative.

20. Annual and special reports of the Commission

(1) The Commission shall submit an annual report to the Central Government and to the State Government concerned and may

at any time submit special reports on any matter which in its opinion, is of such urgency of importance that it should not be deferred till submission of the annual report.

(2) The Central Government and the State Government, as the case may be, shall cause the annual and special reports of the Commission to be laid before each House of Parliament or the State Legislature respectively, as the case may be, along with a memorandum of action taken or propose to be taken on the recommendations of the Commission and the reasons for non-acceptance of the recommendations, if any.

Chapter v

State Human Rights Commisssion

21.Constitution of state Human Rights Commissions

(1) A State Government may constitute a body to be known as the .....(name of the state) Human Rights Commission to exercise the powers conferred upon , and to perform the functions assigned to, A State Commission under this chapter.

(2) The State Commission shall consist of:

(a) a Chairperson who has been a Chief Justice of a High Court;

(b) one Member who is, or has been, a Judge of a High Court;

(c) one Member who is, or has been, a District Judge in that State;

(d) two Members to be appointed from amongst persons having knowledge of, or practical experience in, matters relating to human rights.

(3) There shall be a Secretary who shall be the Chief Executive Officer of the State Commission and shall exercise such powers and discharge such functions of the State Commission as it may delegate to him.

(4) The headquarters of the State Commission shall be at such place as the State Government may, by notification, specify.

(5) A State Commission may inquire into violation of human rights only in respect of matters relatable to any of the entries enumerated in List II and List III in the Seventh Schedule to the Constitution.

Provided that if any such matter is already being inquired into by the Commission or any of the Commission duely constituted under any law for the time being in force, the State Commission shall not inquire into the said matter:

Provided further that in relation to the Jammu and Kashmir Human Rights Commission, this sub-section shall have effected as if for the words and figures "List II and List III in the Seventh Schedule to the Constitution", the words and figures "List III in the Seventh Schedule to the Constitution as applied to the State of Jammu and Kashmir and in respect of matters in relation to which the Legislature of that State has power to make laws" has been substituted.

22. Appointment of Chairperson and other members of State Commission

(1) The Chairperson and other Members of the Commission shall be appointed by the Governor by warrant under his hand and seal;

Provided that every appointment under this subsection shall be after obtaining the recommendation of a Committee consisting of-

(a) The Chief Minister - *Chairperson*

(b) Speaker of the Legislative Assembly - *Member*

(c) Minister- in- charge of the Department of Home in that State - *Member*

(d) Leader of the Opposition in the Legislative Assembly -*Member*

Provided further that where there is a legislative council in a state, the Chairperson of that Council and the leader of the opposition in that Council shall also be members of the committee.

Provided also that no sitting Judge of a High Court or a sitting District Judge shall be appointed except after consultation with the Chief Justice of the High Court of the concerned state.

(2) No appointment of a Chairperson or a Member of the state Commission shall be invalid nearly be reason of any vacancy in the Committee.

23. Removal of the Member of state Commission

(1) Subject to the provisions Subsection (2), the Chairperson or any other Member of a State Commission shall only be removed from his office by an order of the President on the grounds of proved misbehaviour or incapacity after the Supreme Court being made to it by the President, has, on inquiry held in accordance with the procedure prescribed in that behalf by the Supreme Court reported that Chairperson or such other member, as the case may be ought in any such ground to be removed.

(2) Notwithstanding any thing in subsection (1), the President may by order remove from office the chairperson or any other Member if the Chairperson or any other Membre as the case may be.

(a) is adjudged and insolvent; or

(b) engages during his term of office in any paid employment ourside the duties of his offise; or

(c) is unfit to continue by reason of infirmaty of mind or body; or

(d) is of unsound mind and stands so declaired by a competent court; or

(e) is convicted and sentenced to impresonment for an office which in opinion of the president involves moral turpitude.

24.Term of office of Members of the State Commission

(1) A person appointed as Chairperson shall hold office of five years from the date on which he enters upon his officer or until he attains the age of seventy years, whichever is earlier.

(2) A person appointed as a Member shall hold office for a term of five years from the date on which he enters upon his office and shall be eligible for re-appointment for another term of five years.

Provided that no member shall hold office after he has attend the age of seventy years.

(3) On ceasing to hold office, a Chairperson or A member shall be ineligible for further employment under the Government of a state or under the Government of India.

25.Member to act as Chairperson or to Discharge his functions in certain Circumstances

(1) In the event of the occurance of any vacancy in the office of the Chairperson by reason of his death, resignation or otherwise, the Governor may, by notification authorise one of the Members to act as the Chairperson until the appointment of a new chairperson to fill such vacancy.

(2) When the Chairperson is unable to discharct his function owing to absence on leave or otherwise, such one of the Members as the Governor may, by nitification authorise in this behalf shall discgarge the function of the Chairperson until the date on which the Chairperson resumes his duties.

26. Terms and Conditions of Service of Members of the State Commission

The salaries and allownances payable to, and other terms and conditions of service, the Members shall be such as may be prescribed by the State Government.

Provided that neither the salary and allowances nor the other terms and conditions of service of a Member shall be varied to his disadvantage after his appointment.

27. Officers and Staff of the State Commission

(1) The State Government shall make available to the State Commission
  (a) an officer not below the rank of a Secretary to the State Government who shall be the secretary of the State Commission and
  (b) such police and investigative staff under an officer not below the rank of an inspector General of Police and such other officers and staff as may be necessary for the efficient performance of the functions of the State Commission.

(2) subject to such rules as may be by the State Government in this behalf, the State Commission may appoint such other administrative, technique and scientific staff as it may consider necessary.

(3) The salaries, allowances and conditions of service of the officers and other staff appoint under sub-section (2) shall be such as may be prescribed by the State Government.

28. Annual or Special Reports of the Commission

(1) The State Commission shall submit an annual Report to the State Government and may at any time submit Special reports on any matter which in its opinion, is of such urgency or importance that it should not be deferred till submission of the annual report

(2) The State Government shall cause the Annual and Special Reports of the State Human Rights Commission to be laid before each House of State Legislature where it consists of two Houses Or where huch Legislature consists of ona House, before that House alongwith a memorandum of action taken or proposed to be taken on the recommendations of the state Commission and the reasons for nonaccpetance of the recommendations, if any.

29. Application of Certain provisions relating to NHRC to state Commission

The provisions of section 9,10, 12, 13, 14, 15, 16, 17, and 18 shall apply to a State Commission ans shall have effect, subject to the following modifications, namely:

(a) references to "Commission" shall be constructed as references to State Commission";

(b) in section 10, in sub-section (3), for the word "Secretary-General", the word "Secretary" shall be substituted;

(c) in section 12, clause (f) shall be omitted;

(d) in section 17, in clause (i), the words "Central Government or any" shall be omitted;

Chapter VI

30. Human Rights Courts

For the porpose of providing speed trial of offences arising out of violations of human rights, State Governments may with the concurrence of the Chief Justice of the concerned High Court by notification, specify for each District a Court of Session to be a Human Rights Courts to try the said offences.

Provided that nothing in this section shall apply if-

(a) a Court of Session is already specified as a special court; or

(b) a special court is alresdy constituted, for such offences under any other law the time being in force.

31. Special Public Procecutor

For every human rights court the State Government shall by notification specify a public procecure of appoint an advocate who has been in practice as an advocate for not less than seven years as a public procecuter for the purpose of conducting cases in that court.

Chapter VII

Finance, Accounts and Audit

32. Grants by the Central Government

(1) The Central Government shall after due appropriation made by Parliament by law in this behalf, pay to the Commission by way of grants such sums of money as the Central Government may think fit for being utilised for the purposes of this Act.

(2) The Commission may spend such sums as it thinks fit for performing the functions under this Act, and such sum shall be

treated as expenditure payable out of the grants referred to in sub-section (1).

33. Grants by the State Government

(1) The State Government shall, after due appropriation made by Legislature by law in this behalf, pay to the State Commission by way of grants such sums of money as the State Government may think fit for being utilised for the purposes of this Act.

(2) The State Commission may spend such sums as it thinks fit for performing the functions under Chapter V, and such sums shall be treated as expenditure payable out of the grants referred to in sub-section (1).

34. Accounts and audit

(1) The Commission shall maintain proper accounts and other relevant records and prepare an annual statement of account in such form as may be prescribed by the Central Government in consultation with the Comptroller and Auditor-General of India.

(2) The Accounts of the Commission shall be audited by the Comptroller and Auditor-General at such intervals as may be specified by him and any expenditure incurred in connection with such audit shall be payable by the Commission to the Comptroller and Auditor-General.

(3) The Comptroller and Auditor-General and any person appointed by him in connection with the audit of the accounts of the Commission under this Act shall have the same rights and privileges and the authority in connection with such audit as the Comptroller and Auditor-General generally has in connection with the audit of Government accounts and, in particular, shall have the right to demand the Protection of books, accounts, connected vouchers and other documents and papers and to inspect any of the offices of the Commission.

(4) The accounts of the Commission as certified by the Comptroller and Auditor-General or any other person appointed by him in this behalf, together with the audit report thereon shall be forwarded annually to the Central Government by the Commission and the Central Government shall cause the audit report to be laid, as soon as may be after it is received, before each House of Parliament.

35. Accounts and audit of State Commission

(1) The State Commission shall maintain proper accounts and other relevant records and prepare an annual statement of accounts in such form as may be prescribed by the State Government in consultation with the Comptroller and Auditor-General of India.

(2) The accounts of the State Commission shall be audited by the Comptroller and Auditor-General at such intervals as may be specified by him and any expenditure incurred in connection with such audit shall be payable by the State Commission to the Comptroller and Auditor-General.

(3) The Comptroller and Auditor-General and any person appointed by him in connection with the audit of the accounts of the State Commission under this Act shall have the same rights and privileges and the authority in connection with such audit as the Comptroller and Auditor-General generally has in connection with the audit Government accounts and, in particular, shall have the right to demand the production of books, accounts, connected vouchers and other documents and papers and to inspect any of the offices of the State Commission.

(4) The accounts of the State Commission, as certified by the Comptroller and Auditor-General or any other person appointed by him in this behalf, together with the audit report thereon, shall be forwarded annually to the State Government by the State Commission and the State Government shall cause the audit report to be laid, as soon as may be after it is received, before the State Legislature

Chapter VIII

Miscellaneous

36. Matters not subject to jurisdiction of the commission

(1) The Comission shall not inquire into any matter which is pending before a State Commission or any other Commission duly Constituted under any law for the time being in force.

(2) The Commission or the State Commission shall not inquire into any matter after the expiry of one year from the date on which the act constituting violation of human rights is alleged to have been committed.

37. Constitution of special investigation team

Notwithstanding anything contained in any other Law, for the time being in force ,where the Governemnt considers it necessary so to do, it may constitute one ore more special investigation team, consisiting of such police officers as it think necessary for purposes of investigation and prosecution of offences arising out of violations of human rights.

38. Protection of action taken in good faith

No suit or other legal proceeding shall lie against the Central Government, State Government, Commission, the State commission or any Member thereof or any person acting under the direction either of the Central Government, State Government, commission, or the state commission in respect of anything which is in good faith done or intended to be done in pursuance of this Act or of any rules or any order made thereunder or in respect of the publication by or under the authority of the Central Government, State Government, Commission or the state Commission of any report, paper or proceedings.

39. Members and officers to be public servants

Every Member of the Commission , State Commission and every officer appointed or authorised by the Commission or the State Commission to exercise functions under this act shall be deemed to be a public sevant within the meaning of section 21 of the Indian Penal Code (45 of 1860)

40. Power of Central Government of make rules

(1) The Central Government may, by notification, make rules to carry out the provisions of this act.

(2) In particular and without prejudice to the generality of the foregoing power, such rules may provide for all or any of the following matters, namely;

   (a) the salaries and allowances and other terms and conditions of service of the Members under section 8;

   (b) the conditions subject to which other administrative, technical and scientific staff may be appointed by the commission and the salaries and allowances of officers and other staff under sub-section (3) of section 11;

   (c) any other power of a civil court required to be prescribed under clauses (f) of sub-section (1) of section 13;

(d) the form in which the annual statement of accounts is to be prepared by the commission under sub-section (1) of section 34; and

(e) any other matter which has to be, or may be, prescribed.

(3) Every rule made under this Art shall be laid, as soon as may be after it is made, before each House of parliament, while it is in session, for a total period of thirty days which may be comprised in one session or in two or more successive sessions, and if, before the expiry of the session immediately following the session or the successive sessions aforesaid, both Houses agree in making any modification in the rule or both Houses agree that the rule should not be made, the rule shall thereafter have effect only in such modified form or be of no effect, as the case may be; so, however, that any such modification or annulment shall be with out prejudice to the validity of anything previously done under that rule.

41. Power of State Government to make rules

(1) The State Government may, by notification, make rules to out the provisions if this Act.

(2) In particular and without prejudice to the generality of the fore going power, such rules may provide for all or any of the following matters, namely:

(a) the salaries and allowances and other terms and conditiobs of service of the members under section 26;

(b) the condition subject to which other administrative, technical and scientific staff may be appointed by the State Commission and the salaries and allowances of officers and other staff under sub-section (1) of section 35;

(c) the form in which the annual statement of accounts is to be prepared under sub-section (1) of section 35.

(3) Every rule made by the State Government under this section shall be laid, as soon as may be after it is made, before each House of State Legislature where it cinsists of two Houses, or where each legislature consists of one House, before that House.

42. Power to remove difficulties

(1) If any difficulties arises in giving effect to the provisions of this Act,the Central Government may, by order published in the official gazette, make such provisions. Not in consistence with the

provisions of this Act as appeared to it to be necessary expedient for removing the difficulty.

Provided that no such order shall be made after the expiry of the period of two years from the date of commencement of this Act.

(2) Every order made under this section shall. As soon as may be after it is made, be laid before each house of Parliament.

43. Repeal and savings

(1) The protection of human rights ordinance 1993 is hereby repealed.

(2) Notwithstanding such repeal, any thing done or any action taken under the said ordinance (Ord. 30 of 1993), shall be deemed to have been done or taken under the corresponding provisions of this Act.

Appendix-IV

The Right to Information Act, 2005

[Act No. 22 of 2005] ***[15th June 2005]***

New Delhi, the 21st June 2005

The following Act of Parliament received the assent of the President on the 15th June 2005, and is hereby published for general information:

An Act to provide for setting out the practical regime of rights to information for citizens to secure access to information under the control of public authorities, in order to promote transparency and accountability in the working of every public authority, the constitution of a Central Information Commission and State Information Commission and for matters connected therewith or incidental thereto.

WHEREAS the Commission of India has established democratic Republic;

AND WHEREAS democracy requires an informed citizenry and transparency of information which are vital to its functioning and also to contain corruption and to hold Governments and their instrumentalities accountable to the governed;

AND WHEREAS revelation of information in actual practice is likely to conflict with other public interests including efficient operations of the Governments, optimum use of limited fiscal resources and the preservation of confidentiality of sensitive information;

AND WHEREAS it is necessary to harmonise these conflicting interests while preserving the paramount of the democratic ideal;

NOW THEREFORE, it is expedient to provide for furnishing certain information to citizens who desire to have it.

BE it enacted by Parliament in the Fifty-sixth year of the Republic of India as follows:

CHAPTER-I

Preliminary

1. Short title, extent and commencement-

(1) This Act may be called the Right to Information Act, 2005.

2) It extends to the whole of India except the State of Jammu and Kashmir.

(1) The provisions of Sub-section 4, Sub-sections (1) and (2) of section 5, Sections 12, 13, 15, 16, 24, 27 and 28 shall come into force at once, and the remaining provisions of this Act shall come into force on the one hundred and twentieth day of its enactment.

2. Definitions-in this Act, unless the context otherwise requires,

(a) **"Appropriate Government"** means in relation to a public authority which is established, constituted, owned, controlled or substantially financed by funds provided directly or indirectly –

(I) by the Central Government or the Union Territory administration, the central Government;

(II) by the State Government, the State Government;

(b) **"Central Information Commission"** means the Central Information Commission constituted under Sub-section (1) of Section 12;

(c) **"Central Public Information Commission"** means the Central Public Information Officer designated under Sub-section (1) and includes a Central Assistant Public Information Officer designated as such under Sub-section (2) of Section 5;

(d) **"Chief Information Commissioner"** and **"information Commissioner"** mean the Chief Information Commissioner and Information Commissioner appointed under Sub-section (3) of section 12;

(e) **"competent authority"** means –

(I) the Speaker in the case of the House of the People or the Legislative Assembly of a State or a Union Territory having such Assembly and the Chairman in the case of the Council of State of a Legislative Council of States;

(II) the Chief Justice of India in the case of the Supreme Court;

(III) the Chief Justice of the High Court in the Case of a High Court;

(IV) the President or the Governor, as the case may be, in the case of other authorities established or constituted by or under the Constitution;

(V) the administrator appointed under Article 239 of the Constitution;

(f) **"information"** means any material in any from, including records, documents, memos, e-mails, opinions, advices, press releases, circulars, orders, logbooks, contracts, reports, paper releases, circulars, orders logbooks, contracts, reports, papers, samples, models, data material held in any electronic from and information relating to any private body which cal be accessed by a public authority under any other law for the time being in force;

(g) **"prescribed"** means prescribed by rules made under this Act by the appropriate Government or the Competent authority, as the case may be;

(h) **"public authority"** means any authority or body or institution of self-government established or constituted-

(a) by or under the Constitution;

(b) by any other law made by Parliament;

(c) by any other law made by State Legislature;

(d) by notification issued or order made by the appropriate Government,

and includes any-

(I) body owned, controlled or substantially financed;

(II) non-Government organisation substantially financed;

directly or indirectly by funds provided by the appropriate Government;

(i) "**Record**" includes-

(a) any document, manuscript and file;

(b) any microfilm, microfiche and facsimile copy of a document;

(c) any reproduction of image or images embodied in such microfilm (whether enlarged or not); and

(d) any other material produced by a computer or any other device;

(j) **"Right to Information"** means the right to information accessible under that Ace which is held by or under the control of any public authority and includes the right to-
   (I) inspection of work, documents, records;
   (II) taking notes, extracts or certified copies of documents or records;
   (III) taking certified samples of material;
   (IV) obtaining information in the form of diskettes, floppies, tapes, video cassettes or in any other electronic mode or through printouts where such information is stored in a computer or in any other device;

(k) **"State Information Commission"** means the State Information Commission constituted under Sub-section (1) of Section 15;

(l) **"State Chief Information Commission"** and **"State Information Commissioner"** mean the State Chief Information Commissioner and the State information Commissioner appointed under Sub-section (3) of Section 15;

(m) **"State Public Information Officer"** means the State Public Information Officer designated under Sub-section (1) and includes a State Assistant Public Information Officer designated as such under Sub-section (2) of Section 5;

(n) **"Third party"** means a person other than the citizen making a request for information and includes a public authority.

CHAPTER –II

Right to information and obligations of public authorities

3. **Right to information –** Subject to the provisions of this Act, all citizens shall have the right to information.

4. **Obligation of public authorities –** (1) Every public authority shall –
   (a) Maintain all its records duly catalogued and indexed in a manner and the from which facilitates the right to information under this Act and ensure that all records that are appropriate to be computerised are within a reasonable time and subject to availability of resources, computerised and connected through a network all over the country on different systems so that access to such records is facilitated;
   (b) publish within one hundred and twenty days from the enactment of this Act,-

(I) the particulars of its organisation, function and duties;

(II) the powers and duties of its officers and employees;

(III) the procedure followed in the decision making process, including channels of supervision and accountability;

(IV) the norms set by it for the discharge of its functions;

(V) the rules, regulations, instructions and records, held by it or under its control or used by its employees for discharging its functions;

(VI) a statement of the categories of documents that are held by it or under its control;

(VII) the particulars of any arrangement that exists for consultation with, or representation by, the members of the public in relation to the formulation of its policy or implementation thereof;

(VIII) a statement of the boards, councils, committees and other bodies consisting of two or more persons constituted as its part or for the purpose of its advice, and as to whether meetings of those boards, councils, committees and other bodies are open to the public, or the minutes of such meetings are accessible for public;

(IX) a directory of its officers and employees;

(X) the monthly remuneration received each of its officers and employees, including the system of compensation as provided in its regulations;

(XI) the budget allocated to each of its agency, indicating the particulars of all plans, proposed expenditures and reports on disbursements made;

(XII) the manner of execution of subsidy programmes, including the amounts allowed and the details of beneficiaries of such programmes;

(XIII) particulars of recipients of concessions, permits or authorisations granted by it;

(XIV) details in respect of the information, available to or held by it, reduced in an electronic form;

(XV) the particulars of facilities available to citizens for obtaining information, including the working hours of a library or reading room, if maintained for public use;

(XVI) the names, designations and other particulars of the Public Information Officers;

(XVII) such other information as may be prescribed; and thereafter update these publications every year;

(c) publish all relevant facts while formulating important policies or announcing the decisions which affect public;

provide reasons for its administrative or quasi-judicial decisions to affected persons.

(2) It shall be a constant endeavour of every public authority to take steps in accordance with the requirements of Clause (b) of Sub-section (1) to provide as much information ***suo motu*** to the public at regular intervals through various means of communications, including internet, so that the public have minimum resort to the use of this Act to obtain information.

(1) For the purposes of Sub-section (1), every information shall be disseminated widely and in such from and manner which is easily accessible to the public.

(2) All materials shall be disseminated taking into consideration the cost effectiveness, local language and the most effective method of communication in that local area and the information should be easily accessible, to the extent possible in electronic format with the Central Public Information Officer or State Public Information Officer, as the case may be, available free or at such cost of the medium or the print cost price as may be prescribed.

Explanation- For the purposes of Sub-sections (3) and (4), "disseminated" means making known or communicated the information of the public through notice boards, newspapers, public announcements, media broadcasts, the internet or any other means, including inspection of offices of any public authority.

5. Designation of Public Information officers- (1) Every public authority shall, within one hundred days the enactment of this Act, designate as many officers as the Central Public Information Officers of State Public Information Officers, as the case may be, in all administrative units or offices under it as may be necessary to provide information of persons requesting for the information under this Act.

(2) without Prejudice to the provisions of Sub-section (1), every public authority shall designated an officer, within one hundred days of the enactment of this Act, at each sub-divisional level or other sub-district level as a Central Assistant Public Information Officer or a State Assistance Public Information Officer, as the case may be, to receive the applications for information or appeals

under this Act for forwarding the same forthwith to the central public Information officer or the State Public Information Officer or senior officer specified under Sub-section (1) of Section 19 or the Central Information Commission or the State Information Commission, as the case may be:

Provided that where an application for information or appeal is given to a Central Assistant public information Officer or a State Assistant Public Information Officer, as the case may be, a period of five days shall be added in computing the period for response specified under Sub-section (1) of Section 7.

3) Every central Public Information Officer or State Public Information Officer, as the case may be , shall deal with requests from persons seeking information and render reasonable assistance to the persons seeking such information.

4) The Central Public Information Officer or State Public Information Officer, as the case may be, may seek the assistance of any other officer as he or she considers it necessary for the proper discharge of his or her duties.

5) Any officer, whose assistance has been sought under Sub-section (4), shall render all assistance to the Central Public Information Officer or State Public Information Officer, as the case may be, seeking his or her assistance and for the purpose of any contravention of the provision of the Act, such other officer shall be treated as a central Public Information Officer or State Public Information Officer, as the case may be.

2. Respect for obtaining information-(1) A person, who desires to obtain any information under this Act, shall make a request in writing or through electronic means in English or Hindi or in official language of the area in which the application is being made, accompanying such free as may be prescribed, to-

(a) the Central Public information Officer or State Public Information Officer, as the case may be, of the concerned public authority;

(b) the Central Assistant Public Information Officer or State Assistant Public Information Officer, as the case may be, specifying the particulars of the information sought by him or her:

Provided that where such request cannot be made in writing, the Central Public Information Officer or State

Public Information Officer, as the case may be, shall render all reasonable assistance to the person making the request orally to reduce the same in writing.

(2) An applicant making request for information shall not be required to give any reason for requesting the information or any other personal details accept those that may be necessary for contacting him.

(3) Where an application is made to a public authority requesting for an information,-

(i) which is held by another public authority; or

(ii) the Subject matter of which is more closely connected with the functions of another public authority, the public authority, to which such application is made, shall transfer the application or such of it as may be appropriate to that other public authority and inform the applicant immediately about such transfer:

Provided that the transfer of an application pursuant to this sub-section shall be made as soon as practicable but in no case later than five days from the date of receipt of the application.

Comment

A person desirous to obtain any information has to make a request for obtaining such information under this Act either in writing or through electronic means in English of Hindi or any official language of the area with the prescribed fee, to the Central/State Public Information Officer of the concerned public authority or to the Central/ State Assistant Public Information Officer, as the case May be.

3. **Disposal or request-** (1) Subject to the Proviso to Sub-section (2) of Section 5 or the proviso to Sub-section (3) of Section 6, the Central Public Information Officer or State Public Information Officer, as the case may be, on receipt of a request under Section 6 shall, as expeditiously as possible, and in any case within third days of the receipt of the request, either provide the request for any of the reasons specified in Sections 8 and 9:

Provide that where the information sought for concerns the life or liberty of a person, the same shall be provided within forty-eight hours of the receipt of the request.

(2) If the Central Public Information Officer or State Public Information Officer, as the case may be, fails to give decision on

the request for information within the period under Sub-section (1), the Central Public Information Officer or State Public Information Officer, as the case may be, shall be deemed to have refused the request.

(3) Where a decision is taking to provide the information on payment of any further fee representing the cost of providing the information, the Central Public Information Officer or State Public Information Officer, as the case may be, shall send intimation to the person making the request, giving-

   (a) The details of further fees responding the cost of providing the information as determined by him, together with the calculations made to arrive at the amount in accordance with fee prescribed under Sub-section (1), requesting him to deposit that fees, and the period intervening between the despatch of the said intimation and payment of fees shall be excluded for the porpose of calculating the period of thirty days referred to in that sub-section;

   (b) Information concerning his or her right with respect to review the decision as to the amount of fees charged or the form of access provided, including the particulars of the appellate authority, time limit, process and any other forms.

(4) Where access to the record or a part thereof is required to be provided under this Act and the person to whom access is to be provided is sensorily disabled, the Central Public Officer or State Public Information Officer, as the case may be, shall provide assistance to enable access to the information, including providing such assistance as may be appropriate for the inspection.

(5) Where access to information is to be provided in the printed or in any electronic format, the applicant shall, subject to the provisions of Sub-section (6), pay such fee as may be prescribed:

provided that the fee prescribed under sub-sections (1) of Section 6 and Sub-sections (1) and (5) of Section 7 shall be reasonable and no such fee shall be charged from the persons who are of below poverty line as may be determined by the appropriate Government.

(6) Notwithstanding anything contained in Sub-section (5), the person making request for the information shall be provided the

information free of charge where a public authority fails to comply with the time limits specified in sub-section (1).

(7) Before taking any decision under Sub-section (1), the Central Public Information Officer or State Public Information Officer, as the case may be, shall take into consideration the representation made by a third party under Section 11.

(8) Where a request has been rejected under Sub-section (1), the Central Public Information Officer or State Public Information Officer, as the Case may be, shall communicate to the person making the request,-

(i) The reasons for such rejection;

(ii) The period within which an appeal against such rejection may be preferred; and

(iii) The particulars of the appellate authority.

(9) An information shall ordinarily be provided in the form in which it is sought unless it would disproportionately divert the resources of the public authority or would be detrimental to the safety or preservation of the record in question.

4. Exemption from disclosure of information- (1) Notwithstanding anything contained in this Act, there shall be no obligation to give any citizen,-

(a) information disclosure of which would prejudicially affect the sovereignty and integrity of India, the Security, strategic, scientific or economic interests of the State, relation with foreign State or lead to incitement of an offence;

(b) information which has been expressly forbidden to be published by any Court of tribunal or the disclosure of which may constitute contempt of Court;

(c) information, the discloser of which would cause a beach of privilege of Parliament or the State Legislature;

(d) information including commercial confidence, trade secrets or intellectual property, the disclosure of which would harm the competitive position of the third party , unless the competent authority is satisfied that large public interest warrants the disclosure of such information;

(e) information available to the person in his fiduciary relationship, unless the competent authority is satisfied that the larger public interest warrants the disclosure of such information;

(f) information received in confidence from foreign Government;

(g) information, the disclosure of which would endanger the life or physical safety of any person or identify the source of information or assistance given in confidence for law enforcement or security purposes;

(h) information which would impede the process of investigation or apprehension or prosecution of offenders;

(i) cabinet papers including records of deliberation of the Council of Ministers, Secretaries and other officers:

Provided that the decisions of Council of Ministers, the reasons thereof, and the material on the basis of which the decisions were taken shall be made public after the decision has been taken, and the matter is complete, or over:

Provided further that those matters which come under the exemptions specified in this section shall not be disclosed;

(j) information which relates to personal information the disclosure of which has no relationship to any public activity or interest, or which would cause unwarranted invasion of the privacy of the individual unless the Central Public Information Officer or the State Information Officer or the appellate authority, as the case may be, is satisfied that the larger public interest justifies the disclosure of such information:

Provided that the information which cannot be denied to the Parliament or a State Legislature shall not be denied to any person.

(2) Notwithstanding anything in the Official Secrets Act. 1923 nor any of the exemptions permissible in accordance with Sub-section (1), a public authority may allow access to information, if public interests.

(3) Subject to the provisions of Clauses (a), (c), and (i) of Sub-section (1), any information relating to any occurrence, event or matter which has taken place, occurred or happened twenty years before the date on which any request is made under Section 6 shall be provided to any person making a request under that section:

Provided that where any question arises as to the date from which the said period of twenty years has to be computed, the decision of the Central Government shall be final, subject to the usual appeals provided for in this Act.

5. **Grounds for rejection to access in certain cases-** Without prejudice to the provisions of Section 8, a Central Public Information officer or a State Public Information Officer, as the case may be, may reject a request for information where such a request for providing access would involve an infringement of copyright subsisting in a person other than the State.

Comment

The request for any information involving infringement of copyright of any individual other than a State may be rejected by the Central/ State Public Information officer.

6. **Severability-** (1) Where a request for access to information is rejected on the ground that it is in relation to information which is exempt from discloser, then, notwithstanding anything contained in this Act, access may be provided to that part of the record which does not contain any information which is exempt from disclosure under this Act and which can reasonably be severed from any part that contains exempt information.

(2) Where access is granted to a part of the record under Sub-section (1), the Central Public Information Officer or State Public Information Officer, as the case may be, shall give a notice to the applicant, informing-

(a) that only part of the record requested, after severance of the record containing information which is exempt from disclosure, is being provided;

(b) the reasons for the decision, including any findings on any material question of fact, referring to the material on which those findings were based;

(c) the name and decision of the person giving the decision;

(d) the details of the fees calculated by him or her and the amount of fee which the applicant is required to deposit; and

(e) his or her rights with respect to review of the decision regarding non-disclosure of part of the information, the amount of fee charged or the from of access provided, including the particulars of the senior officer specified under Sub-section (1) of Section 19 or the Central Information Commission or the State Information Commission, as the case may be, time limit, process and any other from of access.

Comment

Where a request for access to information is rejected on the ground that such information is exempt from disclosure, than, access may be provided to that part of the record which is not exempted from disclosure under this Act and which can reasonable can reasonably be severed from any part which contains exemption information.\

7. Third party information- (1) Where a Central Public Information Officer or a State public information Officer, as the case may be, intends to disclose any information or record, or part thereof on a request made under this Act, which relates to or has been supplied by third party and has been treated as confidential by that third party, the Central Public Information Officer or State Public Information Officer, as the case may be, shall, within five days from the receipt of the request, give a written notice to such third party of the request and of the fact that the Central Information Officer or State Public Information Officer, as the case may be, intends to disclose the information or record, or part thereof, and invite the third party to make a submission in writing or orally, regarding whether the information should be disclosed, and such submission of the third party shall be kept in view while taking a decision about disclosure of information:

Provided that except in the case of trade or commercial secrets protected by law, disclosure may be allowed if the public interest in disclosure outweighs in importance any possible harm or injury to the interests of such third party.

(2) Where a notice is served by the Central Public Information Officer or state Public Information Officer, as the case may be, under Sub-section (1) to a third party in respect of information or record or part thereof, the third party shall, within ten days from the date of receipt of such notice, be given the opportunity to make representation against the proposed disclosure.

(3) Notwithstanding anything contained in Section 7, the Central Public Information Officer or State Public Information Officer, as the case may be, shall, within forty days after receipt of the request under Section 6, if the third party has been given an opportunity to make representation under Sub-section (2), make a decision as to whether or not to disclose the information or record or part thereof and give writing the notice of his decision to the third party.

(4) A notice given under sub-section (3) shall include a statement that the third party to whom the notice is given is entitled to prefer an appeal under Section 19 against the decision.

Comment

If any information or record or part thereof, of a request made under this Act is related to or has been supplied by a third party and has been treated as confidential by that third party, the Central/State public Information Officer, as the case may be, shall, within five days from the receipt of the request serve a written notice on such third party of the request and of the fact that the central/state public information officer as the case may be, intends to disclose information or record, or part thereof and invite the third party to make a submission in writing or orally, with regard to whether information should be disclosed, and such submission of the third party shall be kept in view while taking a decision about the disclosure of such information.

Chapter- III

The central information commission

12. Constitution of central information commission –(1) The Central Government shall, by notification in the Official Gazette, constitute a body to be known as the central information commission to exercise the powers conferred on, and to perform the functions assigned to, it under this Act.

(2) The central information shall consist of –

1. the chief information commissioner; and
2. such number of central information commissioners, not exceeding ten, as may be deemed necessary.

(3) The chief information commissioner and information commissioners shall be appointed by the president on the recommendation of a committee consisting of -

(i) the prime Minister, who shall be the chairperson of the committee;

(ii) the Leader of opposition in the Lok Sabha; and

(iii) a Union cabinet Minister to be nominated by the prime Minister.

Explanation- For the purposes of removal of doubts, it is hereby declared that where the Leader of opposition in the House of the people has not been recognised as such, the Leader of the single largest group in opposition of the Government in the House of the people shall be deemed to be the Leader of opposition.

(4) The general superintendence, direction and management of the affairs of the central information commission shall vest in the chief information commissioner who shall be assisted by the information commissioners and may exercise all such powers and do all such acts and things which may be exercised or done by the central information commission autonomously without being subjected to directions by any other authority under this Act.

(5) The chief information commissioner and information commissioners shall be persons of eminence in public life with wide knowledge and experience in law, science and technology, social service, management, journalism, mass media or administration and governance.

(6) The chief information commissioner or an information commissioner shall not be a Member of parliament or Member of the Legislature of any state or Union territory, as the case may be, or hold any other office of profit or connected with any political party or carrying on any business or pursuing any profession.

(7) The headquarters of the central information commission shall be at Delhi and the central information commission may, with the previous approval of the central Government, establish offices at other places in India.

13. Term of office of and conditions of service –(1) The chief information commissioner shall hold office for a term of five years from the date on which he enters upon his office and shall not be eligible for reappointment:

Provided that no chief information commissioner shall hold office as such after he has attained the age of sixty-five years.

(ii) Every information commissioner shall hold office for a term of five years from the date on which he enters upon his office or till he attains the age of sixty-five years, whichever is earlier, and shall not be eligible for reappointment as such information commissioner:

Provided that every information commissioner shall, on vacating his office under this sub-section be eligible for appointment as the chief information commissioner in the manner specified in sub-section (3) of section 12:

Provided further that where the information commissioner is appointed as the chief information commissioner, his term of office shall not be more than five years in aggregate as the information commissioner and the chief information commissioner.

(3) The chief information commissioner or an information commissioner shall before he enters upon his office make and subscribe before the president or some other person appointed by him in that behalf, an oath or affirmation according to the form set out for the purpose in the first schedule.

(4) The chief information commissioner or an information commissioner may, at any time, by writing under his hand addressed to the president, resign from his office:

Provided that the chief information commissioner or an information commissioner may be removed in the manner specified under section 14.

(5) The salaries and allowances payable to and other terms and conditions of service of-

(a) the chief information commissioner shall be the same as that of the chief Election commissioner;

(b) an information commissioner shall be the same as that of an Election commissioner:

Provided that if the chief information commissioner or an information commissioner, at the time of his appointment is, in receipt of a pension, other than a disability or wound pension, in respect of any previous service under the Government of India or under the Government of a state, his salary in respect of the service as the chief information commissioner or an information commissioner shall be reduced by the amount of that pension including any portion of pension which was commuted and pension equivalent of other forms of retirement benefits excluding pension equivalent of retirement gratuity:

Provided further that if the Chief Information Commission or an Information Commissioner if, at the time of his appointment is, in receipt of retirement benefits in respect of any previous service rendered in a Corporation established by or under any Central Act or State Act or a Government company owned or controlled by the Central Government or the State Government, his salary in respect of the service as the Chief Information Commissioner or an Information Commissioner shall be reduced by the amount of pension equivalent to the retirement benefits:

Provided also that the salaries, allowances and other conditions of service of the Chief Information Commissioner and the Information Commissioners shall not be varied to their disadvantage after their appointment.

(6) the Central Government shall provide the Chief Information Commissioner and the Information Commissioners with such officers and employees as may be necessary for the efficient performance of their function under this Act, and the salaries and allowances payable to and the terms and conditions of service of the officers and other employees appointed for the purpose of this Act shall be such as may be prescribed.

14. Removal of Chief Information Commissioner or Information Commissioner- (1) Subject to the provisions of Sub-section (3), the Chief Information Commissioner or any Commissioner shall be removed from his office only by order of the President on the ground of proved misbehaviour or incapacity after the Supreme Court, on a reference made to it by the President, has, on inquiry, reported that the Chief Information Commissioner or any Information Commissioner, as the case may be, ought on such ground be removed.

(2) The President may suspend from office, and if deem necessary prohibit also from attending the office during inquiry, the Chief Information Commissioner or Information Commissioner in respect if whom a reference has bee made to the Supreme Court under Sub-section (1) until the President has passed orders on receipt of the report of the supreme Court on such reference.

(3) Notwithstanding anything contained in Sub-section (1), the president may by order remove from office the Chief Information Commissioner or any Information Commissioner if the Chief Information Commissioner or a Information Commissioner, as the Case may be,-

- (a) is adjudged an insolvent; or
- (b) has been convicted of an offence which, in the opinion of the President, involves moral turpitude; or
- (c) engages during his term of office in any paid employment outside the duties of his office; or
- (d) is, in the opinion of the President, unfit to continue in office by reason of infirmity of mind or body; or
- (e) has acquired such financial or other interest as is likely to affect prejudicially his functions as the Chief Information Commissioner or a Information Commissioner.

(4) If the Chief Information Commissioner or an Information Commissioner in any way, concerned or interested in any contract or agreement made by or on behalf of the Government of India or participates in any way in the profit thereof or in any benefit or emolument arising therefrom otherwise than as a member and in common with the other members of an incorporated company, he shall, for the purposes of Sub-section (1), be deemed to be guilty to be guilty of misbehaviour.

Chapter-VI

The State Information Commission

15. Constitution of State Information Commission- (1) Every State Government shall, by notification in the ***Official Gazette,*** constitute, constitute a body to be know as the ....(name of the State) Information Commission to exercise the powers conferred on, and to perform the functions assigned to, it under this Act.

(2) The State Information Commission shall consist of-

(a) the State Chief Information Commissioner, and

(b) such number of State Information Commissioners, not exceeding ten, as may be deemed necessary.

(3) The State Chief Information Commissioner and the State Information Commissioners shall be appointed by the Governor on the recommendation of a committee consisting of-

(i) the Chief Minister, who shall be the Chairperson of the committee;

(ii) the Leader of Opposition in the Legislative Assembly; and

(iii) a Cabinet Minister to be nominated by the Chief Minister.

Explanation- For the purposes of removal of doubts, it is hereby declared that where the Leader of Opposition in the Legislative Assembly has not been recognised as such, the leader of the single largest group in opposition of the Government in the Legislative Assembly shall be deemed to be the Leader of Opposition.

(4) The general superintendence, direction and management of the affairs of the State Information Commission shall vest in the State Chief Information Commissioner who shall be assisted by the State Information Commissioners and may exercise all such powers and do all such acts and things which may be exercised or done by the State Information Commission autonomously without being subjected to directions by any other authority under this Act.

(5) The State Chief Information Commissioner and State Information Commissioners shall be persons of eminence in public life with wide knowledge and experience in law, science and technology, social service, management, journalism, mass media or administration and governance.

(6) The State Chief Information Commissioner or a State Information Commissioner shall not be a Member of Parliament or Member of the Legislature of any State or Union territory, as the case may be, or hold any other office of profit or connected with any political party or carrying on any business or pursuing any profession.

(7) The Headquarters of the State Information Commission shall be at such place in the State as the State Government may, by notification in the ***Official Gazette,*** specify and State Information Commission may, with the previous approval of the State Government, establish offices at other places in the State Government, establish Offices at other places in the State.

Comment

Every state Government has to constitute State Information Communication to exercise the powers conferred on, and the performed functions assigned to it under this Act. The State Information Commission shall consists of – (i) the State Chief Information Commissioner, and (ii) State Information Commissioners, not exceeding ten. The State Chief Information Commissioners and the State Information Commissioners shall be appointed by the Governor on the recommendation of a Committee consisting of :

(i) The Chief Minister who shall be Chairperson of the Committee;

(ii) The Leader of the opposition in the Legislative Assembly; and

(iii) A Cabinet Minister to be nominated by the Chief Minister.

The Headquarters of the State Information Commissioner shall be at such place in the State as the State Government may specify.

16. Term of office and conditions of service – (1) The State Chief Information Commissioner shall hold office for a term of five years from the date on which he enters upon his office and shall not be eligible for reappointment:

Provided that no State Chief Information Commissioner shall hold office as such after he has attained the age of sixty-five years.

(2) Every State Information Commissioner shall hold office for a term of five years from the date on which he enters upon his office or till he attains the age of sixty-five years, whichever is earlier, and shall not be eligible for reappointment as such State Information Commissioner:

provided that every State Information Commissioner shall, on vacating his office under this sub-section, be eligible for appointment as the State Chief Information Commissioner in the manner specified in Sub-section (3) of Section 15:

Provided further that where the State Information Commissioner is appointed as the State Chief Information Commissioner, his term, of office shall not be more than five years in aggregate as the State Information Commissioner and the State Chief information Commissioner.

(3) The State Chief Information Commissioner or a State Information Commissioner shall before he enters upon his office make and subscribe before the Governor or some other person appointed by him in that behalf, an oath or affirmation according to the form set out for the purpose in the First schedule.

(4) The State Chief Information Commissioner or a State Information Commissioner may, at any time, by writing under his hand addressed to the Governor, resign from his office:

Provided that the State Chief Information Commissioner or a State Information Commissioner may be removed in the manner specified under Section 17.

(5) The salaries and allowances payable to and other terms and conditions of service of-

(a) the State Chief Information Commissioner shall be the same as that of an Election Commissioner;

(b) the State Information Commissioner shall be the same as that of the Chief Secretary to the State Government:

Provided that if the State Chief Information Commissioner or a State Information Commissioner, at the time of his appointment is, in receipt of a pension, other than a disability or would pension, in respect of any previous service under the Government of India or under the Government of a State, his salary in respect of the service as the State Chief Information Commissioner or a State Information Commissioner shall be reduced by the amount of that pension including any portion which was commuted and pension equivalent of other forms of retirement benefits excluding pension equivalent of retirement gratuity:

Provided further that where the State Chief Information Commissioner or State Information Commissioner if, at the time of his appointment is, in respect of retirement benefits in respect of any previous service rendered in a Corporation established by or under any Central Act or State Act or a Government Company owned or controlled by the Central Government or the State Government, his salary in respect of the service as the State Chief Information Commissioner or the State Information Commissioner shall be reduced by the amount of pension equivalent to the retirement benefits:

Provided also that the salaries, allowances and other conditions of service of the state Chief Information Commissioner and the State Information Commissioners shall not be varied to their disadvantage after their appointment.

(6) The State Government shall be provide the State Chief Information Commissioner and the State Information Commissioners with such officers and employees as may be necessary for the efficient performance of their function under this Act, and the salaries and allowances payable to and the terms and conditions of service of the officers and other employees appointed for the purpose of this Act shall be such as may be prescribed.

Comment

The State Chief Information Commissioner can hold office for a term of five years from the date which he enters upon his office and cannot be eligible for re-appointment.

17. Removal of State Chief information Commissioner or State Information Commissioner- (1) Subject to the provisions of Sub section (3), the State Chief Information Commissioner or a State Information Commissioner shall be removed from his office only by order of the Governor on the ground of proved misbehaviour or incapacity after the Supreme Court, on a reference made to it by the Governor, has on inquiry, reported that the State Chief Information Commissioner or a State Information Commissioner, as the case may be, ought on such ground be removed.

(2) The Governor may suspend from office, and if deem necessary prohibit also from attending the office during inquiry, the State Chief Information Commissioner or a State Information

Commissioner in respect of whom a reference has been made to the Supreme Court under Sub-section (1) until the Governor has passed orders on receipt of the report of the Supreme Court on Such reference.

(3) Notwithstanding anything contained in Sub-section (1), the Governor may by order remove from office the State Chief Information Commissioner or a State Information Commissioner if a State Chief Information Commissioner or a State Information Commissioner, as the case may be,-

(a) is adjudged an insolvent; or

(b) has been convicted of an offence which, in the opinion of the Governor, involve moral turpitude; or

(c) engages during his term of office in any paid employment outside the duties of his office; or

(d) is, in the opinion of the Governor, unfit to continue in office by reason of infirmity of mind or body; or

(e) has acquired such financial or other interest as is likely to affect prejudicially his functions as the State Chief Information Commissioner or a State Information Commissioner.

(4) If the State Chief Information Commissioner or any State Information Commissioner, is in any way, concerned or interested in any contract or agreement made by or on behalf of the Government of the State or participates in any way in the profit thereof or in any benefit or emoluments arising there from otherwise than as a member and in common with the other members of an incorporated company, he shall, for the purposes of Sub-section (1), be deemed to be guilty of misbehaviour.

Chapter-V

Power and functions of the Information Commissions, appeal and penalties

18. Powers and functions of Information Commissions- (1) Subject to the provisions of this Act, it shall be the duty of the Central Information Commission or State Information Commission, as the case may be, to receive and inquire into a complaint from any person,-

(a) who has been unable to submit a request to a Central Public Information Officer or State Public Information Officer, as the case may be, either by reason that no such officer has been appointed under this Act, or because the Central Assistant Public Information Officer or State Assistant Public Information Officer, as the case may be, has refused to accept his or her application for information or appeal under this Act for forwarding the same to the Central Public Information Officer, or State Public Information Officer or senior officer specified in Sub-section (1) of Section 19 or the Central Information Commissioner or the State Information Commission, as the case may be;

(b) who has been refused access to any information requested under this Act;

(c) who has not been given a response to a request for information or access to information within the time limit specified under this Act;

(d) who has been required to pay an amount of fee which he or she considers unreasonable;

(e) who believes that he or she has been given incomplete, misleading or false information under this Act; and

(f) in respect of any other matter relating to requesting or obtaining access to records under this Act.

(2) Where the Central Information Commission or State Information Commission, as the case may be, is satisfied that there are reasonable grounds to inquire into the matter, it may initiate an inquiry in respect thereof.

(3) The Central Information Commission or State Information Commission, as the Case may be, shall, while inquiring into any matter under this Section, have the same powers as are vested in a Civil Court while trying a suit under the Code of Civil Procedure, 1908, in respect of the following matters, namely:

(a) summoning and enforcing the attendance of persons and compel them to give oral or written evidence on oath and to produce the documents or things;

(b) requiring the discovery and inspection of documents;

(c) receiving evidence on affidavit;

(d) requisitioning any public record or copies thereof from any Court or office;

(e) issuing summons for examination of witnesses or documents; and

(f) any other matter which may be prescribed.

(4) Notwithstanding anything inconsistent contained in any other Act of Parliament or State Legislature, as the case may be, the Central Information Commission or the State Information, as the case may be, the central Information Commission or the State Information Commission, as the case may be, may, during the inquiry of any complaint under this Act, examine any record to which this Act applies which is under the control of the public authority, and no such record may be withheld from it on any grounds.

19. Appeal- (1) Any person who, does not receive a decision within the time specified in Sub-section (1) or Clause (a) of Sub-section (3) of Section 7, or is aggrieved by a decision of the Central Public Information Officer or State Public Information Officer, as the case may be, may within thirty days from the expiry of such period or from the receipt of such a decision prefer an appeal to such officer who is senior in rank to the Central Public Information Officer or State Public Information Officer as the case may be, in each public authority:

provided that such officer may admit the appeal after the expiry of the period of thirty days if he or she is satisfied that the appellant was prevented by sufficient cause from filing the appeal in time.

(2) Where an appeal is preferred against an order made by a Central Public Information Officer or a State Public Information Officer, as the case may be, under Section 11 to disclose third party information, the appeal by the concerned third party shall be made within thirty days from the days from the date of the order.

(3) A second appeal against the decision under Sub-section (1) shall lie within ninety days from the date on which the decision should have been made or was actually received, with the Central Information Commission or the State Information Commission:

Provided that the Central Information Commission or the State Information Commission, as the case may be, may admit the appeal after the expiry of the period of ninety days if it is satisfied that the appellant was prevented by sufficient cause from filing the appeal in time.

(4) If the decision of the Central Public Information Officer or State Public Information Officer, as the case may be, against which an appeal is preferred relates to information of a third party, the Central Information Commission or State Information

Commission, as the case may be, shall give a reasonable opportunity of being heard to that third party.

(5) In any appeal proceedings, the onus to prove that a denial of a request was justified shall be on the Central Public Information Officer or State Public Information Officer, as the case may be, who denied the request.

(6) An appeal under Sub-section (1) or Sub-section (2) shall be disposed of within thirty days of the receipt of the appeal or within such extended period not exceeding a total of forty-five days from the date of filing thereof, as the case may be, for reasons to be recorded in writing.

(7) The decision of the Central Information Commission or State Information Commission, as the case may be, shall be binding.

(8) In its decision, the Central Information Commission or State Information Commission, as the case may be, has the power to-

(a) require the public authority to take any such steps as may be necessary to secure compliance with the provisions of this Act, including-

  (i) by providing access to information, if so requested, in a particular form;

  (ii) by appointing a Central Public Information Officer or State Public Information Officer, as the case may be;

  (iii) by publishing certain information or categories of information;

  (iv) by making necessary changes to its practices in relation to the maintenance, management and destruction of records;

  (v) by enhancing the provision of training on the right to information for its officials;

  (vi) by providing it with an annual report in compliance with Clause (b) of Sub-section (1) of Section 4;

(b) require the public authority to compensate the complainant for any loss or other detriment suffered;

(c) impose any of the penalties provided under this Act;

(d) reject the application.

(9) The Central Information Commission or State Information Commission, as the case may be, shall give notice of its decision, including any right of appeal, to the complainant and the public authority.

(10) The Central Information Commission or State Information Commission, as the case may be, shall decide the appeal in accordance with such procedure as may be prescribed.

Comment

An appeal can be preferred by any person who does not receive a decision within the specified time, or is aggrieved by decisions of the Central/State Public Information Officer as the case may be within 30 days to such Officer who is senior in rank.

20. Penalties- (1) Where the Central Information Commission or the State Information Commission, as the case may be, at the time of deciding any complaint or appeal is of the opinion that the Central Public Information Officer or the State Public Information Officer, as the case may be, has, without any reasonable cause, refused to receive an application for information or has not furnished information within the time specified under Sub-section (1) of Section 7 or ***malafidely*** denied the request for information or knowingly given incorrect, incomplete or misleading information or destroyed information which was the subject of the request or obstructed in any manner in furnishing the information, it shall impose a penalty of two hundred and fifty rupees each day till application is received or information is furnished, so however, the total amount of such penalty shall not exceed twenty-five thousand rupees:

Provided that the Central Public Information Officer or the State Public Information Officer, as the case may be, shall be given a reasonable opportunity of being heard before any penalty is imposed on him:

Provided further that the burden of proving that he acted reasonably and diligently shall be on the Central Public Information Officer or the State Public Information Officer, as the case may be.

ii.Where the Central Information Commission or the State Information Commission, as the case may be, at the time of deciding any complaint or appeal is of the opinion that the Central Public Information Officer or the State Public Information Officer, as the case may be, has, without any reasonable cause and persistently, failed to receive an application for formation or has not furnished information within the time specified under Sub-section (1) of section 7 or

malafidely denied the request for information or knowingly given incorrect, incomplete or misleading information or destroyed information which was the subject of the request or obstructed in any manner in furnishing the information, it shall recommend for disciplinary action against the Central Public Information Officer or the State Public Information Officer, as the case may be, under the service rule applicable to him.

Comment

(i) No legal proceeding shall lie against any person or anything which is done in good faith,

(ii) If any Central/State Public Information Officer has, Without any reasonable cause,

refuses to receive an application for information or has not furnished information within the specified time or mala fidely deny the request for information knowingly given incorrect, incomplete or misleading information or destroyed information which was the subject of the request or obstructed in any manner in furnishing the information, a penalty of Rs.250/- each day till application is received or information is furnished, so however, the total of such penalty shall not exceed Rs. 25,000/- shall be imposed on that officer.

Chapter-VI

Miscellaneous

21. Protection of action taken in good faith- No suit, prosecution or other legal proceeding shall lie against any person for anything which is in good faith done or intended to be done under this Act or any rule made thereunder.

22. Act to have overriding effect- The provisions of this Act shall have effect notwithstanding anything inconsistent therewith contained in the Official Secrets Act, 1923, and any other law for the time being in force or in any instrument having effect by virtue of any law other than this Act.

23. Bar of jurisdiction of Courts- No Court shall entertain any suit, application or other proceeding in respect of any order made under this Act and no such order shall be called in question otherwise than by way of an appeal under this Act.

24. Act not to apply to certain organisations- (1) Nothing contained in this Act shall apply to the intelligence and security organisations specified in the Second Schedule, being organisations established by the Central Government or any information furnished by such organisations to that Government.

Provided that the information pertaining to the allegations of corruption and human rights violations shall not be excluded under this sub-section:

Provided further that in the case of information sought for is in respect of allegations of violation of human rights, the information shall only be provided after the approval of the Central Information Commission, and notwithstanding anything contained Section 7, such information shall be provided within forty-five days from the date of the receipt of request.

(2) The Central Government may, by notification in the Official Gazetted, amend the Schedule by including therein any other intelligence or security organisation established by that Government or omitting therefrom any organisation already specified therin and on the publication of such notification, such organisation shall be deemed to be included in or, as the case may be, omitted from the Schedule.

(3) Every notification issued under Sub-section (2) shall be laid before each House of Parliament.

(4) Nothing contained in this Act shall apply to such intelligence and security organisation being organisations established by the State Government, as that Government may, from time, by notification in the Official Gazetted, specify:

Provided that information pertaining the allegations of corruption and human rights violations shall not be excluded under this sub-section;

Provided further that in the case of information sought for is in respect of allegations of violation of human rights, the information shall only be provided after the approval of the State Information Commission not notwithstanding anything contained in Section 7, such information shall be provided within forty-five days from the date of the receipt of request.

(5) Every notification issued under Sub-section (4) shall be laid before the State Legislature.

25. Monitoring and reporting- (1) The Central InfoOrmation Commission or State Information Commission as the case may be, shall as soon as practicable after the end of each year, prepare a report on the implementation of the provisions of this Act during that year and forward a copy thereof to the appropriate Government.

(2) Each Ministry or Development shall, in relation to the public authorities within their jurisdiction, collect and provide such information to the Central Information Commission or State Information Commission as the case may be, as is required to prepare the report under this Section and comply with requirements concerning the furnishing of that information and keeping of records for the purposes of this section.

(3) Each report shall state in respect of the year to which the report relates,-

- (a) The number of requests made to each public authority;
- (b) The number of decisions where applicants were not entitled to access to the documents pursuant to the requests, the provisions of this Act under which these decisions were made and the number of times such provisions were invoked;
- (c) The number of appeals referred to the Central Information Commission or State Information Commission, as the case may be, for review, the nature of the appeals and the outcome of the appeals;
- (d) Particulars of any disciplinary action taken against any officer in respect of the administration of this Act;
- (e) The amount of changes collected by each public authority under this Act;
- (f) Any facts which indicate an effort by the public authorities to administer and implement the spirit intention of this Act;
- (g) Recommendations for reform, including recommendations in respect of the particular public authorities, for the development, improvement, modernisation, reform or amendment to this Act or other legislation or common law or any other matter relevant for operationalising the right to access information.

(4) The Central Government or the State Government, as the case may be, may, as soon as practicable after the end of each year, cause a copy of the report of the Central Information Commission

or the State Information Commission, as the case may be, referred to in Sub-section (1) to be laid before each House of Parliament or, as the case may be, before each house of the State Legislature, where there are two Houses, and where there is one House of the State Legislature before that House.

(5) If it appears to the Central Information Commission or State Information Commission, as the case may be, that the practice of a public authority in relation to the exercise of its functions under this Act does not conform with the provisions or sprit of this Act, it may give to the authority a recommendation specifying the steps which ought in its opinion to be taken for promoting such conformity.

26. Appropriate Government to prepare programmes- (1) The appropriate Government may, to the extent of availability of financial and other resources,-

(a) Develop and organise educational programmes to advance the understanding of the public, in particular of disadvantaged communities as to how to exercise the rights contemplated under this Act;

(b) Encourage public authorities to participate in the development and organisation of programmes referred to in clause (a) and to undertake such programmes themselves;

(c) Promote timely and effective dissemination of accurate information of accurate information by public authorities about their activities; and

(d) Train Central Public Information Officers or State Public Information Officers, as the case may be, of public authorities and produce relevant training materials for use by the public authorities themselves.

(2) The appropriate Government shall, within eighteen months from the commencement of this Act, compile in its official language a guide containing such information, in an easily comprehensible from and manner, as may reasonable be required by a person who wishes to exercise any rights specified in this Act.

(3) The appropriate Government Shall, if necessary, update and publish the guidelines referred to in Sub-section (2) at regular intervals which shall, in particular and without prejudice to the generality of Sub-section (2), include-

(a) The object of this Act;

(b) The postal and street address, the phone and fax number and, if available, electronic mail address of the Central Public Information Officer or State Public Information Officer as the case may be, of every public authority appointed under Sub-section (1) of Section 5;

(c) The manner and the form in which request for access to an information shall be made to a Central Public Information Officer or State Public Information Officer, as the case may be;

(d) The assistance available from and the duties of the Central Public Information Officer or State Public Information Officer, as the case may be, of a public authority under this Act;

(e) The assistance available from the Central Information Commission or State Information Commission, as the case may be;

(f) All remedies in law available regarding an act or failure to act in respect of a right or duty conferred or imposed by this Act including the manner of filling an appeal to the Commission;

(g) The provisions providing for the voluntary disclosure of categories of records in accordance with Section4;

(h) The notice regarding fee to be paid in relation to requests for access to an information; and

(i) Any additional regulations or circulars made or issued in relation to obtaining access to an information in accordance with this Act.

(4) The appropriate Government must, if necessary, update and publish the guidelines at regular intervals.

27. Power to make rule by appropriate Government- (1) The appropriate Government may, by notification in the ***Official Gazette,*** make rules to carry out the provisions of this Act.

(2) In particular, and without prejudice to the generality of the forgoing power, such rules may provide for all or any of the following matters, namely:

(a) The cost of medium or print cost price of the materials to be disseminated under Sub-section (4) of Section 4;

(b) The fee payable under Sub-section (1) of Section 6;

(c) The fee payable under Sub-sections (1) and (5) of Section 7;
(d) The salaries and allowances payable to and the terms and conditions of service of the officers and other employees under Sub-section (6) of Section 13 and Sub-section (6) of Section 16.
(e) The procedure to be adopted by the Central Information Commission or State Information Commission, as the case may be, in deciding the appeals under Sub-section (10) of Section 19; and
(f) Any other matter which is required to be, or may be, prescribed.

28. Power to make rules by competent authority- (1) The competent authority may, by notification in the official Gazette, make rules to carry out the provisions of this Act.

(2) In particular, and without prejudice to the generality of the foregoing power, such rules may provide for all or any of the following matters, namely:
(i) the cost of the medium or print cost price of the materials to be disseminated under sub-section (4) of section 4;
(ii) the fee payable under sub-section (1) of section 6;
(iii) the fee payable under sub-section (1) of section 7; and
(iv) any other matter which is required to be, or may be, prescribed

29. Laying of rules- (1) Every rule made by the central Government under this Act shall be laid, as soon as may be after it is made, before each house of parliament, while it is in session, for a total period of thirty days which may be comprised in one session or in two or more successive sessions, and if, before the expiry of the session immediately following the session or the successive sessions aforesaid, both houses agree in making any modification in the rule or both Houses agree that the rule should not be made, the rule shall thereafter have effect only in such modified form or be of no effect, as the case may be; so, however, that any such modification or annulment shall be without prejudice to the validity of anything previously done under that rule .

(2) Every rule made under this Act by a state Government shall be laid, as soon as may be after it is notified, before the state Legislature.

30. Power to remove difficulties- (1) If any difficulty arises in giving effect to the provisions of this Act, the central Government may, by order published in the official Gazette, make such provisions not inconsistent with the provisions of this Act as appear to it to be necessary or expedient for removal of the difficulty:

Provided that no such order shall be made after the expiry of a period of two years from the date of the commencement of this Act.

(2) Every order made under this section shall, as soon as may be after it is made, be laid before each house of parliament,

31. Repeal- The freedom of information Act, 2002 is hereby repealed.

THE FIRST SCHEDULE

[See sections 13 (3) and 16 (3)]

From of oath or affirmation to be made by the chief information commissioner/the information commissioner /the state chief information commissioner /the state information commissioner

"I....................., having been appointed chief information commissioner/information commissioner/state chief information commissioner/state information commissioner swear in the name of God/solemnly affirm that I will bear true faith and allegiance to the constitution of India as by law established, that I will uphold the sovereignty and integrity of India, that I will duly and faithfully and to the best of my ability, knowledge and judgment perform the duties of my office without fear or favour, affection or ill-will and that I will uphold the constitution and the laws."

Appendix-V

LIST OF CHAIRPERSONS OF NHRC

First Chairperson - Justice Ranganath Mishra.
Second Chairperson - Justice M. N. Venkatachaliah.
Third Chairperson - Justice J. S. Verma.
Fourth Chairperson - Justice (Dr.) A.S. Anand.
Fifth Charperson – Justice Shri S. Rajendra Babu- 02-04-2007(Present).

LIST OF SECRETARY GENERALS OF NHRC

First Secretary General G.- R.B. Pillai.
Second Secretary General - G. Gopal Swami.
Third Secretary General - P. Thoms.
Fourth Secretary General - Sardar Nirmal Singh.
Fifth Secretary General - R.K. Bhargava. (Present)

Appendix-VI

CONTACT ADDRESS
OF
NHRC AND STATE HUMAN RIGHTS COMMISSIONS

The following information has been collected from NHRC website which were available as on 1st March 2007. The contact address, fax numbers, E. mail address and phone numbers may be changed from time to time. Hence the readers are requested to go through the Commission' s website for upto date information.

National Human Rights Commission
Faridkot House, Copernicus Marg,
New Delhi-110001. (India)
Fax-11-23384863/ 23386521.
Website- www.nhrc nic. in
E. mail: covdnhrc@ nic. in, ionhrc @nic. in
For complaints Filling/status General querries- MADAD: 92-11-23385368.

LIST OF STATE HUMAN RIGHTS COMMISSIONS

1. Assam State Human Rights Commission
   Statfed H.O. Building,
   Bhangarh, Guwahati- 781005.
   Fax –0361-2529450/2527076.
   E. mail- hrca @ sanharnet. In
2. Andhra Pradesh State Human Rights Commission
   Fax-23224325
   E. mail- aphumanrights @ ap.nic.in
3. Himachal Pradesh State Human Rights Commission
   Pines Grove Builading , Shimla-171002.
   Fax-0177-2624908.

E. mail-chairperson_hphrc@ yahoo.com

4. Jammu Kashmir State Human Rights Commission
Dawn Building, Dalgate, Srinagar-119001.
Fax-0194-454046.
E. mail- Not Available at NHRC website as on 01.03.2007.

5. Kerala State Human Rights Commission
M.P. Appan Road, Vazhuthacaud,
Thiruvananathapuram- 695014.
Fax- 0471-2337148.
E. mail-kshrctvpm 2 vsnl.net

6. Madhya Pradesh State Human Rights Commission
Paryavas Bhawan, Arera Hills,
Jail Road, Bhopal-462001.
Fax-0755-574028.
E. mail- mphrc @ sancharnet.in

7. Maharastra State Human Rights Commission
9,Hajarimal Somani Marg,
Near CST Railway Station,Mumbai-400001.
Fax-o22-2885858.
E. mail- Not Available at NHRC website as on 01.03.2007.

8. Manipur State Human Rights Commission
Courts Complex, Lamphel,
Imphal-795004.
Fax- 0385-2410472.
E. mail- mhrc @ man. nic.in

9. Orissa State Human Rights Commission
Gopabandhu Nagar, Unit-8, Bhubaneswar.
Fax – 0674 –2405094.
E. mail- Not Available at NHRC website as on 01.03.2007.

10. Punjab State Human Rights Commission
SCO No. 20-21-22, sector 34 +,
Chandigararh. Fax- 0172- 608520.
E. mail- Not Available at NHRC website as on 01.03.2007.

11. Tamilnadu State Human Rights Commission
Justice Pratap Singh Maaligai
Iind Floor, No-35,
Thiru vi-ka- salai
Roya pettah chennai- 600014.
Fax & e. mail- Not Available at NHRC website as on 01.03.2007.

12. Rajstan State Human Rights Commission
    State Secretariarte, Jaipur.
    Fax –141-2227738.
    E. mail- Not Available at NHRC website as on 01.03.2007.
13. Uttar Pradesh State Human Rights Commission
    1/183, Vincet Khand, gomati Nagar,
    Lucknow- 226010.
    Fax-0522-2726743.
    E. mial- uphrc @ sancharnet.net
14. West Bengal Human Rights Commission
    Bhabani Bhavan, Alipur, Kolkotta-750027.
    Fax –033- 24799633.
    E. mail- wbhrc @ cal.vsnl.net. in
15. Chhatishgarh State Human Rights Commission
    Near Mantranalaya, Raipur-492001.
    Fax-0771-2235590.
    E. mail- cghrcryp @ sify. Com.

Bibliography

Abdulla, Rahim P. (ed.), "Essays on International Human Rights." New Delhi, Asian, Vijaypur, 1991.

Abraham, Henry J. "Freedom and The Court: Civil Rights and Liberties in the United States", 3rd edn. Oxford University Press, 1977.

A penal of legal commentators (ed.), "Law Relating To Human Rights" Asia Law House, 1997.

Agarwal, R.S., "Human Rights in the Modern World", New Delhi, Chetana Publications, 1974.

Aggarwal, H.O. "Implementation of Human Rights Covenants with Special Reference to India", 1st edn. Allahabad, Kitab Mahal, 1983.

A.Natrajan, "Hunan Rights in Interested Perspective", Aavishkar Publishers, Distributor. Jaipur(Raj), 2006.

Arora, L.K.(ed.), "Human Rights Information &Documentation", Isha Books, Delhi, 2006.

Bajwa, G.S., "Human Rights in India: Implementation and Violation", New Delhi, Anmol Publications, 1995.

Bakshi, P.M., "The Constitution of India", Universal Law Publishing Co. Pvt. Ltd., 1991.

Basu, D.D., "Human Rights in Constitutional Law", New Delhi, Prentice Hall of India Pvt. Ltd., 1979.

Baxi, Upendra (ed.), "The Right to the Human", New Delhi, Lancer International, 1987.

Baxi, Upendra "The Future of Human Rights", (2nd Ed.) Oxford University, Ned Delhi, 2006.

Bhagwati, P.N. "Legal Aid as a Human Right." Dharwad, Jagar Bharat, 1985.

Brohi, A.K. "Islam and Human Rights." London, Islam Council of Europe, 1978.

Brownlie, I, (ed.), "Basic Documents on Human Rights", England, Clarendon Press, 1981.

Bunch, Charlotte. 'Women Rights as Human Rights: Toward a Revision of Human Rights'. Human Rights Quarterly 12 (486), 1990.

Casser, Antari, "Human Rights in Changing World", Temple University Press, Philadelphia, 1990.

Chandra, U., "Human Rights", Allhabad, Law Agency Publications, 2002.

Cranston, Maurice, "What are Human Rights?" London, Bodley Head, 1973.

Crowford, James (ed.), "The Rights of Peoples", New York, Oxford University Press, 1995.

Darren JO' Byrne, "Human Rights", Singapore, Pearson Education, 2003.

Das, H., Choudhury, B.C., "Political Theory", New Delhi, Kalyani Publishers, 1990.

Desai, A.R., "Violation of Democratic Right in India", Bombay, Popular Prakashan, 1986.

Dev, Arjun, Dev Indira Arjun and Das Supta (ed.), "Human Rights, A Source Book", New Delhi National Council of Educational Research and Training.

Dr. S. C. Singh "Social Justice & Human Rights In India", Serials Publication, New Delhi, 2006.

Dworkin, R. "Taking Rights Seriously." Cambridge University Press, 1976.

Falk, Richard, "Human Rights and State Sovereignty", New York Holmes and Meier Publishers, 1985.

Gadgil, D.R. "Human Rights in Multi-national Society", Poona, Gokhle Institute of Politics and Economics, 1986.

Garrett Ward Sheldon, "The Encyclopaedia of Political Thought." New Delhi, Vive Books Pvt. Ltd., 2005.

Ghai, K.K., "Indian Polity", Cuttack, Kalyani Publishers, 2003.

Graham, Hugh Davis. "The Civil Rights Era." Oxford University Press, New York, 1990.

Gupta, Vinay, K. (ed.), "Perspectives on Human Rights", New Delhi, Vikas Publishing House Pvt. Ltd., 1996.

Hariss, Davis (ed.), "International Human Rights Reports", Vol. 2, no. 1, January 1995, University of Nottingham, Nottingham, U.K.

Ian Brownlie and Guys. Goodwin-Gill (ed.) "Basic documents on Human Rights" Oxford University Press, New Delhi 2007.

Jaswal, S.P. and Nishtha Jaswal. "Human Rights and the Law." Delhi, APH Publishing Corporation, 1996.

Johari, J.C., "Human Rights and New World Order: Towards Perfection of the Democratic Way of Life", New Delhi, Anmol Publication, 1996.

J. Symonides, "Human Rights, International Protection monitoring", Enforcement (ed.) Rrawat Publications N.D.

Krishna Iyer, V.R., "Human Rights and the Law", Indore, Vedal Wadhwa, 1984.

Krishna Iyer, V.R., "Human Right and Inhuman Wrongs", New Delhi, D.K. Publishers and Distributers, 1990.

Kapur, Devesh and Mehta, Pratap Bhanu (ed.), "Public Institution in India", New Delhi, Oxford University Press, 2005.

Manohar, V.R., "The Indian Penal Code", Nagpur, Wadhwa and Company, 2004.

Martin, J. Paul (ed.). "Human Rights: A Topical Biography." Westvew, CO, 1983.

Milne, A.J.M., "Freedom and Rights", London, George Allen and Unwin, 1968.

Mishra, S.N., "The Code of Criminal Procedure", Allhabad, Criminal Law Publications, 2004.

Noorani, A.G. 'Human Rights During Arm Conflicts'. "Economic and Political Weekly", 27April 1991, P. 1076.

Paine Thomas(ed.), "Rights of Man", Cambridge, Hackett Publishing Company, 1992.

Paranjape, N.V., "Criminology and Penology", Allahabad, Central Law Publications, 2003.

Pandey, J.N., "Constitutional Law of India", Allahabad, Central Law Agency, 1993.

Pandon, M.P., "India and Penal Code", Allhabad, Law Agency, 1994.

Platter, Max F. (ed.), "Human Rights in our Times", Westview Press, London, 1984.

Patil, V.T., "Human Rights", Delhi, Authors Press, 2001.

Pathak, Arun Kumar, "human Rights", Faridabad, Silverling Publications.

Power, Jonathan. "Amnasty International: Human Rights Story." Oxford, Pergamon Press, 1982.

Puri, Kamal. "Human Rights of Indigenous Australians", National Law School Journal, Vol.6, 1994, pp. 25-41.

Ray Arun, "National Human Rights Commission of India" (Vol-I and II), New Delhi, Khama Publishers, 1997.

Rai Rahul, "Globalisation of Human Rights", Authors Press, New Delhi.2006.

Reichert, Elisabeth. "Understanding Human Rights", An Exercise Book, Suge Publication, New Delhi.2006.

Robertson Geoffrey, "Crimes Against Humanity: The Struggle for Global Justice", Harmondsworth: Penguin, 2000.

Sadiq Ahamad Jilani Syed, "Women in India: Legal and Human Rights", Centre for Professional Development in Higher Education and Women's Studies and Development Centre, 2004.

Saksena, K.R. (ed.)., "Human Rights: Perspectives and Challenges", New Delhi, Lancers Books, 1994.

Sastry, T.S.N., "India and Human Rights", New Delhi, Concept Publishing , 2005.

Sabbir Mohammad, (ed) "Quest for Human Rights", Rawat Publications, New Delhi, 2005

Sen, Sankar, "Human Rights and Law Enforcement", New Delhi, Concept Publishing Company, 2002.

Shama Sastry, R. "Kautilya's Arthasastra." Mysore Printing and Publishing House, Mysore, 1967.

Shrma Arvind, "Are Hunan Rights Western", Oxford University Press, New Delhi, 2006.

Shrma S.N. "Personal Liberty under Indian Constitution." Deep and Deep, New Delhi, 1991.

Sharma, Sudesh Kumar. "Distributive Justice Under Indian Constitution: With Reference to Right to Equality and Property." Deep and Deep, New Delhi, 1989.

South Asia Human Rights Document Centre, "Hand Book of Human Rights and Criminal Justice in India", New Delhi, Oxford University Press, 2006.

Subhas, Chandra Khare. "Human Rights and United Nations." Human Rights and United Nations. Metropolitan Book Co., Delhi, 1997.

Thakur Lalitk (ed.), "Culture, Wisdom, Religion and Human Rights", (New Delhi), Indian Institute of Human Rights.

Thakur, Lalit, K. (ed.), "Principles and Theories of Human Rights", New Delhi, Indian Institute of Human Rights.

Thakur, Lalit, K. (ed.), "Introduction of Human Rights", New Delhi, Indian Institute of Human Rights.

Thakur, Lalit, K. (ed.), “State of Human Rights in India”, New Delhi, Indian Institute of Human Rights.

Thakur, Lalit, K. (ed.), “Promotion and Protection of Human Rights and Prevention of its Violations”, New Delhi, Indian Institute of Human Rights.

Thomas, Anna (ed.). “Human Rights in Asia: Women’s Perspectives: “A Report from the Asian Women’s Human Rights Constitution.”

Tripathi, S.C., and Arora, V., “Law Relating to Women and Children”, Allahabad, Central Law Publications, 2004.

Tyagi, Yogesh K. “Human Rights in India – An Overview.” Sage Publications, New Delhi, 1992.

Urik, Peter, “Human Rights & Development”, Kumarian Press, UVC, USA, 2005.

Vasak, Karel (ed.). “The International Dimensions of Human Rights”, 2 Vols. English edn revised and edited By Philip Alston. Greenood Press, Conn., 1982.

Whalen, Mollie. “Counselling to End Violence Against Women: A Subversive Model.” Sage, New Delhi, 1996.

Wronka Joseph, “Human Rights and Social Polity in the 21st Century: A History of the Idea of Human Rights and Comparison of the U.N. Declaration of Human Rights With United States Federal and State Constitutions”, America, Lanham, MD: University Press, 1992.

“Yearbook on Human Rights,” United Nations, 1946-, irreg.

“Year Book of the European Constitution of Human Rights”, M. Nijhoff, Doidrecht, 1980-,

Articles

“Police and Society” Birinder Pal Singh- The Statesman 26 August 1997.

Journals and News Papers

Aihra, “Human Rights”, (Fortnightly), Issue-37 Oct-I, 2005.

Aihra, “Human Rights”, (Fortnightly), Issue-29 June-I, 1005.

Aihra, “Human Rights”, (Fortnightly), Issue-38 Oct-II, 2005.

Aihra, “Human Rights”, (Fortnightly), Issue-35 Sept-I, 2005.

Aihra, “Human Rights”, (Fortnightly), Issue-33 August 2005.

Employment News (Weekly) New Delhi 22-28 November2003.

Employment New (Weekly) New Delhi 15-21 October 2005.

Employment New (Weekly) New Delhi8-14 October 2005.

The Indian Express – 1st June 2006.

The Statesman Orissa Plus April 2006.
The Sunday Statesman Magazine (Weekly) July 2 2006.
News Letter, Human Rights, Vol. 12 No-07 July. 2005 NHRC.
News Letter, Human Rights, Vol. 12 No-08 August. 2005 NHRC.
News Letter, Human Rights, Vol. 12 No-09 Sept. 2005 NHRC
News Letter, Human Rights, Vol. 12 No-11 Nov. 2005 NHRC.
News Letter, Human Rights, Vol. 12 No-12 Dec. 2005 NHRC.
News Letter, Human Rights, Vol.13 No-2 Feb 2006 NHRC.
News Letter, Human Rights, Vol. 13 No-4 April 2006 NHRC.
News Letter, Human Rights, Vol.14 No-5 May 2006 NHRC.
News Letter, Human Rights, Vol.14 No-6 June 2006 NHRC.
News Letter, Human Rights, Vol. 13 No-7 July 2006 NHRC.
News Letter, Human Rights, Vol. 13 No-9 Sept. 2006 NHRC.
News Letter, Human Rights, Vol. 13 No-11 Nov. 2006 NHRC.
News Letter, Human Rights, Vol. 13 No-12 Dec. 2006 NHRC.
News Letter, Human Rights, Vol. 14 No-1 January 2007 NHRC.
News Letter, Human Rights, Vol. 14 No-2 Bebruary 2007NHRC.

Index

C

D

R

V

W

Y

Z